CHALLENGE AND CHANGE FOR THE EARLY YEARS WORKFORCE

The early years sector is going through a period of unprecedented change. This has resulted in significant challenges for the early years workforce and it is crucial that settings, teams, leaders and individual practitioners respond to these if they wish to continue to provide the best care and education for young children.

This timely text identifies and addresses the key challenges for those working with young children from managing personal and professional change, adapting to new legislation and considering new ways of thinking about children's early learning. It considers the core knowledge and understanding of good practice that enables practitioners to respond appropriately and with confidence to issues they face on a daily basis.

Covering a wide range of diverse topics, including professional identity, neuroscience, outdoor education, literacy, special educational needs, the family and the 'risk' factor, the book encourages the reader to reflect upon their own views and attitudes towards change practice and includes:

- Chapter overviews and summary boxes
- Case studies to highlight good practice
- Questions to promote debate
- Annotated further reading

Aimed specifically at those who are studying and working with children from birth to 8, this book will be a core text for Foundation Degrees in early years, early childhood studies and those working towards Early Years Teacher Status.

Christine Ritchie has been working with children and adults in education for over 40 years, including in her role as Senior Lecturer in Childhood Studies at Canterbury Christ Church University, UK.

CHALLENGE AND CHANGE FOR THE EARLY YEARS WORKFORCE

Working with children from birth to 8

Edited by Christine Ritchie

Routledge
Taylor & Francis Group

LONDON AND NEW YORK

First published 2015
by Routledge
2 Park Square, Milton Park, Abingdon, Oxon OX14 4RN

and by Routledge
711 Third Avenue, New York, NY 10017

Routledge is an imprint of the Taylor & Francis Group, an informa business

British Library Cataloguing in Publication Data
A catalogue record for this book is available from the British Library

Library of Congress Cataloging in Publication Data
Challenge and change for the early years workforce: working with children from birth to 8/edited by Christine Ritchie.
pages cm
Includes bibliographical references and index.
1. Education, Primary. 2. Elementary school teachers. I. Ritchie, Christine.
LB1507.C38 2014
372.21–dc23
2014020371

ISBN: 978-1-138-01666-8 (hbk)
ISBN: 978-1-138-01667-5 (pbk)
ISBN: 978-1-131-78074-0 (ebk)

Typeset in Interstate
by Swales & Willis Ltd, Exeter, Devon, UK

Printed and bound in the United States of America by Publishers Graphics, LLC on sustainably sourced paper.

Challenge and change for the
early years workforce

CONTENTS

FIGURES AND TABLES

Figures

Tables

ABOUT THE CONTRIBUTORS

Catherine Carroll-Meehan is a Principal Lecturer in Early Childhood Studies in the School of Childhood and Education Science at Canterbury Christ Church University (CCCU). Catherine is involved in teaching undergraduate and postgraduate students in early childhood and is currently supervising students at Doctoral level. Prior to working at CCCU, Catherine was a Lecturer in Early Childhood Education in Queensland, Australia, and has professional teaching experience with children from birth to 8 years in a range of settings.

Bridget Durell has worked for the past ten years as a Senior Lecturer in Kent, specialising in Education, Childhood Studies and Sustainability. After gaining her English degree from Reading in the 1980s, she qualified as a bi-lingual secretary and spent the following decade working in finance and banking in the private sector. As well as learning to touch-type and write shorthand, she also learned to sell, collect debt and repossess cars during that time – all very useful life skills! Since then, she has gained three children, a PGCE, 12 years' teaching experience in Nottingham and Kent, has worked as a local authority literacy advisor, has acquired a grandson and an MA in Education Studies and is currently working on her doctorate in education. Her interest in neuroscience has been developing since she started lecturing and she believes that, within the field of education, this is an under-researched and little-acknowledged area of human development – even though she believes it helps in so many ways towards our understanding of the puzzle of who we are, how we work and why we do what we do.

Linda Flower has experienced a lifelong career in education in Kent and Hampshire, teaching in primary and middle schools. She taught as a class teacher for several years before going on to a variety of senior leadership roles in a range of primary schools. She has a particular interest in special educational needs and has led a successful inclusive practice over the past fifteen years. Linda is a Qualified Teacher of Visually Impaired (VI) children and has managed and led VI resourced-based provision within mainstream schools as well as working as a county advisory teacher for children with visual impairment. She has worked as a Senior Lecturer at Canterbury Christ Church University in the School of Childhood and Education Science, with a particular focus on special educational needs and inclusive practice to degree level. Linda continues to work in school, advising and leading on inclusion.

Judy Gracey has taught in higher education as a Senior Lecturer in Childhood Studies. Her particular interest and research at university were in the challenges facing the work-based student studying for a degree. She is a Fellow of the Higher Education Academy. Prior to this, Judy trained as a primary school teacher with early years specialism. She has taught in infant schools and worked as deputy head teacher of a primary school in the UK. In addition, she has enjoyed teaching in British schools in Indonesia, Ethiopia and Turkey. This experience and interest also led her to be part of the Teacher Working Group that produced Kent's Agreed Syllabus for Religious Education in schools.

Shona Henderson's working career has been predominantly in education. She began teaching in Scotland in the mid-1970s, having completed teacher training and a further specialism in early years with a focus on the work of Friedrich Froebel. Her various professional roles have been in nurseries and primary schools, engaging in supply work in secondary schools and, currently, teaching in university. Shona also carried out Ofsted inspections for the Early Years and felt privileged to enter the domain of many hard-working practitioners. Additionally, she has lived in various counties where she was able to experience first-hand their education systems and teaching strategies. She engaged in further study seven years ago when accepting a post in university and has subsequently been admitted as a Fellow of the Higher Education Academy. The experience of recent study heightened her recognition of the need to understand personal feelings and to accept challenge when engaging in new learning.

Christine Ritchie has enjoyed a long career in education, working in the UK and Europe, gaining experience in a variety of educational areas, starting as a primary school teacher as well as working in early years education. In 2000 she changed direction, moving from a post as Head of Infants to working with adults as a senior lecturer and Programme Director in higher education. She has valued the experience of working with 'non-traditional' mature students studying on foundation degrees and BA (Hons) programmes related to childhood studies and the early years. Students who 'earn as they learn' bring a particular understanding and capability to study, that links study to practice in an invigorating and exciting way. This has been a driving force for Christine's own professional interests, which include developing study skills for the 'non-traditional' student.

Lin Shaw is a senior registered nurse who has worked in England, Africa and Australia in various specialities, including tropical medicine, maternity and critical care. Paediatric specialism has included neurosurgery, ophthalmics, terminal care and managing residential and home environments for children with complex additional needs. Specialism in early years educare has included Special Needs practitioner within a primary school, managing Mother and Toddler groups, childminding and international voluntary work. Lin is currently a senior lecturer in Early Years Studies at Canterbury Christ Church University.

Clair Stevens' work as an early years teacher draws not simply from her reading and research, undertaken while completing her BA and MA studies, but more importantly from the hands-on experiences and reflections as a mother of six children, five of them boys. Clair's interests extend beyond her teaching at university, and she currently leads practice in a large nursery school with a Forest School attached. The setting opened in 2008 and has been rated as 'outstanding' by Ofsted on the two occasions that it has been inspected. Additionally, in 2013, the nursery was highly commended in the Nursery World awards, highlighting the focus on the use of outdoor environments. The nursery works very closely with other agencies and organisations within the area, including several Children's Centres, local Primary schools and community projects, including allotment projects, coastal walks and the Turner Gallery. She is particularly interested in the benefits of outdoor environments and the opportunities this offers young children and their families. Her concern has been growing over some years, related to the health of young children; this includes a research interest in establishing the 'health rights' of young children. Clair has written several articles for early years publications and, in spring 2013, Routledge published her first book, *The Growing Child*.

Diana Strauss is a Senior Lecturer at Canterbury Christ Church University who specialises in early education and special educational needs. Her teaching career spans 30 years and includes primary, specialist and nursery provision. Diana has a particular interest in professional development and for 18 years she worked across schools in East Kent with teachers and practitioners in classrooms and settings, devising and delivering training and development courses, such as Early Years SENCO, accredited with the Institute of Education. She is a Fellow of the Higher Education Academy and is Year 1 co-ordinator for the Foundation Degree Professional Studies in Early Years and is responsible for a module on the BA Honours Early Years Leadership programme entitled *Leading Alongside Services and Agencies*.

Laurence Taylor worked for 15 years in production in theatre, TV and digital media, and then changed career to become a speech and drama teacher. Alongside this, he has been studying for a BA (Hons) Degree in Childhood Studies, and a Level 5 diploma in Teaching Drama. He will be looking to carry out a Research Masters in his field of interest, digital literacy, and to continue exploring the world of communication.

Clare Wiseman is a Senior Lecturer in the School of Childhood and Education Science at Canterbury Christ Church University, teaching predominantly on the Children Learning Literacy and Children Learning Mathematics modules. She previously taught on both the undergraduate and postgraduate initial teacher education programmes. Prior to joining Canterbury Christ Church University, Clare was a Primary Education Consultant for Kent Local Authority. Previously, she had taught across Key Stage 1 and Key Stage 2 in Kent Primary schools for 12 years.

ACKNOWLEDGEMENTS

The idea that constant challenges and changes in the workplace left educators feeling frustrated and unsure of how to proceed in practice came from an early years focus group, who during discussion produced a long list of concerns and the stress these brought when trying to do the best for the children in their care. Such concerns are not new, but the group's passion and drive inspired this book, so the contributors would like to thank them, and all the other students, participants and teachers who found time to contribute their thoughts through focus group discussions and case study evidence.

Introduction

Catherine Carroll-Meehan

Part 1: About this book

The chapters in this book have been written by tutors who share a range of experiences both in early years care and education settings, as advisors, teachers and early years professionals. The origins of themes explored can be traced back to students who are currently employed, volunteering or planning to work in the early years, who identified some of the issues and dilemmas that they faced in their daily work during group seminars. Tutors and students debating these themes agreed that the challenges faced in the workplace were exciting and stimulating. However, they also agreed that they sometimes felt disempowered or debilitated, as many decisions were difficult to make and seemed to raise further issues, leaving them with the feeling, that as educators, they were going round in circles. As a result, this book was born, with the aim to present contemporary concerns arising out of early years practice, offering some information and questions to assist in finding solutions and to highlight the opportunities for personal and professional improvement and development.

This book, therefore, is aimed at all those working in early years education. It aims to present opportunities for the reader to reflect not only upon professional practice, but also to consider the challenges and issues arising in the locality and to compare these across the wider society and the global issues related to children, their care and education.

The chapters are grouped in three thematic sections:

1   Change = Challenge
2   Challenges for learning and learners in the middle of change
3   Barriers to inclusive practice in times of change

Each section contains three chapters; the first section deals with the concept of change from different perspectives and aims to explore the natural fear and stress that all change seems to bring, whether the change is welcome or not. The changes experienced by the individual – both students and professionals – as a result of changes to the curriculum, qualifications and ideas of leadership are examined in this section.

The second section considers some of the challenges to the way early years teaching and learning is changing as a result of growing understanding about how the brain develops, how new technologies are influencing children in society and how the need to encourage all-round learning through outside play is as important today as it was the past.

The last section explores three of the major concerns encountered in the workplace by those working in the early years that are not directly related to the curriculum, but to the children and families that are at the centre of the whole educational experience. Thus the barriers presented when working with children with special educational needs, the stress of offering support to a wide range of diverse families and the problems associated with protecting and safeguarding children provide the inspiration for the last chapters.

The aim is for each chapter and section to provide a starting place for thinking around each theme. Therefore, it is not necessary for the book to be read in sequence, as the reader may select the chapters that offer a direct challenge to their own personal or professional need. Each chapter has similarities, as well as differences, depending upon the topic; many have case studies to offer examples from practice and most have some 'challenges' – questions arising from the text to support the reader in matching ideas to their own practice.

A final chapter acts as an overall reminder of the main themes and speculates upon challenges that might arise from future change.

Further details about each section and section chapters are outlined below:

Section 1: Change = Challenge

Change = Challenge was a theme highlighted by 100 people when asked about what the word change meant to them. 'Challenge' was the most common response. This first section of the book addresses change in three areas.

In Chapter 1, **Judy Gracey** tackles the '**Challenges of Change**'. As the first chapter of the book, it sets the context for the time of change in which those adults working with young children exist. Recent changes and reforms have been driven by government with the aim of improving quality and outcomes for children. Gracey identifies the importance of considering the 'individual' who faces change. For an educator in the early years, change often is imposed owing to the top-down exertion from external bodies to ensure change is made for compliance.

Currently, a 'patchwork' of qualifications exist in England in the early years sector and this chapter draws on the Nutbrown review (2012) and the government's response, *More Great Childcare* (DfE, 2013). Longitudinal studies such as Effective Provision of Preschool Education (EPPE) provide some clear benefits of qualified staff and the quality of preschool education and the impact on children from disadvantaged backgrounds. The Statutory Framework Early Years Foundation Stage (DfE, 2012) together with supporting guidance, despite frequent changes and updates, has provided statutory and non-statutory requirements for those working with children to deliver a curriculum that supports the learning and development of children from birth to 5 years in England. The EYFS is linked to the Ofsted inspection framework for early years settings. The challenges created by the demand for further qualifications and increased curriculum requirements are two significant changes facing early years educators.

In addition to the personal perspective (including personal values, attitudes and aspirations) on change, other factors that enable or create challenges for change are considered. For example, the ethos, culture and context of the setting impact on how those in the setting feel about the change. It is well established in the literature that these factors impact on how a person acts in practice irrespective of their beliefs (Meehan, 2005; Meehan, 2007).

In Chapter 2, **Shona Henderson** explores '**Understanding feelings: how to accept the challenge**'. This chapter is based on a case study of students exploring feelings of 'being and belonging' and the value of support from peers and networks in times of change. Change produces many emotional responses and, as highlighted in the second part of this section, 'C words for Change' (see Figure 0.2), it is complex and produces uncertainty, which can be discrienting for the person in the middle of the change process. Change can be both personal and organisational. This chapter outlines a brief history of change and in particular the widening participation agenda which has enabled students from diverse and non-traditional backgrounds to access a university education.

Henderson draws on Bourdieu's theory of habitus and, specifically, the personal and social perception that individuals construct about themselves. Students from 'non-traditional' backgrounds often feel like they are living in two worlds – as a university student and in their workplace and family. This provides challenges, pressures and tensions, which are often resolved with new opportunities and outlooks as the process of learning and education boosts their confidence and aspirations. Henderson identified a number of personal factors that impacted on the beliefs, values and attitudes of the students in the case study. It is well supported in the wider literature that demographic factors influence one's perceptions as well as the social and organisational contexts that people exist in (Meehan, 2007).

In Chapter 3, **Lin Shaw** highlights the value and importance of '**Maintaining a vision during times of change**'. This chapter highlights the criticality of leadership and the attributes of leaders during change. In the early years sector there have been significant changes over the past ten years. For example, Shaw highlights that emotional resilience is an attribute required for leaders in the early years.

In England, there has been significant reform in qualifications and more recent changes include having Early Years Teachers and Early Years Educators (More Great Childcare). Shaw raises the issue of nomenclature and the range of often ambiguous titles used in the sector to describe the adults that work with young children.

Shaw explores the role of the leader/manager and the tensions that are inherent in that dual role. The culture or the climate of organisations is also considered, alongside a range of leadership models or approaches. For example, the situational leader (Blanchard and Johnson, 1982), leadership qualities/attributes approach (e.g. Kouzes and Posner, 2007), action-centred approach (Adair, 1998), and empowerment approach (Zhang and Brundett, 2010) and transformational leadership (Bass, 1985). There is a discussion about the aspect of pedagogical leadership and the reality that this is a critical component of leadership in the early years sector, alongside leading and managing people.

Shaw outlines a number of models for supporting people through change and recognition of the difficulty that presents personally and in organisations. The chapter concludes with a vision for the future, and draws on evidence from other countries about possibilities and challenges for the sector.

Section 2: Challenges for learning and learners in the middle of change

In Chapter 4, **Bridget Durell** presents some of the latest research and thinking about '**Neuroscience and young children's learning: what can the early years workforce learn from**

this relatively new area of research?' This highly contemporary and topical chapter presents ideas from this emerging area of research. Many of the previous theories of child development, which have shaped education of the past 100 years, are now being reinterpreted in light of the new knowledge about how the human brain works. This new research confirms the importance of the first 7 to 8 years of life, the time in which the human brain develops at its fastest rates and in complexity.

Children's learning and development has become a part of the political agendas around the world. This period of life is viewed as critical in optimal development and potential for social and economic contributions in adulthood. 'Getting it right in the early years' is now more important than ever, it has been a belief of early years academics for decades but is now a position supported by science.

This chapter unpacks the science behind understanding children's learning and development based on new evidence from research. The process of learning is highlighted, as are the 'critical or sensitive periods' when the child's brain is more receptive for growth and development.

In Chapter 5, **Clair Stevens** presents a case for learning outside of classrooms: '**Taking the learning outdoors: the challenges and the possibilities**'. It argues that outdoor learning is critical in all children's learning and development. Stevens implies that access to learning opportunities in the outdoors is a child's right. Stevens sets up her argument within the context of the early childhood education pioneers who valued children's needs to play and learn with nature.

Stevens highlights the trend in the UK towards Forest Schools, and makes links to the Good Childhood report (The Children's Society, 2012) and the Early Years Foundation Stage curriculum (DfE, 2012). In addition to the educational benefits of learning in the outdoors, reference is also made to the benefits for children's health and well-being. Stevens concludes by articulating the barriers and challenges for not ensuring that children have access and opportunity to learning in the outdoors.

In Chapter 6, **Clare Wiseman** and **Laurence Taylor** explore children's readiness for reading and technology in '**Digital harmony or digital dissonance? Developing literacy skills in the new technological age**'. Technology is part of our lives in the twenty-first century. Children are growing up as 'digital natives' and we, the adults working with them, are 'digital immigrants'. This presents challenges as 'traditional' ways of learning are changing. Wiseman and Taylor highlight these challenges for practitioners with regard to literacy learning. The 'three Rs' form the basis of valued knowledge in schools. Reading is seen as a vital life skill and, with relatively low illiteracy rates in the UK in comparison with other nations, but a poor result in comparison with other OECD countries, the change in preference for digital over paper-based reading materials does present some challenges.

Children in the twenty-first century are multi-modal, multi-literate and multi-taskers. The impact of instant information and the way this is processed is perceived as a barrier to deep learning. Wiseman and Taylor acknowledge the dissonance created by the digital era. Access and equity may be additional factors that add to the dissonance because all children will not have access to the same level of digital media at home.

This chapter highlights challenges for those adults working with children, and new opportunities and challenges for teaching and learning with technology. This is a new concept, and like anything new it will take time to embed in everyday practice, but it is something that cannot be ignored.

Section 3: Barriers to inclusive practice in times of change

In Chapter 7, **Diana Strauss** highlights the '**Complex and challenging: supporting young children identified with special educational needs**'. This first chapter in this section highlight some ways in which barriers to participation in education can be minimised for children identified as having special needs. Children in the UK are beneficiaries of having legislation to protect and support their rights to educational provision which takes into account their disability. The recent Children and Families Act (2014) has meant that there are changes to the education, health and social care provision for children with special needs in England. Changes in legislation and financial pressures, arising from austerity budgets owing to the global financial crisis, have contributed to pressure on the provision of services for children and families by local authorities.

This chapter highlights learning, development and positive action within the context of current policy, procedures and practice which is both statutory and non-statutory in nature. It is supported by a section on assessment and support of children with disabilities that shows a preference for a holistic consideration of individuals and what is best for their learning and development in and out of educational settings.

Disabilities may be life-long. Children born with disabilities usually have these identified in the early years, well before they attend compulsory schooling and then exist beyond schooling into life in the community and employment. Strauss highlights the challenges for those working in the early years sector and, in particular, how communication and information between 'professionals' and parents/carers is critical in ensuring a more seamless experience for children and their families.

In Chapter 8, **Christine Ritchie** considers '**The challenge of supporting diverse families**'. This chapter highlights the demographic changes in family structure, and reports on statistics from national sources in the UK. Ritchie defines a number of 'family types' that have become more prevalent in the twenty-first century, alongside a discussion about parenting styles. Both of these discussions challenge the reader to consider their position about how they define 'family' and 'what good parenting looks like'. This is a core issue for those adults working with children and families as we often encounter families with different values from our own and this can cloud the way we work with them and the assumptions we make about the children and their homes.

Ritchie uses case studies to provide examples to highlight the challenges faced by those adults working with children and families in the current changing context. Bronfenbrenner's ecological systems theory, Bandura's social learning theory and Bowlby's attachment theory support the reader in making sense of how parents raise their children, using a range of theoretical models. Cultural, religious and ethnic variations in child-rearing are also raised in this chapter with increased diversity, not only in family structure but also in globalisation and the results of migration, bringing about tensions between culture and ethnicity and how children, childhood and parenting is viewed.

An increasing issue in the UK is the impact of poverty on children and their families. Ritchie explores the barriers created by poverty to children's social, emotional, educational and economic outcomes. This is a contemporary issue which raises questions for the reader about their own beliefs about poverty and how it is manifest in the lives of young children.

A further contemporary issue raised in this chapter through a case study is the increase in same-sex families. The case study is from the viewpoint of a gay person who works with children. She raises some compelling questions about her own experiences and her future as a mother of a child in a same-sex relationship. Ritchie draws some comparisons between same-sex families and step-families who, historically, have struggled to be accepted in comparison with what society depicts as a 'normal' family.

In Chapter 9, **Linda Flower** and **Christine Ritchie** explore '**Taking risks: living with danger – the benefits and safeguards**'. This chapter highlights the dilemma for those adults working with children with regard to risks. As the chapter title suggests, it is mainly concerned with the health, safety and protection of children. The chapter uses case studies to illustrate a range of health and safety issues that may impact on children's health and well-being. It supports the notion of a common-sense approach to managing risks, with some good pointers for decision-making and risks. It highlights risks and the impact from both the child and adult perspectives.

Resilience is an attribute that supports a person's ability to cope with change, and this chapter considers how resilience and risk-taking can be supported in the context of trusting and enabling relationships between adults and children. This chapter discusses an example of a recent serious case review with regard to children who have been abused and killed in their homes. It raises key questions for practitioners about their role in the care and protection of children and the importance of collaborative working with other professionals to prevent serious cases of child abuse and neglect.

Poverty and the impact on children's health and well-being is also explored in this chapter. This is discussed in terms of the impact on children's life chances educationally and socially, but added to this are factors such as poor health and disability that make it difficult for children to break out of the poverty cycle.

Part 2: The background to 'challenge and change'

This book has been written at a time of unprecedented change. Not just change in one area but in every aspect of life. The chapter themes within the book are situated in the context of a complex set of social, political, economic, technological and global drivers of change. These external forces are forcing rationalisation and improvement agendas and streamlining of public services that are centred on people, learning, education and care. This agenda is not always compatible with the ethics and values associated with care and education. Change provides challenges and uncertainty, but it also allows for opportunities and development.

This part of the introduction sets the context and background with a clear rationale for this book by considering the current context for education and care at four levels, with an adaptation of Bronfenbrenner's (1979) ecological systems model as a framework. This will be followed by an exploration of change as a process that can provide opportunities and at the same time loss. The challenges and complexity of change will be examined to set the scene for the subsequent chapters.

Adults working with young children: who are they and what do we call them?

The choice of words used to describe the adults who work with young children in a range of settings is varied. This small commentary adds to the wider debate which is picked up again in different chapters of the book. The use of 'teacher' in some contexts refers specifically to a person with a relevant qualification or recognised status or professional association membership. Similarly, the word 'practitioner' for one who is engaged in practice is equally problematic. It implies that the person involved is very hands-on, which in itself is suitable, but when it is used next to the word early years' 'professional' there appears to be a gap in status. For example, in England, the introduction of the Early Years Professional Status (EYPS) has introduced an 'elite' group to the children's workforce. These people are viewed as leaders and have had to comply with an assessment against standard and be formally awarded the status by the Children's Workforce Development Council (CWDC)/National College of Teachers. The introduction of the Early Years Teacher Status and the Early Years Initial Teacher Training programmes reinforce the use of the word teacher for those with a specific qualification.

'Educators' is another term used widely, which on the surface appears to be less problematic. If we look at the origins of the word educate, it can mean to 'develop the knowledge, skill or character of'. The word educate has Latin origins (*e-ducere*), meaning 'to lead out'. Early use of the word in ancient Greece by Socrates meant the word was used to describe the process of education through 'drawing out' what was in students and at the same time giving them essential knowledge and skills needed by the society.

For the purpose of this section, and in some chapters, the adults who work with children in a range of ways such as to observe, assess and plan will be referred to as 'educators'. These educators fulfil a number of roles including, facilitating, fostering, nurturing, teaching, instructing, caring, safeguarding, protecting, listening, inspiring, guiding, researching, communicating and the list can continue ad infinitum. Early years educators, as key professionals in children's lives, have a key responsibility to observe, interpret and analyse, to gain an in-depth picture of children. So that all children's complex lives can be taken into account, especially the complexity of the child's social and cultural world.

In the UK and in other countries, there is a constant pressure for accountability, especially with regard to public spending. This book recognises this as a driver of change, underpinning many of the issues raised in its chapters.

So what about children, how are they viewed in this book? The authors' backgrounds and experiences of working with children and families in the UK and internationally have meant that the construction of children and childhood in the book is quite eclectic: drawing on child development perspective, the work of Vygotsky, Montessori, Piaget, Bruner and the latest research from neuroscience all influence the stance taken throughout the text.

The individual's response to change

It is important to reflect on how you, as an individual, respond to change. An awareness of your own beliefs and position is the starting place for understanding, accepting, responding to the challenges brought about by change. As an educator, you bring to your work your own knowledge, skills, values and beliefs about children, in addition to your experience and understanding of the whole education process. These factors will impact on how you respond to the changes and challenges in the workplace.

A central aim here is to give you opportunities to reflect on your beliefs about children, childhood, families, learning, teaching, assessment, care and education. An individual's beliefs are shaped by their experiences as a learner both from childhood and as an adult. The German philosopher and writer Johann Wolfgang von Goethe once wrote, 'To think is easy. To act is hard. But the hardest thing in the world is to act in accordance with your thinking.' This quotation provides a good starting place for adults working with children to reflect upon their own views and to consider better ways of working, based on personal learning and working with young children in an inclusive and diverse context. Goethe's challenge is for educators to be able to step outside of themselves and to have a deep and critical rationale for their actions and act to promote social justice and equity.

Goethe's intentions are not always possible in times of change; as humans we tend to respond to challenge in a reactionary manner rather than with a well-considered response. Kotter in his book *Our Iceberg Is Melting* (Kotter and Rathgeber, 2006), tells a fable about people's responses to change and how those people in leadership can create a positive climate about change. He outlines eight steps for successful change which move from setting the scene and context for change, making a decision about what the change will look like and how it will happen, to making it happen and then embedding the new changes into the culture of the workplace. Kotter articulates the importance of acknowledging 'thinking and feeling' as a means to effecting change (2006, p. 132).

My own doctoral studies (Meehan, 2005; Meehan, 2007) highlighted the importance for those adults working with children to articulate their beliefs and to be reflective in and on action (Ferry and Ross-Gordon, 1998; Schön, 1987). This learning in action and practice is a lifelong endeavour, and continuing professional development needs to be part of the professional responsibilities for those adults working with young children. The book is therefore directed at a wide range of early years educators, from those at the beginning of their studies to others with a wealth of experience and who wish to continue to expand their thinking.

The current early years context

In the field of early childhood education and care, and in wider education, change is rapid and comes from multiple sources. Living in a pluralist and global society diversity of race, culture, language, religion, beliefs, values and traditions present personal and professional challenges to those adults involved in the education and care of young children (Meehan, 2007).

Drawing on Bronfenbrenner's ecological systems model (1979), the adaptation on page 9 highlights the layers involved in the challenging context in which we live. The context will be examined at four levels, starting with the broadest (global and international) and moving down to the children and families who are at the heart of the work and subject of this book. Bronfenbrenner's ecological systems model assumes a level of interaction between the systems. This adaptation of the model shares this assumption, but at the centre of this model, the children and families may adopt a passive or active role in interaction due to a number of personal and contextual factors.

Early childhood education and care typically covers children from birth to 8 years. In the UK, these years are divided into 'pre-school' years and compulsory schooling. The current framework for children from birth to five years is the Early Years Foundation Stage (DfE, 2012), and Key Stage 1 in the National Curriculum covers children up to the end of Year 2 in the primary phase. These documents will be referred to in some of the subsequent chapters in a range of ways.

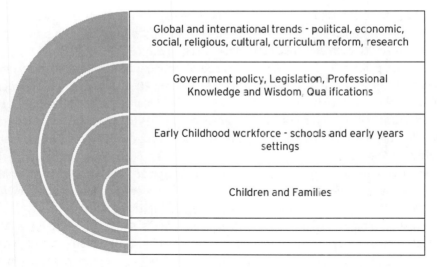

Global and international trends - political, economic, social, religious, cultural, curriculum reform, research

Government policy, Legislation, Professional Knowledge and Wisdom, Qua ifications

Early Childhood workforce - schools and early years settings

Children and Families

Figure 0.1 Four levels of contextual challenge for early years education

Adapted from Bronfenbrenner's ecological systems model (1979)

At a Global and International level, the education and care of children can be found embedded in international treaties and aspirations based on the rights of all children (UNCRC, 1989). Educational aspirations for children internationally can be found in the Four Pillars of Education: 'Learning to be, learning to do, learning to live together and learning to know' (Delors, 1996). These four pillars represent a shift in learning not just for knowledge but also to equip children with skills and attitudes needed in the societies and time they are growing up in. It is these global aspirations that underpin the current drivers in education and care internationally and are measured by tests such as PISA.

Current research and debate

At the government, local policy and field of early childhood level, there are some themes that are the focus of research and debate. These have remained constant for a number of years (Meehan, 2007); for example:

1   reconceptualising children and childhood considering children's rights and participation and the challenge this presents for those working with young children;
2   curriculum and pedagogical issues and an appreciation of good practice from around the world that is shared instantly through the internet;
3   accountability for public funding quality assurance; and
4   current and emerging research and impact on practice, in particular new understanding about neuroscience and brain development.

These four themes are picked up in various ways throughout the text. For example, childhood has been reconceptualised and it is now increasingly recognised that the first years of life are the most critical. This is set within the context of increased diversity of family types as modern society responds to these changes. These changes are indicative of broader societal trends that impact on children, childhood and families, and which are often slowly followed by changes to legislation and policy to reflect the reality.

Major social, political, economic, and technological changes have impacted on children and families since the end of the Second World War (Meehan, 2007). For example, the local and social 'neighbourhood' communities of the 1950s have been replaced by new 'online communities' and social media forums such as Facebook and Twitter. These powerful new forums link people from diverse backgrounds into amorphous groups with learning and the sharing of information being instant and accessible such as at no other time in history. There are many online forums for advice on issues related to children and raising children, learning and teaching, behaviours and disability. These changes have had an impact on children's lives and influenced their identities and how we as adults respond to them.

The question remains whether the 'curriculum' in schools is fit for purpose for children in the twenty-first century. As our understanding of children, the curriculum and pedagogy changes, we need to consider how children learn and how best to prepare for life in a fast-paced world, if in fact that is possible. The question about what 'knowledge' is important leads on to what 'skills and attributes' we can support in the development of children, which may include resilience, valuing social justice and responses to diversity.

The Department for Education (DfE, 2014b) recognises that:

> Education both influences and reflects the values of our society, and the kind of society we want to be. It is therefore important to recognise a set of common aims, values and purposes that underpin the curriculum and the work of schools.

> The school curriculum comprises all learning and other experiences that each school plans for its pupils. The National Curriculum is an important element of the school curriculum.
>
> (DfE, 2014b, p. 5)

The 'core knowledge' contained within the National Curriculum (NS) statutory framework is intended to provide an outline of content, around which educators are 'free to choose' how they organise the day, but assessment procedures and current school culture might restrict any real sense of freedom. How then to be proactive in responding to changes within society, economics and the environment to equip the future generation for the challenges ahead?

Department of Education's Business Plan 2011–2015 (DfE, 2011) opens with the vision for state education which drives its policies and reforms:

> Our vision is for a highly educated society in which opportunity is more equal for children and young people no matter what their background or family circumstances. We will do this by raising standards of educational achievement and closing the achievement gap between rich and poor.
>
> (DfE, 2011, p 1)

The 'raising of standards' has been a common mantra of successive governments, along with increased legislation, so what the future holds will be challenging and, no doubt, hard work!

The political context

The backdrop for the current agendas for young children in the UK is a range of legislative frameworks, policies and curriculum frameworks. For example, in response to its obligations as a signatory of the UNCRC, the government passed the The Children Act (1989), Children Act (2004), and the Education Act (1988) and Education Act (2011), which all set out statutory requirements for the care and education of children in England. For example, these legislative frameworks require all adults working with children to ensure that children's well-being is paramount. Underpinning this legislative requirement, those adults working with young children need to be able to understand and identify children's needs and appreciate the contexts in which they live. Similarly, the Education Reform Act 1988 defines the assessment regimes and curriculum content, and this too has impacted.

One of the products of the Education Reform Act 1988 was the establishment of the Office for Standards in Education, Children's Services and Skills (Ofsted). The stage-based progression through school was also implemented with the National Curriculum. A key feature of the staged schooling is the way in which one stage prepares the student for the next stage. The introduction of the Early Years Foundation Stage framework in 2008 has meant that children from birth are now being prepared for the future education in Key Stages 1, 2 and 3. The Early Years Framework, while containing sound educational principles for young children, ensures that early years educators are compliant and produce evidence that children are fully prepared in the Foundation Stage and 'ready' for Key Stage 1. This became statutory in 2012, with the updated version of the Early Years Foundation Stage.

The Every Child Matters (ECM) policy launched in 2003 enacted the legal responsibilities that were embedded in the health, education and social care policies in the UK. For example, in 2000, the Health Assessment document which outlines the assessment of children in need:

> Securing the wellbeing of children by protecting them from all forms of harm and ensuring their developmental needs are responded to appropriately are primary aims of Government policy. Local authority social services departments working with other local authority departments and health authorities have a duty to safeguard and promote the welfare of children in their area who are in need and to promote the upbringing of such children, wherever possible by their families, through providing an appropriate range of services. A critical task is to ascertain with the family whether a child is in need and how that child and family might best be helped. The effectiveness with which a child's needs are assessed will be key to the effectiveness of subsequent actions and services and, ultimately, to the outcomes for the child.
>
> Hutton (2000, p. 9)

The Education Act was reviewed and updated in 2011, and the Children and Families Act (2014) has implications for the current children's workforce. More Great Childcare (DfE, 2013) sets out the aspirations of the coalition government with regard to the care and education of children in the first five years of life.

Irrespective of current government agendas, a central feature of high-quality early childhood practice internationally is the ability of those adults working with young children to respond to the individual children in the setting that they attend. Therefore, understanding children and their development is a critical component of their work, and has been central to the profession and many early childhood courses historically. Some would argue that a curriculum based on understanding children's development by studying theories of child development restricts the work of practitioners by narrowing their perspectives. However, for the novice practitioner, having a framework to test ideas, theory and practice promotes active reflection.

The media and other prevailing discourses in the UK paint a dichotomous picture of children in the twenty-first century. But remaining at the heart of the issue is the child, or children, with individual needs. The state intervenes in their lives in ways that often depend upon how they are perceived within the context of their 'dysfunctional' families or due to circumstances beyond their control.

The child and family context

The ECM document, hailed as the way forward in 2003, claimed to protect children and to promote a lifestyle for them that would enable them to function as competent members of society. On one hand, children are vulnerable and need to be in the care and protection of the state, because parents all over the UK are not competent to raise them and will do harm to children if the state does not intervene. And yet, as highlighted in both the Victoria Climbé and Baby P cases, the state has failed in its role. On the other hand, a survey commissioned by Barnardo's (2008) found that, overwhelmingly, adults in the UK perceive children as a threat. Words such as 'vermin' and 'danger' were used to describe children and young people. Children are protected and at the same time demonised.

This issue is not new, but accelerated significantly in the media and public discourse with the James Bulger case: in 1993, the unthinkable happened when two children (aged 10 years old) – Robert Thompson and Jon Venables – took a 3-year-old – James Bulger – from a shopping centre and brutally killed him. The case shocked the nation. Retrospective laws were brought in that allowed the two children to be tried as adults.

From the life histories of these two young killers, it could be construed that, sadly, the state had failed them too. In some reports, Thompson was described as being the youngest of seven children, living with his mother. His father had left the family when he was five, and Thompson and siblings had been subjected to abuse and his mother was an alcoholic. Thompson had probably been bullied and had low-attainment levels at school. Venables, similarly came from a dysfunctional family and was described as a loner. His parents were separated; one parent had a mental illness and some siblings had special needs. Venables and Thompson were the very children that the ECM and other policies aimed to protect and nurture. Yet, after ten years of care they committed their crime.

The deliberate reduction of the age of criminal responsibility due to public pressure violates a central principle of common law, namely a right to trial by a jury of one's peers. Given that one must be 18 years of age to serve on a jury and that a child of 12 is not able to purchase a pet, it appears highly incongruous that a child of 10 should be subjected to the full force of the law. It was reported in the media, that the children were seated in the dock, away from parents and did not speak in their own defence. It must have been an intimidating experience for them. The presentation of ideas here is not suggesting that Thompson and Venables should be excused, but rather aims to raise the issue of criminalising children on the one hand, and on the other declaring that children need to be protected.

Other examples from the media in which children and young people were demonised can be seen after the summer riots in 2011. After the riots, the coalition government identified that direct invention was required in the case of some of the most difficult to engage families with children who were at risk of becoming anti-social and lacking in respect for themselves and their community. The rhetoric was about repairing the damage to society by 120,000 of the most troubled families in Britain. References in media reports such as to the 'most troubled families in Britain' highlighted an undercurrent in British society that blamed the riots on children from 'troubled families', although not all of those arrested and charged came from disadvantaged backgrounds. However, the Prime Minister said: 'The sight of those young people looting laughing as they go demonstrated a lack of proper parenting, upbringing, ethics and morals' (www.bbc.co.uk/news/magazine-21 22132).

Such reports on troubled families are accompanied by other reports suggesting that children's lack of emotional attachment is limiting their life chances. A recent report in the media suggested that attachment and in particular poor attachment impacts on children's potential to learn. The Sutton Trust study conducted by Moullin, Waldfogel and Washbrook (2014) highlighted that children's emotional well-being and resilience is linked to bonding with their mother; secure attachments mean that children's educational and life chances will be better. The report suggests that 40 per cent of children in the UK have had a poor start in relation to developing strong bonds or attachment with their mother or primary carer. It is conjectured by the study that attachment and good bonds have a direct impact on learning, behaviour, self-esteem and ultimately the ability of the child to become a productive member of society and the economy (www.bbc.co.uk/news/education-26667036).

The **children** and **families** at the centre of Bronfenbrenner's model receive benefits from society and the economy in terms of education and care. The impact that children and families have on the outer layers connecting to the community and society will depend on engagement beyond the family circle – are they passive recipients of a service or actively involved and influencing the services they are using politically, socially, financially or by other means? Since the 1960s, there has been an increased concern about the nature of formal schooling and when it should start. Governments and countries are being judged internationally based on children's literacy and numeracy skills. There is significant pressure on schools and settings to be accountable for public funding and in the UK Ofsted is the body that regulates the quality of all nurseries, childminders, schools, colleges and universities. An example of how the media reflects upon this is highlighted by this BBC News article related to PISA report in 2013:

Raising the quality of teaching, rather than creating new types of school structure, is the way to raise standards, says Labour's Tristram Hunt. The shadow education secretary said, to catch up with international rivals, teachers needed continuous training. Last week, Mr Hunt announced plans for teachers to be regularly 're-licensed' under a future Labour government. Mr Hunt said he wanted 'world class' teachers to be the 'architects of growth . . . He emphasised the central importance of the standard of teaching – quoting the argument of the OECD's education guru Andreas Schleicher that 'no education system can exceed the quality of its teachers'.

Sean Coughlan, BBC News Education, 15 January 2014

The question to ponder here is whether government intervention, testing or other pressures actually improve the learning environment for children and families or is instead a factor in lowering opportunities and standards.

Context for educators: summary

This introductory section of the book may give you, the reader, a flavour of some of the complex issues that exist in the worlds of children and their families in diverse contexts and communities. All those working with young children should consider the contemporary issues that affect them, and consider how they can make a difference and improve the learning opportunities for all children.

When given the task of writing this section, I turned to Facebook and asked my students, friends and family to give me words that started with 'C' that made them think of change. The word cloud (Figure 0.2) together with Table 0.1 highlights the range of words. The 'C' words have been sorted into words that can be themed as evidence of change, benefits of change, positive and negative words associated with change. You may note that some words can be found in more than one theme.

The title of the book – *Challenge and Change* – conjures up not only feeling about change but also how we as individuals respond to change. Some evidence of change is seen in the development of children, and change is viewed as exciting especially as we anticipate the baby who says their first word or takes their first steps. Change is viewed positively. Similarly, we marvel at the change in seasons when the colours of the leaves on the trees signify beginnings and endings, and this reminds us that change is cyclical. Evidence of change, however, can be viewed negatively, such as loss of control or direction (compass), but on the other hand having a compass can provide comfort in knowing where the change might lead.

Change can be beneficial. Some of the words linked to the benefits of change include the opportunity to collaborate, create and co-produce and find new ways to work with others in order to make a difference. This can create a cohesive approach to change, thereby leading to a change in the culture by building commitment to the community. Change allows for new opportunities, chances for clarity and control over the consequences.

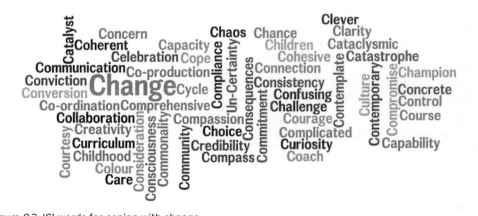

Figure 0.2 'C' words for coping with change

Table 0.1 Change

Evidence of change	Benefits of change	Agents of change	Positives	Negatives
Children	Collaboration	Consideration	Challenge	Concern
Childhood	Credibility	Consistency	Culture	Challenge
Co-ordination	Comprehensive	Capacity	Community	Comprehensive
Conversion	Concrete	Champion	Commonality	Culture
Control	Cohesive	Culture	Choice	Complicated
Consequences	Coherent	Communication	Commitment	Confusing
Compass	Community	Commitment	Clever (innovation)	Compliance
Colour	Commitment	Coach	Compliance	Chance (opportunity)
	Creativity	Curriculum	Care	Un-Certainty
	Care			Chaos
	Chance (opportunity)	Chance (opportunity)	Chance (opportunity)	Control or lack of control
	Celebration	Courage	Capability	Catastrophe
	Clarity	Conviction	Consequences	Consequences
	Compassion	Contemplate	Compromise	Cataclysmic
	Courtesy	Cycle	Catalyst	Compromise
	Consciousness			
	Connection			
	Control			
	Consequences			
	Cope			
	Compromise			
	Co-production			

As agents of change, we all have the capacity to be champions of good practice, to communicate clearly and to show commitment to the changing culture and act courageously in accordance with convictions. We can all contemplate our role in change and think about Mahatma Gandhi's words, 'Be the change we want to see in the world'.

The final two columns of the Table 0.1 highlight the words positively and negatively associated with change. The challenge for those people leading change is that the chances and opportunities created by change are best realised if common goals and vision can be clearly articulated, and that the culture and communication are respectful and supportive of the thoughts and feelings of those involved in the change. If this is the case, then chaos and catastrophes, confusion and perceived lack of control can make complicated change less so and the consequences of change are more likely to be positive.

Bibliography

Barnado's (2008) 'The shame of Britain's intolerance of children'. Available at: www.barnardos.org.uk/news/media_centre/press_releases.htm?ref=42088 (Accessed: 21 April 2014).

Bronfenbrenner, U. (1979) *The Ecology of Human Development: Experiments by Nature and Design.* Cambridge, MA: Harvard University Press.

Coughlan, S. (2014) 'Teacher quality. Hunt's Priority.' Available at: www.bbc.co.uk/news/education-25751988 (Accessed: 6 August 2014).

Delors, J. (1996) *Report to UNESCO of the International Commission of Education for the Twenty-first Century: Learning: The Treasure Within.* Paris: UNESCO.

DfE (Department for Education) (2011) *Business Plan 2011–2015, Department for Education.* Available at: www.gov.uk/government/uploads/system/uploads/attachment_data/file/31930/10-p58-bis-business-plan.pdf (Accessed: 7 August 2014).

DfE (Department for Education) (2012) *The Statutory Early Years Foundation Stage.* Available at: www.education.gov.uk/aboutdfe/statutory/g00213120/eyfs-statutory-framework (Accessed: 21 April 2014).

DfE (Department for Education) (2013) *More Great Childcare: Raising Quality and Giving Parents More Choice.* Available at: www.gov.uk/government/publications/more-great-childcare-raising-quality-and-giving-parents-more-choice (Accessed: 21 April 2014).

DfE (Department for Education) (2014) *Aims, Values and Purposes of Education England* Available at: http://webarchive.nationalarchives.gov.uk/20130903160941/http://www.education.gov.uk/schools/teachingandlearning/curriculum/b00199676/aims-values-and-purposes (Accessed: 21 April 2014).

DfE (Department for Education) (2014a) *Children and Families Act.* Available at: http://www.legislation.gov.uk/ukpga/2014/6/pdfs/ukpga_20140006_en.pdf (Accessed: 21 April 2014).

DfE (Department for Education) (2014b) *National Curriculum in England: Primary Curriculum* [online]. Available at: www.gov.uk/government/collctions/national-curriculum (Accessed: 21 April 2014).

DfEE (Department for Education and Employment) (2000) *The National Curriculum: Handbook for Primary Teachers in England: Key Stages 1 and 2* [online]. Available at: http://webarchive.nationalarchives.gov.uk/20130401151715/https://www.education.gov.uk/publications/standard/publicationDetail/Page1/QCA/99/457 (Accessed: 21 April 2014).

Ferry, N. M. and Ross-Gordon, J. M. (1998) 'An Inquiry into Schön's epistemology of practice: exploring links between experience and reflective practice', *Adult Education Quarterly*, 48(2), pp. 98–103.

Hutton, J. (2000) 'Foreword', in Department of Health, Department of Education and Employment and Home Office, *Framework for the Assessment of Children in Need and Their Families.* London: The Stationery Office.

Kotter, J. and Rathgeber, H. (2006) *Our Iceberg is Melting.* London: Macmillan.

Meehan, C. (2005) 'Early childhood teacher's beliefs about teaching and learning and the factors that impact on their practice', *Journal of the Early Childhood Teachers' Association Inc., Educating Young Children: Learning and Teaching the Early Childhood Years*, 11(3).

Meehan, C. (2007) *Thinking and Acting: Early Childhood Teachers' Beliefs and Practice with Regard to Learning, Teaching and Religious Education*. Published thesis. Brisbane: Australian Catholic University. Available at: http://dlibrary.acu.edu.au/digitaltheses/public/adt-acuvp161.10062008/ (Accessed: 23 March 2014).

Moullin, S., Waldfogel, J. and Washbrook, E. (2014) *Baby Bonds*. Sutton Trust report. Available at: www.suttontrust.com/our-work/research/download/265/ (Accessed: 21 April 2014).

National Archives (2014) Education Reform Act (1988) Available at: www.legislation.gov.uk/ukpga/1988/40/contents (Accessed: 21 April 2014).

National Archives (2014) Children Act (1989) Available at: www.legislation.gov.uk/ukpga/1989/41/contents (Accessed: 21 April 2014).

National Archives (2014) Children Act (2004) Available at: www.legislation.gov.uk/ukpga/2004/31/contents (Accessed: 21 April 2014).

National Archives (2014) Education Act (2011) Available at: http://www.legislation.gov.uk/ukpga/2011/21/contents/enacted (Accessed: 21 April 2014).

National Archives (2014) *Every Child Matters*. Available at: http://webarchive.nationalarchives.gov.uk/20130401151715/https://www.education.gov.uk/publications/standard/publicationDetail/Page1/CM5860 (Accessed: 21 April 2014).

Nutbrown, C. (2012) *Foundations for Quality: The Independent Review of Early Education and Childcare Qualifications: Final Report*. Available at: www.gov.uk/government/uploads/system/uploads/attachment_data/file/175463/Nutbrown-Review.pdf (Accessed: 21 April 2014).

Schön, D. A. (1987) *Educating the Reflective Practitioner.* San Francisco, CA: Jossey-Bass.

The Children's Society (2012) *The Good Childhood Report: A Review of Our Children's Well-Being*. Available at: www.childrenssociety.org.uk (Accessed: 21 April 2014).

UNICEF (1989) Convention on the Rights of the Child. Available at: www.unicef.org/crc/ (Accessed: 21 April 2014).

Section 1

Change = Challenge

The three anonymous quotes given here are motivational to direct your thinking as you begin to read this section of the text. Firstly, 'If it doesn't challenge you, it doesn't change you!'

As you read each of the chapters, think about who you are, the values that you hold and how you can be challenged in your thinking and acting.

Secondly, 'The question isn't can you? It's will you?' Accepting the challenge for change sometimes means that you need to make a decision to change.

Thirdly, 'Challenges are what makes life interesting. Overcoming them is what makes it meaningful.' It is on your journey as a person working with young children and their families that will continue to learn and make meaning.

In this section there are three chapters:

Chapter 1 is written by **Judy Gracey** and explores **'The challenges of change'**.

Chapter 2 is authored by **Shona Henderson** and considers the feelings related to change in **'Understanding feelings: how to accept the challenge'**.

Chapter 3 is written by **Lin Shaw** and highlights the value and importance of **'Maintaining a vision during times of change'**.

1   The challenges of change

Judy Gracey

Overview

This chapter examines the ways in which early years educators are challenged by changes to their roles. It discusses the ways in which the educator, facing changing circumstances, is affected by personal values and attitudes. The context, ethos and culture of the workplace and the impact of various attitudes to change will also be considered. The need to develop personal attributes and skills that assist in meeting these challenges is explored, and the chapter will show how the experience of change can increase personal confidence as well as adding to knowledge and understanding of good practice. Lastly, the chapter discusses the idea that it is the attitude of the practitioner when experiencing change that determines personal well-being and success.

Introduction

The work of the early years practitioner has undergone many changes. From being popularly perceived as a job for those that 'love to work with children', it is now considered to be a profession that plays a crucial role in the care and development of young children and their well-being. However, it is a multi-faceted role. There has been a government-led drive for a more highly qualified workforce, tighter regulations and clear guidelines for practice and accountability to outside agencies for that practice. Nevertheless, caring remains an attribute that is central to the role of the early years practitioner. Moyles (2001, p. 84) states that 'feelings and emotions such as passion are acceptable and indeed desirable', but that it is a mindful passion. It requires deep knowledge and understanding of child development. Moyles links that need for passion with a reasoning mind, able to analyse, reflect, understand, evaluate, learn and engage, and be an inspiration for professionalism.

The individual facing change

Change, fuelled by research, debate and governance has been a constant feature in early years settings. Urban (2008, p. 141) describes distinct layers to our knowledge of early childhood and practice. There is the body of knowledge produced by scholarly research and debate that has to be transferred and then applied in practice. He describes it as a ' powerful top-down stream of knowledge presented as relevant for practice, and a similar downstream of expectations and what needs to be done at practice levels of the hierarchy'. It presents enormous challenges to the early years educator, increasing expectations and requiring them to improve practice based on studying this 'top-down stream' of knowledge, and acquiring deeper understanding of early years development. However, the educator has the satisfaction of seeing how the children respond to the positive changes that enhance their opportunities for development.

In addition, this research has led to improved knowledge and understanding of child development, which has driven the government to increase standards in early years education through inspection and changes to guidelines for practice. Settings are regularly inspected by the Office for Standards in Education, Children's Services and Skills (Ofsted) to ensure the children's well-being, welfare and personal development needs are met. The leadership and management of settings are examined, often resulting in recommendations for more effective practice. This close scrutiny and subsequent reflection and change have often led to the development of clearer management structures and more defined roles and responsibilities for practitioners. The role of the early years educator is increasingly recognised as crucial to raising standards for ensuring the holistic development of the child. This has driven the need for more professional knowledge and understanding of child development through academic study, and increased awareness of an early years career-structure based on qualifications as well as experience.

Childcare qualifications have traditionally been something of a patchwork of levels of knowledge, understanding and skills. In their research concerning effective provision of pre-school education, Sylva *et al*. (2003) found that the quality of early provision was linked to the quality of staff working in the settings. 'Children made more progress in pre-school centres where staff had higher qualifications, particularly if the manager was highly qualified' (2003, p. 3). Consequently, a drive to ensure a more knowledgeable and skilled workforce based on improved understanding of the development needs of young children has been prioritised. For example, England introduced a ten-year strategy to support and improve the lives of families that included increasing the education and skills of those working with the early years (DfES 2005).

In a DfE survey conducted to ascertain the qualifications of group-based early years staff in 2011, researchers found that among the group-based childcare providers and early years settings staff, the difference was relatively small when it came to the proportion of staff holding at least a level 3 qualification (A-level/NVQ level 3). This was 79 per cent among paid childcare staff and 82 per cent among paid early years staff. However, the difference was more pronounced at level 6. Only 10 per cent of paid group-based childcare staff, compared with 42 per cent among paid early years staff, had an Honours degree. Childminders typically had lower levels of qualification than staff in the group-based providers, with 59 per cent of childminders holding at least a level 3 qualification and only 4 per cent holding a relevant level 6 qualification (DfE 2011, p. 90).

The situation is still far from perfect. In the Nutbrown Review, an independent review of early years sector qualifications, it was found that the present qualification system is confusing. Nutbrown (2012) points out that the 'present system is not systematically equipping practitioners with the knowledge, skills and understanding they need to give babies and young children high quality experiences' (2012, p. 5). The UK's economic downturn has eroded the financial support for practitioners' further education and training, and in addition there are few financial incentives for undertaking further learning. However, in her foreword to the report *More Great Childcare* (DfE, 2013), Liz Truss MP promised that the government would:

- build a stronger, more capable workforce, with more rigorous training and qualifications, led by a growing group of Early Years Teachers;
- drive up quality, with rigorous Ofsted inspection and incentives for providers to improve the skills and knowledge of their staff.

The early years practitioner who increases their knowledge and understanding through study is more able to meet the drive for quality that is forcing changes to management and practice. The report promised that the Government 'will improve early years qualifications so that parents and providers can have greater confidence in the calibre of people who are teaching our youngest children' (DfE, 2013, p. 6).

The report cites research undertaken by Sylva *et al.* (2004, 2008) that found:

- The quality of Early Years provision is related to better intellectual/cognitive and social/behavioural development in children at entry to and throughout primary school.
- Children made more progress in pre-school centres where trained teachers were present.
- High quality pre-school is especially beneficial for the most disadvantaged children.

For the early years practitioner, this emphasis on gaining further qualifications comes with higher expectations, more challenges to practice, more guidelines for improving the quality of practice, extensive regulation, accountability and rigorous inspections. These have resulted in exciting but challenging times. In their report 'Early Years and Child Care' (2011, p. 21), Ofsted inspectors also concluded that 'outcomes for children were good or outstanding where practitioners were well-qualified or trained.' Therefore, the practitioner who wishes to improve practice needs to seek out and take advantage of opportunities for continuing professional development.

Moyles (2001, p. 89) wrote that 'if we want professionals then professional understanding itself needs to be nurtured, to be allowed time to develop and opportunity to be applied.' She goes on to say that desire and self-belief are important, 'educational improvement depends upon practitioners feeling they WANT to make a difference: upon them feeling empowered and professional.'

The role of the early years professional has become more complex and is constantly evolving. It is not just a job for those who love working with children, though that attribute remains a central characteristic of those who work with children, but there is now wide recognition of the need for a deeper theoretical understanding of child development in order to fulfil complex requirements. The Early Years Foundation Stage guidance documents support these requirements. Palaiologou wrote that the revised Early Years Foundation Stage (2012) represents:

> a totality and control of learning and development assistance provided through education and care to support children from birth to five years of age and is underpinned by a raft of statutory and non-statutory guidance that forms the framework for inspection and accountability.
>
> Palaiologou (2012, p. xx)

Therefore, alongside and in addition to their daily caring work, practitioners are challenged by the day-to-day responsibilities of meeting the developmental and learning needs of children, together with changes to curriculum and guidance, expectations of parents and carers, pressures from management, accountability to various sources, and an expectation from Ofsted of continuous, excellent performance.

The early years professional is equipped with personal knowledge and understanding of the child, as well as skills, which are enhanced by their personal values and attitudes. Figure 1.1 illustrates how each person can be affected by their role and responsibilities, their personal aspirations, further study, the management structure of the setting, accountability, relationships with other members of their team and the expectations of parents and carers. All these pressures and influences are in turn affected by the context, ethos and culture of the setting. In addition, there are the external pressures from outside the setting such as government directives and guidelines, inspection by Ofsted and the need to work with other agencies such as local authority services.

These responsibilities and accountabilities result in a workforce that requires personal and collective determination, resilience and boundless energy, and the ability to work closely with others. A positive, sensitive and knowledgeable approach can result in the implementation of any necessary changes that enhance practice in accordance with personal values and the ethos and culture of the work setting.

Case study 1

In discussion about the newly introduced Early Years Foundation Stage Framework (2012) Emma said, 'In my experience change is inevitable and often it is for the best. However, the challenge for me is that it is beyond my control. But if I have the means to deal with it effectively, I think that the impact can be managed.'

Challenge

- What personal attributes and professional support do you need in order for the impact of change in your setting to be managed effectively?

Ethos, culture and context of setting

Figure 1.1 illustrates how the context, ethos and culture of a work setting have a direct influence on change taking place within a setting and impact on the individual practitioners and the ways in which they face change.

The context of the setting is constant. It is the community of the setting. A specialism often distinguishes it from other settings. For example, the context of a setting is often influenced by its neighbourhood, whether village or inner city, particular religious beliefs, or the influence of a particular theorist such as Montessori or Froebel. It may have particular links to a specialist environment such as a forest school. It can also be influenced by any specialisms that the practitioners may have, such as art or music. The established context of the setting

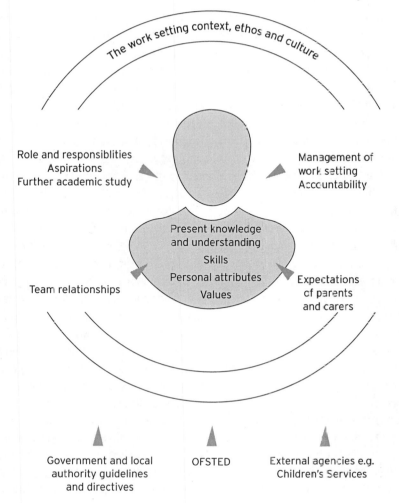

The work setting context, ethos and culture

Role and responsiblities
Aspirations
Further academic study

Management of
work setting
Acccountability

Present knowledge
and understanding

Skills

Personal attributes

Values

Team relationships

Expectations
of parents
and carers

Government and local
authority guidelines
and directives

OFSTED

External agencies e.g.
Children's Services

Figure 1.1 The early years practitioner: influences and challenges

will impact on its ethos, and both context and ethos affect the practitioner and the quality of practice offered to the child.

The ethos of a setting can often be seen on the websites or publicity material of most early years settings. It is typically indicated by a short 'strapline' and a fuller mission statement encapsulating aims and values. It is a concise statement of practice, which the reader can interpret in order to evaluate the setting. Most of these provide statements concerning the well-being and development of the child and the setting's strong links with the parents and carers. These statements are an important tool of communication. However, it is not enough merely to state these principles: they must be supported by like-minded staff. Their determination to uphold the ethos will impact on the effectiveness of the setting. It can become part of the drive to improve practice.

In general, the ethos of a setting is often experienced and not easily articulated. When a person physically enters a setting and spends time with its practitioners and children, a more 'unofficial' ethos emerges, often related to the emotions and feelings of the person in relation to the setting. It arises from their complex experience of interactions with staff, relationships among staff and between staff and children, and between staff and parents and carers. This ethos is often hard to describe and can be subject to change according to any changes experienced in any interactions. So, this aspect of ethos is being constantly negotiated, defined and redefined according to circumstance and experience; it is not static. This 'informal' ethos often has enormous impact on the parents' and carers' beliefs and views about a setting. If the 'informal' ethos strongly supports the more formally stated ethos, it sends a powerful message not only to the community of parents and carers but also any outside agencies. It usually indicates good leadership. It can also inspire the confidence of practitioners, influencing the effectiveness and the quality of their practice, as well as having a positive effect on the children and their parents and carers. A strong, happy and positive ethos that is consistent and permeates a setting carries a robust message concerning the setting's potential to offer good quality provision with the well-being and care of the child at its heart. It also has an impact on those working at the setting. If there is an ethos of support, respect, encouragement, inclusivity and trust, the practitioner will be enabled to give to the best of their abilities. It will increase their confidence and self-esteem. A determination to overcome any problems facing a setting, with each practitioner exploring how to positively support others, will ensure that a strong and positive ethos is maintained. It takes effort by a whole team to ensure that the ethos of a setting is valued and sustained. The workplace then provides an environment where the early years practitioner is enabled and inspired to excel in their practice and provision, with positive consequences for the children in their care.

The culture of a setting can be seen in the process and outcomes of leadership styles, which can range from autocratic to democratic. It can be seen in how the managers and team members interact and communicate with each other. Leadership styles affect the attitudes and enthusiasm of practitioners and thus the quality of provision. Although a practitioner usually has little influence on the leadership style in their setting, the practitioner can still strive for personal excellence based on their increasing knowledge and understanding of good practice. They can influence the culture of the setting by a positive and enthusiastic approach to excellent practice and supportive collaboration with others.

In writing about her experience in successful children's centres, Rudge (2010, p. 133) believes that the key elements for success are:

- Commitment to excellence – a drive to provide the highest possible service . . . enabling the organisation to make significant difference to all.
- Partnership working – the staff of children's centres must agree that all relevant disciplines have a part to play in meeting the needs of children and their families.
- Shared ethos – a team that embraces and owns both a shared ethos and objectives, 'the achievement of a shared ethos is one that requires time, passion and collective ownership'.
- Flexibility – recognising change, embracing challenge with a 'have a go' attitude and a willingness to develop new structures and initiatives.

These elements of success affect the culture of a setting and they take time to establish. They underline the need for a culture that is collaborative and not competitive, that has opportunities for excellent and open communication, that is reflective in practice and supportive of other members of the team. It is important that each member of the team has a role to play in establishing an internal culture that enhances practice and facilitates success.

Case study 2

Zoe was brimming with excitement when she announced to other students on her course that her Nursery school had gained an 'Outstanding' grade from an inspection. She later commented how proud she was of her colleagues, the ways in which they had supported each other and of how hard they had worked together. Over time, it became apparent that these results affected her self esteem and her sense of well being. She appeared to gain confidence in her interactions with her peers and seemed to derive more enjoyment in her study. The resulting determination to achieve well was reflected in her assignment grades. Her achievement at work has resulted in a growing confidence in her formal studies.

Challenge

• Consider the culture of your setting and its impact. In what ways can the culture of your setting be improved? What would your role be in this?

It is important that the practitioner:

• reflects on how the ethos and culture of the setting affect not only the team but also the children in their care;
• considers what can be done to improve and then maintain that ethos and culture.

Personal values, attitudes and aspirations

An individual's personal values and attitudes affect the quality and effectiveness of their practice, the ways in which children are dealt with and team interaction and support. Teams include individuals with different experiences, value systems, attitudes and goals. These aspects guide the behaviour and decisions of practitioners. There has to be awareness that each practitioner may not only have a value system different from colleagues but also from the families with whom the practitioner is in frequent contact. These differences may not be great, but they will emerge and can be divisive in the day-to-day running of a setting. Such differences can be seen, for example, in the way a particular child's behaviour is managed, or the ways in which the expectations of parents are met, or the ways in which an aspect of practice is carried out. There needs to be open discussion about the particular core professional values that a team holds in common. Some of this will be discussed later in the section 'The importance of team relationships'.

Personal values are often strongly held and not easily influenced because they are a culmination of personal lifelong learning, reflection and experience. However, our attitudes, though usually also enduring, can be temporarily affected by those around us. Professional aspirations are strongly influenced by the ethos and culture of the setting. They can be linked to increasing knowledge and understanding through training and study; they can also be linked to improving practice through setting goals, for example, developing positive relationships with children and staff in order to enhance relationships and develop good morale. However, these aspirations can increase workload and or impact on time management, for example, through setting aside time for further studies or meetings. Figure 1.1 shows how aspirations, though a positive influence, are one of the challenges for the practitioner.

Challenge

- How do my personal values and attitudes affect my professional practice?
- What aspirations affect my practice now and how will they affect it in the future?

It is important to question how positive attitudes are developed. Increased knowledge and understanding leads to increasing confidence in practice; this new learning arises not only through formal study but also through reflection on experience, evaluation of practice and discussion with colleagues. Claxton (2007) questioned pupils, head teachers, and national policy-makers about the attributes of the effective learner:

> There is a high degree of consensus in the kinds of attributes or 'dispositions' they suggested. Effective learners are thought to be capable of being:
>
> - curious, adventurous and questioning
> - resilient, determined and focused
> - open-minded, flexible, imaginative and creative
> - critical, sceptical and analytical
> - both methodical and opportunistic
> - reflective, thoughtful and self-evaluative
> - keen to build on their products and performances
> - collaborative but also independent.
>
> Claxton (2007, p. 117)

Challenge

- These attributes of the effective learner are important in establishing more effective practice. Consider which of the above personal dispositions you already have or need to acquire or develop.

Claxton goes on to suggest that 'being questioning' requires self-confidence and an environment that allows you to question. Questioning in a positive spirit of engagement and open-mindedness in order to improve practice is vital. The Scottish Executive (2005) suggested that all practitioners need time to engage in professional dialogue, and pointed out that it takes time and as well as courage. The Executive encouraged 'a reflective and enquiring spirit. A shared understanding of the "why", "what", "how", "when", "where", and "who" of early pedagogy allows us to continue to challenge, to question and review our practice' (2005, p. 13).

Motivation

In order to fulfil aspirations it is important that the practitioner is personally motivated. Motivation is demonstrated in the willingness of practitioners to be prepared to expend effort in response to various goals and new initiatives. In their paper 'Motivation and demotivation of teachers in primary schools: The challenge of change', Addison and Brundrett (2008) point out that staff motivation is essential in order for practice to be effective. Several aspects of their research paper apply to early years practitioners and can be perceived in the culture of the setting. They indicate that a plethora of changes probably affects morale, but that the importance of feedback and of effort being recognised by leaders had a greater impact on morale than the impact of national issues. The research indicated that the respondents also derived motivation from the positive responses of children in their care. In addition, they experienced a sense of achievement from completed tasks and supportive colleagues. From this it can be concluded that it is important for practitioners to 'see tasks through' to completion in order to experience achievement; and that support from colleagues is needed. So, break down any large task into manageable chunks and be prepared to set up a support group if necessary. The researchers found the demotivators were poor response from and poor behaviour among children, and working long hours with a heavy workload. Some of the demotivating factors can be improved by the practice of individual practitioners with support from colleagues, including supportive leadership.

In 'The Baby Room Project' (2013), Goouch and Powell found that practitioners working with babies felt isolated and neglected. They therefore recommended specific training, support and guidance for practitioners that is carefully designed to include opportunities for professional dialogue together with time to disseminate accurate policy and research information. They encouraged practitioners to gain appropriate qualifications and to take part in specialised continuing professional development. Their research showed that practitioners found that opportunities to meet in order to engage in critical reflection on practice were rare. As part of the recommendations, they included time be allowed for 'dialogue exchange and the establishment of networks of practice as a core local requirement'. Later Goouch and Powell wrote that it is important to create:

> opportunities for baby room practitioners to theorise their practice, to engage in reflective exchanges, one which facilitates the kinds of dialogue that mirror the equality of engagement that is argued for all learners and teachers.
>
> Gooch and Powell (2013, p. 61)

This recognises the importance of engaging with others in order to learn together, and reiterates the value of improving practice through reflection and discussion with colleagues in a non-threatening environment. It is motivational. It is important to pause and consider what strategies work well in a setting and what can be done to improve practice, and then take time to plan how these new strategies will be put into place. It is important to evaluate that new practice and continue a cycle of reflection: forward planning, then implementing; evaluating and improving practice. Working together and encouraging each other to enhance practice in a positive environment contributes to well-being. It is motivational and encourages personal resilience.

Resilience

Resilience is a personal attribute which supports the practitioner when facing the challenges that emerge in professional practice such as the changes to the Early Years Foundation Stage and to working practices. The word resilience implies the ability to withstand challenges, overcoming problematic circumstances and emerging stronger. The practitioner needs to be resilient in the face of change, not to be overwhelmed, and to consider problems as a challenge and not a barrier to effective working.

Richardson (2002) describes resilience as the concept of emerging from adversity stronger and more resourceful. It is 'effective coping and adaptation although faced with loss, hardship or adversity' (Tugade and Fredrickson, 2004). The development of resilience is an ongoing process; it is about being able to 'bounce back', to keep going in adverse circumstances. Learning to cope with the challenge of stressful events and anxious times will build up enduring strength. The outcome is a more resilient person.

Challenge

- Reflect on previous experiences, whether professional or personal, and evaluate your ability to 'bounce back' and to persist in difficult circumstances. Ask yourself: What were these situations? How resilient was I? What have I learned about myself in reflecting on these experiences?
- Reflect on the process of becoming more resilient. How does it happen? Can I make myself 'more resilient'?

Reflection on experience may indicate how previous problems have been overcome. The practitioner can build up confidence in their resilience by reflecting on how they have been able to 'keep going' on previous demanding occasions. It is possible to work at increasing the ability to be resilient by positive self-talk: 'I have done this before, I can do it again.' Confidence can be built through successfully completing challenging tasks and thus improving personal resilence. It is important to remember the need for meeting with others in like situations - to collaborate, to encourage and to support - helping each other to build resilience.

Resilience is also helped by positive self-belief. Change can give rise to anxiety and even fear, which affects confidence and self-belief. In her writing about the mature learner, Hoult (2006) suggests that poor self-belief leads to an unconfident learner; however, a confident person with positive self-belief develops a resilience that carries them forward through the changing circumstances of life. She takes the thought 'I will never be successful' and shows how it negatively colours all the learner's assumptions and practices, and she points out that these beliefs must be challenged and replaced by positive self-belief, 'I am capable of succeeding', in order for the student to succeed. This applies to the formal learning situation of study as well as informal learning in the workplace. Ritchie (2013) suggests that by acting with determination on the edge or just beyond personal comfort zones, it is possible to do things that may have once seemed impossible, enjoy the successful outcome and thus enhance positive self-belief. It will prove that success is possible and build resilience.

Case study 3

Jane recalled a previous stressful experience when she talked to an angry parent and failed to proceed to an outcome that helped the situation. Jane felt that she had failed. It affected her self-belief. She believed that she could not handle talking to parents, especially if they were agitated about something. Her manager was encouraging and outlined some ideas for defusing similar situations, and offered to accompany Jane the next time she faced a similar situation. The manager also saw this as a learning experience for the team and they held a session discussing and sharing ideas for developing and sustaining positive relationships with parents and carers.

The next time a troubled parent needed to see Jane, she was offered a quiet place to chat and a cup of tea. The manager made herself available if needed, while Jane listened to and talked with the parent. Jane found that with forethought she was able to manage the situation herself by having a quiet place to talk, making sure the parent felt comfortable and by listening to her anxieties. They talked through a solution to the problem and Jane was able to negotiate a positive outcome. Through carefully considered strategies, Jane has found more confidence in her relationships with all parents and carers. She now feels that she is more capable of succeeding'.

Challenge

- Reflect on past experiences, ascertaining times when anxiety was overcome with positive results. What happened? How did this affect your self-belief?
- Recall experiences when stress caused anxiety and where if you had acted differently there might have been more positive outcomes. How could you have changed the negative outcome? What would you do next time?

This reflection on experiences can help build up personal, positive attitudes to change and help evaluate and challenge negative self-belief. The practitioner needs to work at developing self-awareness, self-regulation and an optimistic attitude.

Positive self-belief results in a willingness to overcome the challenges brought about by change and can help overcome any anxieties or fears about the process or outcomes of change. Resilience is also needed in order to fulfil aspirations for increasing knowledge and understanding through study. Rodd (2013) lists resilience – 'being ready, willing and able to lock on to learning' as being one of the four R's of learning power that was devised by Claxton (2002). Resilience is important for professional development.

The importance of team relationships

It has been acknowledged that working collaboratively, supporting each other in an open and positive environment, and developing 'networks of practice' (Powell and Goouch, 2012) is important. Everyone has different value systems, attitudes and skills, and yet it is vitally important to work consistently together, to have good communication and to be a team that faces change together. It has also been recognised that practitioners need to be valued and empowered; however, like rowers in a boat, there is a need to utilise collective strength and row in unison.

In writing about working with the early years, Edgington (2004, p. 55) suggests:

a successful and effective team

- is value driven
- has good communication
- is collaborative in its dealings
- maximises the use of the abilities of its members
- has the ability to listen to others in an effective way
- has a willingness to solve problems.

Much has been written about the formation of teams. For example, Belbin (2011, 2012) emphasises the importance of the differing roles within a team and that each member brings different strengths and weaknesses.

He includes the roles of:

- The Plant – the creative problem solver
- The Resource Investigator – enthusiastic explorer of opportunities and developer of networks
- The Co-ordinator – mature, promotes decision-making
- The Shaper – challenging, dynamic, seeks to overcome barriers
- Monitor/Evaluator – strategic thinker, discerning, good judgement
- Team Worker – co-operative, avoids conflict, works hard
- Implementer – disciplined, reliable, efficient, implements ideas
- Completer/Finisher – reliable, completes tasks, thorough
- Specialist – provides specialist skills and knowledge, single-minded.

(Further details available www.belbin.com/content/page/4980/
Belbin(uk)-2011-TeamRolesInANutshell.pdf)

Usually team members in early years settings may have to assume more than one role, or there is some overlap of roles. Team members get used to assuming various roles as the situation requires, sometimes operating at the 'edge of their comfort zone'. Belbin (2012) points out that smaller teams often demonstrate greater balance, flexibility and success than larger ones, provided they do not drop below the ideal number of four or the critical number of three.

It is a useful exercise to identify and consider the personal role that each practitioner has in a team. These may be formal or informal, and often reflect the practitioner's strengths. It is important that each member of a team plays their part in supporting the team when addressing fresh challenges.

Edgington (2004) proposes three types of team in early years settings:

- the cosy team: is well established, works well together, is hostile to new ways of working and to new members, ignores the need for change;
- the turbulent team: appears united but strong disagreement appears 'behind the backs' of colleagues, change is difficult because 'there is no clear dialogue for shared decision making';
- the rigorous and challenging team: displays a professional approach, is committed to continuing professional development, reviews practice, employs critical thinking, is thoughtful, open to change and challenge.

Consider your team. In what areas should it improve and how can good team characteristics be sustained?

Tuckman (1965) cited by Cole (2004, p. 63) identified several stages in a team's development towards successful achievement. He suggested that teams develop high levels of effectiveness over time. He named these stages of growth as:

- *forming* – the group starts to come together, consolidating their identity, acquiring relevant information to the task;
- *storming* – settling together, possibly including conflict, establishing leadership and finding a role within the team;
- *norming* – settling into effective and co-operative ways of working;
- *performing* – the team operating at optimum level with solutions found and results implemented.

Tuckman later added the final stage of '*adjourning*' when a team may be disbanded having fulfilled its function or task. It can be useful to identify the present stage of team growth at work and plan how to proceed to the next stage.

The team's ability to cope with changes imposed on them will depend on how they function as a team. It takes time. There needs to be recognition of common professional values, of a collective attitude to issues that commonly arise during practice and of the value of collaboration and active support for other members of the team. Good communication is vital. Open discussions will support the important concept of working together and give each member insight into the attitudes, skills and understanding of other team members. It will give opportunities for members to listen to others and ask for support, and for others to provide that support in a non-threatening way. A fragmented team is weak. Effective teams work together, support each other and recognise and value each others' skills.

Case study 4

Rachel is an enthusiastic early years professional. She respects the new manager of her team and understands the need for some of the changes, but she finds the attitude of a few of her colleagues disheartening. The setting underwent changes after the retirement of the previous popular manager. Some staff were unhappy when the new manager imposed changes without preliminary discussion in order to meet Ofsted recommendations more quickly. It resulted in an unhappy atmosphere within the team and a disintegration into factions, with some willing to work hard in order to meet new goals and others losing enthusiasm. Rachel said, 'There is an unhappy atmosphere at work. I don't enjoy my work as much as I used to. Some colleagues are griping behind the manager's back and some are not pulling their weight. I even heard someone grumbling to a friendly parent about the increased workload. It's getting me down.'

Challenge

1   In what ways might the internal struggles and disagreements of Rachel's team impact on
    • team relationships
    • the quality of provision for the children
    • the practitioner's relationships with parents and carers?
2   What can staff do to support each other?

The ethos of Rachel's workplace is changing, affected by relationships. It is affecting the well-being of staff. Although a manager has a responsibility to support the resolution of conflict and plan a new way forward, each practitioner needs to explore how personal behaviour impacts on attitude to work and the subsequent impact on relationships and provision.

Conclusion

Changes to practice are not peculiar to the early years educator. However, the changes in government guidance and inspection, the recommendations of various reports and reviews, the levels of study and professional qualifications required have increased the workload. In addition, the expectations of parents and carers, as well as management and accountability, have presented huge challenges for the early years practitioner. It requires a positive attitude, high levels of motivation and resilience to achieve and maintain excellence in practice. Practitioners have found that achieving goals with the support of a team has resulted in a fresh enthusiasm for their roles and enhanced confidence in their professional ability. They feel more empowered. Importantly, they have also found that this positive approach not only helps their personal feelings of well-being and success, but in so doing it also enables them to give the children in their care the best quality provision appropriate to the child's development.

> A child's future choices, attainment, well being, happiness and resilience are profoundly affected by the quality of guidance, love and care they receive during these first years.
>
> Tickell (2011, p. 2)

Bibliography

Addison, R., Brundrett, M. (2008) 'Motivation and demotivation of teachers in primary schools: The challenge of change', *Education 3-13: International Journal of Primary, Elementary and Early Years Education*, 36(1), pp. 79–94.

Belbin, R.M, (2011) *Team Roles*. Available at: www.belbin.com/content/page/4980/Belbin(uk)-2011-TeamRolesInANutshell.pdf (Accessed: 11 July 2014).

Belbin, R.M. (2012) *Team Roles at Work*. London: Routledge.

Claxton, G. (2002) *Building Learning Power*. Bristol: Henleaze House.

Claxton, G. (2007) 'Expanding young people's capacity to learn', *British Journal of Educational Studies*, 55(2), pp. 115–134.

Cole, G. (2004) *Management Theory and Practice*, (6th edn) Andover: Centage Learning EMEA.

DfE (Department for Education) (2011) *Childcare and Early Years Providers Survey: 2011*. Available at: www.gov.uk/government/publications/childcare-and-early-years-providers-survey-2011 (Accessed: 11 July 2014).

DfE (Department for Education) (2012) *Early Years Foundation Stage Framework: Until 1 September 2014*. Available at: www.education.gov.uk/aboutdfe/statutory/g00213120/eyfs-statutory-framework (Accessed: 11 July 2014).

DfE (Department for Education) (2013) *More Great Childcare: Raising Quality and Giving Parents More Choice*. Available at: www.gov.uk/government/publications/more-great-childcare-raising-quality-and-giving-parents-more-choice (Accessed: 11 July 2014).

DfES (Department for Education and Skills) (2005) *Support for Parents: The Best Start for Children: A Ten-Year Strategy*. Available at: http://webarchive.nationalarchives.gov.uk/20130401151715/https://www.education.gov.uk/publications/eOrderingDownload/HMT-Support-parents.pdf (Accessed: 11 July 2014).

Edgington, M. (2004) *The Foundation Stage Teacher in Action* (3rd edn). London: Paul Chapman.

Goouch, K., Powell, S. (2013) *The Baby Room Project*. Maidenhead: Open University Press.

Hoult, E. (2006) *Learning Support: A Guide for Mature Students*. London: Sage.

Moyles, J. (2001) 'Passion, paradox and professionalism in Early Years education', *Early Years: An International Research Journal*, 21(2), pp. 81–95.

Nutbrown, C. (2012) *Foundations for Quality: The Independent Review of Early Education and Childcare Qualifications: Final Report*. Available at: www.gov.uk/government/uploads/system/uploads/attachment_data/file/175463/Nutbrown-Review.pdf (Accessed: 11 July 2014).

Ofsted (2011) *The Annual Report of Her Majesty's Chief Inspector of Education, Children's Services and Skills 2010/11*. Available at: http://ofsted.gov.uk/sites/default/files/documents/annual-reports/o/Ofsted%20Annual%20Report%2010-11%20-%20full.pdf (Accessed: 11 July 2014).

Palaiologou, J. (2012) *The Early Years Foundation Stage: Theory and Practice* (2nd edn). London: Sage.

Powell, S., Goouch, K. (2012) 'Whose hand rocks the cradle? Parallel disccurses in the baby room', *Early Years: An International Research Journal*, 32(2), pp. 113–27.

Richardson, G. E. (2002) 'The metatheory of resilience and resiliency', *Journal of Clinical Psychology*, 58(3), pp. 307–21.

Ritchie, C., Thomas, P. (2013) *Successful Study: Skills for Teaching Assistants and Early Years Practitioners*. London: David Fulton Publishers.

Rodd, J. (2013) *Leadership in Early Childhood: The Pathway to Professionalism* (4th edn). Maidenhead: McGraw Hill/Open University Press.

Rudge, C. 'Children's centres' in Pugh, G., Duffy, B. (2010) *Contemporary Issues in the Early Years* (5th edn). London: Sage.

Scottish Executive (2005) *Let's Talk About Pedagogy 1: Towards a Shared Understanding for Early Years Education in Scotland:* Learning and Teaching Scotland. Available at: *www.educationscotland.gov.uk/images/talkpedagogy_tcm4-193218.pdf* (Accessed: 11 July 2014).

Siraj Blatchford, I., Taggart, B., Sylva, K., Sammons, P., Melhuish, E. (2008) 'Towards the transformation of practice in early childhood education: The effective provision of pre school education (EPPE) project', *Cambridge Journal of Education*, 38(1), pp. 23–36.

Sylva, K., Melhuish, E., Sammons, P., Siraj-Blatchford, I., Taggart, B. (2003) *The Effective Provision of Pre-School Education (EPPE) Project: Findings from Pre-school to End of Key Stage 1.* London: DfEE/Institute of Education, University of London.

Sylva, K., Melhuish, E., Sammons, P., Siraj-Blatchford, I., Taggart, B. (2004) *The Effective Provision of Pre-School Education (EPPE) Project: Final Report.* London: DfEE/Institute of Education, University of London.

Sylva, K., Melhuish, E.C., Sammons, P., Siraj-Blatchford, I., Taggart, B. (2008) *Final Report from the Primary Phase: Pre-School, School and Family Influences on Children's Development during Key Stage 2 (Age 7–11) EPPE. Research Report DCSF-RR061* London: DfEE/Institute of Education, University of London.

Tickell, C. (2011) *The Early Years: Foundations for Life, Health and Learning.* London: Department for Education. Available at: www.gov.uk/government/publications/the-early-years-foundations-for-life-health-and-learning-an-independent-report-on-the-early-years-foundation-stage-to-her-majestys-government (Accessed: 11 July 2014).

Tugade, M. M., Fredrickson B. L. (2004) 'Resilient individuals use positive emotions to bounce back from negative emotional experiences', *Journal of Personality and Social Psychology,* 86(2), pp. 320–33.

Urban, M. (2008) 'Dealing with uncertainty: Challenges and possibilities for the early childhood profession', *European Early Childhood Education Research Journal,* 16(2), pp. 135–52.

2 Understanding feelings: how to accept the challenge

Shona Henderson

Overview

This chapter depicts students' reflections on their perceptions and emotions as they begin a new course of study in university. To understand the varied educational backdrop that affects today's learner, an initial commentary is made on historical and societal movement in adult education and training. Thereafter, more personal and practical commentaries expose the concept of 'being and belonging' in new and unfamiliar environments and reveal how 'supportive networks' underpin effective learning. Within the chapter, recognition is made that change is unsettling, and through reflection on the students' stories the transferability of feelings and emotions are acknowledged, as are the numerous opportunities that support and strengthen study aspirations.

Introduction

This chapter illustrates the management of feelings through case study research that discriminates students' perceived barriers to learning from unfolding positions of hope and optimism. The responses gathered from an eclectic group of university undergraduates expose honest, everyday emotions, challenges and triumphs. Some younger students who may not have left education far behind talk of uncertainty that comes from limited life experience and the challenging autonomy required of university study. Others carry the confidence that they assumed from being the 'big fish' in secondary school, yet may face the change in their learning circumstance with trepidation. At the other end of the age profile, many mature students say the changes to their lives brought about by their decision to study are both exciting and uncomfortable as they manage the multiple roles that fall on their shoulders when juggling study, family life and workplace demands. The use of case study responses offers opportunities for reflection and may give reassurances to those embarking on a new course of study and so vitalise confidence. Entering university as a first-time student or when returning to study is both exciting and daunting. Students from a wide range of backgrounds experience, in probable equal measure, doubts and exhilaration when taking their first steps on a higher education course. The stirring of such emotions is no different to those of when starting a new job or joining a new team. Change is uncomfortable regardless of whether it is desired or inflicted.

An initial proposition is that new students stepping into the unfamiliar and demanding environment of university may feel both excited and unnerved. They are not alone in experiencing such emotions. In fact Barnett (2007, p. 173) is emphatic when he states 'anxiety is almost certainly a fact of student life'. Here is a summary of one student's memory of her feelings when first joining a degree course.

Case study 1

'The car radio was loud so blocking out my nerves and thoughts . . . It was obvious that the nerves were really setting in now. All of the thoughts in my head getting mixed up, my heart was racing . . . I was apprehensive about the commitment, excited about the prospect of learning, relieved that the day had finally come, worried that I would not be able to keep up with the pace, hopeful that initial problems were now far away and nothing would get in the way of my education. When I got home later and thought about the day, what best described how I felt was ecstatic.'

Challenge

- Think of a time when you have felt unsure before attempting something new.
- After the event, were you able to put your feelings into perspective?
- Knowing what you now know of yourself, how might you prepare when faced with a similar experience in future?

The student's description of her feelings is indeed visceral and emotional. However, before offering further insight into the perceptions and experiences of her fellow students and the potential reasons for their feelings, it is important to identify some of the pointers that contribute to the challenge and change in becoming a student today, and to grasp recent historical developments in certification of higher education entry degrees.

Brief background history of early years training and study

The concept that history shapes our future is relevant. Looking back 60 years or so in the aftermath of the Second World War, the caring professions such as nursing, primary teaching and nursery provision were predominantly considered female domains; for the latter role, the simple qualifications required to do a good job were love and dedication to the well-being of the child. Notwithstanding, early years practices such as those undertaken by the Froebel Institute, Macmillan Nurseries and Montessori Schools did require structured training with certification underpinning their foundations. This, however, was not the situation nationally at this time. A regular staffing scenario in a nursery hierarchy would be a principal teacher with qualifications and an unskilled team of workers who addressed the welfare of the young children in their care. There was little consideration given to the idea that child workers needed to be trained, as the focus of their engagement was seen as being primarily emotional and social, and not necessarily educational. The view that women should take on this role was unquestioned as looking after children was considered to be natural for them, and therefore training was not considered essential.

However, it was soon widely accepted that children do not only require to be looked after but also need opportunities that nurture their enquiring minds. From as far back as the late 1960s, Plowden policies and rhetoric, such as 'at the heart of the educational process lies the child', in effect assumed fundamental reforms in the economic and social institutions of the country at large (Plowden, 1967, p. 9). Society's attitude is dynamic in guiding and influencing change and education, and its then workforce demanded transformation. Change evolves slowly and has enabled a fairer and richer diversity across the contexts of the home and the workplace. However, change stirs up strong opinions and debate, for example today some maintain that men are viewed with misgiving when they choose to work in childcare roles, such as a stay-at-home father or in early years employment. Equally, some argue that paternity leave and male childcare roles require greater regard before gender equality is reached. Nonetheless, societal attitude has brought about action to secure more parity of opportunity for women and men and has signalled capability in both genders.

Not only did the crossing of conventional gender-role frontiers lead to the acceptance that women and men should be given opportunities to diversify in employment but an added conviction at the same time was that all members of society should be empowered to train and continue in education. Fifty years ago the Robbins Report (Committee on Higher Education, 1963) offered to all who had suitable qualifications the prospect of entering university. In reality it took until the 1980s before students from a wider range of social backgrounds were seen in any significant number in higher education. Before this, university students came mainly from middle-class and higher social standings. However, building on the growing success of widening participation, the Dearing Report (1997) made clear its hope that in the proceeding 20 years, the UK would strive for world-class standards in education. Acting on government needs to see economic rewards translate from any investment in education study, sub-degree certification was created. For many who were thought of as 'non-traditional', those from a background that did not aspire to further education, the first door to a higher education opportunity was opened.

The availability of a study pathway following an entry degree route for instance, has dove-tailed well with the developments in guidance and training related to the early years workforce. Since the 1980s, certificates such as Council for Awards in Children's Care and Education (CACHE) and National Nursery Examination Board (NNEB) have been sought by the workforce, and further acknowledgement of the value of suitably trained staff was identified through the Early Years Professional Status. The development of this qualification led to the Early Years Teacher Status (2014), which attracts full- and part-time students and is the intended goal of many students studying on early years programmes.

The flexibility of study and the range of potential qualifications have appealed to traditional and non-traditional students alike. With any learning prospect comes the challenge of managing emotions and perceptions, and they may be particularly visceral for those students who feel unsure about their 'belonging' in university. Consider now the circumstances of some case studies that demonstrate real and honest emotions of students who are fortunate in having attained a place in university but who nonetheless perceive barriers to their learning, and need to call on inner strength to manage the challenge and change to their circumstances.

Being and belonging

The first barrier to learning that is explored in this chapter is that of 'being and belonging'. Feelings of anxiety are commonplace when in an unfamiliar situation, be it starting a new job, taking on a leadership role or engaging in further education; however, there is a belief that the subconscious mind allows anxiety to be overcome, or not. Some meddling of this phrase suggests 'we are what we know'. This idea is built on the perception that personal and social histories shape the mind and ensuing actions. Bourdieu and Wacquant (1992, p. 126) refer to this concept as 'socialised subjectivity' and indeed Bourdieu in 1985 coined the term 'habitus' to denote status and identity that is drawn from family background, social class and educational standing. Individual histories are the building blocks of habitus, which Bourdieu proposed is not only subliminal but is also embodied and can be demonstrated through actions. Those entering higher education will assume the additional identity of being a student. Possessing a strong student identity is important to success but is something that may take time to develop. In reference to further work of Bourdieu (1996), he talked of 'academic legitimacy' by which he means believing that you truly are a student and have the necessary capabilities to succeed in a university environment. However, the position that new students find themselves in is that of splitting their many identities between university, the workplace, family life and so on, and the pressure felt from being in this situation may weaken the character of 'being and belonging' in any one of these environments.

It takes time to develop a student identity and situational barriers such as location of learning sites, access and general familiarity with the environment are just as significant as the dispositional barriers of self-confidence and belief in being clever enough and having a right to be in university. As noted in the case study research below, access to university was an obstacle to belonging where the student attended university on a part-time basis. The student felt frustrated by the increased challenges that they had to face and the perceived reduction in opportunities to form strong relationships.

Case study 2

'With regard to student identity . . . I'm not like the other students [meaning full-time students], I'm not involved, I'm not on campus regularly, I can't access resources and create student-to-student relationships.'

Challenge

- How are you like or not like other students?
- How does this affect your learning and make you feel?

Situation and access are important elements in belonging and are as significant as the perception of 'legitimacy'. Creating relationships and believing in the right to be in university are essential elements in breaking down perceived barriers. West (1996) and Skeggs (1997) discovered when interviewing students who were from social backgrounds where the structure of widening participation had sanctioned their entry into university, termed as 'non-traditional students', that they possessed fragile student identities. Indeed this fragility is borne out by two further case study comments.

Case study 3

'University wasn't for the likes of me. I worried that I wouldn't fit in with other students.'
'I never thought I would become a university student. It was always something that other people did.'

Challenge

- Are you able to empathise with the emotions expressed, and feel empowered when you reflect on fellow students' comments and actions?

The notion that university is a forbidding environment is evidently not uncommon. It is true that the formal, regulated organisation of higher education can appear austere. Undoubtedly that is because it is unfamiliar. However, as time passes, feelings of anxiety will diminish and the perception of being a 'fish in water', a phrase used by Bourdieu (1990) to describe students who have greater social and cultural capital and who are able to take advantage of the opportunities that are on offer, will hopefully emerge. Happily the notion of habitus is that it is permeable and can be reconstructed through experiences, therefore an adaption of feelings of discomfort in joining the unfamiliar context of university may soon result in greater confidence and engagement. Just as important as being a student is feeling like a student.

Academic habitus: the effects of previous study

A further perceived barrier to learning and 'being and belonging' is the control that previous academic habitus may exert. This is a memory of past school, further education and even previous higher education experiences and success. Taylor (2009) captured the feelings of a group of newly enrolled degree students who displayed a lack of confidence in their cleverness and their fear that at university they are expected to operate with autonomy. Secondary schooling in many cases does little to prepare students to learn through questioning and misconception, and this is often the route to success in the more autonomous environment of higher education. Furthermore, the insecurity of realising that there may not be a correct answer now, or ever, is unsettling for some who rely on and feel comfortable with knowledge being spoon-fed. However, Barnett (2007) reminds that most students feel uncertain and anxious when embarking on a university degree, and may display low self-confidence. The power of an academic habitus is borne out in the testimonies from the following case studies.

Case study 4

'Lack of self-confidence, the fear that I will fail and the worry I am not clever enough has come from past experiences where I have not achieved well.'

'I have had past experiences of study which were not very good and I don't want these to negatively influence my present.'

'I did wonder if I had done the right thing [talking of applying to university]. The other difficulty for me has been my lack of qualifications at GCSE level at least. I have spent most of my adult life studying to improve my knowledge . . . Despite this, I feel almost dogged by my poor results at GCSE level.'

Challenge

* How do you manage feelings of previous successes and failures?

These observations represent the views of many students who have concerns over their academic skills but, despite apparently weak self-confidence, had sufficient self-belief to apply for a place and embark on a university course and seem to be exercising their 'academic legitimacy' (Bourdieu, 1996). They exemplify what Taylor (2009, p. 255) refers to as 'learned helplessness as an inhibitor and learned optimism as an enabler.' It is not surprising that many students appear to have a quixotic personality when learning. Perhaps they can 'bend with the wind' and learn how to adapt to new situations in time. Reay *et al.* (2001, 2002, 2004 and 2010) carried out extensive research into this aspect of learning and propose that despite significant challenges, when talking of students' multiple identities before and within university, most demonstrate resilience and manage their hybrid habituses.

Students' age

A sub-theme that may contribute to an unfavourable 'academic habitus' and fuel low self-confidence appears to be the age students are when studying. Some younger case study students feel they lack life-skills to cope within the very grown-up environment of university or indeed need to enjoy their rite of passage and can be distracted from their study. The transition into student life brings as many benefits as hindrances; however a night on the town preceding a lengthy day of study in university does not generally mix well! Older age group students, who are over the grand age of 30 years, identify the challenges they face of having much to relearn regarding study skills, and many having to manage the multiple roles that they juggle in their everyday lives, for example childcare and employment outside university. Some outline their feelings of guilt as they spend time following their own pursuit of a university course when they could be giving time to their family or workplace. However, for others, this is seen as their time, and an exciting prospect. Younger students too can have similar familial responsibilities and therefore such challenges appear just as pertinent.

Case study 5

'I worried that I may be too old, too busy and too lacking in energy to be able to study [in university].'

'My [old] qualifications and age hindered my self-confidence the most. I was afraid of failing and felt it would take an age for me to digest any relevant material.'

'I'm not sure how I will overcome insecurities that have been imprinted on me over many years.'

'Being a mother is also a large factor [talking about time demands] as I do suffer maternal guilt when slaving over a text and my children are happily avoiding what they should be doing!'

'I do feel sometimes that I may have started [university] too late. I always felt that my education was incomplete because I never got a degree.'

Challenge

• Do you share some of those sentiments or do you feel as suggested above, that 'this is your time'?

In direct contrast to these comments, however, are the views of several students who believe that their university experience enriches their family and workplace lives. Their increased knowledge, their greater awareness of how and why learning occurs and the opportunity they get to learn from and with others all contribute to stronger relationships and outcomes. Reay *et al.* (2010) argue and demonstrate that students can effectively combine family relationships and university expectations and offer similar testimonies to the following case study examples.

Case study 6

'My direct family has had an impact on my learning and doing this course. I feel my family could also benefit . . . , My husband is very supportive . . . My children think it is funny that mummy has gone back to school.'

'My mum is great and she will help me and give advice. I hope I will make my mum proud!'

The examples given show how an 'academic habitus' plays an important role in enabling students to reach their potential in university. It is worth remembering that the construct of habitus is permeable and that early feelings of insecurity can give way to hope and optimism. These uplifting feelings feature within a range of relationships in university and beyond.

Hope and optimism: how supportive networks develop confidence and motivation

Within this section the range of relationships that students may develop are called 'supportive networks'. An initial reminder is given of the concept of identity and the idea of feeling comfortable when with people regarded as like-minded. Gorard *et al.* (2006) warn that the notion of not fitting in can cause potential social and academic barriers. Indeed, Bourdieu (1990) suggests that where social subjectivity is lacking, learning can be curtailed because the power of a dominant habitus may exert such control that a possibility, an opportunity, is discounted. However, Bourdieu equally points out that habitus is indeterminate and flexible, and within its composition an individual can reconstruct, following his or her own mind, or can be buoyed up by others in a group. Without doubt, cohort unity can be considered a 'supportive network' and linked favourably to the concepts of hope and optimism. Despite university sometimes attracting the negative reputation of being formal and elitist, when students find others who share their social subjectivities they may view their cohort group as a safe haven, and in turn this situation can support their learning potential. Reay *et al.* (2010, p. 112) remind of the strength of positive feelings 'where people like us can participate without damaging or changing valued identities'. The following case study examples give an indication of how some students feel about cohort unity.

Case study 7

'I really appreciate that the majority of our group are non-traditional students, [like me] because this was quite a worry prior to starting.'

'What has helped me feel confident is that everyone on the course has the same concerns… We all have busy lives, families, jobs and lack confidence in our academic abilities.'

From these testimonies, what was initially perceived as a barrier to learning, joining an unfamiliar group in a new context, has transformed into a learning scaffold.

Positive perception

A further scaffold to learning is positive perception. Perception is important and positive feelings experienced when in a familiar context or with other like-minded learners can have a significant impact on outcomes. How do you feel about your self-perception?

As a learner, I believe that	Yes/No
knowledge is more important than debate	
each day I become more intelligent	
I am prepared to take risks in my learning	
I see mistakes and failure as reasons to stop learning	
I learn through misconceptions and discussion	

Challenge

- Consider your answers. Do you see similarities between your own perceptions and those in the case studies?

Some learners hold the belief that performance is of greater importance than engagement; whether the context is known to them or not, they only involve themselves in activities where they think they will be successful. Dweck (2000) explores self-theories and motivation and proposes that students demonstrate entity theory when they see their achievement as certain and representative of their intelligence. By contrast, students predisposed to what Dweck calls incremental theory, see their intelligence as malleable and developing with more engagement and therefore offering further opportunities for learning. Entity theory is demonstrated by the student who believes it is important to be praised for achieving a goal, whereas praise for effort is appreciated by the incrementalist. The student who subscribes to entity theory may not chance getting something wrong and consequently tarnish their intelligence label, whereas their counterpart could be motivated by incomplete understanding. As noted at the beginning of this chapter, university learning very often requires risks to be taken, hypotheses to be made and the realisation that answers will not necessarily be reached.

However, when considering the benefits of learning that may be described as 'risky', it is worth acknowledging that if known practices are repeated, the same results are to be expected. The term 'learned helplessness' refers to a trait of the entity theorist or performance goal student who avoids failure and losing face (Yorke and Knight, 2004, p. 27). A better place to be is in a 'virtuous spiral' and to be encouraged by challenge and to attempt more. From the following case study examples, it is clear that students find the learning environment at university a 'supportive network', which advocates an incrementalist learning approach that is derived from the responses of the tutors to the learners' needs.

Case study 9

'My university tutors most definitely have a huge impact on my learning… They teach and guide in small steps and encourage my own thinking.'

'The staff and tutors are very approachable and make you believe it is possible to reach your own goals.'

'I have come to realise that already I have dealt with and overcome my issues that got in the way [of study] when starting uni, and no matter what the problem is, there is always a solution and you have to work hard for it.'

By working in partnership, tutors are able to encourage students to develop self-confidence by proactively employing Dweck's theory and advocating an incremental approach to learning. Indeed, Taylor (2009) vehemently stresses when pinpointing a crucial tutor attribute that 'only a malleable view would have the potential to encourage higher levels of achievement for the student' (p. 265). Tutors will use a range of strategies to increase learning capability and offer the 'supportive network' that brings about success.

Collaborative learning

The final 'supportive network' that will be considered in this chapter is that of collaboration, indeed a scholarship strategy that is believed to be most effective in education and that is strongly advocated by tutors. The concept of collaboration is used regularly in many areas of study and apprentice-type learning. It is possible that this form of knowledge-building is familiar from school activity or from teamwork called upon when playing sport or in a workplace. The practice of working within a learning community is inclusive and can offer short-term security to a learner with little knowledge, who can be nurtured into a confident risk-taker and decision-maker in the long term. Lave and Wenger's (1991) established research focuses on 'situated learning' that is founded on the assumption that effective learning can occur through collaboration within learning communities. They explain the community of practice as an environment that extends beyond the immediate location and that, with time, will overlap other communities. An example could be university learning extending to the workplace and even into less formal social settings such as family life. This can be thought of as the transferability of knowledge.

Learning together can be both symmetrical, where learners who are of very similar levels of understanding discover and debate ideas to make sense of them together, or asymmetrical, where there is a novice and expert learning relationship. It is normal to be rather like a chameleon when learning. At times knowledge will give students confidence and place them within a comfort zone. They may believe that they 'fit' with the ideas under consideration and then venture further by taking risks in hypothesising. On other occasions, they may feel overwhelmed and rely on the support of others to clarify their thoughts. In giving those examples, contrary assumptions are presented where effective learning may occur in secure contexts when emotions are assured, but in other circumstances occurs from the uncomfortable and unexpected. According to communities of practice theory, students need to transcend the complexities of being a newcomer (Lave and Wenger, 1991), become integrated and develop flexibly to reach full membership of the learning community. As identified earlier in this chapter, perceptions of barriers to learning can alter with time. Time is needed to realise the demands of study and to understand the mechanisms of university. Time is also required to build relationships and to reap the rewards of learning from and with colleagues. As demonstrated from the following case study comments, students' feelings appear to alter as they become better adjusted to the demands of study and learning together. The latter comment reflects the sentiments of many students who may initially demonstrate low self-confidence but whose self-belief is shored up through collaborative working.

Case study 10

'My university cohort is supportive . . . If I don't understand something or am a little unsure of what to do, I can always ask someone in my cohort.'

'I have never personally been in a learning group where we've been encouraged to pool our resources and work collaboratively. At first this felt as though it would pose a big challenge to me, but after a couple of weeks I can see how it is going to be OK and helpful.'

'My cohort members are already becoming an important part of my learning . . . looking to each other for guidance and approval that we are on the right track.'

Challenge

- In light of the preceding evidence from students new to higher education, how might you adopt their successful learning strategies?

Summary and conclusions

In summarising the issues covered within this chapter, it is helpful to be reminded of the power of perception. To understand that perception is rooted in past experience is important, as is the need to recognise that an individual's make-up emanates from cultural and pragmatic opportunities. As Bourdieu (1985) proposed, habitus is the layering of past and present experience and is linked to an individual's personal and social history, their 'being and belonging'. Such personal characteristics are examined as diverse degree-level certification has welcomed students from both traditional and non-traditional backgrounds into university in response to societal developments and demands for a better qualified workforce. This arrangement has created many challenges for the institution as well as the student. When considering the opportunity of study, case study participants are drawn to reflect on the challenges and changes that affect their 'being and belonging', their self-perception, and to consider the resilient qualities that persist within the range of hybrid habituses that contribute to their achievement. A strong 'academic habitus' is a powerful commodity. There are many barriers present when joining any new context and it is natural to feel unnerved and anxious; however, it is equally natural to feel excited and motivated by the challenge. Believing in the right to be a student, in being clever enough and in possessing similar traits to fellow students is important. Time is often required to see a shift in perception with regard to being suited to the new environment, as is the awareness that a habitus is permeable and can be reconstructed. Furthermore, self-belief in managing new learning can be influenced by the view that learning is fundamentally valuable. If a student is prepared to take a risk and enjoy the challenge of incremental learning, they will triumph over the learner who demonstrates an entity belief and places value on successful performance alone.

Additionally, 'supportive networks' that offer a scaffold to successful learning and coping with challenge and change are to be found within the practice of collaborative learning. Tutors are duty-bound to support their students but this does not mean they should spoon-feed. It is a recognised truth that there will be times when no complete answer to a question can be found. Some learners will not have been introduced to this concept in their past learning experiences and indeed will feel insecure when confronted by it. They may initially find learning uncomfortable; however, learning that is too conservative and risk-avoidant is perhaps not as effective. The practice of learning in a group can offer both security and confidence. For the learner who is new to a situation, or as Lave and Werger (1991) would say a 'community of practice', they can be supported, be this on a symmetrical or asymmetrical level. The opportunity to collaborate means that learning with and from others becomes an effective self-improvement strategy. Collaboration similarly can have the effect of shoring up a student's 'academic habitus' that in turn can develop into a strong motivator for learning that positively responds to the challenge of study. A final word on the key to accepting this challenge is that feelings are to be reflected upon to be understood and they are integral in achieving success.

Bibliography

Barnett, R. (2007) *A Will to Learn: Being a Student in an Age of Uncertainty.* Buckingham: SRHE/Open University Press.

Bourdieu, P. (1985) in Reay, D. (2004) 'It's all becoming a habitus: Beyond the habitual use of habitus in educational research'. *British Journal of Sociology of Education*, 25(4), pp. 431–44.

Bourdieu, P. (1990) in Reay, D. (2004) 'It's all becoming a habitus: Beyond the habitual use of habitus in educational research'. *British Journal of Sociology of Education*, 25(4), pp. 431–44.

Bourdieu, P. (1996) *The State Nobility: Elite Schools in the Field of Power.* Cambridge: Polity Press.

Bourdieu, P. and Wacquant, L. (1992) *An Invitation to Reflexive Sociology.* Chicago: University of Chicago Press.

Committee on Higher Education (1963) *Report on the Committee on Higher Education (The Robbins Report).* London: Her Majesty's Stationery Office.

Dweck, C. S. (2000) *Self-theories: Their Role in Motivation, Personality and Development.* Philadelphia: Psychology Press.

Gorard, S., Smith. E., May. H., Thomas, L., Adnett, N. and Slack, K. (2006) *Review of Widening Participation Research Addressing the Barriers to Participation to Higher Education.* University of York: Higher Education Academy and Institute for Access Studies.

Lave, J. and Wenger, E. (1991) *Situated Learning: Legitimate Peripheral Participation.* New York: Cambridge University Press.

Plowden, B. (1967) *Children and Their Primary Schools: A Report of the Central Advisory Council for Education (England).* London: Her Majesty's Stationery Office.

Reay, D. (2001) 'Finding or losing yourself?: Working-class relationships to education', *Journal of Education Policy,* 16(4), pp. 333–46

Reay, D., Ball, S. and David, M. (2002) '"It's taking me a long time but I'll get there in the end"': Mature students' access courses and higher education choice', *British Educational Research Journal*, 28(1), pp. 5–19.

Reay, D. (2004) 'It's all becoming a habitus: Beyond the habitual use of habitus in educational research' *British Journal of Sociology of Education*, 25(4), pp. 431–44.

Reay, D., Crozier, G. and Clayton, J. (2010) '"Fitting in" or "standing out": Working-class students in UK higher education', *British Educational Research Journal*, 36 (1), pp. 107–24.

Skeggs, B. (1997) *Formations of Class and Gender.* London: Sage.

Taylor, C. (2009) *Learning through a Foundation Degree.* Available at: http://etheses.nottingham.ac.uk/875/1/C_Taylor_PhD_Thesis_2009_-_Learning_through_a_Foundation_Degree.pdf (Accessed: 11 July 2014).

The Dearing Report Summary (1997). Available at: www.leeds.ac.uk/educol/ncihe/sr_008.htm (Accessed: 11 July 2014).

West, L. (1996) *Beyond Fragments: Adults, Motivation and Higher Education – A Bibliographical Analysis.* London: Taylor Francis.

Yorke, M. and Knight, P. (2004) 'Self-theories: Some implications for teaching and learning in higher education', *Studies in Higher Education* 29(1), pp. 25–37.

3 Maintaining a vision during times of change

Lin Shaw

Overview

Here, the criticality of leadership and the attributes of leaders in times of change are highlighted to show how the workforce has faced the challenge of change over the past ten years while keeping to the core 'vision' of quality provision for children. The chapter recognises the emotional resilience required to take on the role of leader/manager and explores the way in which culture and different leadership approaches support the workforce. Possible future changes and challenges are examined in the conclusion, with the reminder that it should be the child at the centre of education, not politics or policy.

Professional identity and status within the context of political and social change

In the UK, early years practice has evolved from caring for young children to degree-led professional status. This change has influenced quality of education and care provided for children, but just as importantly it has raised the status of those working with the early years sector. Early years practitioners have been empowered by the newly created professional identity and status, although further change is required to establish equality within multi-agency teams.

The term 'professional' is widely used in many aspects of society today. Historically, a profession was defined and monitored by socially accepted criteria and characteristics, with 'true' professions being male-dominated and elitist (Salvage, 2002). However, Burnard and Chapman (2003) argue that an occupation is viewed as professionally dependent upon the skills and specialist knowledge required. The terms 'professions' and 'professional' are changing with time and are now far more fluid and dynamic than in the past. This has permitted entry of previously classed proletarian occupations such as childcare to work towards achieving professional status, thereby meeting the needs of changing circumstances within society (Salvage, 2002). New professional occupations do, however, require a high level of accountability and autonomy for their work to be professionally justified (Burnard and Chapman, 2003). This requires knowledge to be gained through education and practice. Helsby (1995) provides a distinction between professional and professionalism by employing a dichotomy to demonstrate differences in characteristics associated with the two terms. Professions are characterised by pay, status and autonomy, while professional is related to personal or behavioural characteristics such as dedication, commitment and highly skilled practice. In the early years sector, professionalism is reliant upon self-reflection and an altruistic approach to improving practice. Moyles (2001) argues that early years practitioners need to exercise reflection, high levels of professional knowledge, self-esteem and self-confidence in order to establish professionalism.

Social and political context has transformed status and practice within the early years sector in the UK since the mid 1980s (Callan, 2006). Early Childhood Education and Care (ECEC) has been subjected to various centralised government reforms in how it is regulated and inspected. Significant restructuring continues in the early years sector against a backdrop of increased government regulation and demands for performativity. Mahony and Hextall (2000) argue that as a consequence of the National Childcare Strategy (DfEE, 1998) there has been a move towards centralised control and increased steerage from central government which has threatened professional autonomy and morale. The rapid pace of policy reforms within the early years sector has produced increased demands for practitioners to demonstrate competence (Osgood, 2005) and this may impact on professional judgement with its becoming subordinate to the demands of performativity. The changes in entry requirements for Early Years Professional Status (EYPS) – now Early Years Teacher Status (EYTS) – demonstrate state intervention on early years reforms. Since the first EYPS accreditation was conferred in 2007, the criteria for entry requirement relating to general education has risen, to the present requirement of General Certificate in Secondary Education (GCSE) level C or above in English, maths and science (NCTL, 2013a). This will meet the requirements of the state's aspiration to create a highly skilled workforce in the early years sector (DfE, 2012). However, it will impact on the accessibility of the present workforce, as many highly skilled practitioners already holding level 3 qualifications or above are now unable to use equivalency qualifications to obtain Early Years Teacher status. As many of the Early Years qualifications were obtained through non-traditional academic routes the new entry requirements may present barriers to the mature learner. The return to study for GCSE qualifications, requires time and finance, both of which are not often readily available in a low-paid workforce. In addition, mature learners require emotional resilience when returning to traditional routes in education, especially if they have negative memories of attending educational institutions during their childhood.

The impact on widening participation within the early years sector remains to be seen as new entry requirements may limit accessibility for many who wish to enter into a vocational occupation. The DfE confirmed (DfE, 2014) that from 1 August 2014 students receiving government funding to undertake the level 3 Early Years Educator qualification (NCTL, 2013b) will require GCSE English and maths at grade C or above on entry. Functional skills qualifications will not be accepted as equivalent to GCSEs. However, ambiguity on entry level remains as students undertaking apprenticeship in Early Years (DBIS, 2014) will not be required to hold GCSE English and maths A*–C because they can meet the English and maths requirements of their apprenticeship through Functional Skills qualifications (DBIS, 2014). In practice, students will need to obtain the relevant GCSEs before commencing employment if they are to be included in the number ratio (DfE, 2013).

Osgood (2006) argues that participating in continued education will encourage reflexivity and assist in further developing professionalism. However, rather than just pursuing training to satisfy a growing demand for credentialised practitioners, continued education should also promote greater self-awareness and self-confidence. Government discourse for a credentialised Early Years profession may be seen as undermining the emotional nature and intuitive practice that exists within ECEC practice (Claxton, 1999; Freire, 2005). It is noted that in the government documentation relating to Early Years Professional Status (EYPS) (CWDC, 2007), Early Years Teacher Status (EYTS) and Early Years Educator (EYE) (NCTL, 2013b) words relating to caring are notably absent. Without an open culture and ethic of care, practitioners may question the current conceptualisation of professionalism within the early years sector as it fails to recognise the relevance of emotional labour when working with young children (Taggart, 2011). If emotional labour is not recognised, it gives rise to the idea that selfless service is part of professionalism (Colley, 2006) and this in turn may lead to the exploitation of 'feminine capital' (Huppatz, 2009).

The range of titles used for practitioners in Early Years has given rise to ambiguities when developing a professional identity. This was due in part to the historical division of early years care among a range of occupations including nursing and teaching. The lack of professional status has given rise to the social perception that early years practitioners were unskilled female carers, a definition that has been driven by authoritarian and hegemonic discourses that supported gender inequality (Osgood, 2011). The EYE and EYTS (NCTL, 2013a, 2013b) roles have been developed to promote the use of a skilled graduate workforce in all settings and raise the social status of those working in the childcare sector. Cooke and Lawton (2008) suggest that the process of establishing the early years workforce as professional is causing unrest for some of the sectors workers. Career pathways have been seen as working towards manager status without true recognition that professional development in itself was a way to advance an early years practitioner. The early years workforce provides a service that supports economic growth and social justice (Cooke and Lawton, 2008). However, this is not reflected in the pay and conditions of the majority of practitioners in the UK or any of the OECD member countries (OECD, 2012). Miller and Cable (2011) also raise concerns about the term 'professional' in Early Years. They suggest that only those practitioners who achieve Early Years Professional or Teacher status can be considered professional. Moss (2008) disputes this and argues that any member of an Early Years team or workforce should be regarded as professional, although Fenech and Sumsion (2007) urge caution in identifying unqualified practitioners as professionals. In professional occupations it is necessary to determine who is accountable for quality practice and standards of care. It is debatable whether unskilled members of the team should be afforded the same level of accountability and professionalism as staff with EYE or EYTS. The mentoring and supervision of staff yet to achieve level 3 qualifications or above require support and guidance from qualified early years practitioners to ensure that quality care is maintained. Leadership responsibilities should include accountability for the competency of all members of the multidisciplinary teams they lead.

Challenge

- Make a list of your own qualifications and add to this list the qualifications you plan to get in the future.
- Why do you want more qualifications? Is this related to your career or for your own interest?
- Which qualifications do you consider essential for the Early Years professional?
- Are there any qualifications or training that you believe are of little value? Why?

Defining leadership

The professional status of early years practitioners has developed considerably since *The Effective Provision of Preschool Education (EPPE) Project: Final report* (Sylva *et al.*, 2004) highlighted the link between practitioners' levels of qualifications and the quality of provision. In particular, it identified that the quality of provision appeared to be higher in settings that were graduate-led. The reports *Effective Leadership in the Early Years Sector* (ELEYS) (Siraj-Blatchford and Manni, 2006) and *Researching Effective Pedagogy in the Early Years* (REPEY) (Sylva *et al.*, 2010) also identified graduate leadership as enhancing later outcomes for children.

Within the ECEC sector leadership has traditionally been associated with skills, characteristics and personal qualities (Nivala and Hujala, 2002). However, leadership also involves the perception of power, authority and competitive structures within the workforce. The early years sector contains a variety of diverse organisational structures (Muijs *et al.*, 2004) and most employees are women working in a non-hierarchical system (Rodd, 2007). Nurturing environments do not lend themselves to competitive leadership styles that reflect a hierarchical top-down orientation (Osgood, 2004). Instead, early years leaders interpret their leadership and autonomy according to the setting in which they are based. Nurseries, including the voluntary sector, give broader interpretations when defining leadership compared with schools and privately owned settings or childminders, where often an official leader is recognised (Solly, 2003).

Defining leadership within the early years sector requires a distinction to be made between the role of a leader and the role of the manager. Whalley and Allen (2011) suggest that within early years settings the two roles are often intertwined, thereby creating ambiguity and confusion within the workforce. The belief that management and leadership roles are interlinked is supported by Rodd (2007) and upheld by Langston and Smith (1999), who argue that the two roles support each other. However, Solly (2003) suggests that the roles are distinct with leadership promoting enrichment, progress and advancement and managers providing a lead figure for maintaining safeguarding and supervision within an early years setting. Hall (1996) agrees and defines leadership as actively promoting a philosophy but concurs that management is an integral part of this process.

The complementary nature of leadership and management is often assumed within the early years, but this is, in part, due to the diversity of settings. Educational literature, however, draws distinctive differences, perceiving leadership as having a visionary role, based on shared values, while managers focus on the day-to-day running of the organisation. In this respect leaders are in an ideal position to provide motivation and direction towards quality practice for colleagues (Adams, 2008) leaving the manger to take responsibility, authority and accountability for completing tasks efficiently and effectively (Bolden *et al.*, 2003). Rodd (2007) argues that leadership begins with a vision. Vision is identified as the catalyst used by the practitioner to inspire the development of others (practitioners, children and families). Vision promotes self-belief, encourages achievement and a sense of direction. By creating a shared vision the early years community would be able to protect itself when change and uncertainty arises.

Gronn (2003) suggests that culture and society has a key influence on the leadership of individuals. Diversity is regarded as a strength in communities but for this to succeed a cohesive vision among different groups within the early years sector is required. Leithwood *et al.* (2006) suggest that visionary leaders need to work towards creating a collaborative learning community that will involve listening to the many different practitioners who support the early years sector and reflecting on how to make use of the abilities of others. Therefore, as Mistry and Sood (2012) argue, an important challenge for leadership is to create a cohesive framework among the diverse group that shares the same vision. Greenfield and Ribbins (1993) agree that early years workforce needs to bring together individual identities, values and emotions within the social structures and systems of Early Years.

Challenge

- What is your 'vision' for the early years? Can you link this to the individual identity, value and emotion that you (and your colleagues) hold?
- How is the vision that you hold different to that held by other groups? e.g. parents, the 'government' and other outside agencies?

Ebbeck and Waniganayake (2003) debate how successful leaders consider themselves to be equal to other team members, sharing decision-making and giving power to the shared vision. Leadership will then become an all-inclusive and enabling procedure. Whalley and Allen (2011) demonstrate how these factors enable leaders to be visionary when creating change and inspiring the team. However, the development of strong visionary leadership within settings has been hindered by the historical context of feminisation of the early years workforce. Many of the appointed leaders may have been unprepared for the role of leader owing to the lack of training and education available (Ebbeck and Waniganayake, 2003; Rodd, 2007). Female practitioners defining professional identity against learned gendered identity constructs (Osgood, 2005) may be reluctant to enter into leadership roles. The economic reforms and managerialist discourse behind educational policy (DfE, 2011; NCTL, 2013a) in the past ten years focus on developing individualistic and entrepreneurial skills similar to commercial models of organisations (Acker, 1992). This tends to create a difficult challenge within the female-dominated context of Early Years where an ethic of care prevails (Yelland, 1998). The debate on the professional identity in early years settings includes the notion of 'collective identity' (Adams, 2008, p. 208). This raises issues on the challenges and difficulties of uniting a diverse workforce that spreads across the voluntary, private and state sectors. An additional challenge is how to encourage more male leaders within settings (Miller and Cable, 2011). Implementing strategies to defeminise early years practice will promote inclusion and equality while working towards a counterbalance of the largely feminised workforce. This vision will impact on ECEC communities as changes in personal identity and use of genderlect will need to be addressed when defeminising practice.

Leadership skills and attributes

The Department for Education and Skills (DfES, 2006) recognised that effective leadership is vital to the success of quality provision within the early years sector. Without skilled and visionary leaders to help develop high quality learning environments, the opportunity to meet the needs of children under the age of five years will be minimal. Research (Mitgang, 2012) demonstrates that the quality and practice of leadership must be monitored and evaluated to show that it will improve the long-term benefits for children's outcomes and support educational equity (Leithwood *et al.*, 2006).

The traditional concept of a leader has changed and is no longer recognised as the person who must be at the top of a hierarchy of command. Mistry and Sood (2012) recognise that leadership now requires a multifaceted mix of attributes with Whalley and Allen (2011) highlighting the importance of interpersonal skills. Historically, early years setting leaders have been appointed with little consideration for any leadership or management training (Jorebloom, 2003). The criteria for appointment to leader saw consideration given to the amount of time candidates had worked in the industry and their ability to work with children. Leadership is now viewed as both an individual and collective ethical responsibility (Australia DoE, 2013) that encompasses a process in which changes are made that reflect a shared vision and purpose. Siraj-Blatchford and Manni (2006) recognise that leadership requires practices that support vision, shared understanding, effective communication, learning communities and facilitating partnerships with families and the wider community.

Rodd (1998) has identified key elements that she believes are necessary when working towards effective leadership (Figure 3.1). Additional elements to be considered are experience, awareness of current perspectives, knowledge of legislation, effective communication, including interpersonal skills, and creativity in order to offer inspiration and confidence when encouraging community collaboration through times of change. Rodd (2007) states that leaders are successful when they have understanding of the complexities of their team, and the effective leader will reflect upon their own learning and impart their knowledge to the team. Sergiovanni (1999) recommends empowerment within a team where the leader shares responsibility, developing a reciprocal relationship based on trust. The ethics of leadership advocates leaders to be honest, open and truthful to their followers. As Osgood (2006) points out, if leaders are found to have lied then trust will be lost. Trust also relies on the assumption that leaders must be willing to learn and will have in-depth knowledge of all areas relative to their professional role (Rodd, 2007) and will assess the needs of the team and the individual. Moyles (2006) believes that professional leaders who raise the quality of early years practice by empowering the team will also empower the child. This supports Allen *et al.* (2007) who state that an empowered team does not overlook 'any' individual.

Leadership within Early Years focuses on providing quality provision for the children, but it must also lead and support the workforce. Leadership encompasses far more than being responsible for key children or delegated roles within a setting. Leadership requires autonomy and accountability that demonstrates the ability to apply knowledge and skills through reflective practice. Effective leadership will help to ensure that a strong vision is maintained during periods of change. How a leader performs will depend on the style of leadership they practice.

Models of leadership style

Leadership style simply relates to the approach a leader adopts when leading a team. There are many theories and models of leadership available, and a number of factors that might influence the style a person adopts. Style is often based on an individual leader's own beliefs, personality, experiences and working environment, and their assessment of the situation at the time when leadership is required. Some leaders work solely within one style while others are flexible and adapt their style to meet the needs of the environment. Four commonly used leadership styles found in early years settings are:

Situational approach to leadership

Blanchard and Johnson (1982) suggest that leaders should match their leadership style to the development level of the person, or people, being led. Situational leadership takes into account the extent to which followers are able and willing to follow. An everyday example may be the Special Education Needs Co-Ordinator (SENCO) role – if a child within the setting displays behavioural problems, the special skills of the SENCO will enable them to take the lead in the situation (Adair, 2006). This model may best suit a task-orientated approach to

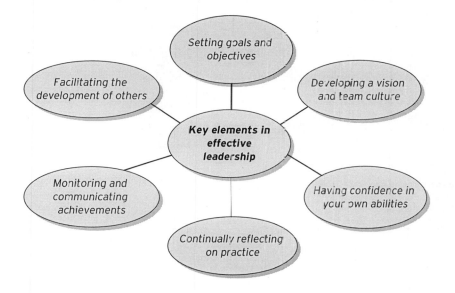

Figure 3.1 Key elements in effective leaders
Adapted from Rodd (1998, p. 12)

work-based practice. The leader must have an understanding of the individual's incentive for working in the early years before delegating roles (Rodd 2007) if this approach is to be successful. One disadvantage is that staff may not be given the opportunity to develop experience in all areas of pedagogy once predetermined roles have been allocated.

Qualities approach to leadership

This approach focuses on the personal attributes (or traits) of leaders, such as physical and personality characteristics, competencies and values. It views leadership solely from the perspective of the individual leader. Leadership traits are considered to be enduring characteristics that people are born with and that remain relatively stable over time. This approach is based on matching an individual's leadership qualities to the qualities required within an early years setting. Unlike skills, personal attributes or innate traits cannot be easily learned, although they may be controlled. For example, you cannot teach someone to have a sense of humour but if they do, skills to ensure that their humour is appropriate in certain situations may be learnt. As identified by Kouzes and Posner (2007) a trait-based approach to leadership has proved unreliable. The common traits required for leaders of political parties would differ from the qualities expected of a leader in an early years setting, particularly as the key traits required would be dependent on the type of EYEC setting. Kouzes and Posner (2007), however, have identified a number of key traits that 'followers' admired in a leader (Figure 3.2).

> **Followers' list of desirable key traits for leaders**
>
> 1 Honesty   6 Supportive
> 2 Forward-looking   7 Broad-minded
> 3 Inspirational   8 Intelligent
> 4 Competent   9 Straightforward
> 5 Fair-minded   10 Dependable

Figure 3.2 Top ten leadership traits
Adapted from Kouzes and Posner (2007)

Challenge

- How do you rate the ten key traits for leaders?
- Are there any that are more important than others?
- Can you put them in order of preference?
- Is this all you need to be a 'good' leader? Is there anything missing from the list?

Action-centred approach

An action-centred approach to leadership focuses on the actions of the leader. According to Adair (1998), there are three elements to all leadership situations. They are:

1   The achievement of a goal or task. This may be the completion of a very practical activity, such as developing an outdoor play area, or it may be a less tangible goal that requires strategic planning. Clear goals shared by all members will often bring a team together. Therefore, within the group, leaders will identify and evaluate the requirements of a task, reviewing or changing plans until the task is achieved.
2   The group of people performing the task. It is likely that the task will only be achieved if all members of the group work together. The group must be viewed as one entity. The leader will communicate with the group and gain their commitment when planning group tasks. Regular group meetings should be held to plan the task, identify resources, and monitor and evaluate progress of the whole group. Communicating feedback to the group on performance and success is essential in order to maintain motivation.
3   Each individual member of the group involved in the task. While the group will take on a life of its own, individuals do not lose their own identity. Their needs as individual human beings must continue to be met if their allegiance to the group, and their motivation to achieve the task, is to be sustained. For example, the leader will allocate responsibility to individuals, monitoring progress so that support, praise and encouragement may be given.

The effective leader has to balance the needs from each of the three elements (Figure 3.3). If any one element is ignored, the others are unlikely to succeed (Adair, 1998).

Empowerment approach

The empowerment approach involves a transfer of decision-making from higher to lower levels. The leader will delegate while expecting people to initiate, create and feel ownership of their role. The empowerment approach supports transformational leadership (Zhang and

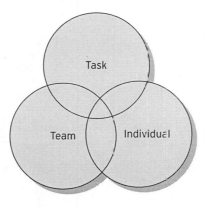

Figure 3.3 Three elements of action-centred leadership

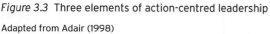
Adapted from Adair (1998)

Brundrett, 2010) where leaders are generally energetic, enthusiastic and passionate, promoting positive changes in those who follow. Transformational leaders are concerned and involved in the process while focusing on helping every member of the group succeed.

> Leaders and followers make each other advance to a higher level of moral and motivation.
>
> Burns (1978 p. ii)

Through the strength of their vision and personality, transformational leaders are able to inspire followers to change expectations, perceptions and motivations, creating an environment where everyone works towards common goals. Bass (1985) developed a model of transformational leadership that demonstrates four central principles (Figure 3.4) to identify the qualities and skills required when using the empowerment approach.

Bass and Riggio (2006) identified the four central principles of transformational leadership as the four 'I's

Idealised Influence (II) – the transformational leader will:

- serve as an ideal role-model for followers;
- possess positive leadership traits;
- demonstrate competence, persistence and determination. Followers will wish to emulate them;
- emphasise the importance of all followers having a sense of working towards a collective mission;
- be willing to take risk while maintaining ethical boundaries.

Inspirational Motivation (IM) – transformational leaders have the ability to:

- inspire and motivate followers;
- communicate high expectations to followers, inspiring them through motivation and commitment to engagement in the shared vision of early years practice;
- combine II and IM to become a charismatic – inspirational leader.

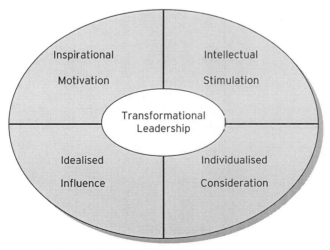

Figure 3.4 Four central principles of transformational leadership
Source: Adapted from Bass (1985)

Individualized Consideration (IC) – transformational leaders demonstrate:

- genuine concern for the needs and feelings of followers;
- personal attention to each follower to bring out their very best efforts;
- effective listening skills to listen to the needs of the followers to help them develop and achieve growth;
- mentoring skills so followers are actively encouraged to achieve higher levels of potential, although the leader will recognise and accept individual differences;
- delegation skills to provide a means of developing an individual who will then be monitored to assess progress or to establish if further support is required;
- the ability to recognise followers as individuals rather than as employees.
- effective communication skills with the ability to speak personally to each individual and encourage two-way conversation.

Intellectual Stimulation (IS) – the leader challenges followers to:

- be innovative and creative. This challenges personal beliefs and values and those of the leader and organisation;
- try new approaches in the process of problem-solving, without fear of criticism if mistakes are made.

Developing leadership skills requires knowledge and practice. In addition, a person must want and need to change before successfully developing a new style of leadership. The Department of Education (e.g. DfE, 2013; NCTL, 2013a) is currently advocating leaders in Early Years that are visionary, and this will be best achieved through the style of transformational leadership. However, the style of leadership practised must take into account the type of EYEC setting and environment. A good team leader will use a variety of styles of leadership to facilitate changing circumstances. Leaders may be faced with barriers to change if they hold no position of authority in settings that are governed by an autocratic or authoritarian style of management. The challenge in this situation is for leaders to maintain a vision that promotes a research-based pedagogical approach to practice.

Challenge

- Which of the four approaches to leadership are you most likely to take?

Situational approach	Qualities approach	Action-centred approach	Empowerment approach

- What about your colleagues?
- Do you believe that any one of these approaches is better than another or are they just different styles?

Transformational leadership in early years practice

Groups led by transformational leaders have been found to have higher levels of performance and satisfaction than groups led by other types of leaders (McDowall-Clark and Murray, 2012).

They inspire, empower and stimulate followers to exceed normal levels of performance. Transformational leaders hold positive expectations for followers, believing that they will do their best. As a result, followers and transformational leaders focus on and care about followers and their personal needs and development. McGregor (2011) states the emphasis is on ethical leadership, thereby encouraging individuals to lead from a human rights perspective. In transformational leadership the style reflects upon the complex and emotional nature of Early Years practice. However, care should be taken as there is a risk of exploitation in that the demands of the leader may impact on the number of hours given by the follower to fulfil the set expectations. This is especially true in a vocational environment such as Early Years where staff value the nurturing and caring aspect of their role.

Leadership and mentoring

> Mentoring is defined as being concerned with 'growing an individual', both professionally and personally. It is linked with professional and career development, and is somewhat characterised by an 'expert–novice' relationship.
>
> Lord *et al.* (2008, p. 6)

Developing transformational leadership qualities requires a creative thought process. Commitment to developing personal creativity and encouraging creativity will help to build confidence. Risk-taking and overcoming negative attitudes will assist in fighting fear of failure, helping to overcome negative attitudes that block creativity. Curiosity should be rewarded as this encourages the realisation that most problems have multiple solutions. Supporting and mentoring practitioners is an important part of the process.

Qualities of the 'ideal' mentor include:

- good communication skills;
- effective interpersonal skills;
- knowledge and competence in subject skills and practices;
- being 'politically' astute in order to understand the wider context.

Mentoring requires leadership skills (Rodd, 2007), with training and support given to staff who are to act as mentors so that they feel confident in supporting others (Jones *et al.*, 2005). Different styles or models of mentoring may be used to support individual needs of mentees (Hobson and Sharp, 2005), demonstrating a humanistic leadership approach. Effective mentoring will provide a useful link with self-appraisal and performance management, helping to implement appropriate staff training and professional development.

Managing change

Human beings tend to be creatures of habit and any change that will influence routines or behaviour may be perceived as threatening on a personal and professional basis. The world of ECEC in the UK has been in a state of constant change and conflict with new policies, laws, guidance and research influencing working conditions, professional identity and pedagogies within every setting. Although change is inevitable and necessary the rate and extent of change will precipitate different emotions.

Fisher (2005) defines the process of change as a series of emotional stages that everyone will experience to a certain degree (Table 3.1). Much of a person's reaction to change is subconscious and the emotions and behaviour through times of transition will depend on factors such as locus of control (Rotter, 1966), resilience and past experiences.

Table 3.1 Emotions involved when change occurs

Emotion	Cause
Anxiety	When a person is aware that change is not under their control and they cannot anticipate how the change will influence their work and behaviour. Staff may question what the future holds for them.
Happiness	When a person thinks something is going to be done to improve the working environment, allowing a bright future to be envisaged, with individual or team success. Staff will believe that they may be able to contribute and take more control.
Fear	Uncertainty around the change may impact on beliefs and behaviour. Staff may wonder how owners, manager, colleagues or parents will judge them.
Threatened	Fear that the change may affect life style or any future choices.
Guilt	Awareness of past failings may cause feelings of guilt, especially if the staff believe that old practices have had a detrimental effect rather than a positive influence on the children they care for.
Depression	Uncertainty of what may happen in the future can impact on personal and professional identity. With no clear vision of what lies ahead, lack of motivation and confusion may occur. Morale may decline, and individuals may demonstrate signs of stress.
Disillusionment	Awareness that personal values, beliefs and goals are incompatible with the changes, creating a feeling of dissatisfaction. In this stage criticising and complaining and doing minimum labour are common. Staff turnover may increase as individuals will not be able to see any future in remaining in the setting.
Hostility	If no effective change is seen, the new processes are ignored or actively undermined. Leadership will be challenged and conflict will ensue.
Denial	Lack of acceptance of any change. Staff continue to use old practices and act as if change has not happened.
Excitement	The change represents a challenge to move forward.

Source: Adapted from Fisher (2005)

The different stages of emotions throughout the transition of transformational change may be applied to staff, parents and children. The role of the leader is to ensure that all those affected are supported throughout the transition period by minimising stress and conflict.

Case study: Resistance to change

As a room leader in a privately owned nursery I wanted to encourage children in their creative and imaginative play and was excited with the prospect of using part of the outdoor area as a 'mud kitchen'. I presented my ideas to the nursery manager who agreed to let me build the resource in the garden. I talked to the other staff about my idea and put articles relating to mud kitchens and a brief explanation of my vision for the resource up on the notice board. I began searching for items that I could use and was fortunate to come across a selection of old sinks and kitchen equipment that I was able to have for free. I employed the help of a friend, a carpenter, to make the frame for the sink and over the course of a weekend we were able to build my 'dream kitchen'. I was pleased with the finished resource although slightly apprehensive about how the children would react. I should not have worried because as soon as they saw the kitchen they ran outside to investigate amid shouts of delight and laughter. Within a short space of time I noticed that not only were they making mud concoctions, they were also using mathematical language as they mixed 'ingredients'. The kitchen was a success with the children but the staff were not as enthusiastic. Comments such as 'we will have mud tramped all across the floor' to 'I suppose all the plastic fruit and vegetables will have to go outside now' deflated my enthusiasm. It is so difficult to be inspired by effective pedagogy at university only to meet resistance and challenge when I take new ideas back to the setting.

Student on Early Years Professional Studies Foundation Degree

Challenge

* Consider your own feelings when change has been introduced to your setting.
* What factors do you feel cause the most stress and conflict when change is implemented?
* How would you inspire staff to embrace new ideas that support research-based practice?

Dealing with resistance to change

Some resistance to change is usually inevitable and this depends on the emotional state of individuals. It may become obvious that a group of people within the team share a similar attitude and are reluctant to change (See Table 3.1). This is often due to feelings of fear as they perceive the change as a threat to their personal or professional identity. Fear may also arise if their knowledge is questioned, making them feel aware of their own limitations. This is especially true of staff who may have worked in a similar role for a long period of time and believe that practical experience should be considered before new pedagogical approaches are enforced upon them. People may become demotivated and challenge change or improvement if they feel that their input such as time, reliability, loyalty and 'heart' is not fairly rewarded with the balance of pay, recognition, praise, responsibility and enjoyment they receive. The use of reflective practice as a means of identifying ways of improving how things are done is a useful tool for practitioners to see practice in a new perspective and make connections with larger issues (Nutbrown, 2012).

In all cases where change is planned, the leader must ensure that effective communication and interpersonal skills are employed. Rodd (2007) suggests that early years leaders should consider the 'Six Cs of Change' adapted from Schrag *et al.* (1985) (Table 3.2) when planning a strategy to implement change.

Adams (2008) believes that the balance between give and take must be viewed as equitable if motivation through change is to be maintained. Transformational leadership is viewed as the ideal style to manage change as it enhances self-confidence and skills, builds team capacity through the efficient use of staff and resources, and promotes active engagement in self-directed change in a blend of learning environments and values individuality and creativity (NCTL, 2013a, 2013b).

Pedagogical leadership

Government policies, reports and statutory guidance aim to embed the role of the visionary and transformational leader within ECEC. The introduction of the EYTS (NCTL, 2013a), demonstrated an ethos of pedagogic leadership (a leader of practice) that was not previously associated with an organisational position. This would allow pedagogical leadership to form a fundamental part of education and training, embedded in professional identity. However, although including a leadership role in professional status is seen as a way to raise quality standards, the term pedagogical leadership is not a concept that is internationally understood (Heikka and Waniganayake, 2011; Nutbrown, 2012).

Table 3.2 The six Cs of change

Challenge	Ensure the whole team clearly understands the aim, objective and benefit of the change.
Communicate	Keep the team informed of the change and how it will be implemented to manage fear.
Commitment	Involve staff in the planning and implementation of change to give them ownership through participation and ownership.
Control	Promote locus of control through opportunities to express ideas and concerns relating to the change.
Confidence	Ensure training and other necessary support is available to build upon self-awareness and self-acceptance.
Connect	Involve the staff, children, parents and the wider community to ensure that all primary users are fully aware of the inevitability of the change. Link with other settings or multi-professional partners so that a support network may be formed.

Source: Adapted from Schrag *et al.* (1985)

Interpretations of leadership are varied within ECEC and Murray and McDonald Clark (2013) argue that the term must be made more meaningful to the early years sector. This will necessitate changing the traditional view of leadership as a position of power and authority within a hierarchical framework. Research was gathered from practitioners (Mathers *et al.*, 2011), and the consensus was that for leaders to be most effective they would need to be in a managerial or hierarchical position, supporting the old traditional notions that power and authority are required if change is to be made. Viewing leaders as an elite group will exclude the notion that all practitioners are leaders of child pedagogy. To support transformational leadership within the diverse nature of ECEC a conceptual framework that includes values of care and nurturing within a loving environment would be advocated. Passionate care allows practitioners to use emotional drive and a commitment to an ethic of care (McDowall-Clark and Murray, 2012) rather than a power-driven basis for personal and professional development. The passion and caring concept of care is based upon enthusiasm and high motivation rather than a feminine trait (Taggart, 2011) and should be supported. The need for an inclusive and uniform style of leadership is essential if practitioners are to develop areas of common understanding and pedagogies that may be shared and developed within an international professional context.

The range of multi-professional and multi-agency situations that are required to develop a holistic approach to ECEC is ever increasing, and leaders in ECEC must be able to move forward to a social perspective of practice and learning. This will develop skills required to engage with different professional bodies and the wider community when identifying common issues and possible solutions for children under their professional leadership. Professional autonomy will be enhanced within the ECEC sector if leadership and professionalism are viewed as reciprocal relationships in which participative pedagogy is embedded within the context of professional practice. This includes specialist pathways in ECEC such as special educational needs and safeguarding where guidance on the joint planning and commissioning of services to ensure close co-operation between education, health services and social care is viewed as a priority within UK's social policies.

Vision for the future

The international dialogue and debate on leadership and pedagogy demonstrates concern for the ways to develop leadership in ECEC. ECEC professionals and practitioners have recognised that the sector requires all who work within it to build on their professional knowledge-base and engage in ongoing learning and development. This includes making children's learning, development and well-being the core focus of their work, and collaboratively developing a culture of ethical inquiry and community of learners (Australia DoE, 2013). The limited availability of child development and care routes for early years teacher training in UK is in sharp contrast to the training available in countries such as New Zealand and Denmark (Miller and Cable, 2008). The introduction of EYTS will not give ECEC professionals the opportunity to take a Post-Graduate Certificate in Education nor receive Qualified Teacher Status. This may lead to a two-tier system existing, with EYTS practitioners receiving lower pay and recognition than Qualified Teacher Status (QTS). It may also limit opportunities for career progression and working in countries that demand ECEC graduates have QTS or equivalent.

In the UK, the government's commitment to raising the status of the profession, the introduction of more rigorous entry requirements and a simplification of early years qualifications (NCTL, 2013a; NCTL, 2013b) has the potential to promote autonomous ECEC leaders. However, pay and conditions of the early years workforce needs to be addressed as no matter how passionate highly skilled professionals may be, the financial reward needs to be on parity with other caring professionals. In 2013, the UK Office for Standards in Education, Children's Services and Skills (Ofsted) stated that strong and effective leadership was the key to making a setting good or outstanding. It added that settings should be subject to rigorous assessment to ensure standards remain high and are continually challenged, while an experienced and well-qualified workforce is essential to providing a quality learning experience for children. The government's Wider Vision for Early Years (NCTL, 2013a) includes the implementation of a rigorous regulatory and inspection regime that will be used to provide evidence to Ofsted (2013). This maintains previous 'tick box culture' practices (Power, 1999) and challenges the perceived role of the visionary leader. By supporting statutorily imposed frameworks, a mentality of compliance is generated and promotes an environment of learned helplessness. Current government rhetoric for the early years sector in the UK (DfE, 2013) advocates professional autonomy, graduate workforce, visionary leadership and effective pedagogy. However, by the nature of the power-based government management structure, it has taken autonomy away by embedding hierarchical leadership practices with a focus on target-led policies.

The challenge for early years practitioners is to develop a strong vision to support an autonomous graduate-led professional rather than a state-led professional body that creates barriers to visionary and transformational leadership in ECEC provision. Within a changing social environment the role of the transformational leader in ECEC will need to include discussion on how to satisfy the demands for performativity and research-based pedagogical practice while complying with a regulated and controlled state agenda. Promoting a holistic approach to meeting the needs of every child will always be the challenge and ultimate vision for all who work within the ECEC sector. Discussion and debate on the vision for Early Years in the UK is set to continue however the one voice that must be heard over all others is that of the child.

Further reading

The following books are suggested to widen critical debate on professional identity and leadership skills within early years practice.

Dalli, C., Urban, M. (Ed.) (2013) *Professionalism in Early Childhood Education and Care*. Padstow: Routledge.

McDowall Clark, R., Murray, J. (2012) *Reconceptualising Leadership in the Early Years*. Glasgow: Open University Press.

Miller, L., Cable, C. (Ed.) (2011) *Professionalization, Leadership and Management in the Early Years*. London: Sage.

Bibliography

Acker, J. (1992) 'Gendered organisational theory', in Mills, A. J., Tancred, P. (Eds) *Gendering Organizational Analysis*, pp. 248–60. London: Sage.

Adair, J. (1998) *Leadership Skills*. London: Chartered Institute of Personnel and Development.

Adair, J. E. (2006) *Leadership and Motivation: The Fifty-Fifty Rule and the Eight Key Principles of Motivating Others*. London: Kogan Page.

Adams, K. (2008). 'What's in a Name? Seeking professional status through degree studies within the Scottish early years context.' *European Early Childhood Education Research Journal*, 16(2), pp. 196–209.

Allen, D., Chen, G., Kanfer, R., Kirkman, B., Rosen, B. (2007) 'A multilevel study of leadership, empowerment and performance in teams', *Journal of Applied Psychology*, 92(2), pp. 331–46.

Australia DoE (Department of Education) (2013) *National Quality Framework for Early Childhood Education and Care*. Available at https://education.gov.au/legislation-ratings-and-standards-information-national-quality-framework (Accessed: 13 July 2014).

Bass, E. M. (1985) *Leadership and Performance Beyond Expectation*. New York: Free Press.

Bass, B. M., Riggio, R. E. (2006) *Transformational Leadership* (2nd edn). New Jersey: Erlbaum.

Blanchard, K. H., Johnson, S. (1982) *The One Minute Manager*. New York: Berkley Books.

Bolden, R., Gosling, J., Marturano, A., Dennison, P. (2003) *A Review of Leadership Theory and Competency Framework*. University of Exeter: Centre for Leadership Studies.

Burnard, P., Chapman, C. (2003) *Professional and Ethical Issues in Nursing* (3rd edn). London: Balliere Tindal.

Burns, J. M. (1978) 'Leadership, 1978', *The New Yorker*. New York: Harper & Row.

Callan, S. (2006) *Mentoring in the Early Years*, Robins, A. (Ed.). London: Sage.

Claxton, G. (1999) 'The anatomy of intuition', in Atkinson, T and Claxton, G. (Eds) *The Intuitive Practitioner: On the Value of Not Always Knowing What One Is Doing*. Buckingham: Open University Press.

Colley, H. (2006) 'Learning to labour with feeling: Class, gender and emotion in childcare education and training', *Contemporary Issues in Early Childhood*, 1, pp. 15–29.

Cooke, G., Lawton, K. (2008). *For Love or Money: Pay, Progression and Professionalization in the 'Early Years' Workforce*. Available at: www.ippr.org (Accessed 15 July 2014).

CWDC (Children's Workforce Development Council) (2007) *Guidance to the Standards for the Award of Early Years Professional Status*. London: The Stationery Office.

DBIS (Department Business Initiative Schemes) (2014) *Apprenticeship Grant for Employers*. Available at: www.gov.uk/government/organisation/department-for-business-innovation-skills> (Accessed: 14 July 2014).

DfE (Department for Education) (2011) *Business Plan 2011–2015, Department for Education*. Available at: www.gov.uk/government/uploads/system/uploads/attachment_data/file/31930/10-p58-bis-business-plan.pdf (Accessed: 7 August 2014).

DfE (Department for Education) (2012) *Early Years Foundation Framework*. Available at www.gov.uk/government/publications/early-years-foundation-stage-framework (Accessed: 14 July 2014).

DfE (Department for Education) (2013) *More Great Childcare: Raising Quality and Giving Parents More Choice*. Available at: www.gov.uk/government/uploads/system/uploads/attachment_data/file/219660/More_20Great_20Childcare_20v2.pdf (Accessed: 7 August 2014).

DfE (Department for Education) (2014) *Children and Family Act*. London. Available at http://www.legislation.gov.uk (Accessed: 14 July 2014).

DfEE (Department for Education and Employment) (1998) *National Childcare Strategy. Green Paper: 'Meeting the Childcare Challenge'*. Available at: http://webarchive.nationalarchives.gov.uk/20130401151715/https://education.go.uk (Accessed 21 July 2014).

DfES (Department for Education and Skills) (2006) Children's Workforce Strategy: *Building a World-class Workforce for Children, Young People and Families. The Government's Response to the Consultation*. Nottingham: DfES Publications.

Ebbeck, M., Waniganayake. (2003). *Early Childhood Professions: Leading Today and Tomorrow.* Australia: Elsevier.

Fenech, M., Sumsion, J. (2007) 'Early childhood teachers and regulation: Complicating power relations using a Foucauldian lens', *Contemporary Issues in Early Childhood,* 8(2), pp. 109-22.

Fisher, J. M. (2005) *A Time for Change,* Human Resource Development International, 8(2), pp. 257-64.

Freire, P. (2005) *Education for Critical Consciousness.* London. Continuum.

Greenfield, T., Ribbins, P., Eds. (1993) *Greenfield on Educational Administration: Towards a Humane Craft.* London: Routledge.

Gronn, P. (2003) *The New World of Educational Leaders.* London: Sage.

Hall, V. (1996) *Dancing on the Ceiling: A Study of Women Managers in Education.* London: Paul Chapman Publishing.

Heikka, J., Waniganayake, M. (2011) 'Pedagogical leadership from a distributed perspective within the context of early childhood education', *International Journal of Leadership in Education* 14(4), pp. 499-512.

Helsby, G. (1995) 'Teachers' construction of professionalism in England in the 1990s', *Journal of Education for Teaching: International Research and Pedagogy,* 21(3), pp. 317-32.

Hobson, A. J., Sharp, C. (2005) 'Head to Head: A systematic review of the research evidence on mentoring new head teachers', *School Leadership and Management,* 25(1), pp. 25-42.

Huppaz, K. (2009) 'Reworking Bourdieu's Capital: Feminine and female capitals in the field of paid caring work', *Sociology,* 43(1), pp. 45-66.

Jones, L., Browne, K., Aitken, S., Keating, I., Hodson, E. (2005) 'Working with parents and carers, in Jones, L., Homes, R. And Powell, J. (Eds), *Early Childhood Studies: A Multiprofessional Perspective.* Maidenhead: Open University Press.

Jorebloom, P. (2003) *Leadership in Action: How Effective Directors Get Things Done.* USA: New Horizons.

Kouzes, J. M. and Posner, B. Z. (2007) *The Leadership Challenge* (4th edn). San Francisco, CA: Jossey-Bass.

Langston , A., Smith, A. (1999) *Managing Staff in the Early Years Setting.* Abingdon: Routledge.

Leithwood, K., Day, C., Sammons, P., Harris, A., Hopkins, D. (2006) *Seven Strong Claims About Successful School Leadership.* England: National College for School Leadership.

Lord, P., Atkinson, M., Mitchell, H. (2008) *Mentoring and Coaching for Professionals: A Study of the Research Evidence.* Available at: www.environmentalconclusions.com/resources/MCM01.pdf (Accessed: 14 July 2014).

Mahoney, P., Hextall, I. (2000) *Reconstructing Teaching.* London: Routledge Falmer.

Mathers, S., Ranns, H., Karemaker, A., Moody, A., Sylva, K., Graham, J., Siraj-Blatchford, I. (2011) 'Evaluation of the graduate leader fund: Final report', *Research Brief DFE-RE144.* London: The Stationery Office, DFE.

McDowall Clark, R., Murray, J. (2012) *Reconceptualizing Leadership in the Early Years.* Glasgow, Open University Press.

McGregor, D. (2011) *The Human Side of Enterprise.* New York: McGraw-Hill.

Miller, L., Cable, C. (Eds) (2011) *Professionalization, Leadership and Management in the Early Years.* London: Sage.

Miller, M., Cable, C. (2008) *Professionalism in the Early Years Workforce.* London: Hodder.

Mistry , M., Sood, K. (2012) *Challenges of Early Years Leadership Preparation: A Comparison between Early and Experienced Early Years Practitioners in England.* London: Sage.

Mitgang, L. (2012) *The Making of the Principal: Five Lessons in Leadership Training. Perspective,* The Wallace Foundation. Available at: www.wallacefoundation.org/knowledge-center/school-leadership/effective-principal-leadership/Documents/The-Making-of-the-Principal-Five-Lessons-in-Leadership-Training.pdf (Accessed: 14 July 2014).

Moss, P. (2008). 'What future for the relationship between early childhood education and care and compulsory schooling?', *Research in Comparative International Education,* 3(3), pp. 224–34.

Moyles, J. (2006) *Effective Leadership and Management in the Early Years.* Maidenhead: Open University Press.

Moyles, P. (2001) 'Ethics in the Nursery', *Every Child,* 7(3), pp. 6–7.

Muijis, D., Aubrey, C., Harris, A., Briggs, M. (2004) 'How do they manage? A review of the research on leadership in early childhood', *Journal of Early Childhood Research,* 2(2), pp. 157–60.

Murray, J., McDonald Clark, R. (2013) 'Reframing leadership as a participative pedagogy: The working theories of early years professionals, *Early Years,* 33(3), pp. 289–301.

NCTL (National College for Teaching and Leadership) (2013a) *Teachers' Standards (Early Years).* Available at: www.gov.uk/government/uploads/system/uploads/attachment_data/file/211646/Early_Years_Teachers__Standards.pdf (Accessed: 14 July 2014).

NCTL (National College for Teaching and Leadership) (2013b) *Early Years Educator (Level 3): Qualifications criteria.* Available at: www.gov.uk/government/uploads/system/uploads/attachment_data/file/211644/Early_Years_Educator_Criteria.pdf (Accessed: 14 July 2014).

Nivala, V., Hujala, E. (Eds) (2002) *Leadership in Early Childhood Education: Cross-cultural Perspectives.* Oulu, Finland: Department of Educational Sciences and Teacher Education, Early Childhood Education, University of Oulu.

Nutbrown, C. (2012) *Foundations for Quality: The Independent Review of Early Education and Childcare Qualifications: Final Report.* Cheshire: Department for Education. Available at: www.gov.uk/government/uploads/system/uploads/attachment_data/file/175463/Nutbrown-Review.pdf (Accessed: 11 July 2014).

OECD (Organisation for Economic Co-operation and Development) (2012) *Closing the Gender Gap: Act Now.* Paris, OECD Publishing. Available at: http://dx.doi.org/10.1787/9789264179370-en (Accessed: 14 July 2014).

Ofsted (Office for Standards in Education, Children's Services and Skills) (2013) 'Getting it right first time: Achieving and maintaining high-quality early years provision' (July 2013). Available at: www.ofsted.gov.uk/resources/getting-it-right-first-time-achieving-and-maintaining-high-quality-early-years-provision (Accessed: 14 July 2014).

Osgood, J. (2004) 'Time to get down to business? The responses of Early Years practitioners to entrepreneurial approaches to professionalism', *Journal of Early Childhood Research,* 2(1), pp. 5–24.

Osgood, J. (2005) 'Who cares? The classed nature of childcare', *Gender and Education,* 17(3), pp. 289–303.

Osgood, J. (2006) 'Rethinking "professionalism" in the Early Years: Perspectives from the United Kingdom', Editorial in *Contemporary Issues in Early Childhood,* 7(1), pp. 1–4.

Osgood, J. (2011) *Narratives from the Nursery.* London: Routledge.

Power, M. (1999) *The Audit Society: Rituals of Verification* (2nd edn). Oxford: Oxford University Press.

Rodd , J. (1998) *Leadership in Early Childhood: The Pathway to Professionalism* (2nd edn). Buckingham: Open University Press.

Rodd, J. (2007) *Leadership in Early Childhood* (3rd edn). Glasgow: Open University Press.

Rotter, J. (1966) 'Generalised expectancies for internal versus external control of reinforcement', *Psychological Monographs,* 30(1), pp. 1–26.

Salvage, J. (2002) *Rethinking Professionalism: The First Step for Patient Focused Care.* London: Institute for Public Policy Research.

Schrag, L., Nelson, E., Siminowsky, T. (1985) *Helping Employees Cope with Change.* Redmond: Child Care Information Exchange.

Sergiovanni, T. (1999) *Rethinking Leadership: A Collection of Articles. K-College.* Illinois: Skylight Professional Development.

Siraj-Blatchford, I., Manni, L. (2006). *Effective Leadership in the Early Years Sector (ELEYS) Study: Research Report*. London: Institute of Education, University of London/General Teaching Council for England.

Solly, K. (2003) *What Do Early Years Leaders Do to Maintain and Enhance the Significance of the Early Years?* A paper on a conversation with Kathryn Solly held at the Institute of Education, University of London, on 22 May 2003.

Sylva, K., Melhuish, E., Sammons, P., Siraj-Blatchford, I., Taggart, B. (2004) *The Effective Provision of Pre-school Education (EPPE) Project: Final Report*, London, DfEE/Institute of Education, University of London.

Sylva, K., Melhuish, E., Sammons, P., Siraj-Blatchford, I., Taggart, B. (Eds) (2010) *Early Childhood Matters: Evidence from the Effective Pre-School and Primary Education Project*. Abingdon: Routledge.

Taggart, G. (2011) 'Don't we care? The ethics and emotional labour of early years professionalism', *Early Years*, 31(1), pp. 85–95.

Whalley. M. E., Allen, S (2011) *Leading Practice in Early Years Settings*. Exeter: Learning Matters.

Yelland, N. (Ed) (1998) *Gender in Early Childhood*. London: Routledge Falmer.

Zhang, W., Brundrett, M. (2010) 'School leaders' perspectives on leadership learning: The case for informal and experiential learning', *Management and Education*, 24(4), pp. 154–8.

Section 2

Challenges for learning and learners in the middle of change

This section considers learning and learners who are beneficiaries of change over which they have little input or control.

Jane Austen, in her novel *Sense and Sensibility*, said: 'I will be calm. I will be mistress of myself.' This is something to consider as you read this section. Again, think about your view, values, beliefs and practice, and think about your role when working with others in change.

In this section there are three chapters:

Chapter 4 is written by **Bridget Durell** and explores **'Neuroscience and young children's learning: what can the early years workforce learn from this relatively new area of research?'**

Chapter 5 is authored by **Clair Stevens** and presents a case for learning outside classrooms: **'Taking the learning outdoors: the challenges and the possibilities'**.

Chapter 6 is jointly written by **Clare Wiseman** and **Laurence Taylor**, who explore **'Digital harmony or digital dissonance? Developing literacy skills in the new technological age'**.

4 Neuroscience and young children's learning: what can the early years workforce learn from this relatively new area of research?

Bridget Durell

Overview

This chapter aims to encourage those who are part of the early years workforce, in one capacity or another, to acknowledge, critically evaluate and apply to practice some potentially valuable and exciting emerging research evidence from the relatively new discipline of neuroscience. The argument put forward is that such research evidence can enhance and broaden our understanding of how young children learn and develop. It can, therefore, provide us with some new ideas to try out in order to improve not only our own practice, but, by doing so, also improve learning and development outcomes for the young children in our care – for better/the greater good. Hilary Leevers from the Wellcome Trust has drawn attention to the 'evidence gap' (Coughlan, 2014) that currently exists, identifying an urgent need for the children's workforce – and especially those in the Early Years – to start to apply research findings from the field of neuroscience to inform their practice, and so it is with this challenge in mind that it is appropriate and timely to consider the ways in which neuroscience can be used in positive ways to improve practice.

The chapter will begin by defining and contextualising the concepts of children's learning and 'neuroscience', placing both within the wider political, disciplinary and historical contexts of social and educational research. Key themes within neuroscience will be discussed and applied to young children's brain development, namely synaptic proliferation, neurogenesis, synaptic pruning, sensitive periods of brain development and brain plasticity. These themes will be further developed through consideration of 'cases' based on examples of neuro-scientific research. Some possible implications for the workplace and practical suggestions based thereon will be identified for each case, with identification of the ways in which neuro-scientific studies could help to develop a deeper understanding of how young children learn and develop. Implications for practice will also be identified with the objective of improving practice when working with children, especially within early childhood contexts. This pragmatic, theory-into-practice approach will provide ideas about how to move from the 'why', to the 'what' and the 'how' of real-life practice in the Early Years.

Part 1 The context: children's learning and neuroscience

Children's learning

The term 'learning' is used to reflect a bias in this chapter towards young children's cognitive development. This is a deliberate choice, although full acknowledgement is also given to the holistic view of child development. Clearly, the links between allegedly different aspects of young children's development reflect, for example, Benjamin Bloom's theory of cognitive, affective and psychomotor domains and taxonomies (Bloom *et al.*, 1956) and also Rudolf Steiner's earlier 'head, heart and hands' concept of child development (Morrison, 2009, p. 161); and these key figures in childhood studies (among others) also acknowledge the inter-relatedness of these domains of development. However, more recent national and international comparisons of children's academic achievement in later life, such as recent reports from the OECD, have put children's educational achievement in this country under scrutiny. Having become a key focus of national political interest, it is inevitable that these issues will form part of the wider debate about how best to ensure high levels of achievement in our children. While the focus of the reports is on older children's academic achievements, it is almost too easy, sometimes, to forget that the very children being judged as inadequate academically compared with other countries were not so long ago being taught in our early years settings. They are the same children, despite artificial separation by policymakers of their lives into discrete segments, ages and stages (with all their attendant guidance and separate criteria for success). It is often argued by early years experts that the first few years of a child's life are crucial to their later achievements and, if they are to be believed, then it could be argued that the early years workforce needs to acknowledge that their practice has a significant influence on our children's outcomes – not just in the here and now, but also in the future – for better or for worse.

Neuroscience

So, what is 'neuroscience'? A general definition would describe it as the scientific study of the neurological, or nervous, system. So the two key features involve 'scientific study', which we will return to in a while, and the 'nervous system', which, although related to the whole body, often focuses on brain activity and response, as explored by Sarah-Jayne Blakemore and Uta Frith in their book *The Learning Brain* (2005). Some of the scientific studies carried out under the umbrella of neuroscience include research into growth, genetics, physiology, socio-emotional development or cognition, and researchers also try to identify how environments might impact on human development. A complex area of study, then, and one which becomes more complicated as new branches of neuroscience emerge over time. For example, a key branch of neuroscience which is of particular interest to those working with children right now is the field of 'social neuroscience'. This involves the study of relationships between neural/biological and social processes. The field of 'cognitive neuroscience' is also an area of interest for those working in different childhood contexts as it focuses on the study of relationships between neural/biological and behavioural processes.

And so, although still in its own 'early years', neuroscience is becoming a key source of information which has the potential to help the early years workforce to gain better understanding of factors that might influence not only children's early learning and development, but also their later relationships, behaviour, health, achievements and successes across the lifespan. It is as if neuroscience is a late arrival at a party, joining earlier theorists from the social sciences. But it is also important to remember that the discipline of neuroscience did not develop in isolation. As with all developments through history, it is part of the wider picture of social, political and cultural developments that have undergone exponential change, especially in more recent times. In particular, technological developments have played an important part in the development of the field of neuroscience; for example, if we consider the technical environment in which key thinkers in the twentieth century (such as Pavlov, Vygotsky, Chomsky or even Gardner) were conducting their studies, their experiments were subject to the available technologies of the day – and many of their experimental theories derived from externally observed behaviours under experimental conditions. But if we move our focus to more recent researchers such as Stephen Pinker, whose work involves using technical advances such as brain scans to inform his ideas about human learning and development, it is clear to see how neuroscientific research has developed as a result of our increasing ability to see inside the brain; what was only visible from the outside is now accessible from within – and that is hugely significant.

The 'scientific' method of study mentioned earlier in this chapter as playing a key role in neuroscience can also be seen in terms of continuity over time; for example, early pioneers in psychology used laboratory experiments and empirical research methods such as observations to help them form their experimental theories – and so many of those became the underpinning of much of successive governments' educational and more general childhood policies. They also informed practice, with ideas from Piaget, Vygotsky, Bruner and Gardner, for example, being adopted and adapted to inform pedagogical practices. So, whatever those of us working with children in the twenty-first century might feel about scientific theory and experimentation, it is clear that we have developed practices which we do almost without thinking these days as a result of them.

One important example of a scientific experiment which is widely used in neuro-scientific research is a method called a randomised controlled trial (RCT). This method uses a control group (to whom nothing is done) and an experimental group (who are participants in the intervention – whatever that intervention may be). This classic scientific method is claimed to be robust because the impact of a certain intervention – or experiment – can be seen through comparison with the control group and, although there have been negative responses from many involved in education and more general childhood studies, others, for example, Ben Goldacre (2011), suggest that much can be learned from this scientific method. He welcomes RCTs as a helpful tool to inform improvements in practice. And he might just have a case as, according to work carried out in 2010 by Jack Shonkoff and colleagues at Harvard University for the National Scientific Council on the Developing Child (Shonkoff et al., 2000), compelling evidence is emerging through the use of RCT findings of a clear link between children's genetic inheritance, early experiences and environmental factors, all of which influence the young child's developing brain. So being able to see into the brain and conducting scientific experiments within the field of neuroscience could help to identify new, inter-disciplinary ways of bringing together the scientific and social fields of research together.

Part 2 Neuroscience and young children's brain development

Synaptic proliferation and pruning

The study of the brain and, in particular, the development of the brain from birth has been a subject of interest to many. Stephen Scoffham in 2007 reminded us that every human has around 100,000 million brain cells. Imagine one million Wembley stadiums, each full of people: that's how many active brain cells each of us has in our brains. Now imagine that each person/brain in the one million Wembleys has 1000 pieces of thread attached to his or her body which can be connected to the threads of others in a variety of ways. The way in which these connections are made is through synapses (see Figure 4.1), so you might want to imagine your own fastening mechanism here to replace the complicated synaptic processes! Hopefully, these examples have helped to illustrate the sheer scale and possible permutations of the human brain from birth – or even before.

When humans are born, it is thought that less than half of their potential brain power exists. However, it is also believed that most human brain cells are formed before birth. It has been established through earlier neuro-scientific research that there are significant periods throughout childhood – especially in early childhood – when the brain goes through important periods of growth where new connections are made between brain cells (see Figure 4.2). These are periods of 'synaptic proliferation' or 'neurogenesis'.

Connections and pathways in the brain that are frequently used become more established and a myelin sheath is created which wraps around these established connections – the

Each brain cell is structured in a special way, as can be seen from the pictures below. The synapses work to make new connections between cells in the human brain. It is a bit like a strawberry plant making new runners.

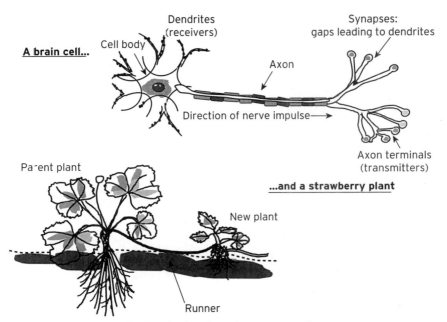

Figure 4.1 Diagram showing how brain cells make new connections

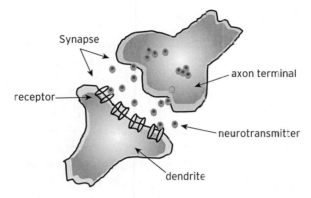

Synapse

axon terminal

receptor

neurotransmitter

dendrite

Figure 4.2 A close-up of the synapse, showing how new connections are made between brain cells

myelin sheath could be seen as a kind of outer cable holding a circuit together (see Figure 4.3). It can be seen how this kind of 'hard-wiring' is significant in setting more established individual human behaviours and habits. And most of this is thought to happen before our long-term memory is developed – much of it before a child is 3 years old.

In addition to periods of synaptic proliferation, there are also significant times throughout early childhood when a phenomenon called 'synaptic pruning' takes place. When children's physical and social environments and experiences change over time, or if an experience no longer becomes frequent, important or significant to a child for whatever reason, the established neural connections will start to deteriorate and the myelin sheath will begin to disintegrate. So a young child's experiences of the world – be they emotional, social or physical, can play an important role in establishing which connections will be kept and which are no longer important. If we continue the electrical wiring analogy here, this process could be likened to the wiring and re-wiring of a house as rooms or circumstances change – in this case, the brain – could be seen as the consumer unit at the centre of the building. Again, once the adapted connections are established, they are reinforced and made more permanent through the growth of a myelin sheath. It can be seen from this that behaviours, habits and beliefs can become more entrenched and, therefore, more difficult to alter.

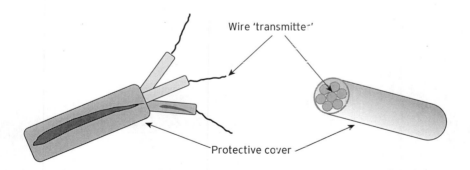

Wire 'transmitter'

Protective cover

Figure 4.3 This diagram shows how a domestic wiring system is similar in some ways to the way in which the myelin sheath in the human brain helps to 'hard-wire' some neural connections

78   *Bridget Durell*

Sensitive periods and plasticity

Until recently, these times in early childhood discussed above, when significant brain development and change occurs, were known as 'critical periods'. But more recently this has been changed to 'sensitive periods', to reflect our developing understanding of how the brain functions and develops. What is being discovered is that, although many of the important developmental brain changes take place at specific points in early childhood and that many established behaviours and beliefs are firmly established at this time (see Figure 4.4), it is now also acknowledged that the brain is able to continue to change and develop outside these periods – not only during childhood but also throughout the human lifespan. This is potentially exciting news for all of us – and it is also clear that biology – or 'nature' – is not a sufficient science to explain these amazing processes in the developing human brain. It would be depressing to think that humans develop only in accordance with a pre-determined, biological and genetic destiny; humans also respond to the world around them, be it physical, emotional or physical, and this is where 'nurture', or the range of environmental influences, plays an important role.

While we should not ignore our genetic heritage, then, evidence from neuroscience suggests that our experiences – whether planned or accidental – also influence and shape human minds and bodies. Some, such as Adele Diamond and Dima Amso (2008), even suggest that lived experience can influence and alter the brain's structure and that this can also cause changes in the biological characteristics that the next generation is born with. This amazing ability of the brain to change and adapt in response to a range of experiences is termed 'plasticity' and the implications are that, although there are opportunities to modify neural connections during the sensitive periods and, as can be seen from Figure 4.4, most of these critical periods for brain development are over or waning by the age of six, it is also possible to change the brain's connections *outside* these times. This is true not only for young children, but also for human learning across the lifespan.

Ultimately, then, human brains – and particularly young human brains – are interactive devices which respond to every sensory and emotional experience that is offered to them. Then, through the mysterious interplay of chemical and electrical activity in response to

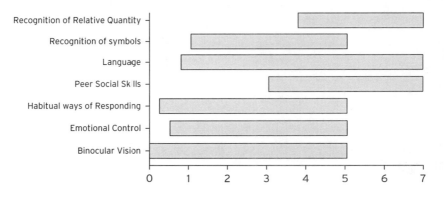

Figure 4.4 Stephen Scoffham's bar chart shows some of the important sensitive periods in children's brain development from birth to 7 years

Adapted from Stephen Scoffham (2007)

these experiences, the brain continuously adapts and switches the way synapses are connected, establishing new connections, reinforcing existing connections and discarding others. An example of this can be seen from research conducted by Tkao Hensch (2004), Professor of neuroscience at Harvard University, who discovered that the brain can be regulated and even 'rewired' during sensitive periods. He and many others believe that it is this very plasticity in the human brain that has enabled us to become the dominant form of life on earth. And, although physical strength may have played an important part in our survival in the past, it is our ability to adapt and change our behaviours through developing ideas both individually and socially that has made us so powerful in more recent history.

Part 3 Cases from neuroscientific research: links to children's learning and implications for practice

In order to address the earlier question of what can be learned from neuroscience, this section will focus on examples of neuroscientific research 'cases' that may have implications for our knowledge, understanding and practice when working with young children. Each case has been selected for its potential to inform aspects of young children's learning and development. The implications are about the 'how', and the suggestions for practice leading from the implications are about the 'what': what can practitioners do as a result of this new knowledge and understanding? Of course, these are only ideas and nothing is set in stone, and a continuation of the ideas is encouraged through the addition of an extra bullet point for each case – and more can be added if desired.

Case study 1: Neuroscience, learning and language development

Summary: Many researchers working in the field of neuroscience have been researching children's language development linked to sensitive periods in brain development. They have found that a combination of intervention and interaction during sensitive periods of neurogenesis, such as phoneme, vocabulary and grammatical development between the age of four and seven, can have a significant impact on children's ability to learn language effectively.

Implications: Language development is one of the key areas where knowledge of sensitive periods and positive intervention during those times can affect how well children learn. Children are born with the potential to make every sound (phoneme) in any language and they also have an innate ability to put words (vocabulary) together into simple sentence structures (syntax).

What practitioners can do:

- Create opportunities for very young children to interact verbally with others on a regular basis;
- Allow time for children to make sounds and participate in turn-taking 'conversations' from birth, even if they do not use real words;
- Provide children with opportunities to listen to and engage with a wide range of sounds in a variety of environments;
- Provide an environment where children can explore physically; as they encounter different objects and experiences, encourage them to respond verbally and support them in the development of naming things;
- What else?

Case study 2: Neuroscience, socio-economic factors and learning

Summary: Neuroscientific research has identified some links between the early social and economic environments children experience and their later brain development; in particular, Michael Meaney (2001) found that family function can either positively or negatively influence children's attention, learning and, particularly, memory.

Implications: Socio-economic factors play an important role in children's learning and cevelopment. Although the proportion of time spent in a more formal childcare setting may not te significant compared with that spent in the home environment, there is still a lot that can be cone to support learning and development.

What practitioners can do:

- Be aware of the social and economic situations of children and use this knowledge to engage sensitively with children and family, building a relationship of mutual trust; of course, there is a fine line between genuine interest for the benefit of the child and pure nosiness, so tread carefully;
- Create an emotional environment which provides for young children's needs – this might include access to food/drink, opportunities for making dens and hiding places or regular access to outside places where children can let off steam. Above all, allow them to have some control over their environment, physical or emotional;
- What else?

Case study 3: Neuroscience, music, rhythmic movement and learning

Summary: Research conducted by Adam Tierney and Nina Kraus in 2013 found that people's ability to move rhythmically to musical beats has a direct link with their linguistic ability.

Implications: These findings suggest that musical training and moving to musical beats can not only contribute to physical development and well-being, but they can also help to sharpen the brain's responses, enhancing learning and language.

What practitioners can do:

- Provide children with opportunities to listen to a range of rhythms and music from a variety of cultures;
- Encourage children to respond (noisily, if necessary) to music using different instruments and objects;
- Provide ample space and time for children to create their own (quite noisy, possibly) music and rhythms, both individually and collaboratively;
- Plan for regular opportunities for children to move their bodies to rhythms and tunes – this might be through directed sessions or more informal in nature, and the where, when and how needs to be carefully thought through;
- What else?

Possible case study 4: Sleep

Korman *et al.* discovered that young children who take regular naps have improved memories.

- What are the implications of this statement, and what could educators do?

Some other more general ideas from neuroscience include the following, which also have implications for practice:

- The first 5 years of a child's life are some of the most important: opportunities for supporting children's well-being, healthy eating and exercise must be made available to enhance both brain development and learning.
- All children are born ready and willing to learn and the best learning and development takes place through positive nurturing environments – emotional, social and physical.
- All children are born ready to use and learn mathematics – believe it or not!
- All children need to have healthy and caring relationships with others that provide opportunities for listening to and using language. In this way, young children's ability and motivation to learn language are both increased.
- All children learn through being engaged and doing, watching and copying – this is also true for older humans as well!

Part 4 Neuroscience and children's learning and development: beware of limitations

So far, an argument for welcoming this relatively new field of enquiry into the fold of early childhood research and practice been presented, but what about the potential costs or risks of this relatively unknown field? As mentioned earlier, much of the neuroscientific landscape is still being discovered and, as with any new ideas, there are also risks involved along the way. It is therefore important to acknowledge some of the limitations or potential costs of a wholesale adoption of neuroscience as the only way forward for improving early years practice:

But we know this already! It is true that much of what is being discovered has already been considered good practice for many years. Perhaps, then, we can celebrate the fact that a lot of what we put down to 'common sense' and earlier-twentieth-century theory is now being confirmed by these newer findings.

But this is potentially dangerous stuff and it may not even be true! Bruno della Chiesa (2006) warned, quite rightly, of the danger of 'neuromyths' such as: we only use 10 per cent of our brain at any one time; there are left-brain and right-brain people; there are gaps in achievement between genders because of differences in the brain; young children's brains can only learn one language at a time; neuroscientific research is only conducted in the interests of economy and politics – not ethical and moral considerations. These are serious issues; ultimately, myths such as these need addressing and the best way to do that is to read as much original source material as possible and to evaluate it critically.

But what about Richard Branson, Steve Jobs, Cher, Oprah Winfrey, J. K. Rowling, Stephen King and Sarah Jessica Parker? Yes, some of world's most successful people suffered adversity in their earlier lives and have become extremely successful despite – or even because of – their experiences. They seem to have developed resilience as a result and this begs the question as to what extent practitioners should intervene in the lives of young children.

But this is all very worrying to me – I've seen too many children being indoctrinated at a young and impressionable age. Should we really play at being gods and take advantage of sensitive periods of brain development? After all, interventions can be used for worse – as well as better.

But this is just kinaesthetic learning, learning styles and phonics all over again. There is, of course, always the risk that practitioners could turn to neuroscience as the latest and only way forward for their work with children; after all, those involved in the care of young children are not necessarily experts in this field and they already have so many other disciplines vying for their attention. Historically, for example, with Howard Gardner's Multiple Intelligence theory (Gardner, 1993), there have been unfortunate examples of this – it is as if one person's ideas or one strategy alone will provide all the answers. There is clearly a need to avoid developing an over-reliance on one context only: we are not always able to judge whether something will work and there is always a danger that children may be put at risk due to our experimental strategies. There is clearly a need to be very careful, then, when working with children.

Conclusion

Debates about the role of neuroscience in contributing to our understanding of children's learning and development are taking place at the moment and will continue to be discussed in the future. Whatever we think about the issues, the field of neuroscientific research is here to stay. Clearly, environments do matter, and significant early adversity can have lifelong consequences for learning, behaviour and health. Opportunities for supporting all aspects of children's development, making sensitive use of our understanding of how the brain works and grows, should be sought by those of us engaged in the care of young children. There is also, of course, a need for researchers to engage in more cross-discipline research in the interests of developing new knowledge about human life, growth and development – and this includes children, of course. But in the meantime, more exciting findings about children's learning are emerging all the time; findings that cannot be achieved through behaviour studies alone. Therefore, despite the limitations, we should cautiously welcome the relatively new discipline of neuroscience to the party, keeping an open mind as to its potential to enhance our knowledge, understanding and practice, especially when working with young children.

Bibliography

Blakemore, S.J. and Frith, U. (2005; reprinted 2007) *The Learning Brain: Lessons for Education*. Oxford: Blackwell Publishing Limited.

Bloom, B.S., Engelhard, M.D., Furst, E.J., Hill, W.H. and Krathwohl, D.R. (1956) *Taxonomy of Educational Objectives: The Classification of Educational Goals. Handbook 1, The Cognitive Domain*. New York: David McKay Company.

Burton, R.A. (2013) *A Skeptic's Guide to the Mind: What Neuroscience Can and Cannot Tell Us About Ourselves*. New York: St. Martin's Press.

Champagne, F.A., Francis, D.D., Mar, A. and Meaney, J. (2003) 'Variations in maternal care in the rat as a mediating influence for the effects of environment and development', *Psychology and Behaviour*, 79, pp. 359-71.

Chechik, G., Meilijison, I. and Ruppin, E. (1999) 'Neuronal Regulation: A mechanism for synaptic pruning during brain maturation'. *Neural Computation*, 11(8), pp. 2061-80.

Coughlan, S. (2014) 'Brian scientists to work with schools on how to learn'. Available at: www.bbc.co.uk/news/business-25627739 (Accessed: 6 August 2014).

Craik, F. and Bialystok, E. (2006) 'Cognition through the lifespan: Mechanisms of change', *Trends in Cognitive Sciences*, 10(3), pp. 131-8.

De Smedt, B., Ansari, D., Grabner, R.H., Hannula, M.N., Schneider, M. and Verschaffel, L. (2010) 'Cognitive neuroscience meets mathematics education', *Education Research Review*, 5, pp. 97-105.

Della Chiesa, B. (2006) *Neuromyths*. Monterey, CA: Monterey Institute of International Studies.

Diamond, A. and Amso, D. (2008) 'Contributions of neuroscience to our understanding of cognitive development', *Current Directions in Psychological Sciences*. 17(2), pp. 136-41.

Gardner, H. (1993) *Multiple Intelligences: The Theory in Practice*. Philadelphia: The Perseus Book Group.

Goldacre, B. (2011) 'How can you tell if a policy is working? Run a trial', *The Guardian*. Available at: www.theguardian.com/commentisfree/2011/may/14/bad-science-ben-goldacre-rancomised-trials (Accessed: 10 February 2014).

Hensch, T.K. (2004) 'Critical period regulation', *Annual Review of Neuroscience*, 27, pp. 549-79.

Illes, J. and Sahakian, J. (2011) (Eds.) *The Oxford Handbook of Neuroethics*. Oxford: Oxford University Press.

Kolb, B., Mychasiuk, R., Mahummed, A., Yilin, L., Frost, D.O. and Gibb, R. (2012) 'Experience and the developing pre-frontal cortex', *Proceedings of the National Academy of Sciences*, 109(2) pp. 17186-93.

Korman, M., Doyon, J., Doljansky, K., Carrier, K. and Dagan, Y. (2007) 'Daytime sleep condenses the time course of motor memory consolidation', *Nature Neuroscience*, 10, pp. 1206-13.

Matthews, L. (2013) 'A new field of developmental neuroscience changes our understanding of the early years of human life', *PNAS*, 109(42). Canadian Institute for Advanced Research.

Meaney, M. J. (2001) 'Maternal care, gene expression, and the transmission of individual differences in stress reactivity across generations', *Annual Review of Neuroscience*, 24, pp. 1161-92.

Miller, G. A. (2003) 'The Cognitive Revolution: A historical perspective', *Trends in Cognitive Sciences*, 7, 3, pp. 141-4.

Morrison, G.S. (2009) *Early Childhood Education Today* (11th edn). Boston: Pearson Education Inc.

OECD (2013) *Education at a Glance 2013: OECD Indicators*. OECD Publishing. Available at: http://dx.doi.org/10.1787/eag-2013-en (Accessed: 20 January 2014).

Palmer, J. A. (2001) (Ed.) *Fifty Major Thinkers on Education: From Confucius to Dewey*. London: Routledge.

Pinker, S. (2002) *The Blank Slate: The Modern Denial of Human Nature*. London: Penguin.

Satel, S. and Lilienfeld, S. (2013) *Brainwashed: The Seductive Appeal of Mindless Neuroscience*. New York: Basic Books Limited.

Scoffham, S. (2007) 'Teaching, learning and the brain'. *Education 3-13: International Journal of Primary, Elementary and Early Years Education*, 31(3) pp. 49–58.

Shonkoff, J.P. and Phillips, D.A. (2000) (Eds) *From Neurons to Neighborhoods: The Science of Early Childhood Development*. Washington, USA: National Academy Press.

Tierney, A. and Kraus, N. (2013) 'The ability to move to a beat is linked to the consistency of neural responses to sound', *Journal of Neuroscience*, 33(38), pp. 14981–8. Available from the Wellcome Trust at: http://blog.wellcome.ac.uk/2013/05/15/what-can-neuroscience-teach-education/ (Accessed: 20 January 2014).

5   Taking the learning outdoors: the challenges and the possibilities

Clair Stevens

Overview

> This chapter is for all those who 'invest daily, deeply and for life in this vital phase of education ... The education of young children matters immeasurably - to them both now and in the future, and to our society'
>
> Robin Alexander, 2010

The aim of this chapter is to emphasise and establish the importance of outdoor learning as a need and requirement for all young children. The application of theory will be strengthened by including examples from practice that will challenge and expand teachers' thinking related to the possibilities and potential of outdoor experiences. It will seek to enhance the understanding and relationship between brain development, movement and the senses and inspire those who work with young children to seek more exciting and rewarding opportunities for those in their care. With the increasing demand for extended hours, and the growing debate related to developing healthy patterns for life, this chapter will explore children's biological need for movement, and seek to create more exciting opportunities for learning. Establishing a love of the outdoors provides strong foundations for future engagement in later life and, as such, the chapter will consider the challenges and possibilities in relation to:

- potential, persistence and perspectives
- provocations, preoccupations and planning.

Background

Taking the learning outdoors is not a new concept; it was recognised and promoted by many pioneers of early education such as Froebel, Montessori, the McMillans and Isaacs who all saw outdoor natural spaces as essential for young children. The view of the child as 'competent' and requiring some 'agency' over their learning has become powerful, particularly in the field of Early Childhood Education, therefore we must question why natural outdoor spaces are not the norm. Dahlberg, Moss and Pence in *Beyond Quality in Early Education and Care* (1999) placed great emphasis on the child's need for independence, suggesting: 'The young child is born equipped to learn and does not ask for permission to start learning' (p. 48).

Enormous progress has been made in recent years to improve the understanding and provision for outdoor play. This drive has been supported by a number of key initiatives from organisations such as Learning through Landscapes, Play England, The National Trust and the Forest School movement. However, it could be argued that such initiatives have been limited to particular areas and specific settings, and that their use is predominantly related to the knowledge, skills and understanding of those running the provision.

> The attitude and behaviour of adults outdoors has a profound impact on what happens there and on children's learning. It is therefore vital that children have the support of attentive and engaged adults who are enthusiastic about the outdoors and understand the importance of outdoor learning.
>
> DCSF (2007, p. 2)

In the past ten years, both the DfES (2006) and Ofsted (2004) have emphasised the importance of outdoor education. Resources relating to risk management and guidance are available on the DfE website for those wishing to offer more challenging play spaces. Additionally, the Early Years framework (DfE, 2012) includes three key indicators or characteristics of effective learning 'playing and exploring, active learning, and creating and thinking critically', all highly relevant to the learning opportunities available outside.

Challenge

- Look at the work of Claire Warden in Scotland. Mindstretchers (www.mindstretchers.co.uk) offer a range of books, resources and equipment to enhance outdoor learning.

However, some confusion still remains over the daily requirement to provide children with the opportunities that outdoor spaces provide. Many have become rather sterile and lack the natural resources that change and grow over seasons. Rather than offering the possibilities children need to engage their senses and enhance their play, the spaces have often been levelled, safety surfaced and fenced, in order to somehow protect children from not only the perceived risks but, regretfully, the exploration and excitement of natural elements, such as mud or water. Recently Sir David Attenborough appealed to the government to halt the loss of green spaces in and around schools (Morpurgo, 2011). As past patron of the charity Learning through Landscapes, he has first-hand experience of the work they have undertaken over the past ten years to 'transform Tarmac playgrounds into places with pools, and earth where children could grow things. Now the government is saying we need more classroom space so the schools are building them on the very nature habitats we've been working to provide.'

I have heard practitioners in England comment that the garden is closed down during the winter or that they haven't been out with the children for months because, they claim, it has been 'too wet or too cold, quite unsuitable'. Even warmer summer weather seems to bring restrictions with some settings establishing rules that prevent children going outside between 11 and 3 owing to the strength of the sun. Surely with consideration and flexibility, all weather offers possibilities and potential for learning and exploration?

The Forest School movement

The growth in the Forest School approach across the UK has enabled children to access environments that offer complementary experiences to the traditional indoor classroom or outdoor areas. They provide regular opportunities for active learning in nearby woodland, enabling children to build up confidence and competence. The children are highly motivated and engaged and it is clear to see that the potential for learning and development is immense. A clear message from the *The Good Childhood Report* (The Children's Society, 2012) suggests that children are happier when given freedom, autonomy and choice, all aspects closely linked to both the Early Years Foundation Stage Framework (EYFS) (2012) and the Forest School principles. According to *The Good Childhood Report*, children need agency and real experiences to connect them to their local community, and this responsibility and trust leads to a more contented, meaningful life.

In September 2013 more than 300 organisations, including the RSPB and the National Trust, launched the Wild Network, with the purpose of encouraging more children and families to reconnect with nature. This is echoed and further supported in a new film, made from the perspective of young children and families today, which suggest that they spend increasing hours indoors in front of screens. The film *Project Wild Thing* was written and released in 2013 by David Bond and highlights the growing concern that many share in terms of children's disconnect with nature and wild outdoor spaces. This chapter therefore, will strive to support those working with young children to look for opportunities, push boundaries, ask questions and adapt practice to further young children's engagement in the real world.

Potential, persistence and perspectives

I begin here with some reflections following a Dimbleby lecture given by the children's author Michael Morpurgo, in 2011, entitled 'Set Our Children Free'. The author describes children as 'the centre of my world', being a parent, grandparent and a storyteller, and explains his belief that education is above all the most fundamental right of children. He talks with great insight about people who 'make a real difference to children's lives', using his own experiences of children around the world in relation to the UN Convention on the Rights of the Child, ratified in the UK in 1991. He questions whether some children in Britain today ever 'know the joys of childhood', and asks whether 'we are doing the best for children in our schools'. His belief in every child as 'a unique genius and personality' is threatened, he maintains, by a system that defines children in terms of success and failure. Instead, he urges us working with young children to 'allow the spark of genius to catch fire, burn brightly and shine'. So as you start this section, I challenge you to think about the 'individuals who made the difference' in your young life? Morpurgo reminds us that, often, those that make the most difference are not seen as important in our society. And he goes further, suggesting that the 'younger the children concerned . . . the less status there is for those involved'.

Health benefits of outdoor play

It is impossible to discuss the potential impact that regular outdoor physical play can have without discussing the increased opportunities provided in terms of tackling contemporary health problems, such as obesity and the return to the UK of rickets. In a recent damning report, 'Our Children Deserve Better: Prevention Pays' (October 2013), Dame Sally Davies said that the country should be 'profoundly ashamed' of the state of children's health. Dr Hilary Cass, President of the Royal College of Paediatrics and Child Health, went further, suggesting that 'the challenge is to ensure that child health is high on the agenda. We have a duty to this generation of children, to the next generation and to generations to come' (2013). The report makes a strong case for change as data collected shows five excess child deaths per day in the UK compared with Sweden. However, the report is not simply calling for improvements in physical health, it also highlights the need to support children to build emotional resilience, and to provide opportunities for children to learn from their mistakes and deal with life's inevitable 'ups and downs'.

> . . . it is obvious that outdoor play experiences contribute to children's physical development, in particular to motor development. Less obvious is the learning that happens as children test their strength, externally and internally: how high can I climb? Why does my heart pound when I run? Am I brave enough to jump from this platform?
>
> Hewes and McEwan (2005, p. 4)

Surely working with young children and families we have a responsibility 'to the future for improving our children's health and well-being'.

The evidence collected in this latest report has previously been highlighted by the World Health Organisation (2009, 2010) and the British Heart Foundation (2011), who suggest that increasing physically active play that incorporates opportunities to run, climb, balance and swing promotes inner body strength, core muscle development, co-ordination and flexibility. In her book *Sensory Integration and the Child* (1979), Jean Ayres describes the importance of physical activities for young children as 'food for the brain'. She maintains that it is our senses that provide the knowledge needed to inform and direct the body and mind, but that it is the brain that must organise and make sense of the messages. Although we are all familiar with the senses involved in taste, sight, smell and sound, many do not realise the importance of the other senses, those relating to movement: force of gravity and body position.

Physical development: EYFS and active learning

A key change in the EYFS (2012) is the distinction made between the prime and specific areas of learning. This new focus on the physical development of young children should encourage each of us to reflect on our existing knowledge of child development and raise questions and discussions in relation to the opportunities we provide. A strong start in the early years increases the probability of positive outcomes in later life. A weak foundation significantly increases the risk of later difficulties (DfE/DH, 2010). In terms of school readiness, young children in the foundation years need daily opportunities to develop their whole bodies. These experiences are essential for developing core strength, which in turn promotes the development of the brain and central nervous system. Growing research from Harvard (Developing Child, 2010) is supporting a new focus on how the brain develops, particularly with regard to the importance of the environment and the different ways in which children learn. New evidence suggests that we need to re-engage children with the world using all of their senses in order for connections and experiences to be joined up and stored.

This focus on 'experiential' or 'real' learning was described by the educator John Dewey almost a 100 years ago, as a vision for 'Schools of Tomorrow' (1915):

> The Teacher and the book are no longer the only instructors; the hands, the eyes, the ears, in fact the whole body, become sources of information, while teacher and textbook become respectively the starter and the tester. No book or map is a substitute for personal experience; they cannot take the place of the actual journey.
>
> Dewey and Dewey (1915, p. 74)

This concept of 'active' learning was further developed through the work of Jean Piaget (1936), Maria Montessori (1946), and later by Carl Rogers (1969, p. 5) whose work focused on the affective components, describing significant learning having a quality of personal involvement:

> Human beings have a natural potentiality for learning. They are curious about their world, until and unless this curiosity is blunted by their experience in our educational system.
>
> Rogers (1969, p. 157)

This example from a setting in Sweden demonstrates how young children, regardless of the weather, work hard outside, both physically and mentally:

> They did not necessarily have sand and water inside, but it was always available outside. When challenged as to what happened when it rained, they said that the children loved it then, they could carry buckets of water from place to place, create waterfalls down slopes, pour it into the sand. They said there were no bad weather conditions, only bad clothes.
>
> Calder (1995 p. 6)

Additionally, children in these settings generally spent far less time on table-top activities that promote fine muscle control, but showed the development of their fine motor skills by regularly undertaking things such as putting on and taking off their own clothes and footwear, fastening buttons and undoing laces.

At a time when there appears to be some discussion of 2 year olds entering the education system in the guise of reducing inequalities, we would be wise to consider the voices from the past as well as the overwhelming new evidence from neuroscience. Both fully support environments that offer active, hands-on real experiences with adults that have established, strong emotional relationships. We must remember that young children's senses are the 'pathways to learning' and the outdoor environment offers daily adaptations, variations and experiences that invite active engagement using all the senses. Young children are intensely curious and need regular opportunities to explore the changing world around them. The potential for learning is maximised if we seek to provide environments that offer the powerful combination of physical, visual and naturalistic ways to play and learn.

The work of Susan Isaacs at the Malting House School allowed each child's curiosity to lead the learning in a rich environment including a large garden. Isaacs found that the freedom and challenge offered to the children in the outdoor area, with real tools, fires and exciting exploration, resulted in the most wonderful questions and scientific investigations (Graham, 2009). Much of the learning and play that I have witnessed outside offers repeated opportunities to develop persistence as it is highly motivating, driving learning forward and giving children a seedbed to germinate ideas and test out theories. The Teaching and Learning in 2020 Review Group (Gilbert, 2006, p. 6) described their vision for the future, where:

> learners are active and curious: they create their own hypothesis, ask their own questions, coach one another, set goals for themselves, monitor their progress and experiment with ideas for taking risks, knowing that mistakes and 'being stuck' are part of learning.

This vision for learning appears to suggest hands-on experimentation, collaboration and problem solving, all highly effective if planned and utilised in outdoor spaces. Furthermore, the review also suggested that education needed to develop key attitudes and skills identified by employers as highly valuable particularly in a growing knowledge-based economy. These include:

- being able to communicate orally at a high level;
- reliability, punctuality and perseverance;
- knowing how to work with others in a team;
- knowing how to evaluate information critically;
- taking responsibility for, and being able to manage, one's own learning and developing the habits of effective learning;
- knowing how to work independently without close supervision;
- being confident and able to investigate problems and find solutions;
- being resilient in the face of difficulties;
- being creative, inventive, enterprising and entrepreneurial.

The Teaching and Learning in 2020 Review Group (2006, p. 10)

I would argue that challenging outdoor spaces provide perfect opportunities for young children to develop these skills and that these experiences should be incorporated into the curriculum throughout primary education. Using children's interests and preoccupations outside allows teachers to come alongside play scenarios and ask questions that open up 'possibility thinking' as proposed by Craft *et al.* (2012). These might be presented to children as leading questions such as 'How can we get across this ditch/stream/river?'; a service question, 'How can we make the structure stronger?'; or a follow-through question, 'Where is the right place to cross?' Surely education for the twenty-first century should echo these reflections from the poet Sean Rafferty (Morpurgo lecture, 2011), concerns shared by so many today:

> Now more than ever it matters that children from the inner cities can experience life in the country. This is a generation that will hear repeatedly of ecological disaster; will be told that the earth itself is threatened. For some of them the earth will not be a globe in

the classroom or a map on the wall but a Devon farm where they scuffled beech leaves along the drive and broke the ice on the puddles in the lane. When they were told of polluted rivers it will be one river, which has had its share of pollution, where they first saw a trout jumping and a wading heron, and plastic bags caught in the branches to mark the level of the last great flood. Last Spring two children went down to the river at dusk to watch for badgers. They did see a badger and they also saw two young otters at play, something many people born and bred in the country have never seen. It was as though nature herself were choosing her champions.

Challenge

• Try reading this beautiful story to children in a range of different outdoor environments and consider how often we invite them to simply listen: *The Other Way to Listen* by B. Baylor and P. Parnall (1997: NewYork, Aladdin).

Many of the skills and attitudes described in Morpurgo's lecture as 'preparing children not simply for employment, . . . for the contribution they can make to the common good . . . but for the difficult decisions they will have to make in their personal lives, in those moments when they have to take responsibility for themselves, and for others.' These attitudes for life are sometimes falsely described as 'soft skills' however they closely link to the 'lifelong learning character' and 'learning-oriented habits of mind' discussed by Claxton and Lucas (2009), and defined below, as essential to develop twenty-first-century explorers.

- Being adventurous
- Discussing with peers
- Working with others
- Imagining possible solutions
- Taking responsibility

- Creating ideas
- Questioning things
- Being active
- Showing initiative
- Self-evaluating

Opportunities for more complex learning do not just occur in classrooms. The school grounds can be designed to afford a range of formal and informal opportunities to ground learning in the messier experiences of gardens, woodlands and other open spaces.

Claxton (2009)

Provocations, preoccupations and planning

Play for the day, learn for a lifetime.

Glasgow Science Centre

I begin here with an example from practice that is personal to my own setting and demonstrates perfectly how a child's thoughts can be used to develop exciting child-led planning. A group of 3 year olds were out in the surrounding park and their adventures that day led them into areas that were dense with shrubs and trees. Once the children had returned to a clearing in the park one child noticed a number of spikey buds attached to his coat. 'Look!', he exclaimed, 'Baby hedgehogs.' The other children were equally captivated by the thought that these tiny buds were indeed hedgehogs. On returning to the setting with the carefully collected buds, the children's thoughts and questions were captured and new planning initiated on the board. The opportunities and investigations that radiated from this initial statement led to discussions around habitat, hibernation, seasons and growth, leading to new activities both inside and out. The children's interests and questions were shared with parents and this resulted in a visit by grandparents with a real hedgehog found in their garden. The children's images, reflections, representations and questions were then displayed in order to share the process of investigation.

Extending thought and creativity

In order for us to truly respect children, we need to provide activities and provocations that stretch and engage children to become enquirers, test theories, uncover connections and think deeply. Adult-driven agendas not only limit opportunities and possibilities for children but are also often irrelevant and futile to children's lives. The idea of using 'provocations' to stimulate learning links to the work of Lois Malaguzzi (1994) and the pre-schools of Reggio Emilia, in northern Italy. Here such 'provocations' are defined as 'deliberate and thoughtful decisions made by the teacher to extend the ideas of children'. As such, teachers seek out materials and resources for children to extend learning, but the direction and exploration of ideas is left to the children. Since 1963, when the municipality of Reggio Emilia first set up a small network of early education centres for young children and families, the reputation and respect has gathered, and now the 'Reggio approach' to early education has a worldwide reputation.

The philosophy in itself provides challenges to our accepted approaches to early education and many visitors are impressed not only by the quality of the pre-school environments considered 'the third teacher' but also by the ethos and respect given to the interests of the children.

> The teachers understood that children like changes in scale, loose parts, new perspectives, places for quiet reflection, passages, intimate playful and creative spaces, a variety of colours, smells, tastes and sounds, multiple pathways and opportunities for risk taking. These qualities of an outdoor space resonated so closely with findings from my own research.
>
> Greenfield (2007; 2011)

The qualities described above are echoed in the voices of the thousands of teachers and practitioners that visit the Reggio centres and marvel at the care and great detail shown in both the indoor and outdoor environments.

The Cambridge Curiosity and Imagination group (CCI) is based in the east of England and is a not-for-profit organisation that has been working creatively with local communities and children since 2002. The group's work has been inspired by the pre-school centres in Reggio

Emilia and the woodland nurseries in Scandinavia. Much of its work has been with pre-school children in woodland and clearly demonstrates the complex and multi-layered nature of their experiences. The group has published a number of books documenting the children's voices and these offer true insight into the individual journeys, stories and preoccupations of those children involved. Another visual example, the short film *Into the Middle of Nowhere*, from Scotland, was filmed in a nursery setting that utilises local woodland on a daily basis. The film clearly shows how confident and capable the children are in their environment: moving items, climbing trees without hesitation and demonstrating considerable skills in communication, collaboration and imagination. A construction built with logs and branches becomes an aeroplane that takes the children wherever they want to go in their imagination. The children look so at home in this wild, free environment – completely at ease and engrossed in their own world – as Laevers (2005) would describe, like 'fish in water'.

It is important when planning for children that we listen carefully; we need careful observations and above all we need to acknowledge the many different ways that children respond and express their thinking. As adults we need to respect young children's interests and carefully confront the difficult power relationships that can exist between adults and children. In Reggio Emilia the teachers first and foremost respect the children as researchers and see their own roles as co-researchers, working alongside the children, following their interests, preoccupations, questions and leads. This change in perception and practice requires courage:

> Taking action as a result of listening to children means sometimes having to change decisions already made. It sometimes shows up gaps in our adult thinking and understanding. Taking action means we have to recognise and acknowledge this or admit that we were wrong and, perhaps more importantly, that we do not have all the knowledge.
>
> Kinney, as cited in Clark *et al.* (2005, p. 122)

Challenge

- Check the blog by 'Teacher Tom', Teaching and Learning from Preschoolers. He regularly shares insights, reflections and examples of practice. He believes his environment should be a place where children learn as much from mud, sticks, rocks and water as they do from books, puzzles or teachers (http://teachertomsblog.blogspot.co.uk/).

Mud leads to clay

As spring approached, after a particularly wet winter, we began to notice changes in the children's engagement with the ever-increasing areas of mud in and around the woodland. Having thawed from the icy temperatures of the winter it now promised something new, and previous experience reminded the children that mud was exciting stuff. For days the properties and texture of the mud provided opportunities to explore depth, force, suction, speed and evaporation as areas exposed to the sunlight dried and contracted. Weekly additions of small world resources (diggers, dinosaurs, elephants, snakes and lizards) extended the opportunities for language, vocabulary and thinking and allowed children time to wallow in ideas and personal interests using the small world additions alongside the natural resources to create play scenarios rich in possibilities. Back in the setting we introduced the children to clay, allowing them to make connections between the experiences and interests outdoors and reinforcing the sensorial aspects of the learning. We then posed the question: What would the children make of the clay if we took it out to the woods? What new opportunities would the natural loose parts abundant in the woodland offer combined with the clay? The creative thinking demonstrated by the children over the following few weeks astounded the adults as they constructed, carved and created a plethora of personal objects combining the clay with treasures collected and scavenged in the surrounding woodland. One child designed and made a bed for fairies with a roof to keep out the rain, while another spent a great deal of time and effort wrapping his clay in large leaves and asking for lengths of string which he repeatedly wrapped around his parcel; this it turned out was a parachute, and needed careful testing as part of the process of construction.

The children were deeply involved and worked intensely with the clay as they had with the mud previously. However, this time the children's learning was extended and facilitated by the staff to try different tools, to use the clay in different ways, to combine other materials and come to reasoned decisions about the ones that worked well with the clay, refining and rejecting materials and skills as they worked. Most importantly, the staff knew the children well so could facilitate and guide; informed by previous knowledge of the child as well as what each child was striving to do and the way he or she handled the clay. The children, through co-construction, gradually formulated and adapted their ideas to produce meaningful representations; however, for some, the clay was uninviting and these children preferred to explore and collect, returning to deposit their treasures in the meeting place. This then led to two children being engrossed in sorting and classifying objects for future use. In this example, teaching and learning went from initial interest, to exploration, then took the form of indirect and, where required, direct facilitation of the learning outdoors in order to support alternative ideas and ways of thinking. Malaguzzi (1994) reminds us that 'what children want, is to be observed while engaged, they do not want the focus of the observation to be on the final product. When we as adults are able to see the children in the process, it's as if we are opening a window and getting a fresh view of things'.

Much of the work in the Reggio pre-schools focuses on children's creativity, drawing the indicators of effective learning together as defined in the EYFS (DfE, 2012). This next example demonstrates how adults can use the outdoor area throughout the year to facilitate representation. The example can be used with individual children or to produce a collaborative piece, and offers children hands-on opportunities to develops spatial awareness, using colours, shades and textures.

Picture that

This is a very effective and easy way to entice children to create or represent in a different way using natural resources. It uses very basic wooden picture frames placed in different outdoor spaces: parkland, woodland, sandy beach, shingle beach, snow. Children are invited to create and represent, using an array of colour and texture. Larger frames are useful for collaboration and encourage children to work together to create a shared image. These can be used throughout the year as the seasons change and different colours fill the spaces. These compositions are equally appealing in the snow as images can be created using salt, sticks and seeds. Photographing the frames and taking these back offer opportunities to reflect, discuss and engage the children in further planning.

Conclusion

> The most important of all the occupations of men is the successful rearing of the next generation.
>
> Stallibrass (1989, p. 263)

It is the job of each and every one of us working with young children and families to make it our highest priority to 'give every child the best start in life' (Marmot Review, 2010). I hope that this chapter enables you to see the potential in every child and to be brave in your approach with all the children you encounter. This new emphasis on developing healthy habits for life in the Foundation years cannot be understated; we must all now recognise the links between health and future development. The chapter introduces the notion that children have health rights: to play outdoors, not in safety surfaced deserts, but in wild exciting places or community spaces that open up possibilities: questions, provocations and excitement. We are quite literally shaping the future for these children and so what we offer now will determine not only their future health but fundamentally their happiness and life chances.

Personal and professional challenges

Challenge

Consider the following list of the main barriers to overcome when planning successful outdoor learning experiences and the challenges present in your workplace:

- Accessibility, time, ease of use and ownership of outdoor spaces
- Place and value of outdoor learning in the culture and ethos of the setting
- Perceptions of team, parents and families in terms of risk/litigation/benefits
- Overemphasis on Health and Safety
- Staff knowledge, understanding, confidence and competence
- Reluctance to use or engage in community spaces
- Lack of resources; suitable for wet/cold weather
- Rigid ratios and lack of flexibility
- Weather conditions.

Challenge

- What needs to change to encourage more active outdoor learning?
- How can you successfully initiate change?

Challenge

Consider your own practice. Do you manage to:

- Resist the top-down pressure to prepare children with structured 'school'-based activities;
- Ensure children are physically active for a minimum of three hours each day;
- Support children to take risks, be adventurous and work as a team;
- Think carefully about how you are developing the dispositions of learning such as perseverance, determination and self-reliance;
- Reflect on the possibilities and inspirations within your community and plan to use these to arouse children's interests?

Challenge

- What can be changed in your outside area to add intrigue, challenge, and awe and wonder?

Further reading

There are several texts available for further study; start by searching out these texts:

Banning, W. and Sullivan, S. (2010) *Lens on Outdoor Learning.* St Paul, MN: Redleaf Press.

Gould, T. (2011) *Effective Practice in Outdoor Learning: If in Doubt, Let Them Out!* Lutterworth: Featherstone.

Harryman, H. (2008) *The Outdoor Classroom: A Place to Learn.* Swindon: Red Robin books.

Knight, S. (2013) *Forest School and Outdoor Learning in the Early Years.* London: Sage.

Nelson, E. (2012) *Cultivating Outdoor Classrooms.* St. Paul, MN: Redleaf Press.

Robertson, J. (2014) *Dirty Teaching: A Beginners Guide to Learning Outdoors.* Carmarthen: Crown House Publishing.

Stevens, C. (2013) *The Growing Child: Laying the Foundations of Active Learning and Physical Health.* Abingdon: Routledge.

White, J. (2007) *Being, Playing and Learning Outdoors: Making Provision for High Quality Experiences in the Outdoor Environment.* Abingdon: Routledge.

Rosenow, N. (2012) *Heart-Centered Teaching Inspired by Nature: Using Nature's Wisdom to Bring More Joy and Effectiveness to Our Work with Children.* Lincoln, NE: Dimensions Educational Research Foundation.

Bibliography

Alexander, R. (2010) *Children, their World, their Education: Final Report and Recommendations of the Cambridge Primary Review.* Abingdon: Routledge.

Ayres, J. (1979) *Sensory Integration and the Child: Understanding Hidden Sensory Challenges.* Los Angeles: Western Psychological Services.

British Heart Foundation (2011) *Stay Active, Stay Alive. National Centre for Physical Activity and Health,* Loughborough University.

Calder, P. (1995) *Using the Early Childhood Environment Rating Scale as a Measure to Make Cross-National Evaluations of Quality: Advantages and Limitations.* Paper presented at the European Conference on the Quality of Early Childhood Education. Paris, France, 7–9 September 1995.

Clark, A., Kjorholt, A.T. and Moss, P. (Eds) (2005) *Beyond Listening*. Bristol: Policy Press.

Claxton, G. and Lucas, B. (2009) *School as a Foundation for Lifelong Learning: The Implications of a Lifelong Learning Perspective for the Re-Imagining of School-Age Education*. Centre for Real-World Learning: University of Winchester.

Craft, A., McConnon, L. and Paige-Smith, A. (2012) 'Child-initiated play and professional creativity: Enabling four-year-olds' possibility thinking', *Thinking Skills and Creativity*, 7(1), pp. 48–61.

Dahlberg, G.P., Moss, P. and Pence, A. (1999) *Beyond Quality in Early Childhood Education and Care: Postmodern Perspectives*. London: Falmer.

Davis, S. (2013) *Chief Medical Officer's annual report 2012: Our Children Deserve Better: Prevention Pays*. London: Department of Health.

DCSF (Department for Children Schools and Families) (2007) *Effective Practice: Outdoor Learning*. Nottingham: Department for Children, Schools and Families. Available at www.urbanforestschool.co.uk/PDF/3_3b_ep.pdf (Accessed: 12 December 2013).

Dewey, J. and Dewey, E. (1915) *Schools of Tomorrow*. California: Dent.

DfE (Department for Education) (2012) *Early Years Foundation Stage Framework*. Cheshire: Department of Education.

DfES (Department for Education and Skills) (2006) *Learning Outside the Classroom: Manifesto*. London: Department for Education and Skills. Available at www.education.gov.uk/publications/standard/publicationdetail/page1/DFES-04232-2006 (Accessed: 12 December 2013).

Gilbert, C. (2006) *2020 Vision Report of the Teaching and Learning in 2020 Review Group*, DfES, http://dera.ioe.ac.uk/6347/1/6856-DfES-Teaching%20and%20Learning.pdf (Accessed: 12 December 2013).

Graham, P. (2009) *Susan Isaacs: A Life Freeing the Minds of Children*. London: Karnac Books.

Greenfield, C. (2010) 'The outdoor playground through children's eyes'. *Encounters*, Summer 2011/12.

Harvard University (2010) *The Foundations of Lifelong Health are Built in Early Childhood*. Cambridge, MA: Centre for the Developing Child.

Hewes, P.J., MacEwan, G. (2005) *Let the Children Play: Nature's Answer to Early Learning*, Early Childhood Learning Knowledge Centre, http://tinyurl.com/an46p8 (Accessed: 12 December 2014).

Into the Middle of Nowhere (2010) Film. Directed by A. F. Ewert. AEON Films.

Laevers, F. (2005) *Well-being and Involvement in Care Settings: A Process-oriented Self-evaluation Instrument*. Research Centre for Experiental Education, Leuven University.

Learning and Teaching Scotland (2007) *Taking Learning Outdoors: Partnerships for Excellence*. Available at www.educationscotland.gov.uk/Images/TknLrnOutA4_tcm4-402066.pdf (Accessed: 25 January 2014).

Malaguzzi, L. (1994) 'Your image of the child: Where teaching begins', *Child Care Information Exchange*, 96, pp. 52–6.

Marmot Review (2010) *Fair Society, Healthy Lives: Strategic Review of Health Inequalities*. London: Global Health Equity; UCL Research Department of Epidemiology and Public Health.

Montessori, M. (1946) *The Absorbent Mind*. Adyar, India: The Theosophical Publishing House.

Morpurgo, M. (2011) *35th annual Richard Dimbleby lecture: Set Our Children Free*, www.bbc.co.uk/programmes/b00ymf57 (Accessed: 23 February 2014).

Ofsted (2004) *Outdoor Education: Aspects of Good Practice, HMI 2151*. London: Ofsted. Available at www.ofsted.gov.uk/resources/outdoor-education-aspects-of-good-practice (Accessed: 12 December 2013).

Piaget, J. (1936) *Origins of Intelligence in the Child*. London: Routledge & Kegan Paul.

Plowden, B. (1967) *Children and their Primary Schools: A Report of the Central Advisory Council for Education (England)*. London: Her Majesty's Stationery Office.

Project Wild Thing (2013) Film. Directed by D. Bond. Green Lions Ltd.

Rafferty, S. as cited in Morpurgo, M. (2011) *35th annual Richard Dimbleby lecture, Set Our Children Free*. Available at: www.bbc.co.uk/programmes/b00ymf57 (Accessed: 23 February 2014).

Rogers, C. (1969) *Freedom to Learn: A View of What Education Might Become* (1st edn). Columbus, OH: Charles Merill.

Stallibrass, A. (1989) *The Self-Respecting Child: Development Through Spontaneous Play*. Reading: Addison-Wesley.

Steedman, C. (1990) *Childhood, Culture and Class in Britain: Margaret McMillan*. Cambridge: Virago.

The Children's Society (2012) *The Good Childhood Report: A Review of Our Children's Wellbeing*. Available at www.childrenssociety.org.uk (Accessed: 14 February 2014).

Wilenski, D. and Wendling, C. (2013) *Ways into Hinchingbrooke Country Park: Fantastical Guides for the Wildly Curious*. Cambridge: Cambridge Curiosity and Imagination.

World Health Organisation (2009) *Interventions on Diet and Physical Activity: What Works: Summary Report*. Geneva: World Health Organisation.

World Health Organisation (2010) *Global Recommendations for Physical Activity for Health*. Geneva: World Health Organisation.

6   Digital harmony or digital dissonance? Developing literacy skills in the new technological age

Clare Wiseman and Laurence Taylor

Overview

Through discussion and case studies this chapter will help you to think about the potential challenge to practitioners that arises from the increasing trend of young people choosing to read on-screen print via devices such as smart phones, tablets and consoles, for example, in preference to paper print. Research has revealed that there has been a year-on-year increase in children choosing to read daily using an electronic device, such as text messages, websites, instant messages and e-books (Clark, 2014). The same research also suggests that a link exists between the greater involvement with on-screen print and low levels of both reading attainment and reading for enjoyment. Therefore, the challenges for practitioners addressed in this chapter are two-fold:

- How can practitioners develop and adapt long-established literacy practices and pedagogies with young children to encompass and build on the competencies that interaction with screen print allows?
- How can a balance between using books and technological devices be incorporated into a curriculum and assessment system that strongly favours traditional approaches to the acquisition of literacy skills?

The historical background to the current practice for developing young readers

With the introduction of the 'three Rs' (reading, writing and 'rithmatic) to the elementary school curriculum in 1875 as 'obligatory subjects', the place of the acquisition of 'reading' as a necessary and important skill for all children was firmly established, although definitions of what constitutes being a 'reader' have continued to be debated into the present day. Little has changed in this respect; the current twenty-first-century primary school curriculum still has at its core the study of 'English', including spoken language, reading, writing and vocabulary, and states that 'fluency in the English language is an essential foundation for success in all subjects' (DfE, 2014, p. 6). There are very few who would argue against the need for children to gain competency in English, and the role of the practitioner in supporting children in attaining this success is concerned not only with the acquisition of both de-coding and comprehension skills for reading, but also in ensuring that pupils leave the education system as literate members of society. What it means to be 'literate' in today's society involves a greater engagement with texts than the ability to de-code words and understand them. Socio-cultural approaches to learning have encouraged us to think much more widely about the 'non-print' aspects of engaging with text, such as values, gestures, actions, contexts, meanings, talk and interaction, tools and spaces (Lankshear and Knoble, 2006). As Kress (2003, p. 9) suggested more than a decade ago, the book was 'ordered by the logic of writing', but the screen is 'ordered by the logic of image'; being 'literate' in contemporary society is an ever-changing concept. Pupils now need to be multi-literate; the challenge that we now face suggests that some of the practices and pedagogies which practitioners have tradition-ally utilised to support children in becoming literate may need to be updated and adapted to provide a relevant and engaging language experience for all children, many of whom now arrive in schools and settings with expertise of digital forms of literacy and who will enter a society where the rapid progress of the digital exchange of information continues.

Historically, the use of printed text as a resource and medium for the teaching and learning of language has been paramount. The 1928 Hadow Report recognised that if children were to be taught to read and write, then the provision of books in schools that appealed to children's imaginations and curiosity needed to be addressed. It suggested the establishment of both a 'Book List Committee' to help practitioners make choices about the books to be used in their classrooms and also that local authorities set up 'book rooms' where books could be borrowed by schools to meet the needs of the children. The 1928 Report also highlighted the importance of close co-operation between public libraries and schools, and pioneered the idea of allowing children to take books from school to be read and enjoyed in the home. These practices, initiated nearly 100 years ago, are still in place today and are highly useful and important in developing young readers. Indeed, the revised statutory National Curriculum (implemented in schools in September 2014) makes central the use of books as a means to develop young readers. For example, the Year 2 Programme of Study for English (DfE, 2014, p. 25) states that 'practitioners should . . . make sure that pupils listen to and discuss a wide range of stories, poems and plays and information books, this should include whole books'.

The idea that educators need guidance and support in choosing the most appropriate books with which to develop young readers has not diminished over the years, and the recommendation that children should read established and quality texts is firmly embedded in the National Curriculum orders (DfEE, 2000, p. 54) which state that the range of reading provided for children should include: modern fiction by significant children's authors; long-established children's fiction; good-quality modern poetry; classic poetry; texts from a variety of cultures and traditions, myths, legends and traditional stories and play-scripts. While it would be foolish to discount the practice of sharing 'good quality' books with children of all ages, it is becoming increasingly evident that the model of the narrative book and the linear reader is a small representation of the range and relevance of literacy events now available to children. Many children now have access to computers, consoles, tablets, televisions, DVDs and smart-phones, which provide multi-modal, interactive literacy experiences in a way in which conventional print media is unable to do. These fresh and emerging forms of literacy, which integrate media and technology, are often referred to as 'New Media Literacies' (NMLs), or 'digital literacies'. It is vital that today's practitioners have an understanding of how children make meaning in their translation of ideas across a range of mediums and to recognise the potential for learning contained therein. However, it is also necessary to accept that even if practitioners can embrace the pedagogical and learning potential provided by NMLs and digital literacies, there still exist barriers to change that will need to be explored if the full potential for integration of these new literacies is to be fully realised. Some of the features of the skills that can be developed out of these NMLs are presented in Table 6.1.

From Table 6.1 it is therefore possible to see how NMLs or digital forms of literacy can support the learning that is currently addressed mainly in the form of printed material, but more importantly, it indicates some of the higher order thinking skills involved in organising ideas, critical analysis and creating new meaning that can be developed through engagement with different media and a variety of representations of information.

Potential barriers to change

It might be suggested that one of the potential barriers preventing practitioners from sincerely adopting NMLs or digital literacies as a pedagogical approach to developing children's emerging literacy skills are the many concerns surrounding the impact of the proliferation of NMLs on aspects of children's learning and development. Concerns exist that on-screen reading encourages a 'passive reader', where the critical engagement of the reader with the text is reduced and the highly visual nature of the medium diminishes imagination, weakens

Table 6.1 Features of NMLs or digital literacies

Multi-modality	• Making sense of the 'grammar' of expressive formats, such as graphics, sound and moving images (Crook, 2012; Appel, 2012) • Manipulating expressive formats into non-linear, parallel and highly playful ways to create meaning (Craft, 2012; Lotherington and Ronda, 2009)
Information-seeking	• Navigation of digital environments to find and analyse free information, pursuing thought threads from hyper-link to hyper-link (Craft, 2012; Lotherington and Ronda, 2009; Proserpio and Gioia, 2007; Appel, 2012)
Critical analysis skills	• Research and reflection skills (Gee, 2010) • Adoption of a critical position to things presented, rather than rote memorisation or simple comprehension (Appel, 2012; Paraskeva et al., 2010)
Collaboration	• Participation and connection to develop social skills (Merchant, 2013; Jenkins, 2006)
Critical engagement	• With media and text, including playfulness to expand the possible interpretations and creations of texts (Lotherington and Ronda, 2009; Merchant, 2013; Alper, 2011)

concentration and heightens distractibility (The Pearson Foundation, 2010). Alongside this, the potentially solitary or individualistic nature of learning through digital forms can lead to anxieties that the rich social interactions which formerly characterised children's learning and play are declining (National Association for the Education of Young Children, 2009, cited in Alper, 2011). Additionally, concerns about the content of screen media as a catalyst for such social ills as violence, obesity, reinforcement of stereotypes and advertising have often been raised, although definitive empirical research that confirms this simplistic and problematic link is lacking (Alper, 2011). Indeed, these concerns exist and need to be acknowledged, but the extent to which they impact on children's development is contested. Moreover, the perceived barriers to wholeheartedly adopting new approaches to teaching literacy through NMLs have created what is described by some as 'digital dissonance'. The following section looks more closely at this notion and may explain why greater integration of digital technology and media in the classroom has not yet occurred.

The resistances to digital technology and media

Digital dissonance can be described as the divide, disconnect (Helspar and Eynon, 2009), or tension (Clark *et al.*, 2009) felt by pupils and practitioners over how digital technology and media is used informally outside of school and formally in the classroom, and the potential non-transferability of skills between the two settings (Clark *et al.*, 2009). In other words, new generations of pupils are developing knowledge and skills from their everyday social and cultural practices that increasingly diverge from, in particular, the literacy practices they are taught at school (Owston *et al.*, 2009, Lotherington and Ronda, 2009).

This dissonance may be explained by resistances from three groups: pupils, practitioners and parents.

1 Resistance from pupils

Much of this can be put down to two interrelated ideas: firstly, that children prefer having exhilarating experiences playing games (Prensky, 2006) independently and informally, away from parental supervision (Chambers 2012) and away from the classroom, as they see the integration of gaming into a formal culture as diluting those experiences (Royle, 2008); and secondly, that they feel that the commercial games they play at home are far more sophisticated and attractive (Lotherington and Ronda, 2009) than educational or 'serious games' that strive to get learning into games (Royle, 2008) but which suffer from having much lower production and marketing budgets.

Case study 1

An interview with a high ability Year 3 group in which all six had access to laptops or a PC, five had access to an iPad, and five to a Wii.

Their favourite activities included: Temple Run (escaping from monsters, collecting), Angry Birds, Minecraft (building), NOVA 3 (collecting), Eden (building), Doodle Pad, Bin Weevils (collecting), *Movie Maker, Time To Create, Club Penguin* and *Moshi Monsters* were dismissed as being 'for babies'. Most preferred having levels to complete even if these levels were infinite (as found in console games such as Wii *Skylanders*) rather than coming to a definite end, and collecting and printing were acceptable end results. They were mostly sceptical about using games in the classrooms, especially when it was suggested that serious games would most likely oblige them to actively engage in an external educational task or homework assignment (Paraskeva *et al.* 2010) before continuing play. When the term 'teacherised' was used and explained in relation to games played in the classroom, they were all in agreement, describing such games as 'lame' and 'uncool'. Hence, it can be seen that games designed to educate do not engage children, and truly engaging games do not have enough educational value (Royle, 2008).

Some researchers conclude that children mostly want to use digital media informally for mundane reasons, passively viewing entertainment or communicating (Buckingham 2007, cited Clark *et al.*, 2009) with only cursory interactivity, and consuming rather than creating (Crook, 2012).

2 Resistance from practitioners

This can be broken down into three broad categories: how confident practitioners are in their own skills; how disruptive they view pupils' use of digital technology and media; and how reliant they are on traditional classroom pedagogy.

First, as technology becomes more complicated and unfamiliar, most adults in general feel less capable in using it than children (Chambers, 2012) and are unsure about what is best practice (Alper, 2011). Although it is oversimplifying matters to say that all 'digital natives' know more than all adults (Merchant, 2013), there is much clear evidence that children are radically different in the ways they use and process information (Helspar and Eynon, 2009). Many commentators have suggested that when practitioners perceive themselves to be less proficient than their pupils, then that undermines their confidence in their ability to use digital technology and media and to integrate it into their classrooms (Becker 2007, McDougall 2010), which puts their self-image at odds with the 'sage on the stage' (Proserpio and Gioia, 2007). This is often a result of limited technical and pedagogical training for practitioners (Monsivais *et al.*, 2014), although The British Educational Communications and Technology Agency (BECTA) Review suggest that significant progress is being made in teacher confidence and competence (BECTA, 2005 p. 4).

Second, practitioners used to leading whole-class instruction are apprehensive about the disruptive potentials (Clark *et al.*, 2009) of pupils using digital technology, either through the physical presence of laptops or devices, or students working independently but multitasking. There are several studies reporting on how increased laptop use has correlated negatively to student learning (Fried 2008, cited Lee *et al.*, 2012), how laptops become a focal point for non-users (Lindroth and Bergquist, 2010), and how laptop users use the screen as a shield (*ibid.*), especially to prevent the teacher from seeing them active in other ways, such as instant messaging and Facebook, both of which have been related to more distractibility for academic reading (Bowman 2007, cited Lee *et al.*, 2012) and lower grade point averages (*ibid.*). Some claim that multitasking does not interfere with pupils' learning (Prensky, 2006), some that there are limits to how much our brains can process at once (Foehr, 2006, cited Lee *et al.*, 2012), but most practitioners seem to believe instinctively that digital technology and media are potentially distracting.

Third, many practitioners share an inherently conservative mindset towards classroom pedagogy (McDougall, 2010), identifying their 'core business' or top priority as teaching, in the case of primary level, basic literacy, and believing that games, for example, do not have the correct learning outcomes (Royle, 2008). Merchant's study (2010) saw that when practitioners used a game and had to create support materials, they were based on the standard practices (shared text work, guided writing activities, and so on). This could be explained by practitioners being confused about the gap in expectations between the digital culture of pupils and the traditional culture of schools and curricula (McDougall, 2010). However, as a new generation of practitioners closer in age and temperament to the digital culture enters the profession, this mindset may change (*ibid.*).

Case study 2

An interview with a Year 3 teacher in her twenties

Her main issue was knowing where to start and go to for advice on resources, and having the time to research and trial. She felt that unless all pupils had a device then it was difficult to share out, and when they all were working on their own then it was difficult to keep track, especially as there was often a wide variety of digital skills. More knowledgeable pupils were always trying to advise 'this is how you do it', and once they were immersed in a task they tended to 'zone out', as she saw it.

3 Resistance from parents

This is part of a wider 'childhood at risk' discourse (Craft, 2012), and is fed by a 'moral panic' in the wider media about the supposed corrosive effect of social media, gaming and other new technology (Merchant, 2013). This deficit view of digital technology and media suggests that practitioners and parents typically loathe it (Steinkuehler, 2010) and would prefer to stamp it out rather than nourish it. They feel it deflects from activities that may seem more important to development (Alper, 2011), and may negatively affect academic performance (Paraskeva *et al.*, 2010). The moral panic often centres around the suitability of content and controls over it – particularly relating to violence and gender stereotypes (Alper, 2011) – even in the classroom, although it is the case that there are as many traditional books and films that are clearly inappropriate for classroom use as there are commercial games (Becker, 2007).

All of this resistance undermines the 'crucial partnership between school, after-school, and home' (Alper, 2011, p. 180), and has failed to 'maintain a level of continuity and consistency' (Girard *et al.* 2012, p. 207) between pupils' digital experiences at home and at school. It seems that it has also resulted in most computers and interactive whiteboards being used at this time by practitioners for routine administrative tasks and assessment purposes rather than creative, resource-rich lessons (Becker, 2007), as they are significantly constrained by institutional rules and routines (Merchant, 2010) including restrictive network firewalls.

An additional factor that creates a challenge for practitioners in terms of developing a digital harmony is the current curricula and assessment regimes which are still rooted in traditional approaches to the teaching and learning of literacy.

The Department for Education, backed by Ofsted, have been driving curricula towards more and more standardised assessment over the past two decades. Increasingly, this now has a global element as part of what can be termed the wider performative discourse (Ball, 2003), where countries are increasingly measuring each other's performance in maths, science, and reading in the Programme for International Student Assessment (PISA), and where pupils' formal test results act as a 'key arbiter of educational quality' (Craft, 2012, p. 179). The 'literacy crises' that this has thrown up, such as when the UK found itself in 23rd place for reading in 2012, have given momentum to an 'agenda of assessment measures designed to ensure accountability in terms of the basics' (McDougall, 2010, p. 679).

To put it another way: the policy-makers require simple and measurable pupil performance (Merchant, 2013); this is best achieved by focusing on basic skills instruction (McDougall, 2010) and the reading and writing of print-based texts (Walsh, 2009). This canonical print literacy (McDougall, 2010) then gets written up into curriculum documents and assessment requirements, and the result is a narrowing down of schooled literacy (Merchant, 2013), and a 'growing separation between the everyday meaning-making practices of children and those that are valued in the school system' (Merchant, 2010, p. 137). This process of social control of pedagogic practice (Merchant, 2010) mitigates against any significant innovation, and, it can be argued, has formally enshrined digital dissonance.

The policy-makers make the occasional cursory nod to digital literacy, such as Education Secretary Michael Gove's speech in 2012, in which he made three major points: about how technology can disseminate learning wider than ever before, how it prompts thoughts about pedagogical practice, but his third point, tellingly, was how it brings unprecedented opportunities for assessment. His remark that 'while the technology is unpredictable, Government must not wade in to prescribe to schools exactly what they should be doing and how' (DfE, 2012) seems to contradict the evidence of 'social control of pedagogic practice' that minister after minister has put into place. While Gove's recognition that digital technology offers a huge opportunity that comes with responsibility is fine on paper, the reality of practice does not suggest such a harmonious picture and is, to a large extent, still stuck in a narrow and traditional print literacy.

How can policy makers and practitioners achieve a sense of digital harmony?

The benefits of digital literacy are manifold and can combine to form a very sound peda-gogical approach, but maybe the way in which they have tended to be excitably expressed as the answer to all classroom woes has been overwhelming for the traditional practitioner struggling to cover the literacy basics and achieve acceptable results. However, the argument for foregrounding digital literacy cannot be lost because it offers the most significant oppor-tunity that has possibly ever existed to deliver a truly creative curriculum. Hence, in order for there to be a paradigm shift away from policy-driven outcomes that favour a traditional and assessment-led approach, this argument needs to be won on three grounds:

1 That there will always be 'digital dissonance' and it is not a problem.

There needs to be recognition that there will always be issues with new and evolving technologies, as there were historically with using video and so on, as well as a divide between the experiences of children at home and at school. There are many reasons why schools cannot be expected to replicate those experiences (Walsh, 2009), such as the fact that hardware and bandwidth in schools will always be less up-to-date or powerful than in homes, so it is not simply a case of trying to jump on the bandwagon of the latest fad.

2 That unless digital literacy can be equitably and efficiently assessed, then it will never be accepted in the classroom or adopted by policy-makers.

The need for assessment will always be present, so research needs to be undertaken into how digital expression can be assessed. Generally, practitioners need to know how multimodal texts can be incorporated into literacy assessment (Walsh, 2009) without falling back on to familiar literacy assessment practices (Owston *et al.*, 2009), and specifically as to how:

- questions can be framed using different media;
- multiple expressions (text/image/film/audio) can be compared; and
- collaborative acts of problem-solving rather than individual performances of ability (Lotherington and Ronda, 2009, Merchant, 2010) can be tested.

3 That a sharply-defined pedagogy needs to be proposed, allowing practitioners to 'see the point' of fostering digital literacy.

The fact is that digital technology and media is here to stay in the classroom, so that the main issue is not so much developing technical skills across media but more how to use them in ways that are pedagogically meaningful (McDougall, 2010). This is an attitudinal approach that encompasses committing practitioners to the value of the approach (Proserpio and Gioia, 2007) by understanding why using digital technology and media is important (Morsivais *et al.*, 2014) and is integral to the modern classroom (Walsh, 2009), as well as developing 'more generic dispositions' towards learning in this way (Merchant, 2010, p. 148).

Perhaps good exemplars of digital literacy in the classroom are needed (Merchant, 2010), as well as a simple encapsulation of a pedagogical approach that allows practitioners to be as creative and innovative with the digital technology and media as they are comfortable with, which Proserpio and Gioia (2007) suggest might involve:

- active participation by pupils in the learning process;
- facilitative social settings; and
- a problem-solving focus.

In this way, pupils can be guided to develop interpretations and personally relevant solutions in a context of collaborative learning through discussion and comparison.

Facing the challenge of achieving digital harmony

It is wrong to suggest that the impact of technology depends on how it fits with existing pedagogic purposes (Jewett and Moss, 2009) or that new 'e-pedagogies' should only make slight changes in syllabuses (Pena-Lopez, 2010). Unless curriculum priorities are challenged (McDougall, 2010) to produce radical reform (Merchant, 2010) and significant changes in curriculum and assessment practices are embraced (Walsh, 2009), some commentators warn that classrooms are in danger of becoming redundant, as the gap between school and everyday literacy practices increasingly diverge to create scenarios where pupils may be successful in a digital literacy context while still being 'at risk' in terms of schooled literacy (Merchant, 2013).

Rather, the emphasis should be on digital literacy as the fundamental component in preparing pupils in the very literacies necessary for social and professional communication (Lotherington and Ronda, 2009), employment (Merchant, 2013), and becoming responsible citizens (Lotherington and Ronda, 2009) in the twenty-first century. It should be obvious that to be digitally literate is to be prepared for the future, but the skills demanded for an increasingly technological and changing workplace are not being learned in schools, rather 'through children's engagement in virtual worlds' (Beavis *et al.*, 2009: 164). Kellner (2004), however, contends that schools must be the primary agents of change that take the lead (Owston *et al.*, 2009).

Digital literacy has been maturing as a concept. It is difficult and disruptive and is therefore a challenge, particularly as it introduces 'communicative practices that are difficult to control and integrate into dominant classroom routines' (Merchant, 2010: 147). Nevertheless, it is based on a sound premise, practitioners are now more familiar with the technology from both school and home use, and it allows children to behave creatively as 'possibility thinkers' (Craft, 2012).

The case for trying to establish digital literacy as a harmonious classroom practice needs to be presented in a clear way to practitioners so that they can embrace it, but there are three strong pull factors that might indicate that education is already poised for change: 'pupils are oriented today to their use: educational theory encourages taking advantage of their possibilities and industry is hungry for pupils experienced in these ways of thinking and interacting' (Crook, 2012 p. 65).

Further reading

Parvin, T. (2011) 'Lights, camera, action . . . take 9!', in Bower, V. (Ed.), *Creative Ways to Teach Literacy*. London: Sage.

Bibliography

Alper, M. (2011) 'Developmentally appropriate New Media Literacies: Supporting cultural competencies and social skills in early childhood education', *Journal of Early Childhood Literacy* 13(2), pp. 175–96.

Appel, M. (2012) 'Are heavy users of computer games and social media more computer literate?' *Computers & Education*, 59, pp. 1339–49. Philadelphia: Elsevier.

Ball, S. (2003) 'The teacher's soul and the terrors of performativity.' *Journal of Education Policy*, 18(2), pp. 215–28.

Beavis C., Apperley, T., Bradford, C., O'Mara, J., and Walsh, C. (2009) 'Literacy in the digital age: Learning from computer games', *English in Education*, 43(2), pp. 162–75.

Becker, K. (2007) 'Digital game-based learning once removed: Teaching teachers', *British Journal of Educational Technology*, 38(3), pp. 478–88.

BECTA (British Educational Communications and Technology Agency) (2005) *The Becta Review 2005: Evidence on the Progress of ICT in Education*. Coventry: Becta ICT Research. Available at: http://dera.ioe.ac.uk/1428/1/becta_2005_bectareview_report.pdf (Accessed: 23 March 2014).

Chambers, D. (2012) 'Wii play as a family: The rise in family-centred video gaming', *Leisure Studies*, 31(1), pp. 69–82.

Clark, C. (2014) *Children and Young People's Reading in 2013*. Findings from the 2013 National Literacy Trust's Annual Survey. London: National Literacy Trust.

Clark, W., Logan, K., Luckin, R., Mee, A., and Oliver, M. (2009) 'Beyond Web 2.0: Mapping the technology landscapes of young learners', *Journal of Computer Assisted Learning*, 25, pp. 56–69.

Craft, A. (2012) 'Childhood in a digital age: Creative challenges for educational futures', *London Review of Education*, 10(2), pp. 173–90.

Crook C. (2012) 'The "digital native" in context: Tensions associated with importing Web 2.0 practices into the school setting', *Oxford Review of Education*, 38(1), pp. 63–80.

DfE (Department for Education) (2012) *Reforming Qualifications and the Curriculum to Better Prepare Pupils for Life After School*. Available at: www.gov.uk/governmentspeeches/Michael-gove-at-the-bett-show-2012 (Accessed: 23 March 2014).

DfE (Department for Education) (2014) *National Curriculum in England: Primary Curriculum*. Available at: www.gov.uk/government/collctions/national-curriculum (Accessed: 1 March 2014).

DfEE (Department for Education and Employment) (2000) *The National Curriculum: Handbook for Primary Teachers in England: Key Stages 1 & 2*. Available at: http://webarchive.nationalarchives.gov.uk/20130401151715/https://www.education.gov.uk/publications/standard/publicationDetail/Page1/QCA/99/457 (Accessed: 23 March 2014).

Gee, J. (2010) *New Digital Media and Learning as an Emerging Area*. Cambridge, MA: MIT Press.

Girard, C., Ecalle, J., and Magnan, A. (2012) 'Serious games as new educational tools: How effective are they?' *Journal of Computer Assisted Learning*, 29, pp. 207–19.

Hadow Report (1928) *Books in Public Elementary Schools*. Available at: www.educationengland.org.uk/documents/hadow1928/html (Accessed: 3 February 2014).

Helsper E. and Eynon R. (2009) 'Digital natives: Where is the evidence?' *British Educational Research Journal*, 36(3), pp. 503–20.

Jenkins, H. (2006) *Confronting the Challenges of Participatory Culture: Media Education for the 21st Century*. Chicago: MacArthur Foundation.

Jewitt, C., and Moss, G. (2009) 'Teachers' pedagogic use of the technological possibilities of interactive whiteboards in UK secondary schools'. Research into Teaching with Whole class Interactive Technologies International Conference, Cambridge.

Kellner, D. M. (2004) 'Technological revolution, multiple literacies and the re-visioning of education', *E-Learning*, 1(1), 9–37.

Kress G. (2003) *Literacy in the New Media Age*. London: Routledge.

Lankshear, C. and Knoble, M. (2006) *New Literacies – Everyday Practices and Classroom Learning* (2nd edn). Maidenhead: Open University Press.

Lee, J., Lin, L., and Robertson, T. (2012) 'The impact of media multitasking on learning', *Learning, Media and Technology*, 37(1), pp. 94–104.

Lindroth, T. and Bergquist, M. (2010) 'Laptopers in an educational practice: Promoting the personal learning situation', *Computers & Education*, 54, pp. 311–20.

Lotherington, H. and Ronda, N. (2009) 'Gaming geography: Educational games and literacy development in the Grade 4 classroom', *Canadian Journal of Learning and Technology*, 35(3).

McDougall, J. (2010) 'A crisis of professional identity: How primary teachers are coming to terms with changing views of literacy', *Teaching and Teacher Education*, 26, pp. 679–87.

Merchant, G. (2010) '3D virtual worlds as environments for literacy learning.' *Educational Research*, 52(2), pp. 135–50.

Merchant, G. (2013) 'The Trashmaster: Literacy and new media.' *Language and Education*, 27(2), pp. 144–60.

Monsivais, M., Salas, L. and Lavigne, G. (2014) 'Application and validation of a techno-pedagogical lecturer training model using a virtual learning environment', *Revista de Universidad y Sociedad del Conocimiento*, 11(1), pp. 91–107.

Owston, R., Wideman, H., Ronda, N., and Brown, C. (2009) 'Computer game development as a literacy activity', *Computers & Education*, 53, pp. 977–89.

Paraskeva, F., Mysirlaki, S. and Papagianni, A. (2010) 'Multiplayer online games as educational tools: facing new challenges in learning', *Computers & Education*, 54, pp. 498–505.

Pena-Lopez, I. (2010) 'From laptops to competences: Bridging the digital divide in education', *Revista de Universidad y Sociedad del Conocimiento*, 7(1), pp. 21–32.

Prensky, M. (2006) *Don't Bother Me Mom – I'm Learning!* New York: Paragon House.

Proserpio, L. and Gioia, D. (2007) 'Teaching the virtual generation', *Academy of Management Learning & Education*, 6(1), pp. 69–80.

Royle, K. (2008) 'Game-based learning: A different perspective', *Innovate*, 4(4). Available at: http://wlv. openrepository.com/wlv/handle/2436/47420 (Accessed: 3 February 2014).

Steinkuehler, C. (2010) 'Video games and digital literacies', *Journal of Adolescent & Adult Literacy*, 54(1), pp. 61–3.

The Pearson Foundation (2010) *The Digital World of Young Children: Impact on Emergent Literacy*. Available at www.pearsonfoundation.org (Accessed: 3 February 2014).

Walsh, M. (2009) *Pedagogic Potentials of Multimodal Literacy*. Hershey, PA: IGI Global.

Section 3

Barriers to inclusive practice in times of change

The anonymous quote 'The biggest obstacles in our lives are the barriers we create in our minds' establishes a way of thinking about the chapters in this section. The challenge remains in this section where you as a reader are encouraged to let go of the things you cannot change and focus on what difference you can make.

In this section, there are three chapters:

Chapter 7 written by **Diana Strauss** highlights the **'Complex and challenging: supporting young children identified with special educational needs'**.

Chapter 8 authored by **Christine Ritchie** considers **'The challenge of supporting diverse families'**.

Chapter 9 co-written by **Linda Flower** and **Christine Ritchie** explores **'Taking risks: Living with danger – the benefits and safeguards'**.

7 Complex and challenging: supporting young children identified with special educational needs

Diana Strauss

Overview

The need for improved training opportunities has been a dominant theme in the field of special educational needs and disability awareness. This chapter draws together the most current developments, reflections and evaluations from case study evidence conducted by mature students in Kent who are in employment in this sector. A discussion of special education in the context of change makes reference to policy and current procedure. Sample observation schedules are used to discuss effective approaches that can be implemented in formative and summative assessment. Positive strategies are presented to promote mutual respect and trust between parents and teacher/practitioners. This will include debate regarding a shared vision and a collaborative approach to ensure more effective information sharing and *early help*, previously referred to as early intervention, and identification of young children identified with special needs. A *can do approach* is highlighted when investigating the challenges surrounding access to training. Facing such challenges can provide possible opportunities, and in this regard, examples of complex real-life scenarios illustrate such opportunities. It is important to avoid oversimplifying this challenging topic; more effective is to explore positive action as this can help demystify the subject and so reduce fear among some teacher/practitioners working in early education. As a result, early years professionals can examine their practices, identify their personal and professional values and, in so doing, be able to provide genuinely inclusive experiences for young children with special educational needs guided by the imperative to find ways forward for future optimism during unsettling and changing times. Collectively it is possible to establish a vision that supports genuine and empathic working practices.

Provision for children with Special Educational Needs in Context

Anti-discrimination legislation protects children with disabilities; all schools and settings must make reasonable adjustments and prevent less favourable treatment deemed to be discriminatory under the Great Britain Equality Act (2010). Currently, legal requirements are implemented to meet standards set out in Codes of Practice, (2001, 2005, revisions due 2014/15). However, from September 2014, the Children and Families Act (2014) will take effect and, as the Council for Disabled Children (2014) rightly states, the significant revisions and changes for all stakeholders are:

- Giving parents and young people control over the decisions about the support they are given;
- The introduction of Education, Health and Care plans in replacement of Statements;
- Personal budgets for parents and young people to carry out their Education and Health Care plans;
- A requirement on local authorities to provide a Local Offer which will include the education, health and care services.

Council for Disabled Children (2014 blog news)

The statutory duty under the *Special Educational Needs and Disability Code of Practice: 0 to 25 Years* (DfE and DoH, 2014) strengthens an existing anticipatory requirement on teachers/practitioners to achieve genuine consultation and full participation of young children and their parents in educational and social experiences. High quality teaching and collaborative practices, are identified as key principles that can secure positive outcomes for all (2014, pp. 19–25). This chapter can prompt teachers and practitioners to participate in the decision-making process for support in schools and Early Years settings. Children, young people and parents need confidence in Local Authority provision because the support provided must be early, helpful and the best possible. Teachers/practitioners must achieve greater levels of confidence by actively seeking more detailed knowledge, so this chapter recommends sources available online as well as guidance in the form of approaches to facilitate up-to-date training opportunities.

Arguably (as highlighted by Wall, 2011), training in special educational needs and disability in schools is available for teachers, whereas equivalent professional development is less evident in early education and care settings. Early years practitioners report that their access to training has evolved more slowly and the provision has been variable. For example, from 1998, central government first devolved funds to pay for training resources, to be disseminated by Local Authorities. Authorities were responsible for appointing Area Early Years Special Educational Needs Co-ordinators (SENCOs) to deliver the training and distribute the resources. This was to be achieved across England by 2004. The training consisted of the equivalent of three-days input to enable every Early Years setting to appoint a designated (and setting-based) SENCO who would ensure the setting met the welfare requirements and the duties outlined in the *Special Educational Needs Code of Practice* (DfES, 2001). Across Kent, one of the largest education authorities in England, these roles were first advertised as late as 2004; while in the London boroughs, Early Years Area SENCOs were appointed from the outset in 1998, and teams in London were trialling effective approaches within professional networks. As a result they were able to:

provide dedicated support and practical advice to early years and childcare settings, helping them to access specialist support to assist with the early identification of special educational needs and the action required to meet those needs.

Association of Teachers and Lecturers (1998, p. 17)

This perceived disparity may indicate a wider and less than equal provision in essential training across local authorities in England. Access to such training can now only be achieved through positive action and a *can do approach*. An additional layer of challenge is the whole notion of the designated SENCO role. It is important to guard against a possible unintended consequence of isolating an individual by designating the SENCO as the only expert. Teachers and practitioners report that when they access high quality training and participate in supportive professional networks they are much more likely to gain more professional confidence and therefore they are equipped to advance their skills and knowledge base.

Challenge

- Consider your training, experience and expertise AND the equality policy within your workplace.
- Are you confident in your knowledge and understanding of the provision that is, or should be, available for children with special educational needs?
- When was your (a) last training and (b) next training related to SEN?

Policy - procedure - practice

Teachers and practitioners are well-versed in the need for sound policy to inform procedure that then ensures best practice. Individualised learning as a concept is familiar to the majority of practitioners, especially from birth to 8 years. The *additional and different* provision within individualised planning as very small steps is often more appropriately the responsibility of the key person and class teacher, rather than a designated SENCO. As a co-ordinator of provision, this specific role is more accurately defined as one of leadership. The role must inspire and inform others to take responsibility and ownership in the day-to-day 'action' associated with the provision of support. This is the only effective approach to ensure positive outcomes for young children. With regards to the regulation of Early Years provision, practitioners should refer to (and be guided by) the detail in non-statutory guidance such as Department for Education (DfE) (2013) *Early Years Outcomes*, written to help practitioners and inspectors understand child development. In addition, parent/carers (as well as professionals) can access detailed information when planning small step targets outlined in the *development journals* for children from birth to 8 years, published by *Early Support*. This journal, with the accompanying guidance document, provides specific information for diagnosed conditions and impairments and these are all available as free downloads from the *Early Support* website. The inspection schedule published by Ofsted (2013a) emphasises the responsibility of all practitioners to demonstrate positive outcomes regardless of special educational need and/ or disability/impairment. In terms of the impact of what practitioners do, to demonstrate children's learning and development, inspectors must evaluate and report on:

> whether children make the best possible progress taking into account their starting points and capabilities, the length of time they have been at the setting, and how often they attend; and how well they are prepared for school or the next steps in their learning.
>
> Ofsted (2013a, p. 6)

This emphasis by regulatory bodies places a requirement upon school and setting leaders to ensure that all practitioners can demonstrate sound and detailed knowledge of child progress. The tension here arises from a lack of knowledge in aspects of progress. Consideration must be given to time for consolidation and *periods of plateaux*. Sometimes learning is clearly visible; however children and adults will (at times) level out and stay the same, before showing that learning has progressed further. Teachers/practitioners can show their levels of confidence by describing the children's actions and behaviours with this knowledge. This then inspires confidence from parents/carers who can see that their own child is the starting point in the planning process. Practitioners can build an excellent understanding through a process of reflection, analysis and evaluation. This is achieved through discussion and consultation, both with the children themselves and with the significant adults in their lives – sharing examples and scenarios, both within the school/setting (and beyond). This can form the essential basis for analysis – and where possible, these examples should illustrate the observable differences made for the child in terms of their experiences. Ongoing formative assessment must be robust and transparent. Children, parent/carers and professionals must all be consulted, and every contribution must be balanced for an accurate summative profile. The tension here is the issue of *perceived* progress undermining *intrinsic rhythms* and *swings of development* referred to by Mead (2013) (see below).

Assessment: formative and summative

The selective use of observations, together with significant information that is exchanged, provides a solid foundation for knowledge that is secure and well-founded. This information exchange puts summative judgements into context so the most suitable strategies can be identified. It is the quality of this analysis that determines the effective support by adults for young children. The Early Years Framework, which identifies *Prime Areas* of development and describes what constitutes the *Characteristics of Effective Learning* (DfE, 2012, pp. 5-7), focuses attention on universal principles that may be overlooked once a diagnosis is sought for children with special educational needs. Accuracy and detailed knowledge of *typical* key developmental stages must be embedded in all provision and practice. Therefore, high quality formative assessments ensure that teachers and practitioners are equipped to examine developmental pathways and individualise support, which is grounded in young children's interests, their need for peer support and evolving groups of friends. In addition, and this is crucial, adults must be skilled and confident in their communication skills to work collaboratively with colleagues and develop a method of analysis to determine the interventions and actions that must be taken. The manner and approach must demonstrate deep and sound empathy or understanding of young children's life experiences in the varied, and often complicated, scenarios.

Misdiagnosis and labelling must be avoided. Teachers/practitioners must recognise the potential for many significant events in a young child's life, such as the arrival of a new sibling or family bereavement, resulting in developmental *swings*. This is widely recognised in literature (Mead, 2013), including education and healthcare guidance that underpins relevant reports commissioned by government. For example, Tickell (2011) emphasises:

Children's development therefore is seen to occur not in a predictable linear progression, but in a web of multiple strands with rates of progress varying between children, and subject to influences by factors both within and outside of the child.

Tickell (2011, p. 1)

The earliest and most important intervention is therefore to build up an accurate profile (over time) but without delay. The professional judgement required here is complicated and challenging, and it highlights the tension between intervening early enough to achieve good outcomes without rushing to label learning difficulty or impairment.

Pitfalls to avoid when trying to intervene early:

- Over-simplification. Ensure information is *developmentally* explained and behaviours that indicate the stage of development are acknowledged.
- Insufficient knowledge leading to possible misinterpretation of need. Question and evaluate the observations. Discuss the interpretations fully. Check the findings with family members; be cautious, yet confident as a professional in the detail of observed information; gather this across a range of experiences. Avoid *snapshots*, particularly when gathering information when building a case for additional support.
- Achieve genuine consultation with the children. Demonstrate to them through your actions that you are actively listening. Do not rely on speech. Interpret the behaviour of young children because this is their preferred method of communication.
- Do not assume that *conforming* or *compliant* behaviour is evidence of understanding or a *level of intellect*.
- Guard against possible tedium arising from *low aspiration* for children. Plan so every child is at the centre of the *play-action*. Explain to all the supporting adults that it is their attitudes and their behaviours that will make the most significant difference. Positive outcomes are achieved in the small actions taken by adults on a daily basis.

An example of an observation template (see Table 7.1) here requires the adult to record the actions they have taken in the observation process.

Current challenges for the early years

- Time! In the words of a leading Early Years setting-based SENCO, 'There is always more that you want to do for the child.' A visual timetable that details the events can build a picture for key members of staff. However, trying to manage time more efficiently does not create the hours in the day that are needed to liaise and consult with parent/carers, specialist teachers and therapists or specialist nurses. This ongoing challenge pervades all aspects of education across all areas. Strategies such as delegation and collaboration apply here, and the familiar adage *do your best and acknowledge the limitations* is worth remembering.
- Regular updates! Teams in schools and settings must receive information at regular and timely intervals, and within practical sessions. Find ways to make the knowledge meaningful by providing examples through discussions and demonstration.

Table 7.1 Adapted template used in a setting to record actions taken by adult in the observation/assessment process

Date:	Child's name:
Photos of targets	
How did the child achieve the target shown in the photo?	What did the key person do to support the child?
Which experiences involve me the most?	What has to happen for my well-being to be high?

Adapted from J.J. observation sheet

- Money, staffing and resources. At the outset, costs are invariably met by Early Years providers. Maintained schools receive funding from local authorities; however, high staff ratios, specialist equipment and adaptions to the environment may place an additional financial burden upon the organisation.

Personal budgets are to be paid directly to parents of children in receipt of Education Health Care Plans. The anxiety of parents is quoted here as a blog entry.

> There is no way I would want anything to do with that. James's needs amount to hundreds of pounds of care and equipment. I would not want to have to co-ordinate all the people and work out their budgets.
>
> Jane Raca, author of *Standing up for James* (2012)
> www.standingupforjames.co.uk

The threat of diminishing resources, shrinking services and the potential loss of specialist, knowledgeable and experienced personnel requires positive action in response. Networks of expertise must be established so families and professionals come together to learn from each other and empathise for greater mutual understanding. Aim to be honest and open, and work hard to establish channels of communication. Avoid blame and try not to pre-judge. A process of trial and error can sometimes reassure everyone concerned that the solution is rather like a jig-saw and the pieces must be gently eased into place before the whole picture can emerge. Feelings can run high and it is not helpful or constructive when parents blame themselves. Find out relevant information to empathise but avoid labelling parents. The behaviours and attitudes they experience could support them in the process when acknowledging that their child has special educational needs.

Communication for professional trust

The professional conversations and interactions should work towards open and factual sharing of information. The only way to achieve trust is to:

> Always, always, always, talk to parents before talking to 'outside experts'; gather your thoughts; think about what is going well as well as what is proving difficult; be honest; be assertive; if you don't understand, ask; be willing to try things out, even if you suspect they might not work; don't expect any magic wands or silver bullet.
>
> Primary head teacher, Nottingham

Find ways for the new knowledge to consolidate trusting relationships. Documents such as *Learning journeys* in Early Years settings and *Communication passports* for transition, in both schools and settings, can be highly effective when engaging parent/carers in the process of acceptance. Some conversations can be difficult, so provide a photograph journal and focus attention that is shared. This joint-focus that depicts the child's experiences and learning opportunities can make difficult conversations more consensual. Open the conversation with phrases that all parties will agree upon so that everyone is smiling in consent from the outset. For example, there will always be consensus that the purpose of meeting is to ensure that the child could be supported to make friends and participate fully in early education experiences. Acknowledging that this can be difficult when a child has severe communication needs could lead to a discussion regarding referral and assessment routes.

Case study 1: Reflections of a mature student in employment

I have a fresh understanding of the challenges which the whole family face when dealing with the needs of a child with leaning difficulties and disabilities. With a deeper knowledge of how children learn I can now see the importance of planning for specific children's individual needs using individual education plans. I will continue to value, listen and communicate regularly with parent/carers to ensure there is a consistent approach towards support for children's learning and development. I intend to ensure that different storytelling methods incorporating resources are included on the planning to enable all children to be included.

Challenge

- How 'fresh' does your knowledge and understanding of the challenges facing families with a child with learning difficulties feel?
- How do you plan learning, communicate with parents and adapt resources to accommodate the inclusion of all children?

Professional development

Tackling the challenge to access training and development endures. I advocate a change of emphasis towards a genuine shift away from an expectation that training will just appear. There is a new imperative to believe in young children with special educational needs. They have their own will and can be the *authors of their own life stories,* Early Support (2013).

Through consultation and participation, practical strategies can be deduced and environments can be created that are potentially both *deaf friendly* and *autism friendly*. This approach is likely to have a universal appeal. *Friendliness* is a concept that can be tried in all approaches and in all settings: mainstream, specialist and beyond (leisure centres, clubs and activity groups and after school clubs). What must be demonstrated is a willingness to find ways forward, rather than restrict and limit the opportunities or experiences of young children with special educational needs.

So-called, *in-house* and continuing professional development is required under the *anticipatory duty* of the (DfES, 2001) Special Educational Needs Code of Practice (now revised) and highlighted in evaluation schedules for regulation under Ofsted (2013). The point here is, an individual must take responsibility to remain informed and aware, and equally, an entire team must work together. These points are vital:

- Senior managers lead by identifying training needs across staff teams through supervision.
- A teacher/practitioner must be proactive and show initiative:
  - Request professional development opportunities.
  - Take significant actions to improve outcomes for children with learning impairments and difficulties and/or disabilities.
  - Sign up for online training.

The following steps can make actions more effective and maximise impact of training:

- Clearly communicate the importance and the significance of the training.
- Consider that teacher/practitioner motivation may be higher if the imperative for the training is understood and shared among the team.
- Structure the delivery to include practical elements, so find ways to deliver the learning in active and practical ways.

These steps will help to reduce anxiety, therefore building more confidence. Demystifying difficult subjects and certain aspects of specialist and specific conditions/impairments is positive. This is especially important for children who have medical and health needs without special educational needs. In this scenario, a medical and/or *health-care plan* must be drawn up. This should not be confused with the new Education Health and Care Plans that will replace Statements of Special Educational Need. A school nurse, health visitor and specialist nurse adviser must work with parent/carers and agree the plan. This must be shared with the key person or teacher. If information-sharing is good, then the education professionals need not be fearful. Remember:

- Talk openly about what is appropriate and pinpoint the strategies that can be tried.
- Decide which battles are really worth engaging in.
- Agree the boundaries and aim for consistency between parent/carers, school and setting.
- Acknowledge that there is likely to be a process of trial and error.
- A fear of *getting it wrong* is linked to a reluctance to talk about the difficulty in real terms.

Case study 2: Reflections of a parent

There is a particular look of fear in some practitioners, more fearful of getting it wrong than empowered to try a number of strategies that work for individual children. There is likely to be conversation about 'conformity' and a need to understand the perspectives of the family, their own behaviours and patterns in relation to the difficulties, and crucially, whether there is 'acceptance', or not. For many families and people working with SEN, there is the fear of not being able to affect it positively. In the culture in which we live and work, we are measured, and we measure ourselves, by the positive impact we can have on others. Not being able to visibly or measurably help frightens people.

Challenge

- Write an action plan towards a vision that would provide support that is based upon genuine and empathic communication. Which communication style and vocabulary might be most supportive?
- Describe key behaviours that families would recognise and appreciate as your efforts to show compassion and care.
- Reflect upon examples that you can recall when your perspective has shifted because you have learnt some important new insights from the young children you teach. Share these examples with their parents who will also learn from these experiences.
- Try to find ways for all the adults to be *attuned* and *mindful* with, and for, children. What is required here is much greater imagination, determination and responsiveness.

Case study 3: Reflections of a mature student in employment

Inclusion diversity and SEN is a very 'hot topic' in our society today. The SEN code of practice is under review, following the EYFS review. There are so many specialised areas and more seem to be appearing. Many years ago and even now we still hear the conversation about how we are not allowed to call children 'just naughty': we need to get a diagnostic reason for their behaviour.

As part of a case study I reflected upon a conversation with a GP about a child and he said it was boundaries the child had difficulties with and maybe our nursery was not the right place for her. This statement really worried me and the other staff and all sorts of doubts came up in our discussions. Very importantly we questioned whether we were meeting her needs, whilst trying to be fully inclusive. I am fully aware that some environments are not suited to all children but we do strive to be fully inclusive. It feels like we have failed if the child and family leave the nursery. This was resolved with careful discussion with other professionals and parents. I believe we were unsettled; it is clear we are passionate about the subject and strive to get it right for our young people.

Terminology was also a worry for me as this seems to change regularly and when having discussions in the classroom sometimes things were not said in fear of criticising others or not getting the right terminology. This made me realise how it must be for these children and parents when we talk, for example about an IEP, if we have not explained it in full. Through listening to other professionals [SENCO specialist teachers], and reflecting on the process of children's IEPs, I feel a little more confident to speak to the parents when very sensitive issues arise. Through doing a case study I have learnt a lot about sensory processing disorder and the effects this can have on the everyday life of some adults and children.

Challenge

- Think about some of the terminology that you might use that parents are unfamiliar with. How can you make this clearer?
- Think about the words or terminology related to SEN that is now considered taboo; why is this? What is the consequence for the child or others if the wrong term is used? Also consider any damage that might be caused if the subject (rather than the word) is so sensitive that it remains hidden.

Examples of resource strategies categorised as *universal, beyond universal* and *specialist*

The training that consistently has the greatest impact is that which is delivered jointly by trainer and parent/carers who can talk about a specific condition. The information that is shared can provide the detail about how the child and family learn to manage living with the condition or impairment. This leads to deeper understanding and greater empathy for the child(ren) and family. The session works best when the information is delivered by the parent alongside a specialist healthcare professional, involved and delivering medical intervention and support. Common understanding enables a child's experience at home to be extended into the education setting and then back again. Remember to balance the *measuring* of individual targets performed by young children with the measuring of adult understanding, in effect *piecing the jigsaw* together. Observe closely and try to find order, shape, pattern and form. Try turning the fragments of what you think you know upside down and move your perceptions around. Keep making adjustments and celebrate even the smallest steps forward. Note down what actions have made a positive impact and keep a record of the outcomes.

Strategies: some are universal and for all children

- Know your child(ren): check the information and avoid assumptions; check these are not value judgements that lead to stereotyping attitudes and behaviours.
- Be responsive: this may require more careful consideration of all possible and often variable factors.
- Be flexible and imaginative: remember to bring the fun into learning and development. Often the small step target-setting process is so *watched* and assessed that it has the effect of suppressing any joy.

Keep professional practice up to date by regularly browsing resource-based websites. In the case of speech, language and communication, log on to talkingpoint.org.uk, I CAN and Every Child a Talker (see below). It can be very challenging for adults to try to interpret children's behaviours accurately. This is because young children's *intended communications* (which they express through their actions and behaviour) are frequently misunderstood by the adults around them. Adults may have to undertake a considerable amount of detective work to forensically piece together information for a satisfactory conclusion. Aim to be consistent in responses to children. Try to be careful and considered. Provoke some deep reflection by (respectfully and confidentially) seeking more information and background knowledge.

- Discover all the local support services and promote these in the school and setting.
- Advertise the services in ways that are accessible.
- Encourage more families to ask for help.
- Provide parent/carers with contact names and numbers.
- Design and print leaflets and posters with images, diagrams and prompts for parent/carers to use when requesting support.
- Audit the environment and check that the routines are displayed visually.
- Ensure that abstract concepts such as *waiting for a turn*, *what is next* and ideas such as *finished* are communicated visually. Use egg-timers, visual prompts, build a structure that can be anticipated, make a *Now* and *Next* board.
- Rules and boundaries must be visual with images and examples. Keep rules to a minimum so make them count, turn all negative language into positive statements: Reflect upon the instinctive reaction to shout 'Don't run!' when a child dashes onto wet surfaces in swimming pools or play areas. Make a conscious effort to tell the child in such a way that the word they hear is the action you want them to do, '*Walk – it's slippery*'.
- Ask parent/carers what home routines and boundaries can be *mimicked* in the setting.

Possible sources to search for practical strategies and information website links:

- Every Child a Talker: Guidance for Early Language Lead Practitioners, www.nationalarchives. gov.uk/20130401151715/https://www.education.gov.uk/publications/eOrderingDownload/ DCSF-00854-2008.pdf.
- I CAN resources www.ican.org.uk/resources
- Inclusion Development Programme, www.nationalarchives.gov.uk/20110202093118/http:/ nationalstrategies.standards.dcsf.gov.uk/search/inclusion/results/nav:46335
- Write Dance Training, www.writedancetraining.com

Strategies beyond universal: individualised support

- Jointly and accurately assess observable need(s). Collaborate with parent/carers from the outset so there are absolutely no surprises for the family.
- Empower parent/carers to understand why and how positive outcomes can be achieved through early information sharing. Celebrate the work of colleagues in health and social care. Avoid the pitfall of a blame culture between service providers.
- Offer regular contact with families and be prepared to liaise on a daily basis.
- Be prepared to make and provide resources for family members to use at home to achieve consistency for the child.
- Audit staff knowledge on criteria for Common Assessment Framework (CAF) and Early Help Assessment processes and systems. Seek local advice from the lead professionals in the region.
- Plan a rolling programme of professional development opportunities and appoint *lead teacher/practitioners* to take responsibility for staff briefings and the production of information leaflets and posters so *frontline* teachers and practitioners are fully confident in specific knowledge of special educational needs.
- Most importantly offer *timely* support and always ask for clarification or help. It really isn't helpful (although it is frequently well intentioned) to guess and act without accurate knowledge.
- Guard against assumptions that the parent/carers sharing responsibility for a child will always share the same views. Remember to check before making any assumptions. Different perspectives are also common between parents and grandparents. Professional conduct and boundaries are required here and this does not preclude some emotional support, using genuine and active listening skills.
- Consider *opening up* the school and setting-based training opportunities and invite other settings in the locality to attend. This could lead to regular network sessions that focus on professional development. It may open up some opportunities mutual support by sharing scarce resources. One way to be entrepreneurial as a school/setting is to charge a small training fee to fund some of the costs incurred.
- Audit staff team members on their levels of confidence regarding knowledge of specific conditions such as autism spectrum conditions, the prevalence of glue ear, sensory integration difficulties and specific high-incidence needs such as dyslexia and dyscalculia.

Possible sources to search for practical strategies and information weblinks:

- National Autistic Education Trust, www.autismeducationtrust.org.uk
- National Deaf Association (search for family support) www.ndcs.org.uk/family_support/index.html
- Signs and symbols (search for Makaton Sign Supported Communication) www.sencobooks.com/catalogue/253/books/makaton-sign-supported-communication.html
- Writing with symbols (search for Welcome to Widget) www.widgit.com

Medical care planning for children with no learning needs

Draft statutory guidance is available from the Department for Education. A comprehensive list of information that must be considered when drawing up an individual healthcare plan is available from the Department for Education (DfE, 2014, p. 8).

Strategies towards gaining specialist knowledge

- Seek specialist nurse adviser for medical training, the use of 'epi-pens', administering all medication.
- Ensure all practitioners have peer/buddy support when administering medication and/or moving and handling children with physical impairment.
- Identify core skill training for all *face-to-face* and frontline members of staff to enhance the trusting relationships and prevent anxiety or fear among the team.
- Avoid labelling or stigmatising attitudes and behaviours. Example scenarios to avoid can range from adults talking dismissively about children, to staff members only focusing on known impairments or only seeing the *condition*. Much more effective is to get to know children and try to find ways to engage and stimulate some episodes that can be described as *shared attention* for educational experiences that motivate greater participation in the *day-to-day action* in the class or setting.
- Lead and provide supervision for all members of staff. Ensure the staffing ratios provide peer support.
- Open the school and setting as a venue to host local network meetings and parent support group sessions for the area. These are especially important for parent/carers who have recently received a diagnosis for their child.

Advice and specialist knowledge should be available from health and social care professionals. Charitable organisations and national advocacy/support groups publish practical and professional booklets and guidance documents describing actions. These are accessible from the internet as well as in hard copy. In summary the outcome could look like this example scenario below:

> The pre-school individual education plan was clear and specific with well-defined objectives agreed with parents. The teacher of the deaf worked closely and effectively with the nursery manager and key workers to identify specific actions that could be taken to enable her to hear better within the nursery environment. This was particularly

important as she had not previously socialised very often outside of the family environment. Some simple actions taken in the nursery included the provision of soft furnishings to improve the acoustics.

Ofsted (2012, p. 16)

Accredited and advanced skills training for designated roles

Original and positive outcomes are achieved when designated SENCOs and frontline teacher/practitioners share and exchange expertise. The example case study below illustrates action taken by a Forest School leader to include a young boy on the autism spectrum in active-learning sessions outdoors, without his assigned support worker. New and fresh information was generated from the observations in this outdoor environment. Knowledge of the child was secure; it had been well established that he was able to relax in the outdoor environment; it was not a threat. As a result, he had more space, more autonomy, and this facilitated a step towards greater awareness of his own peer group.

Case study 4: Effective and positive – a Forest School leader's story of transition planning for a young child on the autism spectrum

The systems in place at the setting in this case study have been judged to be outstanding. The support for children with special educational needs is especially strong and effective. The support and full engagement with and for parents is celebrated here. A strong emphasis is upon developing a child's relationship with their key person. The key person captures detailed knowledge and talks confidently about their understanding of the child, thus tailoring the care and early educational experiences to engage and foster good relationships. These extend to the family. Parents can see that their preferences are acted upon. Parents learn how the individualised and developmental targets are designed to enable interaction through 'playful' exploration and 'active participation' as this is capturing the child's curiosity and attention.

This particular child loves outdoor spaces, bugs and animals. Observations during forest school sessions noted his calm mood in this natural environment where 'disturbing-experiences' are removed. The observations show that he is noticing other children and approaching them to try and 'join-in'. This environment has reduced his stress and distress. Observations show his increased attention and awareness giving the key person some clues for possible next steps in his social communication. The forest school leader was successful in developing this child's learning and 'life skills'. Parents engaged with nursery staff, and were then helped to voice their preferences and views. The SENCO provided guidance to the key person, when agreeing targets with parents for 'pocket-sized' plans that documented the evidence for future funding and intervention. It was vitally important that the role of the key person was understood in helping the child to develop a secure, secondary attachment. This made the greatest impact on his individual needs. It also provided the opportunity for a strong working relationship with parents, which culminated in home visits in order to really gain an insight into what the setting could provide by way of the greatest 'early-help'. The key person listened to the parents and together they agreed the most appropriate strategies.

Roles can be complicated and it is the joint responsibility of a key person and the SENCO to document and gather strong information for sharing. The records show small achievements; tiny progress and aspirational goals within areas that still need to develop (but only the ones that are 'reachable' and reasonable). This formed the foundation and basis for transition. The communication between home and setting, setting and school was found to be the best that could have been hoped for. The views of the parents and the child were captured and interpreted. Parents' views about their child's experiences in education were reflected in the decisions that affected their child. Regular meetings and discussions provided significant support. The child's behaviours and responses guided the learning and the developmental targets. These were recorded on transition documents and, as a consequence, the process of transition was well supported. This Forest School leader recommends that:

a   All children's views must be interpreted and captured on 'profile' documentation.
b   Parent/carer(s) must see that their comments are recorded when planning for transition.
c   'Profiles' must identify that children are children first; therefore transition documents must summarise significant and specific information regarding special educational needs and diagnosed conditions, without losing sight of, 'who the child is and what makes them tick'.
d   Genuine collaboration between parent, child, key person and SENCO must be achieved when planning for transition.

Challenge

* What steps are taken in your setting to ensure that the interests of children are uncovered and then used in a similar way to help the child to access learning?
* How are the children's views recorded, shared and acted upon?

Challenges ahead: Education Health Care Plans

At the time of writing this chapter, the discussion surrounding the proposed Education Health Care Plans to replace Statements of Special Educational Needs is forming a lively debate and eliciting a range of responses. The ICAN blog page reported in January 2014 that:

> Guidance says that Education Health Care Plans should be given when the local authority thinks that the mainstream early years setting, school or college can't give a child all of the extra support they need for learning (e.g. they need extra help and/or money). We understand from the information we have at the moment that children and young people whose main needs are to do with health or care will not be given a plan, unless the difficulties they have affect their education.

> I CAN (2014)

The Children Act (2004) preceded the guidance for practitioners published by Children's Workforce Development Council (2009) and identified the need for early intervention in a Common Assessment Framework. Local authorities have retained the function to integrate and co-ordinate services through this process by adopting *a personal education plan* approach. This is an extension of the Early Support model for integrated service provision. The approach is characterised by the parent/carers taking the central role, alongside their key-worker, to share information and make requests for support from the team working with the child. The discussions are formalised as family plans and are intended to be well informed and joined up and specifically focused *around a child*. In areas where this approach is already working well, the proposed Education Health Care Plan model could be adopted seamlessly. In local authorities where this model is not working well, positive action is urgently needed in response to the proposed removal of the DfES (2001) *Special Educational Needs Code of Practice*. A starting point is to work towards a common language, shared goals and strong aspirations for children and their families. This is a prerequisite for frontline teacher/practitioners who can take the initiative and seek out training and development opportunities in order to develop confidence through increased knowledge and skills. Only then will there be a shift away from the current single assessment that is conducted in professional isolation, known as the Statement of Special Educational Need, and that is criticised as it does not prevent *less favourable treatment* in the form of discrimination, as illustrated by the case studies published by the Local Government Ombudsman (2013).

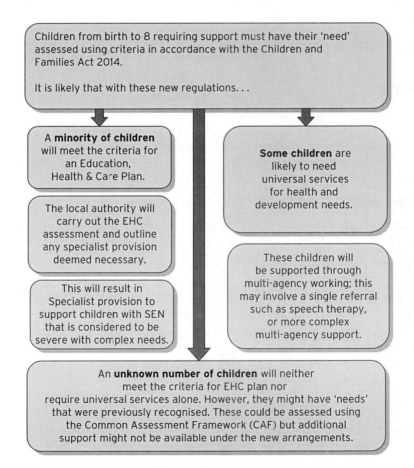

Figure 7.1 The distribution of support offered to children with SEN

An ever-increasing challenge is that of the workload and the escalating demands placed upon members of staff across many service providers. This stress adds to the anxiety associated with the delivery of any new system. One way forward is to agree a common language, which is free of jargon, to achieve integrated service delivery. Furthermore, staffing levels, in the Early Years, must allow flexibility for those teacher/practitioners, who have invaluable knowledge and experience, to attend planning meetings and case conferences.

Case study 5: Reflections of a practitioner

All professionals should not underestimate this challenge. They must also recognise and understand that the non-maintained early years settings do not have the capacity to release members of staff for planning meetings and case conferences.

Challenge

- Are there other (realistic and achievable) ways to communicate and share information? Or can funding for staff cover be found from external sources to allow key staff to attend critical meetings?
- What are the implications of not being able to take part in planning meetings and case conferences?

Conclusion

The school or setting approach and ethos must be supported by strong leadership. Managers must prioritise supervision and training opportunities for frontline teacher/practitioners. Examples in the chapter make a case for positive action in the form of shared values and heightened levels of knowledge in order to achieve skilled early-help for young children's special educational needs. Attention has focused upon a commitment to ensure that young children with special educational needs are securely visible in the centre of the class action and/or the play action. Teachers and practitioners can take positive steps when consulting with children and their parents to identify individualised early help, thereby implementing informed strategies that make a difference, ensuring *favourable* and *equal* caring, educational experiences.

Challenge

- Find the motivation, confidence and perseverance to challenge unreasonable and inappropriate situations.
- Consult with children by requesting photographs taken in the home learning environment, then help young children to choose the photographs for their own communication passport'.
- Try to identify possible principles and values that matter to young children themselves. Arguably, the most important priority for a child is to have dignity. Therefore, evaluate the practices in schools and settings to ensure that children experience a sense of *belonging*.

> Guard against interventions and targets that isolate children as these have the unintended consequence of neglecting opportunities for emerging peer support networks and early friendship groups. Try to experience the world through the perceptions of the child with special educational needs.
> - Attend meetings with family members to plan and review together, wherever possible.
> - Be guided by what is genuine, meaningful, achievable and realistic.
>
> Above all, try to be available, open to new ideas and be prepared to be flexible.

Further reading

This short list offers four essential support documents:

Children's Workforce Matters (2014) *Common Assessment Framework*. Available at: www.childrensworkforcematters.org.uk/workforce-matters/common-assessment-framework (Accessed: 6 August 2014).

Department of Health (2014) *Getting to Know Your Health Visiting and School Visiting Service*, www.foundationyears.org.uk/files/2014/03/Parent-Fact-Sheet_v0-12.pdf (Accessed: 6 August 2014).

Talking Point website Parents tab 'Primary School Checklist', www.talkingpoint.org.uk/parents/finding-right-school/primary-school-checklist (Accessed: 6 August 2014).

Working Together to Safeguard Children (2013), Chapter 1: 'Assessing need and providing help: A guide to inter-agency working to safeguard and promote the welfare of children', www.workingtogetheronline.co.uk/chapters/chapter_one.html (Accessed: 7 August 2014).

Bibliography

Association of Teachers and Lecturers (1998) *Right From the Start Early Years Education: Policy and Practice*. Available at: www.atl.org.uk/Images/Right%20from%20the%20start.pdf (Accessed: 31 March 2014).

Children Act (2004) London: The Stationery Office. Available at: www.legislation.gov.uk/ukpga/2004/31/contents. The National Archives (Accessed: 31 March 2014).

Children and Families Act (2014) London: The Stationery Office. Available at: www.legislation.gov.uk/ukpga/2014/6/contents/enacted (Accessed: 31 March 2014).

Council for Disabled Children (2014) News January–June 2014, 'Children and Families Bill receives Royal Assent'. Available at: www.councilfordisabledchildren.org.uk/news/january-june-2014/children-and-families-bill-receives-royal-assent (Accessed: 31 March 2014).

Department for Education and Skills (DfES) (2001) *Special Educational Needs Code of Practice*. Available at: http://media.education.gov.uk/assets/files/pdf/s/special%20educational%20needs%20code%20of%20practice.pdf (Accessed: 23 October 2013).

Department for Education (DfE) (2012) *Statutory Framework for the Early Years Foundation Stage: Setting the Standards for Learning and Development and Care from Birth to Five*. Nottingham: DfE Publications.

Department for Education (DfE) (2013) *Early Years Outcomes: A non-statutory guide for practitioners and inspectors to help inform understanding of child development through the* early year. Available at: www.gov.uk/government/publications (Accessed: 31 March 2014).

Department for Education (DfE) (2014) *Supporting Pupils at School with Medical Conditions Statutory Guidance for Governing Bodies of Maintained Schools and Proprietors of Academies in England.* Available at: www.gov.uk/government/uploads/system/uploads/attachment_data/file/277025/draft_statutory_guidance_on_supporting_pupils_at_school_with_medical_conditions_for_consultation.pdf (Accessed: 6 August 2014).

Department for Education (DfE) and Department of Health (DoH) (2014) *Special Educational Needs and Disability Code Of Practice: 0 to 25 years: Statutory Guidance for Organisations who Work with and Support Children and Young People with Special Educational Needs and Disabilities.* Available at: www.gov.uk/government/uploads/system/uploads/attachment_data/file/341058/Code_of_Practice_approved_by_Parliament_290714.pdf (Accessed: 7 August 2014).

Early Support (2013) *How to Use the Developmental Journal.* Available at: http://ncb.org.uk/media/884281/how_to_use_the_early_years_developmental_journalv2.pdf and http://ncb.org.uk/media/994609/eydj_practice_guidev2.pdf (Accessed: 23 October 2013).

Equality Act (2010) London: The Stationery Office. Available at: www.gov.uk/government/uploads/system/uploads/attachment_data/file/269341/Equality_Act_2010_-_advice.pcf (Accessed: 31 March 2014).

Local Government Ombudsman (2013) 'Ombudsman calls for fair treatment for children with SEN'. Available at: www.lgo.org.uk/news/2014/mar/ombudsman-cal s-fair-treatment-children-sen/?scmOverrideRecord=22005MDdoQ (Accessed: 31 March 2014).

Mead, A. (2013) Keynote Conference address, Baby Room Conference, July 2013, Canterbury Christ Church University.

Office for Standards in Education (Ofsted) (2012) 'Communication is the key: A good practice survey of services for deaf children. Available at: www.ofsted.gov.uk/resources/communication-key (Accessed: 23 April 2014).

Office for Standards in Education (Ofsted) (2013) 'Unseen children: access and achievement 20 years on'. Available at: www.ofsted.gov.uk/resources/unseen-children-access-and-achievement-20-years (Accessed: 23 October 2013).

Office for Standards in Education (Ofsted) (2013a) 'Evaluation schedule for inspections of registered early years provision'. Available at: www.ofsted.gov.uk/resources/evaluation-schedule-for-inspections-of-registered-early-years-provision (Accessed: 23 October 2013).

Raca, J. (2012) Standing up for James Articles and Letters. Available at: www.standingupforjames.co.uk/33812.html (Accessed: 6 August 2014).

Tickell, D.C. (2011) *The Early Years: Foundations for Life Health and Learning: An Independent Report on the Early Years to Her Majesty's Government:* DfE.

Wall, K. (2011) *Special Needs and Early Years: A Practitioners Guide,* (3rd edn). Thousand Oaks, CA: Sage Publications.

8   The challenge of supporting diverse families

Christine Ritchie

Overview

Supporting children and their families has always been an important aspect of early years childcare and education but changes in family structures and parenting styles provide new challenges: first, in understanding the diverse nature of families and second, in building relationships and guidance to support all families. The aim of this chapter is to assist the practitioner in identifying the range of differences between family structures and to examine some of the pressures felt by families and the possible effect that these may have on educational outcomes for children.

Family structure

Society today no longer relies upon the traditional family set up of husband, wife and two children to function effectively, if at all, so practitioners and teachers over time have had to adjust to changing families within a changing society. There are several academic definitions to explain the constitution of a 'family', but within this chapter the definition of a family is taken to mean a group of people who share a legal or blood bond and usually live in the same household. In some ways, the composition of a family unit should not matter for the education of a child, provided that the family unit is stable and supportive, but research and media views have contributed towards society's thinking and action when dealing with different family groups. Understanding the range of family groupings and how they might influence the child within an educational context should assist those in education in supporting both the child and the family.

Historically, the traditional nuclear family and its sub-groups (e.g. widow and children) has been at the centre of British society and has often been supported by an extended family consisting of siblings, grandparents, aunts, uncles and their offspring. In more recent times different family groupings have emerged with many non-traditional family groupings becoming more acceptable, and in some localities more common than the traditional 'nuclear' family. The Office for National Statistics (OFNS) (2013) groups families with dependent children into three types:

- Married or civil partner couple family (4.7 million)
- Cohabiting couple family (1.8 million)
- Lone parent family (1.9 million).

These statistics show that although there has been a steady increase in cohabiting and lone parent families since 2003, married couple families are still the most common type of family in the UK (OFNS, 2013, p. 7). But statistics like this, however helpful, do not fully represent the range of family structures that a practitioner may encounter in their workplace. It is important to respect all types of family groupings, and also to understand their different issues, needs, strengths and values. Therefore, the three types of families can be further divided:

- Nuclear family: married or cohabiting couple in stable relationship
- Lone parent family: either mother or father raising children alone
- Blended or step-family: made up of members of previous family units
- Co-custody family: parents are divorced/legally separated and share custody of the children
- Adoptive family: where one or more children has been legally adopted
- Foster family: where one or more of the children is a temporary member of the family unit
- Black, Asian or minority ethnic family: may be second or third generation, or a part of a more recent immigrant/migrant group
- Immigrant or migrant family: with a language and cultural background that may/may not be different from the local population
- Single-sex family: either gay or lesbian, and may be part of an adoptive family
- Mixed/multi-racial/inter-ethnic family: parents are members of different ethnic groups
- Transnational family: where the parents and/or children may move regularly between two countries or be separated from each other and live in different parts of the world
- Multi-family households: the data from the 2013 Statistical Bulletin (OFNS) states that this is one of the fastest growing types of household, where two or more families live together.

These family groups could be further divided or combined, demonstrating the complexity of the family structures that contribute to the fabric of UK society. Within these structures lie a variety of attitudes towards parenting, education and gender that affects the child and could contribute towards their future attainment and achievement within education and society. Some of the attitudes are defined by culture and some by other factors, for example, poverty or prejudice. Respecting and understanding the differences in family composition, culture and aspirations and the changing shift away from the traditional nuclear family are an important part of early years practice and support systems, presenting a challenge to early years educators.

Diverse parenting styles

The importance of any child/adult relationship in nurturing development is well established, with the Early Years Foundation Framework (EYFS) 2012 (DfE, 2012) underpinning the care and education of children through assigning each child a key person (DfE, 2012, para 1.11) and establishing 'positive relationships' as one of EYFS's four themes. It is, however, possible that the key person and others in the workplace have a different view of 'parenting' than the parent/carer and this may provoke thinking that becomes critical and disrespectful on both sides. This may produce a subtle wedge between practitioner and parent that affects their relationship and ultimately the child. Undoubtedly, the apparent rise in children who are unable to concentrate, seem to lack basic skills such as naming of colours or counting, who are still in nappies when they start school and who present 'challenging' behaviour is frequently blamed upon a lack of parenting skills, with educators often feeling that they have to do the job of 'parent' as well as being the teacher.

Government sources also recognise that some groups in society are not aware of their responsibilities in terms of 'good' parenting. The 'Unsure Start' speech given by Sir Michael Wilshaw to herald the first Office for Standards in Education (Ofsted) Children's Services and Skills Early Years Annual Report (Ofsted, 2014) declares that some parents from disadvantaged backgrounds do not know how to 'teach' their children basic skills and that advice and support available does not reach them. He proposed that more should be done, and that there should be more accountability placed upon children's centres and nurseries to educate young children and their parents. Wilshaw lists ten minimum requirements for 4 year olds to master as a preparation for school (Wilshaw, 2014 p. 9-10) and outlined a renewed 'baseline' test for literacy and numeracy as children enter the reception class. No doubt there will be debates and arguments about the effectiveness and desirability of such initiatives, but this still reflects upon the lack of 'parenting skills' apparent in some parts of society and the expectation that this can be corrected, and the UK can become like other European countries, where 'A teacher is there to teach. A parent is there to parent' (Harvey, 2014).

Support and advice for parents from a range of sources, from health visitors and other professionals to self-help books, all reflect the view that parenting does not come naturally and is hard work. However, all suppose that all parents can, or want to access such advice and then follow it. How a family raises their children starts with the parents' own experience of parenting, and their view of what was 'negative' or 'positive' about their own upbringing is personal to them, as well as reflecting the community and time in which they were children. There are also two likely polarised reactions from parents being offered support: one being 'it's none of your business how I bring up my children!'; the other, 'I feel too ashamed to admit my problems.' Finding the middle ground can be a challenge!

Research that dominates the parent–child relationship is focused in the work of Diana Baumrind (Baumrind, 1966, 1991) who, in observing the interactions between young children and their parents, described three main types of parenting styles based upon the warmth and control within their relationships. Subsequent research (e.g. Maccoby and Martin, 1983; Darling, 1977) added a fourth dimension usually included in descriptions of parenting styles. The four styles are necessarily generalised, and it is likely that most parents will employ different methods and styles in different situations (see below). Despite this, it is interesting to note that the 'authoritative' style often described as being 'just right' as a parenting style is the style most similar to that used when describing 'high quality teaching and learning'. This could have the effect of making educators consider themselves better than the parents, although once practitioners and teachers have their own children they may come to realise just how different and difficult parenting can be; knowing the 'rules' of good parenting is not sufficient in itself to become a good parent.

The four parenting styles may be described as:

1   **Authoritarian:** this is associated with strict parenting, placing a high demand on children to behave in 'acceptable' ways. The parent style is rigid and harsh, placing importance

on following rules. In some cases this style of parenting may be seen as harsh or abusive, but this is not necessarily always the case.

2   **Permissive or indulgent:** often this is seen as a parent being too 'soft' with children and giving in too easily to their demands. It is categorised by few rules and inconsistent boundaries. Children of such parents are frequently described as being 'spoilt' or 'wild'.

3   **Authoritative**: this is represented by parents who give appropriate, clear and consistent rules to their children to follow. The parenting style is supportive but not overly restrictive, allowing children to respond and become independent members of society.

4   **Uninvolved:** this category has been used to describe parents who are neglectful of their children and unconcerned about their behaviours and development. Parents may make few demands on the children and are unlikely to respond to the needs of the children.

Looking over these parenting styles, you might find it useful to briefly consider what style you consider to be dominant in today's society and compare this to the parenting style that you most favour.

Since the 1960s when these descriptions of styles were first identified by Baumrind (Baumrind, 1966, 1991) society has changed rapidly. The 'swinging 60s' was a time noted for its rise in the permissive society and children born during this period might have had a more permissive upbringing, guided by Dr Spock (Spock, 1946), compared with the children raised in the more authoritarian society up to the 1950s. The changes in society from that time towards the current more tolerant, open society have led to more variation in parenting styles and family structures than in the past. This brings its challenges, as a practitioner may encounter a group of parents with differing views on education; some may want the child to be taught in a rigid and authoritarian way and place a high value on the acquisition of knowledge, while other parents may request a more relaxed and exploration-led education without too many demands being placed upon the child. Other parents may not be interested and contribute little to the education of their child, declining to come to parent/school meetings and not offering support or praise to their child. Balancing out the needs of the parents and ensuring that the developmental and educational demands of the Early Years Foundation Stage (EYFS) curriculum are met for every child can prove taxing at times.

However, the variety of parenting styles should not be considered 'wrong', but rather a choice made by the parent, or deriving from the culture or background of the family group. What might be considered more important are the positive outcomes of parenting, rather than the 'rules', as suggested to parents by the popular author Dr Tanya Byron in her book, *Your Child, Your Way* (Byron, 2008). Some cultural practices within families that lead to a particular parent style are admired and emulated, often resulting from families striving to provide the best future for their children. For example, the publicity surrounding the books by the American 'tiger mother' Amy Chua (Chua, 2011: Chua and Rubenfeld, 2014) brought great controversy, some considering the strict regime of parenting akin to child abuse but others seeing value in hard work and discipline and admiring the high academic attainment that follows. Parental monitoring, where the parent is aware of their child's behaviours and interests and interacts positively with the child, was seen by Bronfenbrenner to be one of the most consistent predictors of positive child development (Darling, 2007 p. 209). Perhaps the intensity of the mother/child relationship and monitoring of behaviour, along with the strong belief in a child's potential as described by Amy Chua may be considered extreme, but it explains, in part, the achievement of her children. Attainment statistics released by the Department of Education (DfE, 2011, 2013, 2014) all show that Chinese pupils are the highest attaining ethnic group in the UK, supporting the view that 'tiger parenting' is a common feature within this ethnic group, with a strong motivation to succeed academically within the culture. The statistics also indicate that other ethnic groups achieve highly, for example, Indian, white and Asian children, while others, notably traveler and Roma children, achieve less academically. This difference in academic achievement is due, in part, to the attitude of parents and the value placed upon education within the different ethnic and community groups. This also appears to be connected to socio-economic status, with 'richer' parents being more involved with their children than those from 'poorer' families. Indeed, it may be argued that the whole idea of 'value' in education is based upon upper/middle class perception, even though most working class/poorer parents value education and have high aspirations for their children (Gorard *et al.*, 2012; Menzies, 2013). Despite the fact that some ethnic groups out-perform others, the DfE statistical release shows that the achievement of all defined groups in society has been raised since 2008/9, with pupils from any black background seeing the largest improvement. It is over-simplistic to credit educational achievement solely upon parenting or economics or indeed, education, but those working within education can perhaps influence future academic performance through offering strong role models and guidance for supporting learning (Sylva *et al.*, 2008; Siraj-Blatchford *et al.*, 2009; Siraj-Blatchford *et al.*, 2010), teaching children how to learn and helping them to acquire new knowledge.

As indicated, children being brought up in families with different parenting styles will themselves have different expectations and attitudes towards education. Gregg and Washbrook (2009) conclude that the aspirations and attitudes of parents vary across socio-economic groups; this not only affects the attitudes, but also the behaviour of children. The 'ideal' child that teachers dream of, who is ready to learn, full of questions and ready to follow 'rules' does exist, but children from a deprived or different cultural background might be more demanding, less likely to conform and follow rules and not be ready to engage in learning. This may be noticeable in one individual or family, but in some areas it may influence a larger group of children. This is reflected in the case study below, illustrating the challenges faced when working in an area of social deprivation:

Case study 1: Part a

I recently moved to a new setting that presents new challenges that are very different from my previous workplace. The new setting is in an area of social deprivation, with many parents out of work and living in some degree of poverty and the children's learning seems affected by an atmosphere of failure. As a new manager I am struck by the differences in achievement and behaviour between my previous setting and this one. Swearing and mild aggression is commonplace amongst the children and creating a calm learning environment seems to be difficult. The whole setting seems to be affected by the area of deprivation, with low staff morale and lack of team spirit.

Challenge

- What challenges are set by the family and community that dominate your setting?
- How do they affect the team and individual members of staff?

The importance of bringing quality early years provision to lift the expectations of staff and parents, and the academic achievement of the children is demonstrated in the follow-up to the story, indicating that one practitioner/leader can make a difference over time. It is also important not to make a judgement about a child's potential ability or intelligence based upon family or community backgrounds, but rather to question attitudes and to improve the quality of teaching and learning.

Case study 1: Part b

I am pleased to say nearly a year on and things are very different. Staff have higher expectations of children and children are encouraged to have an 'I can do attitude'. Parents are warming to the changes and have commented that the atmosphere within the setting is calmer. Parents feel listened to instead of been rushed out of the door. Overall the staff have adopted a more consistent approach when supporting children in following the boundaries and this has resulted in minimal unwanted behaviour. From a manager's perspective it has been a roller coaster ride, however the journey is now slowing down and everything feels much more settled.

Challenge

- How can staff raise expectations and encourage children and adults to have an 'I can do attitude'? What does this mean?

The two parts of case study 1 clearly indicate that practitioners make a positive difference to the educational environment and potential outcomes for children. What makes the 'difference' for young children has been the focus of research, including, among others, the Effective Pre-School and Primary Education (EPPE) 3-11 project (Sylva *et al.*, 2004). The recommendations to improve outcomes for children, such as improving parenting skills and providing quality education, seem sound common sense, but require a quality workforce to put into practice. The three strategies listed in the second part of case study 1 (high expectations, relationship with parents, consistent approach to acceptable behaviour) seem simple enough, but may be underpinned by more subtle strategies and behaviours and confident leadership. Bronfenbrenner (Bronfenbrenner, 1994: Bronfenbrenner and Morris, 1998) emphasises the influence on child development from birth onwards that starts with the mother in the home and radiates out to encompass other people and environments. The child in this process is not passive, but active, and each child will respond differently to the same stimuli. Within Bronfenbrenner's ecological theory, it is the interrelationship of different processes and relationships that helps to determine development. Within this model, the child and others are continually changing; therefore the relationship with an early years practitioner over time can also bring about change in parent, child and even practitioner. Such relationships are described as being a part of 'quality provision' (Sylva *et al.*, 2004; Tickell, 2011) and a confident workforce with highly qualified staff are proving to be strong role models for children and their families. Children respond to the learning environment that they are in, and research indicates that children in high quality provision are more likely to achieve academically than those who do not have a similar learning opportunity (Sylva *et al.*, 2004, 2008; Tickell, 2011; Nutbrown, 2012).

Social learning theory

Understanding of parent-child relationships has also been greatly influenced by the social learning theory following on from Bandura's work (Bandura, 1977). Social learning theory argues that child (and adult) behaviour is modified as the result of both negative and positive reinforcement. The basic belief is that if a child engaged in any activity/behaviour gets an immediate reward (e.g. attention or praise) then the behaviour is repeated, but if the activity/behaviour is ignored or punished then the behaviour is less likely to occur again. The idea that the principles of reinforcement and conditioning determine the behaviour of children in families has also been explored by Gerald Patterson, who established the Oregon Social Learning Center in the USA in 1977. This centre continues to provide research into the social interaction of parents and children concentrating on the traditional theory of 'reinforcement and conditioning' as well as developing systems of positive intervention with children and families (www.oslc.org). It is perhaps easy to see how the use of 'reward and punishment' can influence the behaviour of children, as this has long been a part of school practice. That parents can 'reward' the type of behaviours that may be considered undesirable by education is perhaps an inevitable consequence of some parenting styles and behaviours. For example, parents may not encourage young children to look at books, engage in much intellectual questioning or they may laugh at inappropriate behaviour, thus encouraging a repeat. However, as the two parts of case study 1 show, early years settings and schools can provide role models and strategies that support parents to engage more 'academically' with their children and raise the value of learning.

Attachment and emotional development

Another major feature when considering parenting is the importance of attachment theory, first established by Bowlby and Ainsworth (Bretherton, 1992). Attachment theory is concerned with the emotional bond that develops between parent/carer and child, that sense of warmth that makes a child feel safe and secure. Bronfenbrenner also made it clear that the child requires emotional nurturing as part of the parenting 'package'. The importance of an emotional bond is familiar to practitioners and endorsed by the EYFS (DfE, 2012) within the key person structure, which encourages professional relationships to develop between family, child and practitioner. Although primarily introduced as a safeguarding measure, the key person, while remaining professional, makes an emotional connection with the child and the family. This has the benefit of providing something of a safe haven for the child if the emotional support given by parents is temporarily disrupted, for example, through emotional stress brought on by poverty, relationship breakdown, physical or mental health problems or other events. The child may no longer feel safe and protected if their sense of emotional security is disrupted and this can halt development and learning. The key worker is likely to be the first person to notice signs of emotional deprivation and be able to offer a consistent and stable environment for the child to help reduce some of the feelings of insecurity and also to seek help for both parents and child. Of course, the parent who is unable or unwilling to provide emotional support for their child must be of greater concern, and the subject of much more rigorous investigation than can be explored here.

So, understanding the connections between parenting styles, the emotional bond between parent and child, plus how a child learns to behave in social situations through the reinforcement strategies used by parents, is an important aspect of understanding how a child develops and learns to learn. When one of these 'systems' is broken, the effect on the child can lead to challenging behaviours and/or lack of development and learning. When more than one is broken, then the child will face significant challenges to their development that might produce a long-term effect on their learning and future prospects for health and wealth. Parenting styles can make a difference to the cognitive, social and behavioural development of children (ESRC, 2012), but so can education.

Cultural influences on the family

There are a range of factors that influence the way parents bring up their children, and determine the parenting styles and behaviours adopted by the family. The diverse family groups within British society face many influences, some from established traditional practices, religion and culture, and others from changes in society, such as the acceptance of gay marriage, the rise of the 'working mother' and the multi-cultural, multi-ethnic society that has grown as a result of immigration. Some changes are blamed for the perceived anti-social behaviours of groups within the community, with changes such as the increase in technological devices from television and social media sites being seen as detrimental to family life and a threat to childhood itself (Byron, 2010). And, as in the past, parent and child behaviours are often perceived as being worse than in previous generations. However, when looking at the influences and resulting change in society and family life, it is important to take a balanced view and accept that there are different ways of doing things and absolutes, such as being 'right' or 'wrong', often do not exist.

Religion, for example, has an influence on the family and parenting with wide-ranging benefits or disadvantages, depending upon one's viewpoint. The diverse nature of society in the UK today means that educators will encounter a range of expectations from parents as to how their children should be taught, including those related to the religious beliefs of the parents. This requires sensitivity and understanding on the part of the educator when planning activities and building communication links.

Ethnicity, that is the cultural values, attitudes and behaviours that define a person's idea of 'self' and their membership of a particular group in society (Burton *et al.*, 2008, pp. 4–5), offers a ready-made stereotypical image that could lead to a set of assumptions and expectations being applied to children and families. Ethnic groups, however, are as complex a group to define as family groups; generalities drawn should be tempered with the knowledge that individuals are just that – individuals – regardless of their background. Also, as Burton *et al.* (2008) observe, as any ethnic group becomes integrated into society, the less meaningful the ethnic group identities become (Burton *et al.*, 2008, p. 5). However, cultural background inevitably influences the attitudes and behaviours of parents and these are passed on to children. It is important therefore that practitioners adjust their own understanding of the community they work in so they are able to relate to the needs of the whole family, not just the child, as this case study illustrates:

Case study 2

We had a child from mixed-race parents, who, from the school's perspective, clearly had learning difficulties. The parents' views on his difficulties were at opposite ends of the spectrum. The child had been struggling to read and write over a lengthy period alongside associated difficulties of attention and concentration and possible underlying speech and language difficulties. The white British mother recognised this and was prepared to work with the school staff to support the child in assessment of his needs and the subsequent support needed to help him to progress. However, the Asian father saw his child's problem as one of laziness which working harder and more diligently, including lengthy periods of home tutoring every evening, would rectify. This resulted in the child being too tired to learn next day and struggling more than ever. There was also increasing tension between the parents themselves which made the situation worse. In order to help the child, who was rapidly losing self-esteem and confidence, the school staff needed to build a relationship with the father and enable him to see his child's difficulties from a new perspective. This took time as he was not inclined to come into school, possibly seeing this as the mother's role. Eventually he was encouraged to meet with teachers who built a rapport with him and gradually helped to build his understanding of his child's underlying needs. His culture, values and upbringing was clearly different to ours but this needed to be recognised and managed in school successfully in order for the child to move forward. There was a successful outcome for everyone but especially the child.

Challenge

- How can you ensure that those working with the best interests of the child in mind work together successfully and 'sing the same song'?
- How do you 'educate' parents and carers? What is provided in terms of booklets, handouts and other guidance?

Same-sex parenting and families

One of the family structures that has increased over the past 20 years is that of same sex family grouping (OFNS, 2013). The high-profile gay personalities who have publicly announced the addition of children to their relationships have helped to raise awareness of this desire to expand as families. Society recognises gay and lesbian civil partnership and marriage and more same-sex couples are fulfilling their dream of having children. The difficulties faced once a child is part of the family unit are similar to those of other families; lying in the complexity of close relationships and the interface with others outside of the family. Same-sex parents may face the surprise and possibly censure of other families as they take children to pre-school or school, and although this can be difficult, Case study 3 shows that same-sex parents are being absorbed into normal family groupings with comparative ease.

Case study 3

In the 16 years that I have been working with children and their families in the early years, I have worked closely with some families whose make up has been more contemporary than that of the 'traditional family'. I have worked with single-parent families, families of differing cultures and religions, step-families and same-gendered parents. As a gay female woman who is civil partnered and has two step-children (my partner's biological children), I am familiar with the issues that arise within our family set-up, and therefore felt more prepared to deal with same-gender families. From my own experience it has been at times difficult to come into a well-established one-parent family (my partner and her two children who are now 16 and 17 years old) and be a step-mum, without the added anxieties of sexuality issues.

My partner was extremely nervous to tell her children that she was gay for fear of rejection. As a parent you want your children to love you unconditionally, and she felt breaking this news to them would have an impact on that. At the time the children were 10 and 11, and my partner's biggest fears were how the children's peers would react to this information; if they would be bullied because they had 'two mums' would their friends' parents stop them from coming over to play or have sleepovers, etc. In hindsight we have been amazingly lucky that both children being fairly resilient took the news extremely well, and have grown to accept their family set-up as normal. Now in their mid- to late-teens they share this information freely with their friends and say they are proud of our family. They both have peers who have struggled with their sexualities and are either gay or bisexual and their experiences at home have enabled them to deal with these issues more effectively. As a step-parent, I dealt with the difficulty of coming in and being a 'second mum' to these children. At times it has felt like the three of them and me, but mostly we have grown together with good and bad times and have established ourselves as a family unit. The children were very involved in our civil partnership and without their support and acceptance we would never have been able to make that commitment.

My partner and I are on a new adventure now and are trying to have a baby. I will carry the pregnancy but the child will be ours and will become part of our loving and diverse family. I hope that my experiences of being a biological parent as a gay woman will be the same as any other woman in the world regardless of sexuality, and I hope that our child will grow up in a world where they will not see their family as 'different' or 'diverse' but 'normal' and their experiences of being part of a same-gendered family will enable them to teach others about acceptance and understanding.

In many ways, the case study has similarities to the stories of step-families: of being accepted and building new relationships based upon trust and mutual affection and love. Some step-families initially struggle to bond together, others quickly assume 'normality'. This is just how families are! As far as educational outcomes are concerned, research looking at children raised in a same-sex relationship, although based upon small numbers, indicates high levels of achievement (Potter, 2012; OFNS, 2013). Parents who may have had to work hard to have children through adoption, IVF or surrogacy are likely to be determined, well-educated and want to provide a protective and supportive environment for their children. The parents may already have survived prejudice and so may be able to teach their children to be resilient in the face of adversity, and resilience generally leads to self-confidence and success.

Supporting same-sex parents, therefore, is one of acceptance; adjusting some activities to meet the needs of the family in the same way that settings and schools accommodate events and situations for all families. It involves being a good listener and thinking ahead to ensure equality and good practice prevails. For example, events such as Mother's Day need to be thought through, with changes made to include all parents from all religions and all family structures. This should not mean that some traditional British events should be abandoned, rather they should be adapted to include all children and families. Case study 4 illustrates some of these points:

Case study 4

I have cared for two different children whose families are same-gendered. One mum had a biological child and another couple adopted a child. My own experiences as a gay parent enabled me to understand the issues and concerns they had for their children integrating into the early years setting. Both families recognised that there was a limited amount of recognition for same-gendered families in terms of positive images and stories of same-gendered families in books which can be freely accessed by children in their book corners.

Both families had concerns about events such as Mother's Day and Father's Day, and the impact these events might have on their children. Would they be allowed to make two Mother's Day cards, could they make a grandfather or uncle card on Father's Day, or if they had no male models in their lives would they be offered alternatives in a supportive way? Again these parents were anxious about comments from their children's peers and as a practitioner I have witnessed comments such as 'girls can't marry girls', 'you have to have a mum and a dad', etc., because that is what is 'normal' to those other children. I recognise that there is a great need for children to see and experience different families as they do for other religions and cultures, but I'm also aware that at this young age this needs to be done gently and naturally rather than as something which is 'taught'. Being open, having positive images and stories and challenging stereotypes in the early years setting is an effective way of promoting 'different' types of families so that eventually all types of families will appear 'normal' to all children.

Challenge

- How do you meet the needs of children in similar situations? Do you have access to, and use, storybooks that reflect the diverse nature of families?
- How do you ensure 'equality' for all children and families attending your setting/school?

The case study clearly shows how British society is adapting to encompass the different families that make up that society, and educators have a large part to play in helping communities to embrace diversity. Educational institutions are reflections of society; what happens within them happens outside too. Communities vary across the country, and different communities are made up of clusters of families. Although it is dangerous to generalise, areas of social deprivation may be made up of a large proportion of families out of work and single parent families; inner-city areas may be more multicultural than rural areas: and the South Coast may have more same sex-parents than the north of England. However, in preparing children to grow up in society it is necessary to educate them as part of the composition of the whole of society. Case study 5 suggests doing this 'normally', through stories, images and discussion. To do this successfully, the educator needs to be aware of the different family types that make up their intake, and those that exist in wider society.

The effect of poverty on children and families

This final section considers poverty, something that may affect any family, although the risk of poverty is higher for some groups, including some ethnic groups and those from areas of social deprivation. There is overwhelming evidence that poverty is one of the most destructive elements in education; children living in poverty are less likely to succeed academically compared with their counterparts, offer more challenging behaviours for staff, and are more likely to end up as poor, uneducated adults (Sylva *et al.*, 2004, 2008; Coghlan *et al.*, 2009; Egan *et al.*, 2012; DfE, 2011, 2014; DWP, 2014, 2014a; Ofsted, 2014). While there has always been poverty in the UK, this has increased because of the national economic situation. Poverty has been defined in several ways for example, as 'relative poverty, absolute poverty, persistent poverty, and material deprivation' (Child Poverty Act, 2010, p. 2-3), however, within government and research papers poverty is linked to the number of children who are entitled to free school meals. The statistics show that children eligible for Free School Meals (FSM) perform less well than and make less progress between stages than other groups of pupils (DfE, 2011, 2013, 2014). The current government declares its commitment to 'end poverty by 2020' (DWP, 2014, p. 11) through a range of strategies designed to break the cycle of 'poor children growing up to be poor adults'. The Department of Work and Pensions (DWP, 2014a) examined the drivers of persistent child poverty and acknowledged the parental characteristics that influence a child's educational attainment; these include parental qualifications, the home learning environment and the under-development of a child's non-cognitive skills. The identification of parental characteristics to determine a child's progress and learning are not new; recognition that the 'home is the first school and the parent is the first teacher' and that having an interested parent and book-friendly home life gives children motivation and readiness to learn. Parents who themselves were poorly educated have difficulty knowing how to support child development, and poverty prevents expenditure on books or 'educational' activities. What continues to prove difficult is reaching poorer parents and providing them with the knowledge and skills to help improve the future prospects for their children.

Families in poverty face other difficulties that prevent them from being as supportive as other more affluent or better-educated parents. These difficulties include emotional barriers that bring despair and a sense of hopelessness and can exacerbate non-cognitive skills such as motivation, self-control, aspirations and inter-personal relationships (DWP, 2014a, p. 89). Non-cognitive skills are a pre-requisite for learning, and if not passed on to children, may have a detrimental effect upon their schooling. Considering a child's well-being and engaging in activities that promote non-cognitive skills has become part of everyday practice in education, and can make education more accessible for many children. Other initiatives that support families in poverty have some consensus among government sources and researchers as being able to break the cycle of poverty and make a difference for children. This includes the recognition that high-quality early years provision with well-qualified staff improves the educational chances for all children, but particularly for disadvantaged children. The focus of several research and practice documents, including the EPPE project (Sylvia *et al.*, 2004), the Tickell Report (Tickell, 2011, p. 7) and the Early Years Foundation Stage curriculum (DfE, 2012) all link quality practice to well-qualified staff. Improved training opportunities have followed demands for further qualifications for the workforce (Nutbrown, 2012). The development of the Early Years Foundation Stage Curriculum (DfE, 2012) and Ofsted inspections are aimed at raising standards and improving provision for all, but especially for 'deprived' children. Early years educators are expected to engage in professional training opportunities to increase their own qualifications and level of expertise for what constitutes 'good quality practice' and adopt strategies that support children in poverty to 'close the gap' and succeed academically (Sharples *et al.*, 2011).

In addition to the research findings demonstrating that high-quality provision makes a difference, is the statistical and research data that shows that well-educated parents, particularly mothers, who provide a stimulating home learning environment, raise the academic and economic outcomes for their children (Siraj-Blatchford *et al.*, 2009; Coghlan *et al.*, 2009; Tickell, 2011; DWP, 2014). Therefore, considerable effort to 'educate' parents by government has been tried, all with the aim of improving outcomes for all children. One such initiative was the Sure Start Children Centres, introduced in 2004 amid optimistic promises of improving outcomes for children by providing universal integrated services (DfE, 2013a, p. 3). Improving 'outcomes for young children and their families and reduce inequalities between families in the greatest need ... in parenting aspirations and parenting skills' (House of Commons, 2013, p. 11) remains part of the core purpose of the Sure Start Children's Centres programme, although Sir Michael Wilshaw, speaking in April 2014, said that we cannot rely upon them to actually give children a 'sure start' (Wilshaw, 2014). Sure Start has been criticised for not being cost-effective and for not meeting its primary aims despite being popular with communities, with anecdotal evidence indicating success (House of Commons, 2013, p. 7). The National Evaluation of Sure Start Team (NESS) indicate that while families reported benefits, including engaging in less harsh discipline and providing a more stimulating environment for their children, who are happier as a result, there is no evidence of improved academic outcomes for children at age 7 (DfE, 2012a). This, coupled with the economic climate, has brought about a shift in government thinking, one that still considers a poor home environment as a reason children fail to do well at school, but seeing parental worklessness, low earnings and low parental qualifications as major inhibitors of future success. One solution for improving outcomes for children is now seen to be getting people into work or education (DWP, 2014, 2014a). Spending, therefore, has moved away from children's centres and services, with many being closed or moved to cluster groups (Hopwood and Pharaoh, 2012; Hannon, 2013). Cuts in local spending that impinge upon universal services mean fewer local opportunities to directly intervene and support families, which could potentially create problems for the future. Case study 5 illustrates how practitioners are noticing the changes in services resulting from changes in funding levels and availability of support staff.

Case study 5

Just a few years ago, if we had a child or family that was experiencing difficulties in our nursery setting, for example, with speech or behaviour, we used to be able to phone our local services for advice, and a visit to our setting would be arranged to assess the problem. Often someone would visit that same week and, if necessary, an intervention programme would be put into place. At the very least we would be offered support and guidance. Now we find it so much harder to get help and support; you can phone for help but there is no one to provide the support that we need any more. I undertook training for speech therapy, as I have an interest in this area, but I cannot do as much for children as the professional speech therapist can. Other colleagues have also taken on extra responsibilities and training to support children and families in difficulties, but unless the problem is considered serious, or a safeguarding/welfare issue, there is little out there to help us!

Challenge

- Local cuts in children's services, plus shortages of specialists in some areas, seem to be the result of an 'economic' crisis. Can you identify any such cuts in your local area and comment upon media coverage of cuts and your perception of need?

For practitioners and teachers, regardless of the economics, there is a belief that the home environment makes a difference to the development of the child, so early years settings create strong home/school links to inform parents of ways to support their children (Sharples *et al.*, 2011, p. 3; DfE, 2012, p. 17). The aim behind supporting parents is twofold: first, it offers the opportunity to educate parents, to guide them in creating a more stimulating home environment in tune with education, and second, it helps to create and maintain realistic parental aspirations for their child's future. High aspirations for their children are held by most parents, regardless of socio-economic background (Carter-Wall and Whitfield, 2012; Gorard *et al.*, 2012; Menzies, 2013), and later by children themselves, but, 'the real difficulty for many children was in knowing how to fulfil their ambitions' (Carter-Wall and Whitfield, 2012, p. 4). All parents may have high aspirations for their offspring, but other research shows that children aged 3 years from poor backgrounds already have a noticeable gap in cognitive performance when compared with children from better-off backgrounds (Sharples *et al.*, 2001, p. 8). The early years environment may close this gap, but some children may struggle to catch up lost ground.

The government seems to wish to close this gap by introducing a more rigid curriculum and tougher testing, including the re-introduction of a baseline assessment for Reception-aged children in 2016. As a strategy to improve the chance of success for the poorest children, this could be flawed. Progress that is 'graded' and liable to lead to comparison between children may well dent the aspirations of the parents as well as the children. It may reinforce feelings of failure, rather than celebrate success. It is difficult at this time to see the government providing resources to support children and families who do not meet the baseline standards. Breaking the cycle of underachievement by poorer families and those from disadvantaged groups is likely to continue to be difficut, with educators again in the front line with the ability to 'make a difference'.

Summary and strategies to support families

This chapter has demonstrated some of the complexities related to the family structure and the relationships that contribute towards the academic success or failure of a child within education and the challenges in understanding such complexities for the early years educator. Barriers that inhibit learning are well known, but it is clear that 'quality provision' can ease away some of the barriers and make learning relevant and accessible for all children. The diagram below summarises some of these barriers.

This chapter cannot present the whole picture, of course; other issues can impinge on the outcomes for children, including, for example, child health and disability, housing, extended family, the role of grandparents and gender issues. However, it is clear from the research that strategies used to support children and families under stress benefit all children and families. This is particularly relevant when considering aspects of 'quality provision' and 'good practice'. Key ideas that promote achievement and learning in early childhood include:

- Knowing the community that you are working in; listening to the parents and the children.
- Building strong relationships with parents and encouraging learning activities at home to raise and maintain parental aspirations for children.
- Introducing activities that help children to understand different types of families: e.g. story books, games and discussion.

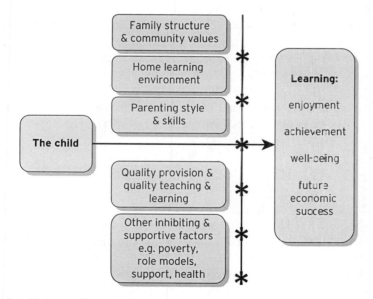

Figure 8.1 Factors that can either inhibit or encourage engagement with learning

- Introducing activities that develop non-cognitive skills (motivation, concentration, self-control, confidence, etc.) as well as those that develop cognitive skills.
- Developing clear teaching objectives to implement in a developmentally appropriate way; that is, remember that young children learn through play, so provide activities that fully engage children in a rich play-based learning environment.
- Being clear about the learning you hope to achieve with children and keeping records of progress to plan the next steps in learning.
- Having high expectations of children and direct support to achieve those expectations for children who are underachieving as quickly as possible.
- Engaging in 'early intervention' strategies as soon as possible and using one-to-one learning strategies with children when appropriate.
- Planning activities that develop social and emotional competences.
- Employing formative assessment methods to ensure that teaching and learning is meaningful and successful.

Recommended reading

1   Although showing its age, the 'Family Diversity Reading Resource: 100+ pictures books to value children's families' from 2005 is a good starting place to identify story books to read with young children. It contains a list of 100 books grouped by family types. It is available as a download from Bishop Grosseteste University College, Lincoln, at: www.bishopg.ac.uk/docs/Research/Family%20Diversity%20Reading%20Resource.pdf.
2   Several organisations produce research and recommend strategies to support children in families from a range of diverse backgrounds. All can be found using simple online search methods and include:

  - Joseph Roundtree Foundation
  - London Centre for Excellence and Outcomes in Children and Young People's Services
  - Family and Parenting Institute
3   A 'quick read' of the literature review below will give you a summary of the findings from seven pieces of research that look into the influence of parenting on child's lives:

Utting, D. (2007) *Parenting and the Different Ways It Can Affect Children's Lives: Research Evidence.* London: Joseph Rountree Foundation. Available at: www.jrf.org.uk/system/files/2132-parenting-literature-reviews.pdf (Accessed: 17 July 2014).

Bibliography

Bandura, A. (1977) 'Self-efficacy: Toward a unifying theory of behavioral change'. *Psychological Review,* 84(2), pp. 191–215.

Baumrind, D. (1966) 'Effects of authoritative parental control on child behaviour', *Child Development,* 37(4), pp. 887–907.

Baumrind, D. (1991) 'The influence of parenting style on adolescent competence and substance use', *Journal of Early Adolescence,* 11(1), pp. 56–95.

Bretherton, I. (1992) 'The origins of attachment theory: John Bowlby and Mary Ainsworth', *Developmental Psychology,* 28(5), pp. 759–75.

Bronfenbrenner, U. (1994) 'Ecological models of human development', in *International Encyclopedia of Education*, Vol. 3 (2nd edn). Oxford: Elsevier.

Bronfenbrenner, U. and Morris, P.A. (1998) 'The ecology of developmental processes' in Damon, W., Lerner, R.M. (Eds) *Handbook of Child Psychology: Vol. 1: Theoretical Models of Human Development*, pp. 993-1028. New York: Wiley.

Burton, J., Nandi, A. and Platt, L. (2008) *Who Are the UK's Minority Ethnic Groups? Issues of Identification and Measurement in a Longitudinal Study*. Essex University, Colchester: Institute for Social & Economic Research/Economic and Social Research Council.

Byron, T. (2007) *Your Child, Your Way*. London: Penguin Books.

Byron, T. (2010) *Do We Have Safer Children in a Digital World? A Review of Progress Since the Byron Review 2008*. Nottingham: DCFS Publications. Available at: http://webarchive.nationalarchives.gov.uk/20130401151715/https://www.education.gov.uk/publications/eOrderingDownload/DCSF-00290-2010.pdf (Accessed: 7 April 2014).

Carter-Wall, C. and Whitfield, G. (2012) *The Role of Aspirations, Attitudes and Eehaviour in Closing the Educational Attainment Gap*. London: Joseph Rowntree Foundation. Available at www.jrf.org.uk/sites/files/jrf/education-achievement-poverty-summary.pdf (Accessed: 10 January 2014).

Child Poverty Act (2010) Available at www.legislation.gov.uk/ukpga/2010/9/pdfs/ukpga_20100009_en.pdf (Accessed: 12 April 2014).

Chua, A. (2011) *The Battle Hymn of the Tiger Mother*. London: Penguin Books.

Chua, A. and Rubenfeld, J. (2014) *The Triple Package*. London: Penguin Books.

Coghlan, M., Bergeron, C.M. White, K., Sharp, C., Morris, M. and Rutt, S. (2009) *Narrowing the Gap in Outcomes for Young Children Through Effective Practices in the Early Years*. London: Centre for Excellence and Outcomes in Children and Young People's Services (C4EO).

Darling, N. (2007) 'Ecological systems theory: The person in the center of the circles', in *Research in Human Development*, 4(3-4), pp. 203-7.

DfE (Department of Education) (2011) *Statistical First Release: National Curriculum Assessments at Key Stage 1 in England, 2011*. Released 29 September 2011. London: Department for Education. Available at: www.gov.uk/government/uploads/system/uploads/attachment_data/file/219034/main_20text_20sfr222011.pdf (Accessed: 17 July 2014.)

DfE (Department of Education) (2012) *Statutory Framework for the Early Years Foundation Stage: Setting the Standards for Learning and Development and Care from Birth to Five*. Nottingham: DfE Publications.

DfE (Department of Education) (2012a) *Research Brief DFE-RB220: The Impact of Sure Start Local Programmes on Seven Year Olds and Their Families:* London: Department for Education. Available at: https://www.gov.uk/government/uploads/system/uploads/attachment_data/file/184073/DFE-RR220.pdf (Accessed: 12 February 2014).

DfE (Department of Education) (2013) *Statistical First Release. National Curriculum Assessments at Key Stage 2 in England, 2013 (Revised)*. Released 12 December 2013. London: Department for Education. Available at www.gov.uk/government/uploads/system/uploads/attachment_data/file/264987/SFR51_2013_KS2_Text.pdf (Accessed: 12 February 2014).

DfE (Department of Education) (2013a) *Sure Start Centres Statutory Guidance; for Local Authorities, Commissioners of Local Health Services and Jobcentre Plus*. London: Department for Education. Available at: www.gov.uk/government/uploads/system/uploads/attachment_data/file/273768/childrens_centre_stat_guidance_april_2013.pdf (Accessed: 12 February 2014).

DfE (Department of Education) (2014) *Statistical First Release: GCSE and Equivalent Attainment by Pupil Characteristics in England 2012/13*. Released 23 January 2014. London: Department for Education. Available at: https://www.gov.uk/government/uploads/system/uploads/attachment_data/file/280689/SFR05_2014_Text_FINAL.pdf (Accessed: 12 February 2014).

DWP (Department of Work and Pensions) (2014) *An Evidence Review of the Drivers of Child Poverty for Families in Poverty Now and for Poor Children Growing Up to Be Poor Adults.* Department for Work and Pensions. Available at: www.gov.uk/government/uploads/system/uploads/attachment_data/file/285389/Cm_8781_Child_Poverty_Evidence_Review_Print.pdf (Accessed: 14 April 2014).

DWP (Department of Work and Pensions) (2014a) *Consultation on the Child Poverty Strategy 2012–2017.* Department for Work and Pensions. Available at: www.gov.uk/government/uploads/system/uploads/attachment_data/file/302911/35696_Cm_8782_accessible.pdf (Accessed: 14 April 2014).

Egan, D. (2013) *Poverty and Low Educational Achievement in Wales: Student, Family and Community Interventions.* London: Joseph Rowntree Foundation.

ESRC (Economic & Social Research Council) (2012) *Evidence Briefing: Parenting Style Influences Child Development and Social Mobility.* Available at: www.esrc.ac.uk/_images/parenting-style-social-mobility_tcm8-20071.pdf (Accessed: 8 October 2013).

Gorard, S., See, B. H., and Davies, P. (2012) *The Impact of Attitudes and Aspirations on Education Attainment and Participation.* York: University of Birmingham and Joseph Rowntree Foundation. Available at: www.jrf.org.uk/sites/files/jrf/education-young-people-parents-full.pdf (Accessed: 16 March 2014).

Gregg, P. and Washbrook, E. (2009) *The Socio-economic Gradient in Child Outcomes: The Role of Attitudes, Behaviours and Beliefs – The Primary School Years: Report for the JRF.* London: Joseph Rowntree Trust. Available at: www.bristol.ac.uk/cmpo/publications/other/jrf.pdf (Accessed: 16 March 2014).

Hannon, C. (Ed.) (2013) Living Precariously: Families in an Age of Austerity. Family and Childcare Trust. Available at http://cdn.basw.co.uk/upload/basw_13700-6.pdf (Accessed: 17 July 2014).

Harvey, G. (2014) 'In France, a parent is a parent and a teacher is a teacher'. *The Telegraph Online* 8 April 2014. Available at: www.telegraph.co.uk/education/expateducation/10745471/In-France-a-parent-is-a-parent-and-a-teacher-is-a-teacher.html (Accessed: 20 April 2014).

Hopwood, O. and Pharaoh, R. (2012) *Families on the Front Line? Local Spending on Children's Services in Austerity.* London: Family & Parenting Institute and ESRO. Available at: www.niace.org.uk/sites/default/files/documents/projects/Family/External_research/FAMILY-AND-PARENTING-INSTITUTE-Local-Spending-on-Childrens-Service-in-Austerity.pdf (Accessed: 16 March 2014).

House of Commons (2013) *Foundation Years: Sure Start Children's Centres; Fifth Report of Session 2013–2014,* Vol. 1. London: The Stationery Office. Available from: www.publications.parliament.uk (Accessed: 14 April 2014).

Maccoby, E. E., and Martin, J. A. (1983) 'Socialization in the context of the family: Parent–child interaction', in P. H. Mussen (Ed.) and E. M. Hetherington (Vol. Ed.), *Handbook of Child Psychology: Vol. 4. Socialization, Personality, and Social Development* (4th edn), pp. 1–101. New York: Wiley.

Menzies, L. (2013) *Educational Aspirations: How English Schools Can Work with Parents to Keep Them on Track.* London: Joseph Rowntree Foundation. Available at: www.jrf.org.uk/sites/files/jrf/england-ecucation-aspirations-summary.pdf (Accessed: 15 April 2014).

Nutbrown, C. (2012) *Foundations for Quality: The Independent Review of Early Education and Childcare Qualifications: Final Report.* Cheshire: Department for Education. Available at: www.gov.uk/government/uploads/system/uploads/attachment_data/file/175463/Nutbrown-Review.pdf (Accessed: 11 July 2014).

OFNS (Office for National Statistics) (2013) *Statistical Bulletin: Families and Households, 2013.* 31 October 2013. Available at: www.ons.gov.uk/ons/rel/family-demography/families-and-households/2013/stb-families.html (Accessed: 10 January 2014).

Ofsted (2014) *The Report of Her Majesty's Chief Inspector of Education, Children's Services and Skills: Early Years, 2012/13.* 3 April, 2014. Available at: www.ofsted.gov.uk/earlyyearsannualreport1213 (Accessed: 10 April 2014).

Potter, D. (2012) 'Same-sex parent families and children's academic achievement', *Journal of Marriage and Family*, 74(3), pp. 556–71.

Sharples, J., Slavin, R., Chambers, B. and Sharp, C. (2011) *Effective Classroom Strategies for Closing the Gap in Educational Achievement for Children and Young People Living in Poverty, Including White Working-Class Boys.* London: Centre for Excellence and Outcomes in Children and Young People's Services.

Siraj-Blatchford, I. and Siraj-Blatchford, J. (2009) *Improving Children's Attainment Through a Better Quality of Family-based Support for Early Learning.* London: Centre for Excellence and Outcomes in Children and Young People's Services (C4EO).

Siraj-Blatchford, I., Mayo, A., Melhuish, E., Taggart, B., Sammons, P. and Sylva, K. (2010) *Performing Against the Odds: Developmental Trajectories of Children in the EPPSE 3–16 Study.* London: Department for Education.

Spock, B. (1946) *The Common Sense Book of Baby and Child Care.* New York: Duell, Sloan & Pearce.

Sylva, K., Melhuish, E., Sammons, P., Siraj-Blatchford, I. and Taggart, B. (2004) *The Effective Provision of Pre-School Education (EPPE) Project: Final Report.* London: DfEE/Institute of Education, University of London.

Sylva, K., Melhuish, E., Sammons, P., Siraj-Blatchford, I. and Taggart, B. (2008) *The Effective Provision of Pre-School Education 3–11 Project: Final Report from the Primary Phase: Pre-school, School and Family Influences on Children's Development during Key Stage 2 (age 7–11)*, Research Report DCSF-RR061. London: DfEE/Institute of Education, University of London.

Tickell, C. (2011) *The Early Years: Foundations for Life, Health and Learning. An Independent Report on the Early Years Foundation Stage to Her Majesty's Government.* London: DfE. Available at: www.educationengland.org.uk/documents/pdfs/2011-tickell-report-eyfs.pdf (Accessed: 7 January 2014).

Wilshaw, M. (2014) *Unsure Start: HMCI's Early Years Annual Report 2012/13 speech.* 3rd April 2014, Church House, Westminster. Office for Standards in Education, Children's Services and Skills (Ofsted). Available at: www.ofsted.gov.uk/sites/default/files/documents/about-ofsted/speeches/Earlyper cent20Yearsper cent20Annualper cent20Reportper cent201213per cent20-per cent20Unsureper cent20startper cent20-per cent20HMCIper cent20speech.pdf (Accessed: 6 April 2014).

9   Taking risks: living with danger – the benefits and safeguards

Linda Flower and Christine Ritchie

Overview

Considering the benefits of taking a risk within an educational framework is often challenging and can contribute to the stress felt by adults working with children. This chapter explores the worries raised by a group of educators and considers some of the background issues to their concerns. It highlights a 'common-sense' approach to risk that considers the benefits for children who are allowed to engage in risk-taking activities while emphasising the importance of dealing with any significant risk to children's well-being and safety. The need to protect and safeguard children is established as a 'non-negotiable' part of early years practice, and some of the problems associated with rising poverty are explored. The case studies used to illustrate this chapter have been collected from focus groups across Kent, comprising practitioners, teachers and students.

Introduction

It seems that modern life and education are both under constant threat from a range of sources, ranging from too many addictive computer games and inappropriate access to media to lack of safe play areas in the community and from poor parenting and education to those intent on bringing harm to children. Sorting out the very real risks and the perceived risks in children's lives seems to have become a major occupation of parents, educators and society to the extent that they feel that any 'risk' in the care of children is to be avoided. This leads to situations where children become less confident in their own judgements, less independent and more 'helpless', and may conversely make children more vulnerable in risky situations because they lack the experience and confidence in how to respond. Generally, adults may hope that children are never put in a risky situation, but at the same time it is accepted that children often 'learn by doing' rather than by being told. There are many undesirable activities that we do not want children to 'learn by doing', but children who are confident and able to act independently and say 'no' when necessary are safer than those who have always relied on others and adults to make decisions for them.

Identifying types/levels of risk for both children and adults

When considering the risks facing children it is impossible to also deny that these are linked closely with risks that the adult faces, particularly in a care or educational setting.

Once, it seemed that those 'teaching' children only needed to concern themselves with the content and manner of 'teaching'. Now, adults working with children within education have a much greater responsibility and expectation for the all-round care, well-being, safety and development of children. This is clearly indicated in successive government initiatives, including the five universal ambitions from 'Every Child Matters' (National Archives, 2014) 'to be healthy, be safe, enjoy and achieve, make a positive contribution and achieve economic wellbeing'. Although these five outcomes were intended to be the joint responsibility of all agencies working for children this has been somewhat lost in the coalition government rhetoric since 2010, but the outcomes still remain embedded in the practice of education today. Wide-sweeping aims such as these, alongside the teaching needs of the curriculum, may also contribute to the stress felt by the workforce as they strive to provide education, care and sometimes counselling to all children and parents/carers. It could be argued that staff adjusted to the demands placed upon them by taking a 'safe' approach, covering with care what seemed to be necessary, and putting to one side the activities that felt extraneous. This awareness that educators have weighty responsibilities has a down-side that often results in a risk-avoidance attitude, which at its worst, significantly limits the opportunities provided for children and thereby effects their development. The voices of those in a case study discussion group conducted September 2013 expressed a range of issues and situations that prevented them from engaging in some activities, including:

- Teachers now are far more aware of 'risk-taking' – it's in the forefront of their minds.
- Risk of court proceedings – suing culture. We have to limit children's experiences by having more rules so that we are not risking teachers' careers.
- School governors are always around the place checking health and safety – it makes me panic and stops me offering experiences that I might otherwise feel valuable.
- Press/media make parents over-aware of risk. Parents are frightened of letting their children do things they did readily in the past (e.g. children can't ride scooters now – never having been allowed to learn in case they hurt themselves; snowball throwing; conkers; climbing trees; just 'playing outside').
- We talk a lot about Baby P and similar sad stories – we don't want to be named and shamed. We are really anxious about child protection issues and so we fill in green forms (CP forms used in school) at the slightest issue – we are covering our backs. We have to as we have a huge responsibility and we can't mess up.
- Talking about children with a high level of need – what do you do? It stops us doing things (especially outside visits) as it would be unsafe or cause too many problems. Do we 'include' or 'exclude'? We can't exclude so we don't do it. Taking lots of extra adults would help but that costs money.

These risks, whether perceived or real, indicate the challenge to staff who want to do more for the children and the creeping nature of a risk-avoidance culture. Changing attitudes and actions in such a culture, where everyone seems frightened of making even the slightest mistake is difficult, but there is a move towards taking a more proactive and common-sense approach to risk-taking opportunities that is supported by government and many experts in child development, as illustrated by four points in the list on page 156. However, case study 1 reveals the stress felt by staff organising a visit, even if the effort is worth it:

Case study 1: The welly walk

In our team planning we were all very excited in coming up with the idea of taking the children on a 'welly walk'. We had a local volunteer group contact us asking if our children would like to take part in a project they had put together where children would have the opportunity to visit a local nature reserve. It was in fact across the road from the school; therefore we felt it would be a great opportunity for our children to take part in.

We sent a letter out to parents informing them and asking for helpers to help us with our small trip. This was the first out of school trip I had organised and I was naively unaware of what I was signing myself up for. The whole process from then on was, in my opinion, less than enjoyable. I had to ask each helper to fill in a form at the office to enable them to be CRB-checked before the date we went. I did my best to cobble together a risk assessment where I had to visit the site myself and then answer a series of questions about the level of hazards I felt there might be. After filling in this form, I sent it to the office to be checked and signed off. They then informed me that because one of the children in one of the classes would need to take a wheelchair, I needed to fill in a separate risk assessment form for this child. This I did, answering similar questions about the levels of dangers, etc. I then sorted all of the first aid kits out so that members of staff would have resources available should there be any accidents. I wrote all phone numbers on a generic sheet so that, in case of any accidents, we could all contact each other. I sat with the children and talked about the dangers we may face and how the children would need to behave on this trip in order to remain safe. The office then contacted me for a third time informing me that because a member of staff was pregnant I needed to fill out a third risk assessment for this trip. Again I answered similar questions, handing this in to be signed. Copies of all three risks assessments were made so that all members of staff could be briefed and made aware of how to keep their classes out of any harm. I wrote up a list of safety measures for all parent-helpers, detailing what to do in the case of an emergency and how to keep the children in their groups safe.

By this point I was completely worn out. I had thought about the risks so much that actually I really didn't even feel like going anymore. I had filled out so many pieces of paper that it had now become more of an onerous task rather than the initial fun trip out to experience local nature. I felt drained, and my excitement for the trip was now no longer there.

The morning of the trip arrived and the children were extremely happy, looking forward to going out for the morning. A parent grabbed hold of my arm and asked, 'You will keep my baby safe won't you?' I sighed inside at this lack of trust I was feeling from the parent and took the time to reassure her. Another parent provided me with a wrist strap for their child (this child had speech problems but as far I was concerned this child never showed me any signs of running away), and spoke to me at length about their child's tendencies to run into roads. I took the strap and rearranged the groups so that I could have this child with me.

We finally set off and walked out of the school gates, across the road and arrived at our destination. The children explored the nature area and had the best time collecting bugs carefully and drawing the plants they could see. The children had the most wonderful time and we gained so much from our trip with the drawings, the talk it generated and the write ups. It made it really worth it. However, I did go home feeling drained and stressed after the events leading up to the trip, and I have to admit I didn't feel like organising another one again . . . although of course I did . . .

To encourage more outdoor visits, the policy paper, 'Common Sense, Common Safety' (Cabinet Office, 2010) not only recommended a simplified risk assessment and process for school trips and for classrooms but also suggested 'a shift from a system of risk assessment to a system of risk-benefit assessment'. The template risk benefit assessment tools to download from the Department of Education and the Health and Safety Executive websites demonstrate how the government is trying to minimise paperwork and improve clarity. However, many staff continue to complete full, written risk assessments for any 'risky' activity to provide evidence of care for parents or other questioning groups. This goes against the trend of simplifying paperwork that was recommended in the Tickell Report (2011) and included in the Statutory Framework for the Early Years Foundation Stage (EYFS) (DfE, 2014a), which suggests that 'providers must determine where it is helpful to make some written risk assessments' (DfE 2014a, para. 3.64, p. 28), indicating that not all risk assessments should be paper-based, and goes on to state that for outings, 'the risk assessment does not necessarily need to be in writing' (DfE, 2014a, para. 3.65 p. 29). This is in line with Department of Education's response to the 'Common Sense, Common Safety 2010' report (Cabinet Office, 2010), which recognised how an undue amount of bureaucracy can stifle school activities, especially outside visits, stressing the unlikelihood of legal action if despite all the care that a teacher may take something goes wrong. The report recognised that there was a fear of litigation, recommending the need to clarify and simplify risk assessment. This has been put in place: The latest Health and Safety advice on legal duties and powers makes these key points:

- Children should be able to experience a wide range of activities. Health and safety measures should help them to do this safely, not stop them.
- It is important that children learn to understand and manage the risks that are a normal part of life.
- Common sense should be used in assessing and managing the risks of any activity. Health and safety procedures should always be proportionate to the risks of an activity.
- Staff should be given the training they need so they can keep themselves and children safe and manage risks effectively.

DfE (2014, p. 4)

These points all indicate a strong sense of shared responsibility towards risk-taking that also includes children, an approach that has been adopted by many schools. The guidance is encouraging, but some staff do not feel confident in taking measured risks, as case study members explain:

- Use of large apparatus for PE – staff feel that they are actively encouraged not to use the large apparatus because of health and safety issues that could arise, i.e. children falling off, whether to put mats underneath or not. When asked if this was official they felt it wasn't but nobody uses apparatus because of the 'risk' involved – it's easier and safer not to use it. This is also linked to the 'time' it takes to get out apparatus and put away again – children need to be in the classroom learning and achieving – they are missing 'learning time'.

- Greater parent awareness (and at times over-awareness) of off-site visits, e.g. visit to local fire station and hazards that might be met on way; walk to local church (a distance of just over half a mile) – many parents felt it was too far for their children to walk which led to the visit being cancelled. A 'welly walk' caused all sorts of similar issues (see case study 1 on page 155).
- Cooking is great for the children but allergies, use of potentially risky equipment all cause worries, e.g. do I let them chop or not chop – should they be allowed to use a knife?
- As a young NQT I am frightened to use/put out small items (e.g. seeds, buttons, marbles): 'How much risk do I take? I need to keep the parents happy and balance this with giving children a range of experiences.'
- I used to keep children in (as opposed to outdoor play) because I was too scared. I now feel that knowing the class helps and I have increased in confidence with experience. I also feel that parents trust me more as an 'older' teacher.

All indicate that perceptions of risk between politicians, parents and the workforce vary considerably. However, weighing up the potential risk in any environment or activity and the possible benefits for risk-takers for both children and adults may be problematic, but well thought out health and safety policies and risk-management guidance can highlight essential points so that a decision can be made as to whether a risk is worth taking or not. Workplace policy, together with official guidance (e.g. HSE, 2011, 2011a) will be a starting point for making decisions. It might help to classify risks into three categories: minor, moderate or significant, and then decisions taken as to whether to proceed, or not, with an activity.

Identifying the category of risk is part of an individual's 'common sense' but within education it is also part of policy and practice and relies on strong teamwork and communication in liaison with leadership teams. By working together, both experienced and inexperienced staff can grow in confidence and improve their judgements in risk management. An ongoing

Table 9.1 Classifying risks

	Minor risk	Moderate risk	Significant risk
Identifying the risk	Unlikely to cause long-term problems	Risk worth accepting	Risk that needs careful planning and consideration before going ahead
Managing the risk	Just do it!	Complete risk assessment and proceed with care	Involve others in decision making, follow policy guidance and practice, identify roles and responsibilities
Monitoring the risk	Observe and adjust as necessary	Monitor with care and adjust if necessary	Take care with supervision; monitor and record feedback

pattern of training should be provided by the workplace (DfE, 2014: DfE, 2014a), and children should also be encouraged to be part of the risk-assessment process where appropriate.

Risk faced by children

The risks that children face in society as a whole can be classified as (a) risks arising from everyday experiences and living and (b) risks that no child should face, that is, the harm associated with all forms of abuse. The type of risk faced by children in the workplace is of the first kind, although wide-ranging, as it is in real life! Risks are also relative; what might be a serious risk to one child might be a minor risk to another, depending upon age, experience and the environment. When categorising risk, even those considered to be 'minor' will therefore require appropriate, adequate supervision, and this becomes the responsibility of all staff. Risk-taking might be temporary or permanent in outcome or can change as any activity progresses, further illustrating how the continued management and monitoring of any situation or activity is important. The types of risk faced by children in early years settings fall into four main categories, and may depend upon the environment, buildings and staff:

Table 9.2 Types of risk a child may face in an educational setting

What?	Cause?
Accident	from equipment, classroom layout, poorly supervised activity, action of others, playground activities
General health	unknown allergies, lack of understanding of a health issue (e.g. asthma, epilepsy), spread of disease, accident
Emotional stress	bullying, intimidation from other child/adult, fear of failure, unrealistic expectations by parents/adults, unable to relate to peers or make friends, inadequate adult support in stressful situations
Development	poor teaching, lack of appropriate resources or support, lack of opportunities to develop via risk-taking activities, over reliance on adult support, beginning a 'learned helplessness' approach to life

- When considering the level of risk, which of the risks in Table 9.2 might be minor, moderate or significant?

Risk faced by adults

The adult too, in the educational world faces risk, and both the organisation and the individual have responsibilities to ensure that any workplace risks are considered and managed as 'far as reasonably practical' (HSE, 2014, p. 12). Although there may be several risk factors within an educational workplace (see Table 9.3), indicators point towards stress as being an outcome of considering risk management itself, which may be relieved by better management (HSE, 2007, p. 11). Shin and Liberzon (2010) demonstrate how fear and anxiety lead to stress, a condition that is 'extremely common', that in turn affects not only the individual, but is also associated with 'impaired workplace performance' (Shin and Liberzon, 2010, p. 169). It is reasonable to assume therefore, that teachers under stress may not provide the best learning conditions for the children in their care, and may pass on their fears and anxiety to the children and parents/carers and so create a cycle of stress, even if this is unintentional. Understanding the benefits of risk, feeling supported through training and practice and teamwork may alleviate some of the stress associated with risk management in both adults and children.

Health and Safety and risk analysis; school policy and personal responsibility

There is little doubt of the importance of team and individual responsibility in being aware of the risks connected with any activity and of any policy in place in minimising the risk involved. It would be of little comfort after any mischance to say, 'Well, I believed that was X's responsibility, not mine.' Risk assessment or risk-benefit assessment becomes the duty of all and the monitoring of safety is the concern of all staff at all times under the leadership of the head teacher or setting manager. Completing risk assessment forms, however, does not remove all the anxiety felt by staff:

- Completing risk assessment forms – we 'get grief' if we haven't filled them in quickly enough. They take so much time to complete and are so detailed now – you have to think of everything – but we haven't been trained in completing them. We need it to make sure we are doing them properly – due to possibility of being sued if we get it wrong or miss something.
- If you miss an 'issue' you constantly feel you are on dodgy ground.

Table 9.3 Types of risk an adult may face in an educational setting

What?	Cause?
Accident & general health	from equipment (e.g. too low furniture, lifting, poorly maintained flooring, asbestos), classroom layout & design, actions of others, ill health
Emotional stress	bullying, intimidation/harassment, fear of failure, unrealistic expectations of SMT, new initiatives to implement, Ofsted, 'pushy' or over anxious parents, ill health
Development	lack of appropriate training, resources or support
Legal/job loss	poor teaching, not following policy & practice guidelines, parents complain or sue, issues of unfair dismissal

- Adult/child ratio – there are so many unpredictable children – you need to feel you have others to support you or to be witnesses. Sometimes we don't feel safe.
- Children help in the writing of risk assessments now at the school but we are still in the process or learning how this can be made more effective.

These comments suggest that the word 'risk' has more power to prohibit an activity than the perceived 'benefit'. Clear policies, procedures and training should go some way towards reducing such feelings of stress and risk-anxiety, as advocated by recent government policy and guidance.

Risk-taking vs. risk avoidance: benefits of risk-taking for children

It seems clear that the word 'risk' is associated with stress, even danger, for both staff and children, but many researchers and writers, including government departments (HSE, 2012) suggest that linking 'risk' with 'benefit' is one way to change attitudes and behaviours and move away from a risk-avoidance culture. In 'Common Sense, Common Safety' (Cabinet Office, 2010) it was made clear that benefits gained by activities should take precedence. Benefits gained by risk-taking can be also be found in the abundant literature on this subject (Tovey, 2007; Ungar, 2007; Lester and Russell, 2008, 2013; Guldberg, 2009; Lindon, 2011; Waite, 2011; Gill, 2012; Ball *et al.*, 2013) suggesting taking risks includes:

- an increase in confidence, self-efficacy and resilience;
- enhanced learning with greater achievement;
- children who are more likely to engage in new experiences and new challenges in the future;
- development of social and emotional skills that may reduce chances of poor mental health in the future;
- a greater awareness and understanding of risk; and
- improved physical health; less obesity and better general health.

The literature makes it clear that allowing children to take some risks in their everyday activities has long-term benefits. Some research relates to studies of older children and young people, but building attitude towards taking a risk can begin at an early age, helping a child feel more optimistic and avoiding feelings of helplessness (Seligman, 1990, 1995). The 'risk' taken might be emotional, as in whether to share toys or a game with a new playmate, or it might be physical, such as balancing on stepping stones, but each new challenge a child decides to take for themselves builds confidence and skill. Those working with children can support their decision-making in positive ways, particularly in the language and tone of voice that might be used. Adults who frequently say, 'Be careful!' and 'Don't do that!' may give the impression that risk is always to be avoided. Alternatively, the adult who offers guidance and support and says, 'Well done, you took care!' and calmly accepts that sometimes minor things go wrong, is more likely to encourage a safe and positive attitude towards risk.

Some risks are worth taking as they enhance learning, such as the example given in case study 2, 'The great fire of London'. This indicates how a group approach can enable staff and children to engage in a 'risky' activity together. The activity highlights how the children's motivation and concentration developed and was sustained by the anticipation of the risk added to the activity, followed by the long-remembered historical facts that were part of the objective for learning. The case study also illustrates the risk felt by the staff and the anxiety and excitement generated as a result. Both children and adults appear to have experienced similar feelings and it could be presumed that there were as many benefits for the adults as for the children: increased motivation and concentration plus enhanced memory of the event. Sustaining such strong shared learning experiences during day-to-day activities may not only enhance learning, but may also build feelings of confidence and trust.

The Forest School movement (Massey, 2005) along with the learning approach established by Reggio Emilia (Edwards *et al.*, 1998) have both promoted the idea of children being independent learners with decision-making capabilities that offer some degree of risk. For example, the Forest School experience offers camp fire activities as a core part of their philosophy and the Reggio Emilia approach gives children time to follow and explore their own interests. Children are taught the rules that are essential to safety but not denied the opportunity to experience risk, albeit within a safe environment and under appropriate supervision. As the children come to understand the inherent dangers associated with an activity they are able to make their own risk judgements and also to share the experience with others.

Case study 2: The great fire of London

This case study example indicates that taking a calculated risk benefits learning. It demonstrates the worried thinking prior to taking on the risk but also the excitement for both the adults and children when engaging in something unusual and potentially threatening.

In PPA we had an exciting idea that we would get the children to build 'London' and then we would have our very own great fire of London in school! We sat in our planning meeting all shrieking at the possible idea: 'Can we really do this?' 'Are we going to be allowed?' 'Will the parents mind?' We debated these questions, but there was something inside me that really wanted to venture out and do this for the children. 'It will be FUN!!!!!', I remember saying. We discussed it with our deputy head and she seemed to agree with the idea. This made it all the more exciting as we realised it could actually happen. She helped us follow the relevant procedures in carrying out the correct safety measures and completing the correct risk assessments. I commented, 'Do we need the fire brigade here?', actually worrying a little about what we were going to do. She reassured me it was going to be OK and this not your 'usual day' idea really sent a real buzz through the team. We were excited. We communicated the idea with the children and they shrieked and gasped and shouted 'YES!!!'. I couldn't wait and nor could they. We worked as a class to recreate the houses, talking about what they would have looked liked and what they were really made out of back then. We recreated London Bridge and St Paul's Cathedral. We even made road signs drawing on the knowledge we now had about the event. The children wanted to make a baker's shop so that we could start the fire there. The build-up was incredible, and all children and staff were so engaged with this project.

The day finally came when we were to have the fire. We invited a few extra members of staff outside to help us, one with a fire extinguisher. One member of staff suggested a bucket of water and some metal sheets to help contain the fire. Children all stood well back and we waited and watched while the fire was started. It was a windy day; the fire went up quite quickly and the children screamed and gasped in complete amazement. They shouted 'Wow!', and some put their hands over their mouths in complete shock. I videoed their reactions, and to watch it back makes me tearful. Those children were so amazed. They jumped up and down in excitement. Yes, there was a moment when the wind picked up and the fire went quite high and we all thought, 'Oops!! Is this going to be OK?' But it was, and all children were safe and we had it all under control.

The impact that had on their learning was astonishing. They wrote up pages and pages about what had happened. They spoke about what had happened and now had a true understanding of the historical event. Those children will never forget that and, as staff, nor will we. Sometimes daring to do something a little dangerous with the children can have such a positive impact on their learning. Of course, safety is key and those children were safe, but having the confidence to step out and do something like that can be extremely rewarding. I am so glad my deputy head said, 'Yes, do it!' We showed the footage to the parents in our sharing assembly and parents cried at the reaction their children had had on that day in their learning. I felt so proud we had dared to do it.

However, as the case study group reported, parenting concerns related to perceived dangers within present society and the modern environment have influenced educational practice. Some parents are opposed to their children taking risks, particularly in activities associated with outdoor play or off-site visits. Many children spend more time in 'safe' activities (see Palmer, 2006) within the home than in the past and as a result may be less able to estimate the level of risks encountered in the wider community:

- The older teacher said that children do not get the same experiences nowadays because parents are too frightened to allow them to play outside and this prevents them learning things that they would have done in the past – an example was learning/knowing that brambles can hurt you – if you don't 'play out' you don't learn such things. She felt it is the way society is now – stay indoors it's safer. Her colleagues agreed.
- Keeping children clean is an issue – at least a third of the current parents don't like them getting muddy. This has become more of an issue as years have gone by. The parents say that they like the outside play area (it is highlighted when the parents choose the school) but some are not keen on the children getting dirty. Comments have included 'it is the third jumper I've had to wash this week.' It has even been commented on during Ofsted inspection – parents have complained about it.
- Across the range of parents some are very over-protective at this stage of children's school life (Reception) – they seem to calm down a bit by Year 1 or 2. We have to build trust in Year R.

This results in children who are less able to safely engage in risk-taking activities and adults feeling more apprehensive about giving children the freedom to do so as the children are more accident-prone, or more likely to engage in risky behaviours, when they cannot accurately judge the risk for themselves.

Resisting the urge to keep children too safe and helping parents to understand the importance of risk-taking as part of becoming independent and safe is an important part of children's education. As well as supporting parents to understand the need for children to become independent is the desire to help them to understand the benefits of risk for the future. One of the many benefits of providing 'healthy' risk opportunities throughout childhood is that older children may be less likely to engage in more risky behaviours because they are bored and unchallenged (Ungar, 2007). Young people growing up often search for something that gives a sense of danger or personal responsibility to move away from adult control. This is usually associated with early teenage years, but children of all ages can at times reject the 'safe option' and take the challenge offered by a more exciting alternative that could lead to real danger. Giving children responsibility for any age-appropriate risk-taking activity will build their sense of personal control and offer experiences so that they can learn and estimate future risks. Lester and Russell (2013) make the point that there are times when adults should allow growing children 'time and space' to be on their own and not always be closely observed by an adult. This may not apply to very young children, but there are times when the adult needs to step back and allow children the freedom to make their own decisions. Lindon (2011) recognises that assessing risk starts in the early years and lasts throughout childhood into adulthood. The Heath and Safety Executive (HSE, 2012) offers this practical key message:

> Play is great for children's well-being and development. When planning and providing play opportunities, the goal is not to eliminate risk, but to weigh up the risks and benefits. No child will learn about risk if they are wrapped in cotton wool.
>
> HSE, 2012, para. 5

The presumption here is that if children are allowed to take acceptable risks, there will be consequences; these may be immediate resulting in some hurt, but the long-term benefits outweigh the short-term cost. The idea here is perhaps comparable with a child learning to walk; they may fall over, but the adult encourages the child to attempt more steps rather than stop the child from trying. The point here also is that the urge to engage in the risky pursuit of walking comes from the child, not the adult.

The goal of providing more freedom to engage in some type of risky play is endorsed by the Play Safety Forum (PSF) along with researchers and experts (Thom *et al.*, 2007; Tovey, 2007; Lester and Russell, 2008; Guldberg, 2009; Play England, 2011). It is up to practitioners and teachers to assess the risk and to ensure there is an appropriate balance between the level of risk and adequate supervision.

However, teaching all children how to be safe is not without problems for the practitioner, as this comment shows:

- Greater 'inclusion' of children with greater and more complex needs (including low levels of understanding) means that teaching children to keep themselves safe (part of EY curriculum) is harder to cover and achieve. This means that children who understand about how to keep themselves safe are subjected to staff constantly going over the same ground for the sake of those less able to understand it. It takes a huge amount of teacher time and is constantly in the teachers' minds as under-pinning everything else that goes on.

So perhaps there is a need to work out how to focus teaching and supervision in a more individualised way to meet the needs of all children as well as considering what might be a differentiated risk for different groups of children.

Building resilience in young children

Among the many benefits of taking a risk is the idea that succeeding in a risk situation or activity builds resilience. Resilience as a concept has complex definitions (Liebenberg and Ungar, 2009 p. 6; LeBuffe *et al.*, 2013 p. 242), but here resilience is taken to mean an ability to recover from adversity or failure and find the strength to carry on and have another go. In many ways, resilience could be considered a partner to risk, one that is more outgoing and positive, rather than inward looking and negative. Whether children grow up to be resilient or not, relies upon many factors primarily linked to three attributes:

- the individual
- the family
- and the educational/ community influences

and the interaction between these attributes (Masten, 2014). Research into parent's attitudes indicates that the language of resilience and emotional well-being is expressed in terms of social skills and confidence, as well as the ability to bounce back and school readiness (Gosling and Khor, 2008, p. 1). Such attributes are often described as being part of the main purpose of early years education, and weave through all aspects of care and education. Early years settings and government initiatives are often credited with supporting the family in the bringing up of children, resulting in greater levels of academic and social attainment that can provide a route to future economic and personal success (e.g. Best Start Resource Centre, 2012). The importance of quality teaching and learning within the early years in binding the individual and the family to education is crucial to the success of such initiatives (Sylva *et al.*, 2004, 2008). This includes promoting resilience, which is embedded within the four guiding principles of the EYFS (DfE, 2014a, p. 6) and in Dame Clare Tickell's opening response to her 2011 report:

> A child's future choices, attainment, wellbeing, happiness and *resilience* are profoundly affected by the quality of the guidance, love and care they receive during these first years.
>
> Tickell, 2011, p. 2

Encouraging and developing resilience in children starts with the relationship developed between adult and child, which is why the key person/child/family connection is important. The quality of the interaction between the adult and the child in building resilience is illustrated by these key dealings:

- by offering choices so the child experiences control (would you like apple or banana?);
- giving responsibilities to the child by encouraging small tasks (could you put the book away?);
- by identifying competence for the child (well done, you remembered to walk round Peter so you did not upset his play – you are thinking about others);
- and by encouraging some risk in play (well done, today you held on carefully and you climbed up the slide by yourself!).

Interactions that provide choice for the child demonstrate to the child that they are important and that their views matter. Showing that a child is trusted to 'do the right thing' and giving them opportunities to experience this brings about feelings of trust within the child in their own capabilities. Sometimes taking the child beyond their comfort zone to gain experience in other areas will help them to feel successful, boost their confidence f successful, and build confidence and resilience further. There are times when we all need to stretch ourselves just a bit further!

Safeguarding and protection issues

The risks faced by children that have been considered so far in this chapter relate generally to everyday activities presented as part of a rich learning environment. There has been an assumption that the educational setting is safe and the adults working within the setting pose no threat. However, safeguarding and welfare requirements demand that staff are vigilant in the workplace, focusing upon protecting children's safety and well-being by ensuring that equipment and the environment remain safe, that staff behave appropriately and that policies and records are efficient and effective (Tickell, 2011, p. 37). As Tickell (2011, p. 6) writes, 'Keeping children safe is ... a non-negotiable element of any early years framework.' In addition, there is the requirement that all staff working in early years settings are trained to recognise behaviours that might indicate abuse or neglect that would warrant further enquiry (Tickell, 2011, pp. 37–8; DfE, 2014, pp. 20–1). Statutory guidance makes the point that for children who need help and support, 'every day matters' and that professionals should share appropriate information with colleagues and the local authority children's social care team so that decisions and action can be taken at the earliest opportunity (DfE, 2014b, pp. 3–10). This requires staff to be 'on the ball', keenly observant, good listeners and with up-to-date child protection training. Robust record keeping and communication between the designated person responsible for safeguarding, practitioners, and relevant agencies, are also vital components of good practice. Although few in number, at serious case reviews considering the death of a child from abuse, it is often reported that signs of abuse had been observed without their significance being fully understood. For example, the Serious Case Review into the death of Daniel Pelka (Lock, 2013) noted that the school had observed minor injuries and loss of weight but believed the mother's explanation of medical problems. The review makes it clear that if these had been formally recorded and a child protection referral made, it is possible that a different course of action might have been taken by linking together evidence from other sources. The review notes that raising concerns frequently within an organisation might not be enough, and states, 'this may have led staff members into a false sense of security that they were doing more than they actually were' (Lock, 2013, p. 60, 7.18). Among the lessons learned from this case, as in others, is the importance of ensuring concerns are shared across agency working and this means that the designated person for safeguarding and protection has a greater responsibility than individuals for checking the accurate reporting and filing of concerns. However, practitioners passing information to the designated person also have a responsibility to check that information is acted upon and not assume that knowledge passed on is sufficient in itself. This is not always easy, as Ward *et al.* (2012) records that head teachers report poor responses from social care when referring children thought to be seriously neglected (Ward *et al.*, 2012, p. 84).

Effective support for children and families often relies upon local agencies working together to identify and support children and their families. Local Safeguarding Children Boards are responsible for monitoring and evaluating training in the area and inter-agency assessments should be provided to ensure co-ordinated support (Barlow *et al.*, 2012). One such assessment, the Common Assessment Framework (CAF) was designed to prevent needs escalating to a point intervention would be needed via a statutory assessment under the Children's Act 1989 (National Archives, 2014a, para. 26). Using CAF or similar assessment procedure is more likely to ensure effective sharing of information between professionals and local agencies and puts the child at the centre of the process to consider three aspects of care: the child's developmental needs, parenting capacity and the family and environmental factors (see Figure 9.1). It is clear that to get an overall picture of how these three elements fit together different agencies must work together; practitioners and teachers may have an understanding of the child's developmental progress, but rely on hearsay and assumptions when assessing other areas. Also, there is the issue of staffing, noted by a case study member:

- We need staff to support the 'well-being' of children and parents at the beginning and end of the day as this takes up a lot of time. The FLO (Family Liaison Officer) being there takes the pressure off staff but she cannot be everywhere. Many parents need this level of support and need to feel listened to, etc.

Contexts for assessment for safeguarding and promoting welfare

Staff, however dedicated, cannot be everywhere nor do everything, but adopting a 'child and family welfare approach' is more likely to lead to effective ways of working with children who might be at risk of abuse or neglect (Ward, 2012, p. 88). Being alert to signs of danger and accurately recording, reporting and sharing data with relevant authorities is essential to the safeguarding and protection of children. Relevant and appropriate training for staff at all levels is crucial to understanding how to observe and respond to safeguarding concerns. The sort of serious abuse that leads to a child's death may not be as common as feared, but undoubtedly, many forms of abuse slip under the radar. The Action for Children report (Action for Children, 2014) suggests that as many as one in ten children suffer from neglect and that many children, parents and professionals feel frustrated by the lack of support available owing to 'thresholds, lack of resources, constant changes in social workers' (2014, p. 16). As Berger and Slack state, 'child protection refers to a society's efforts to respond to child abuse

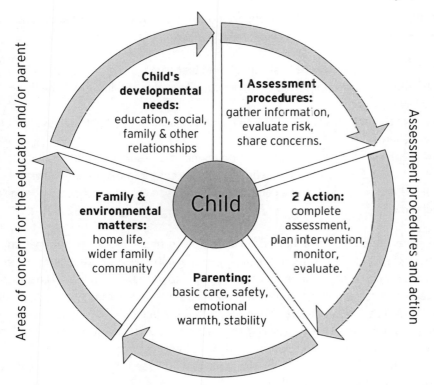

Figure 9.1 Contexts for assessment for safeguarding and promoting welfare

Adapted from CAF assessment triangle (available at webarchive.nationalarchives.gov.uk)

and neglect' (in Ben-Arieh *et al.*, 2014, p. 105) and this must be a combined effort with all parties, indeed, all individuals, responsible for looking out for, and taking steps to protect all children, and demanding some action. Accessing training is one step forward.

Poverty and other risks

Sadly, there are many other risks that children face in society today that can impact upon their education and their well-being. The Child Poverty Strategy 2014–2017 (DfE, 2014c) indicates the continuing concerns of the government in the number of children and families living in poverty and underlines the educational attainment gaps from the early years through to adulthood for those reared in poverty (Lupton, 2010, pp. 12–14). While poverty is not in itself a cause of maltreatment, it can increase the risk factors than lead to abuse and neglect (Ward *et al.*, 2012, p. 91). Respected organisations, including Barnardo's and the Joseph Rowntree Foundation, as well as other research findings, also link poverty with low educational achievement. Barnardo's organisation goes as far as declaring that poverty is the 'single greatest threat to wellbeing of children and families ... that affects every aspect of a child's development – social, educational and emotional' (www.barnardos.org.uk). In areas of high risk, it is agencies working together alongside the community that can make a difference for children and break the cycle of need. Tickell and Lupton (2010, p.14) suggest a list of six educational strategies that could support progress in tackling deprivation and helping children to escape poverty traps. These include ensuring that:

- the poorest areas have the best schools and teachers;
- integrated support through health visitors and high quality childcare is regularly available;
- the curriculum builds a love of learning, and assessment highlights achievement rather than failure;
- where necessary, primary schools continue one-to-one support where required;
- costs of childcare through to higher education is cut for low-income families;
- schools make the most of the contact with parents to link to other services and reduce isolation.

These strategies are not new but perceived as being under threat as national and local budgets are cut, so rather than expanding, some initiatives are reducing in size. The importance of early intervention programmes is recognised and the difference made by early years education valued (Jackson, 2012). There is much that the practitioner and teacher can do to support children by ensuring that the immediate working environment is welcoming and builds a love of learning that leads to success, by developing relationships with parents and carers to offer support and share information about services, and in being open to training and professional development that will keep them fresh and ensure that they are 'best teachers' for all children.

To end this section, comes the warning arising from the millennium cohort study (Sabates and Dex, 2012) that children who are exposed to two or more risks (see Table 9.4) in the first years of life are likely to be disadvantaged both cognitively and behaviourally as they grow up (Sabates and Dex, 2012, p. 22). The study also concludes that children facing a single risk factor would not 'end up with a major development problem' (Sabates and Dex, 2012, p. 6) – in other words, the more risks the more significant the long-term damage to development. A

Table 9.4 Causes of risks faced by children

Risks faced by children may be caused by:	
	Examples
Poverty	Unemployed; low income; insufficient food, clothing, warmth; overcrowding; financial stress
Parent's health	Depression; alcohol or drug addiction; mental or physical ill-health; domestic violence
Neglect, harm or Emotional stress	Poor parental skills; instability of parental relationship; emotional and/or physical abuse, neglect
Child's health	Premature birth; long-term illness; physical disability; developmental delay; SEN

single disadvantage may be overcome over time, but all children facing risk factors are more likely to need additional support to make educational progress. This support is often provided through the range of services targeted at vulnerable children and families, such as looked-after children or those with disabilities. When economic times are tough or when there is a shortage of specialists, then the support is targeted at the group of children most at risk as their long-term future is bleaker than other groups of children. This is not always easy to explain to parents or others why one child gets support while another is on a long waiting list. Sensitivity and tact is essential in dealing with such issues and a long-term view of the outcome of support is required when resources are limited.

Conclusions

This chapter has two main points to make:

1   Sometimes a calculated and well-thought out risk is a risk worth taking and the benefits for children in learning to be independent 'risk-takers' is important for their long-term development;
2   Risks related to safeguarding and the protection of children are never worth taking and all adults working with children should constantly be vigilant for any signs that a child or family is in need and not hesitate to follow reporting guidelines to activate appropriate support.

The practitioners from the case study group discussed the issues surrounding risk assessment and risk management and came up with the following list of what might help them in their workplaces:

- More adults in the school/nursery setting
- Reduce the curriculum - this would breed a less stressed nation
- Make learning less like a conveyor belt and more individual and local
- Reduce testing to take the pressure off
- Regular meetings with the social care team so that we get to know each other and can share concerns.

The challenge for all those working with young children is not just to create such lists, but to take responsibility to ensure that all children are supported, that policy is regularly updated and understood and that robust communication links are opened and maintained between team members. This is no easy task, but as one student remarked, 'working with young children is not rocket science - it is much more difficult; rewarding when you get it right, devastating when it goes wrong.'

Recommended reading

1   When considering risk benefit assessment or welfare and safeguarding issues, the online guidance documents provided by the Health and Safety Executive (HSE) and government websites are a 'must read', for example:

National Archives (2014a) Children Act (1989) Available at: www.legislation.gov.uk/ukpga/1989/41/contents (Accessed: 10 January 2014).

Palmer, S. (2006) *Toxic Childhood: How the Modern World Is Damaging Our Children and What We Can Do About It.* London: Orion House.

Play England (2011) *Make Time to Play: A World Without Play: A Report from Play England.* Available at: www.playengland.org.uk/resources/a-world-without-play-literature-review.aspx (Accessed: 10 December 2013).

Sabates, R. and Dex, S. (2012) *Multiple risk factors in young children's development: CLS cohort studies working paper 2012/1.* London: Centre for Longitudinal Studies.

Seligman, M. (1990) *Learned Optimism.* New York: Simon and Schuster.

Seligman, M. (1995) *The Optimistic Child.* New York: Harper Collins.

Shin, L.M. and Liberzon, I. (2010) 'The neurocircuitry of fear, stress, and anxiety disorders', *Neuropsychopharmacology Reviews*, 35, pp. 169–91.

Sylva, K., Melhuish, E., Sammons, P., Siraj-Blatchford, I. and Taggart, B. (2004) *The Effective Provision of Pre-School Education (EPPE) Project: Final Report.* London: DfEE/Institute of Education, University of London.

Sylva, K., Melhuish, E., Sammons, P., Siraj-Blatchford, I. and Taggart, B. (2008) *The Effective Provision of Pre-School Education 3–11 Project: Final Report from the Primary Phase: Pre-school, School and Family Influences on Children's Development during Key Stage 2 (age 7–11) Research Report DCSF-RR061.* London: Department for Children Schools and Families. Available at: https://www.gov.uk/government/uploads/system/uploads/attachment_data/file/222225/DCSF-RR061.pdf (Accessed: 26 March 2014).

Thom, S., Sales, R., and Pearce, J.J. (2007) *Growing up with Risk.* Bristol: The Policy Press.

Tickell, C. and Lupton, R. (2010) *Deprivation and Risk: The Case for Early Intervention.* London: Action for Children.

Tickell, C. (2011) *The Early Years: Foundations for life, health and learning. An Independent Report on the Early Years Foundation Stage to Her Majesty's Government.* London: DfE. Available at: www.educationengland.org.uk/documents/pdfs/2011-tickell-report-eyfs.pdf (Accessed: 7 January 2014).

Tovey, H. (2007) *Playing Outdoors: Spaces and Places, Risks and Challenge (Debating Play).* Berkshire: Open University Press.

Ungar, M. (2007) *Too Safe for Their Own Good: How Risks and Responsibilities Help Teens Thrive.* Toronto, Ontario: McClelland & Stewart.

Ungar, M. (2010) *Too Safe Schools, Too Safe Families: Denying Children the Risk-Taker's Advantage.* In Education Canada, Vol. 18. p. 1. Canadian Education Association (www.cea-acd.ca).

Ward, H., Brown, R. and Maskell-Graham, D. (2012) *Research Report DFE-RR209: Young Children Suffering, or Likely to Suffer, Significant Harm: Experiences on Entering Education.* London: Department for Education.

Waite, S. (2011) *Children Learning Outside the Classroom: From Birth to 11.* London: Sage.

Conclusion

Christine Ritchie

Overview

This concluding chapter takes a brief look at some of the issues raised in the three sections of the book. It draws together some of the main themes and looks towards challenges and changes that may come in the future.

Background to this book

The notion of challenge and change as the focus for this book was initially inspired by students studying on a Foundation Degree programme, who during animated discussion raised issues about the everyday challenges they came across in their workplaces. These 'challenges' were in many ways outside of their studies, even the 'curriculum', yet were still connected to their learning. How could they do what they felt was right, they asked, when they were bombarded with problems, changes and support systems that were being eroded, and their own power to affect or resist change felt so limited? The issues were then taken to other groups of students, practitioners and teachers, who all raised similar questions during discussion and produced a wide range of real examples used as the 'case studies' throughout the book. The challenges were grouped as the three main themes of this book:

- Change = Challenge:
  How can I cope with change? A changing curriculum, change in responsibilities, changes in my thinking and working practices? And, especially, how do I cope with the changes that I do not want and did not ask for?
- Challenges for learning and learners in the middle of change:
  The curriculum and ideas of teaching and learning seem to be constantly changing; how do I keep up with all the new strategies and testing regimes, stay true to my own principles about early learning and make it all work?
- Barriers to inclusive practice in times of change:
  How can I help all children to learn in the diverse society that we live in? How can I possibly meet the needs of all children when so many face problems in their lives that impact upon learning?

Obviously, the book has not been able to deal with all the possible questions or issues that were raised by those working in early years education, but, instead, each section has dipped into the most current and pressing concerns. This book does not claim to have all the answers – if only that were possible, the world (or at least education) would be perfect! It does, however, hope to assist the reader in identifying their own concerns and give them a glimpse of the bigger picture. Sometimes, identifying the issues is one step towards overcoming the perceived challenge.

Certainties and changes

If one thing about education is certain, it is that educators will be buffeted by the winds of change with the constant expectation of new challenges. Politicians will present 'new' ideas to raise standards, demand that practitioners change their pedagogy to accommodate new 'research', and work hard to win society over to their way of thinking. This pattern is not new, as even a cursory look at the history of education will show how past practices have been influenced by groups of politicians, social reformers as well as businessmen looking ahead to employ an appropriately educated workforce.

Some things do remain constant, fortunately, including factors that contribute to the formation of strong human relationships; for example, the love between parents and their children. Strong relationships are also developed in the formation teams of educators; this not only supports staff members through the process of change but also provides a forum for problem solving. Importantly, good teamwork also makes the workplace a happy, productive environment that welcomes staff, parents and others to share in the same goals for the benefit of the children. Also, despite all of the changes and challenges faced by educators today, it could be argued that the child at the heart of education remains constant. The way a child develops, learns and builds relationships with those around them is timeless, a never-ending story. Children need the same now as they did in the past: love and care, food and sustenance, clothing and warmth, someone to learn from and stimulation to arouse their natural curiosity. The challenge now, as it always has been, is to determine how best to provide this environment for all the children in a diverse society and world. Perhaps after all, it is just the adults and society that change, not the 'child'.

To change or not to change

Change and challenge are neither new concepts nor necessarily bad things. If you have ever worked with colleagues who when asked to consider a change to their practice remarked, 'Well, I've been doing it like this for 20 years and I seen no reason to change now', you will realise how this sounds and that standing still is never an option. Taking a step out of your 'comfort zone' – the place where you feel professionally competent and confident – is difficult; stepping into the unknown and taking a risk, even a carefully thought-out and conservative risk, takes some courage. This is when the leaders and the team members that you work with really count, providing a secure sounding board for ideas and a well-considered response to any question about what to do in a given situation. Being informed about the issues is one step towards creating and planning for change, as although sometimes it is good to step into the dark and 'go for it', it is often better to devise an adaptable plan with Specific, Manageable, Achievable, Realistic, Time bound (SMART) targets. The chapters in this book all outline the changes in thinking and practice that impact upon educators and consider different aspects of change related to the chapter topic.

Looking to the future

So, where next? Where is the next set of changes and challenges coming from? The government, that almost anonymous and fluctuating mass of ministers and officials that determine the direction of education in the UK, will continue to debate solutions to the battle of continually raising standards. Some solutions will be adopted as initiatives or strategies, some will become statutory and others will fade away and be consigned to distant memory in the government online 'archives' despite any upheaval that they may cause when first introduced. If the sheer volume of strategies, initiatives and Acts of Parliament that has been produced over the past 20 years continues, then those working in early years education will continue to face feelings of uncertainty that has almost been taken for granted as being part of education. However, as the wheel of change turns, it is interesting to watch the same ideas return, albeit with a changed vocabulary or different wrapping. For example, the idea of a baseline assessment as children start school has been around for a long time. The National Curriculum in 1998 established a statutory requirement for schools to carry out baseline assessments in the first weeks of starting school, which quickly merged into the Foundation Stage Profile (2000), and later was renamed as the Early Years Foundation Stage (EYFS) Profile. The idea of a baseline assessment resurfaced again in 2014 with announcements that the EYFS Profile will no longer be compulsory after 2016 as it will be replaced by Reception class baseline assessment (DfE, 2014). The aim of a baseline assessment is essentially one of accountability with the measurement of any 'added value' from schooling becoming important; these measures have in the past been shown to be flawed and it is questionable whether very young children can be accurately 'measured' in any meaningful way in the first few weeks of school. It may also mean that any pre-school learning becomes marginalised and seen as unimportant. Regardless, however, of any debate upon the validity or desirability of such assessments, it still provides an example of how ideas are introduced as being 'new' but are really just repeats of previous strategies or initiatives. In addition to this is the uncertainty of implementation, as governments and ideas may change before they reach the early years workplace, or even worse, just as they reach the workplace!

The chapters in this book have, therefore, tried to look at the challenges and changes that are sweeping through the early years in the knowledge that some changes are just re-branding of previous ideas, but some basic principles remain constant. Spotting the difference can often be a challenge, and this is where experience and knowing past, recent history helps.

Challenges to ideas of learners and learning

Throughout the chapters, there have been key words that reflect the preoccupation with learning that is the main focus for those working in education. Words such as 'resilience', which are to be found throughout the literature for learning and within the EYFS documentation. The need to build up self-esteem so that young children grow up to be confident and competent learners is very much a part of the everyday educational experience. However, there are some adults and children who are not as resilient as others, and the effect of this on learning features in several chapters. Such ideas are born out of the understanding of the emotional response to new experiences, including learning, and the ways in which very young children learn to trust in others and then trust in themselves to be independent in thought and action.

E-literacy

One area that seems to excite and interest all children regardless of age is technology. From simple flashing lights on many toys to the interactive games and stories available on tablet devices, the appeal of technology is powerful. Chapter 6 asks why 'e-literacy' is not more widely accepted in education as legitimate learning, and explores the rise in technology as a literacy tool. It does seem that adults often see technology as a corruption of 'real' literacy with only a place in leisure activities. The speed of change in society as a result of technology also provides a challenge, in that children seem to be able to absorb and adapt to the technological advances so much faster than adults. Children are exposed to technology at a very early age in the home, with children as young as two or three being able to switch on gadgets and find their favourite games to play. It is interesting to watch how they navigate the screen, pressing the 'start' button and controlling the action. The debate about whether this is 'good' or 'bad' for children has plenty of voices from both sides! It may be, like many things, that a little of what you like is OK, but too much is harmful.

Challenge

- Compare what your setting has to offer in technology with what the children are able to use at home. Do you have an 'old' computer for the children to play on at counting or shape games or similar activities? How does it compare with a touch screen computer or tablet?
- In an experiment, a small group of 3/4-year olds had access to a tablet. They could switch it on, find the folders for games and stories; locate YouTube to find favourite film clips and generally navigate round the screen with ease. What does this say about the old computer in the corner or about the 'computer literacy' of the children?
- Try this experiment yourself – can children use a tablet or similar device independently?

One thing is certain, technology is a part of society and likely to continue to develop at a fast rate, rather than diminish. The challenge for those working within early years is to learn to live with the technology, and embrace the aspects that may have a direct bearing on the education of children. Providing young children with access to tablet or similar device is expensive and electronic tools may be considered too much trouble to be of use with young children. There is, of course, also the question of whether it is desirable to encourage use of such technology with children. However, change in production processes generally results in cheaper, smaller and more robust devices being made, so new e-tools may be just around the corner ready for your workplace soon!

Go outside and play to learn

In direct contrast to the challenge of the 'sit-down-and-play' technology is the 'go-out-and-play' message of Chapter 5. The benefits of outdoor play and exploration are very clear, although it still seems that many children do not have the opportunity to develop through outdoor learning as educators would wish. Changes in government thinking seem to be steering a way towards more a formal educational approach for young children, with educators fearing that the value of play, particularly outdoor play and learning, will be pushed aside to accommodate a narrow curriculum that favours testing to identify failure. In an open letter to *The Telegraph* signed by 128 leading early years professionals, a call to reject formal teaching designed to promote 'school-readiness' was made (*The Telegraph*, 2013). This, along with other pressure groups, including the newly formed 'Too much, Too soon' campaign (www.toomuchtoosoon.org), argue against early 'teaching' and 'testing' and call for learning through play to be protected for the under-fives. David Whitebread followed up the *Telegraph*'s open letter with a short review of the evidence of the consequences of starting school too early (Whitebread, 2013). Whitebread notes how evidence from anthropological, psychological, neuro-scientific and educational studies all indicate the importance of the different components of play for human development and for inducing lasting feelings of well-being. His report *The Importance of Play* (2012) argues that an understanding of the importance of play in relation to human development and learning is growing among researchers and educators, but increased urbanisation, stress in family life and changes in educational systems mean that children's play opportunities may be under threat (Whitebread, 2012, pp. 3–4). The challenge for educators is to be confident and assertive about what they believe is important for early childhood development and to find the research evidence and the voice to withstand the pressures of those who wish education to be confined to more formal literacy and numeracy learning. This is where Chapter 5 may help. The early years workforce is generally a compliant one, but as the workforce becomes more qualified and confident with the acquisition of knowledge there may be a time when early years leaders can truly lead the way for parents, children and even the politicians. Chapter 3 also hints at such transformational possibilities, along with parity of pay across the teaching and care professions.

Educational 'scientists'

The chapter looking at neuroscience goes further than considering an emotional response to learning to look at the ways in which a brain functions. Much is now known about the developing brain, and this knowledge is woven more carefully into the business of teaching and learning. Not all educators feel that they are qualified as 'scientists' in terms of fully understanding all the workings of something as complex as a brain, but that is changing, as new research spreads across society and many of the strategies used by educationalists have been developed from a foundation based upon neurological studies. Well-tried and tested strategies following the ideas of the traditional theorists, including Vygotsky, Bloom and Bandura (as explained in Chapter 4) are now supplemented by a greater understanding of why such strategies might work. Neuroscience has some interesting messages to help with the understanding of learning, particularly for those working with very young children, and no doubt there will be more challenges in the future as those working within the early years sector use the information to support their activities and planning.

Challenge

As a persuasion for educators to understand more about how the brain functions, think about the following:

- Compare the response of two workers: one is a car mechanic and the other an educator. If you ask the car mechanic to explain how a car works, the mechanic will probably go into detail about how engines work, etc., and not a lot about how to drive the car. However, if you ask an educator about how a child works/learns it is unlikely that the answer will contain much information about how the brain works. The answer is more likely to be about strategies for learning.

So, the challenge is:

- If the brain is the 'engine' which controls the body, thinking and learning, how much about the brain do you understand?

Science support for teaching and learning

So, what is coming up on the horizon of scientific thinking for the future? It would seem that the use of genetics to predict outcomes is rising in prominence. The understanding of genetics is already influential in medical circles, with society accepting that DNA can help predict a heightened risk of diseases for some people. Examples include breast cancer, as well as inheritable diseases that can be identified before birth, such as cystic fibrosis. Gene therapy is increasingly offered as a form of treatment giving hope to many where in the past no help was available. It would seem logical then, that genetics might do the same for education, with a DNA test at birth providing a 'road map for education' (Rutherford, 2014) that could help to predict which children might have a problem with learning, and trigger a set of very early support and interventions to be put into place for each and every child. This is not to suggest that a 'cure' is required, just a greater understanding of how the mind and body works for each individual.

Such ideas as DNA-testing of children at birth to assess whether they might have a gene that affects their learning seems to belong to the realm of science fiction and films like *Gattaca* – where individuals screened at birth have their future lives planned for them without any possibility of personal choice. It also brings the spectre of Nazi Germany, with the idea of promoting the 'perfect' man above all others and destroying others. This is anathema to those who believe that children might be born different, but are born equal. The polarised notions of knowing all about a person from birth (a) in order to be able to support them to achieve their potential, as opposed to (b) being able to attach value to those with a higher intelligence or ability, is the danger inherent in all forms of labelling. Science is now able to read genomes with comparative ease compared with just a few years ago and the prospect of using the information to be able to improve strategies for teaching in the future may be a tempting one. As Professor Robert Plumen said in a BBC radio programme, ' . . . we need to recognise that genetics is one of the reasons why children differ in how easily they learn . . . it is becoming increasingly possible to predict learning difficulties, e.g. reading, and match this to the environment', indicating how educators might be able to 'personalise' the learning environment to match individual learning needs (Rutherford, 2014). Plomen *et al.* (2013) also writes about the danger of the 'pendulum swing' in giving more significance to the importance of 'nature' as opposed to 'nurture' that might be on the horizon owing to such new discoveries. This book, however, is more concerned with how children are supported and nurtured as they develop and grow. Whether new genome studies can change this balance for early years educators is something for the future.

Barriers to inclusion

Like the 'nature vs nurture' debate, the discussion about who and what makes a difference to improve the educational outcomes of children is likely to continue for some time. Some strategies are well established and others are being developed to improve the learning environment for different groups of children, including children with disabilities, as highlighted in Chapter 7. The Equality Act 2010 (DfE, 2013) brought together and simplified the previous regulations related to equality, so making 'equality duty' clearer to follow. The effect the law has had on educational practice has been profound, but as Chapter 7 argues, more training and understanding of the nature of disabilities and the support children and families require is needed now and in the future. Attitudes towards those with disability are steadily changing in society, partly due to the inclusion of all children in education and legislation but also because of public events such as the Paralympic games. Watching athletes with disabilities achieve success in sports is a timely reminder of the power of role models in society, where even the seemingly impossible becomes a reality. Where once children and adults with disability were side-lined by society and kept out of sight, spending lifetimes living in institutions, it is now accepted that they have a valued place in the community. The challenges for those in education is to hold high expectations for all children, regardless of ability or disability, and not just to settle for the mundane or ordinary. This requires knowledge, understanding and continuous learning on part of the educator, as it has become necessary for all to be aware of needs of the different children across the learning spectrum. The history of the treatment of the disabled is one of missed opportunities and locked doors; the future must be one of celebration, openness and achievement.

Chapter 7 highlights another of the broad themes of this book that weaves through the chapters, that of being prepared for any future challenge and change by accessing training and gaining qualifications. The demand for the early years workforce to move from an experienced but unqualified majority to a highly qualified workforce has gathered momentum over the past 20 years. The first three chapters dealt with the different effects of this in some detail, but the idea that just having experience of working with children is no longer sufficient is also implicit in other chapters. This is a change that is not going to go away as research argues that quality provision and high standards are the end results when experienced and qualified staff are involved in the education of young children.

Challenge

Chapter 7 calls for action to be taken to positively face the new challenges of including all children in education. This includes greater understanding and knowledge of disabilities and support strategies.

- How will this call for action affect you?
- What training opportunities have you accessed, and what plans have you made for the future?

Further barriers

It is clear to see how a child with a disability requires additional support, but there are other barriers to inclusion that are more subtle. Chapter 8 considers other barriers to learning that can affect children, such as parenting and poverty. Poverty is not just about a lack of money and resources, of course, but also about an absence of education and lack of ambition. Trying to break a cycle of poverty through education is not a new idea, but it is one that all UK governments have tried to achieve. Much of the rhetoric and the actions of the coalition government have been aimed at providing support for areas of social and economic deprivation and raising standards in education for all children. To be optimistic is to believe that poverty can be eradicated and all children will be in a position to reach their full potential and go on to become successful and economically stable adults. To be pessimistic is to believe nothing will change.

That successive governments want to improve the situation for children and families in need is not disputed, but how to do this is not always clear. Clare Tickell, when chief executive of Action for Children, wrote the forward for *For As Long As It Takes: A New Politics for Children* (Action for Children, 2008), which lists uncertainties caused by the avalanche of legislation and advice handed down to those trying to work across the range of children's services. Tickell writes that, over a 21-year-period, there were:

> 98 separate Acts of Parliament passed across the UK that affect the services that they [children] use, 82 different strategies for various areas of children and youth services, 77 initiatives and over 50 new funding streams. That equals over 400 different major announcements – around 20 every year – with each new initiative lasting, on average, a little over two years.

Tickell calls for a pause in the legislation and a time to consolidate practice and reduce change. This illustrates one of the other challenges for those working with children, that of keeping up with the rapid changes in policy and ideas. Each new government and each new minister perceives a problem and tries to fix it with a new solution. Some problems seem to grow rather than shrink, such as poverty, owing to the economic situation of the country, and little seems to change the underlying problems, no matter how many initiatives are introduced. Each chapter considers some of these issues to help the reader to decide what is relevant to their own practice.

Conclusion: taking a risk

Taking on new challenges and accepting change is to be open to risk, but to stand still and do nothing also poses the risk of getting left behind or failing to meet the needs of children and families. However, as Chapter 9 illustrates, sometimes risk-taking has benefits by encouraging personal growth, confidence and independence. Well-planned change and risk assessment is what is required by educators for the future of the early years profession. The acquisition of knowledge and development of understanding through experience are powerful protectors both for children and adults. All the chapters in this book urge the reader to consider change, to develop knowledge and understanding and take a calculated risk towards the future. Of course, accepting the challenge may mean persuading others to accept what should not change, and sometimes it is the small, subtle changes, as in attitudes, that make a real difference. As the reader and as an educator, you have the power to decide what challenges to accept and what changes you wish to make.

Overall, this book may seem to have a disparate group of chapters, each with its own view of early years teaching and learning with its own agenda. These represent the wide range of challenges present for early years educators. However, as shown, the chapters have many common elements:

- a set of common key words and key terms;
- a view of change that is positive and transformative;
- a series of challenges for educators, including adapting to a stream of changing initiatives and strategies;
- a call for continuous training and development for those working with young children; and
- a positive attitude towards the future of early years education.

As stated, the original purpose for this book was to address some of the concerns raised by practitioners, teachers and students. Hopefully, dipping into this text will have helped you, the reader, to stop and think about your own approach to some of these challenges and changes. Perhaps other issues will be just as urgent and worrying for you, but reading about change will help you to manage the changes necessary in your own work life. One change to look forward to in the future might be a time of 'no change', to allow for consolidation and the development of existing strategies. This might also allow time to debate the important things in early years education – the children.

Bibliography

Action for Children (2008) *For As Long As It Takes: A New Politics for Children* (Available at: www.actionforchildren.org.uk (Accessed: 23 May 2014).

DfE (Department of Education) (2013) *The Equality Act 2010: Departmental Advice for School Leaders, School Staff and Governing Bodies in Maintained Schools and Academies.* Available at: www.gov.uk/government/uploads/system/uploads/attachment_data/file/269341/Equality_Act_2010_-_advice.pdf (Accessed: 25 May 2014).

DfE (Department for Education) (2014) *Reforming Assessment and Accountability for Primary Schools; Government Response to Consultation on Primary School Assessment and Accountability.* March 2014.

Available at: www.gov.uk/government/uploads/system/uploads/attachment_data/file/297595/ Primary_Accountability_and_Assessment_Consultation_Response.pdf (Accessed: 19 May 2014).

Plomin, R., Shakeshaft, N.G., McMillan, A. and Trzaskowski, M. (2013) 'Nature, nurture, and expertise', *Intelligence*. Vol. n/a, no. n/a, 2013, p. n/a. Available at: www.sciencedirect.com/science/article/pii/ S0160289613000810 (Accessed: 24 May 2014).

Rutherford, A. (2014) 'Intelligence: Born Smart, Born Equal, Born Different', Episode 3, BBC Radio 4. First broadcast Tuesday, 13 May 2014.

The Telegraph (2013) 'Open letter to the Telegraph: The Government should stop intervening in early education; earlier starts to formal learning can affect the health and wellbeing of young children', *The Telegraph*, 11 September 2013. Available at: www.telegraph.co.uk/comment/letters/10302844/The-Government-should-stop-intervening-in-early-education.html (Accessed: 23 May 2014).

Whitebread, D. (2012) *The Importance of Play*. Belgium: Toy Industries of Europe (TIE). Available at: www. importanceofplay.eu/IMG/pdf/dr_david_whitebread_-_the_importance_of_play.pdf (Accessed: 25 May 2014).

Whitebread, D. (2013) *Too much, Too soon: school starting age: the evidence*. Available at: www. toomuchtoosoon.org/uploads/2/0/3/8/20381265/school_starting_age_-_the_evidence.pdf (Accessed: 20 May 2014).

INDEX

Giants *in the* Nursery

Giants *in the* Nursery

A Biographical History of Developmentally Appropriate Practice

David Elkind, PhD

Redleaf Press®
www.redleafpress.org
800-423-8309

Published by Redleaf Press
10 Yorkton Court
St. Paul, MN 55117
www.redleafpress.org

First edition 2015
Cover design by Jim Handrigan
Cover art by Hakki Arsian/ThinkStock
Interior design by Dorie McClelland, Spring Book Design
Typeset in Adobe Minion Pro
Photo on page 176 © Ted Streshinsky/Corbis
Photo on page 194 © Heritage Images/Corbis

Printed in the United States of America
22 21 20 19 18 17 16 15   1 2 3 4 5 6 7 8

Library of Congress Cataloging-in-Publication Data
Elkind, David, 1931-
  Giants in the nursery : a biographical history of developmentally appropriate practice / David Elkind.
      pages cm
   Summary: "Examine the evolution of developmentally appropriate practice with this biographical history of early childhood education. This book explores the theory's progression--from its beginnings in writings of sixteenth- and seventeenth-century philosophers, its experimental implementation by eighteenth- and nineteenth-century practitioners, and its scientific grounding in contemporary theory and research"— Provided by publisher.
   Includes bibliographical references and index.
   ISBN 978-1-60554-370-3 (paperback)
   ISBN 978-1-60554-371-0 (ebook)
1. Early childhood education 2. Early childhood educators. 3. Child development. I. Title.
   LB1139.23.E56 2015
   372.21--dc23
                                      2014030734
Printed on acid-free paper

To Nancy McCormick Rambusch

dear friend

trusted and admired colleague

originator of the American Montessori Association

Contents

Acknowledgments

Acknowledging all the many friends and colleagues who have contributed to the conceptualization of this book over the years is impossible. But I must thank several people in particular who have helped to make it a reality. I am most indebted to Barbara Beatty, who insisted I read and include John Amos Comenius. I also want to thank George Scarlett for reading and commenting on many of the chapters. Punum Banta was kind enough to read the Montessori chapter and make many valuable suggestions. I owe enormous thanks to Kyra Ostendorf and Elena Futz for their thoughtful and thorough editing and fact-checking of all the chapters. They have made it a much better book than it would have been without their help. Last, but certainly not least, I want to thank my wife, Debra, for her gracious willingness to serve as a sounding board for, and gentle challenger to, my ruminations about each of the Giants.

Let the main object of this, our Didactic, be as follows: To seek and to find a method of instruction, by which teachers can teach less, but learners learn more; by which schools may be the scene of less noise, aversion, and useless labor, but of more leisure, enjoyment, and solid progress; and through which the Christian community may have less darkness, perplexity, and dissension, but on the other hand more light, orderliness, peace, and rest.

JOHN AMOS COMENIUS, DEDICATION TO *THE GREAT DIDACTIC*

Introduction

Over the last few centuries, early childhood education—the instruction of young children outside the home—has become an internationally accepted level of schooling. Yet the first years of life are unique in that they include the most accelerated pace of physical, intellectual, emotional, and social growth and development of all stages of the human life cycle. Consider the progress from a squalling bundle of wants at birth to a walking, talking, socially accept child by age five or six. These rapid changes make it necessary to take growth and development into greater account in the education of this age group than any other level of pedagogy.

It was John Amos Comenius in the seventeenth century who not only first recognized the educational importance of the early years but also articulated the teaching practices, skills, and subject matter most appropriate for this age group. First and foremost, he argued that both child rearing and education should be adapted to the growing abilities, needs, and interests of the child. In accord with this principle, he contended that subjects should be presented from the simple to the complex and in a way that is made interesting and enjoyable to the student. He was also adamant that education should be for everyone, male and female from whatever station in life, and for those of limited as well as exceptional ability.

These ideas were progressively elaborated, articulated, and given philosophical, practical, research, and theoretical support by those individuals whom I am calling the Giants of early childhood education. The work of these Giants further clarified, extended, and enriched Comenius's original vision of child-centered education. To be sure, early childhood was not the major concern of many of the Giants. Nonetheless, they all recognized, in their own ways and from their own perspectives, the crucial importance of age-appropriate child-rearing and early childhood instruction for later healthy development. Yet despite four centuries of arguments for constructing pedagogy in accordance with the psychology of the developing child at all age levels, this idea has yet to be fully implemented.

In the United States, the negative legacy of humanism and the reliance on books, recitation, and role learning have been difficult to overcome. This has been particularly true of elementary and secondary education. The difficulty has been aided and abetted by the introduction of standardized tests of academic achievement—suggesting that education is a measurable quantity. As a consequence, major efforts at educational reform have not been fully successful. As Diane Ravitch (2011) explains, the problem is that each reform movement is followed by a counterrevolutionary one aimed at correcting the errors of its predecessor. With this in mind, perhaps the best we can hope for is that we take what is of value in each of these efforts to progressively craft a more humane and effective educational system.

Early childhood education has had its own problems. Because of its focus on very young children, long thought to be the province of the family, the education of young children outside the home has challenged traditional gender roles and religious values. It also has not been spared the intrusion of politics, economics, and social and historical forces (Pound 2011). As a result, the history of early childhood education has been diverse and discontinuous. For example, in many countries, including the United States, support for educating young children outside the home has waxed and waned depending on the particular political party in office at the local, state, and federal levels.

The fortunes of early childhood education have also suffered because of the many competing child-centered programs claiming to best meet the needs of young children. The success of these competing programs (for example, Froebel, Montessori, Waldorf, and Reggio) has made it difficult to argue that one is undeniably better than any other. That being the case, it has been hard to present a united front against the pressures to make early childhood education a "size smaller" elementary education.

The Introduction of DAP

In 1987 the National Association for the Education of Young Children (NAEYC) reintroduced some of Comenius's ideas under the rubric of developmentally appropriate practice (DAP) (Bredekamp 1987). In 2010 this concept was expanded (Bredekamp and Copple 2010) to encompass the philosophical, practical, theoretical, and research contributions of the later Giants. What this integration has made clear is that all of the child-centered early childhood programs, regardless of the particular Giant to whom they owe allegiance, share the same core principles:

namely, child rearing and education have to be adapted to the growing needs, abilities, and interests of the child, and children are best served when they are actively involved in their own learning. This commonality makes it clear that beneath the appearance of diversity and discontinuity in the history of early childhood education, there is an underlying unity and continuity.

The Giants of Developmentally Appropriate Practice

The progressive elaboration and integration of the philosophical insights, experimental innovations, theoretical ideas, and research evidence of the twelve principles brought together by NAEYC is the untold history of early childhood education. To be sure, these philosophical, practical, theoretical, and research ideas were not formulated exclusively for the education of young children. Indeed, the Giants thought of their ideas as applicable to all levels of child rearing and education. Comenius himself proposed that his ideas were applicable from infancy through the university level (Keatinge 1910). That DAP can be employed at least up to the high school level is supported by the fact that many of the descendants of the schools first introduced by two of the Giants, Montessori and Steiner (Waldorf schools), today serve the K–12 age groups.

I am very well aware that, over the years, a great many distinguished educators both in the United Sates and abroad have made important contributions to early childhood education. But in every discipline there are only a few individuals whose work marks major turning points in their field. I believe this is true for early childhood education. From this perspective, there are eleven individuals whose work has shaped the discipline. These are the philosophers, practitioners, researchers, and theorists whom I am calling Giants. By focusing on the work of the Giants, I by no means intend to belittle the significance of other contributors. It just seems necessary to call on the authority of the Giants in support of DAP at a time when DAP principles are being overlooked, ignored, or rejected—witness national achievement standards.

In choosing the Giants, I used three criteria. First, they were persuaded, far ahead of their times, that education had to be based on an understanding of the child. In the absence of a science of child psychology, they employed analogies, such as the growth of plants and the change of seasons, to illustrate developmental changes and to suggest age-appropriate child-rearing and educational practices.

Second, each has made a unique contribution to our conception of the child and to our understanding of experiential learning. To be sure, all learning is experiential in a broad sense. Yet, since the time of Francis Bacon (1561–1626), it has been tradition to distinguish book learning and deductive reasoning from experiential learning based on sensory observation, experiment, and inductive reasoning.

Finally, they are all Giants inasmuch as they have all found a prominent and lasting place in the theory and practice of early childhood education. Coming from different backgrounds and living in different times and places, each Giant conceptualized the child and experiential learning from his or her unique orientation. Each successive conception has added to our knowledge of the complexity and variety of child nature and of the ways in which young children learn. Thanks to these ideas, we have a more comprehensive picture of the young learner than students at any other age level.

Ten individuals meet the criteria outlined above. John Amos Comenius, John Locke, and Jean-Jacques Rousseau contributed the philosophical foundations of experiential learning and modern education in general. Johann Heinrich Pestalozzi, Friedrich Froebel, Maria Montessori, and Rudolf Steiner carried out the experimental groundwork of early childhood education. Most recently, early childhood education was scientifically rooted in the research and theory of Sigmund Freud, Jean Piaget, and Erik Erikson. I have also added a chapter on the Russian Lev Vygotsky, even though he was not a Giant in the sense described above. This seemed appropriate both because of his influence and because he might well have been a Giant had he lived long enough to fully articulate his theories and complete his research program.

The Aims of This Book

My aims in this book are threefold. First, as described above, one core problem in early childhood education is that most, if not all, historians of early education give accounts of the diversity and controversy in the field at the expense of a comprehensive picture of the discipline as a whole. From the perspective of DAP, however, early childhood education does have a historical and a conceptual continuity and unity. All the Giants contributed significant ideas about the nature of the child and about learning and instruction that have been progressively assimilated into the principles of DAP. In detailing the lives and works of these Giants, I aim to provide a much-needed coherent and compelling narrative of the progressive formulation, application, and theoretical or research support for the foundational principles of DAP.

Second, another longstanding problem in early childhood education is that there are a number of competing child-centered camps linked to the work of Froebel, Steiner, Montessori, Freud, Piaget, Vygotsky, and Erikson. The proponents of these methods seldom communicate or interact with one another. Many educators working under these rubrics are unfamiliar with the other methods' histories and shapers. This book addresses this problem by bringing together a brief biography and work summary of the Giants of each of these programs. This integrative approach will afford both students and workers in any early childhood specialty an opportunity to learn about the Giants of other approaches. This is particularly true for the contributions of little-known and exceedingly original Comenius. Likewise, there is little recognition of Pestalozzi's introduction of manipulatives and field trips as methods of experiential learning. Finally, outside of Waldorf-trained educators, few early childhood professionals know much about Rudolf Steiner and his holistic educational contributions.

A third aim of this book is to provide early childhood educators three powerful arguments in defense of DAP:

1. DAP is more solidly grounded in philosophy, theory, research, and practice than any other approach to education or any other early education program.
2. DAP provides the most integrated curricula of socialization, individualization, work, and play than does any other approach to education.
3. DAP offers students the greatest possible combination of learning experiences (social, natural, personal, and unconscious) than any other approach to education.

I believe these three considerations taken together enable early childhood educators to make a powerful case for the superiority of DAP over any other educational programs for young children.

I fully appreciate that there are many approaches to the education of young children other than DAP. But in my fifty years of engaging in child-development research, teaching child development, and supervising students, I have become convinced that the science of child psychology is the science of education.

This conviction was further reinforced when I began lecturing to parents and teachers in the United States and other countries. I was particularly impressed by my visits to Scandinavian countries where DAP is the norm for their educational systems. Throughout these countries, formal education does not begin until age six or seven, and early childhood programs are play based. One of the most powerful observations I have made is that effective early childhood educators, regardless of their theoretical persuasion, practice what we now call DAP. Finally, I have yet to see any research evidence to show that any non-DAP approaches are more effective in the long or short term than DAP approaches that adapt to the growing needs, abilities, and interests of children.

Despite all the above considerations, the pressure to push academics into early childhood has increased rather than abated. In my talks at early childhood centers and in numerous letters and e-mails from experienced early childhood professionals, I hear the same sad story. The pressures for testing, homework, and the elimination of play are unrelenting. Too many of our best early childhood educators are leaving the field because they cannot, in good conscience, engage in the age-inappropriate practices they are being forced to impose on young children.

It is because DAP has the weight of history, philosophy, practice, theory, and research to recommend it that I believe it is superior to any other educational approach for young children—indeed, for students at all age levels. And it is because I see this approach in jeopardy that I wrote this book.

Organization of the Book

The organization of the book is as follows. An introductory chapter provides a brief history of Western education from the Greeks and Romans until the modern era introduced by the Reformation, the printing press, and the exploration of the New World. The next few chapters of the book offer brief accounts of the lives and work of Moravian philosopher and educator John Amos Comenius, English philosopher John Locke, and Swiss French social philosopher Jean-Jacques Rousseau. The following chapters give similar accounts of the lives and work of the shapers of early childhood pedagogy: Swiss Johann Heinrich Pestalozzi, German Friedrich Froebel, Austrian German Rudolf Steiner, and Italian Maria Montessori. The last chapters are devoted to the lives and work of the researchers and theorists: Austrian Sigmund Freud, Swiss Jean Piaget, Danish American Erik Erikson, and Russian Lev Vygotsky.

At the end of each chapter, I summarize how each Giant viewed the nature of the child, the aims of education, and the role of play. I chose the nature of the child because each Giant held his or her own view of what was essential to childhood. Like the blind man and the elephant, each Giant saw the child in a somewhat different way. Together, their perspectives give us a fuller and richer appreciation of the child than we might otherwise have.

I chose the aims of education because the modern recognition of individual rights has raised the issue of whether education should focus on individualization, socialization, or some combination of the two. Over the years, individual rights versus social obligations has become a major issue addressed in different ways by modern major educational figures. Herbart (McMurry 1893) suggested that the issue was a character (education) versus academic (teaching) issue; Dewey ([1899] 1900) put it as an issue of the child and society. More recently, Freire (1970) has argued that it is a political issue of liberation versus domestication. What is important from the perspective of this book is that regardless of how each Giant viewed the aims of education, they all believed these aims could be achieved in developmentally appropriate ways.

I have included the Giants' ideas on the role of play because their views of play complement their views on the aims of education. Each Giant's perspective also gives weight to the idea that our stances on perennial issues in education derive, in part at least, from our personal predispositions.

Each chapter concludes with how the writings of the Giants link to one or more of the twelve principles of early childhood education given in *Developmentally Appropriate Practice in Early Childhood Programs Serving Children from Birth through Age 8* (Bredekamp and Copple 2010). For the later Giants in particular, the origination is often readily apparent. For example, the principle "Development and learning result from a dynamic and continuous interaction of biological maturation and experience" is a basic proposition of Piaget's theory. The principle "Early experiences have profound effects, both cumulative and delayed, on a child's development and learning; and optimal periods exist for certain types of development and learning to occur" is surely a reference to Montessori's sensitive periods. Likewise, the principle "Development and learning advance when children are challenged to achieve at a level just beyond their current mastery and also when they have many opportunities to practice newly acquired skills" is clearly taken from Vygotsky's zone of proximal development (ZPD) concept. For the earlier Giants, the links to the DAP principles are not as direct but are clearly anticipated in their writings.

The book's concluding chapter describes some of the personality traits that the Giants had in common and details each Giant's individual contribution to the concept of experiential learning. The chapter also compares and contrasts the Giants' contributions to our conception of child nature as well as their views on the aims of education and the role of play. A final section in the last chapter concludes that history supports the employment of DAP and reiterates the warning of the great philosopher George Santayana: those who ignore the mistakes of the past are bound to repeat them. The chapters that follow teach again how much we have to learn from history.

References

Bredekamp, Sue. 1987. *Developmentally Appropriate Practice in Early Childhood Programs Serving Children from Birth through Age 8.* Washington, DC: NAEYC.

Bredekamp, Sue, and Carol Copple. 2010. *Developmentally Appropriate Practice in Early Childhood Programs Serving Children from Birth through Age 8.* Washington, DC: NAEYC.

Dewey, John. (1899) 1900. *The School and Society.* Chicago: University of Chicago Press.

Freire, Paulo. 1970. *Pedagogy of the Oppressed.* New York: Herder and Herder.

Keatinge, Maurice Walter. 1910. *The Great Didactic of John Amos Comenius.* London: Adam and Charles Black.

McMurry, Charles Alexander. 1893. *The Elements of General Method Based on Principles of Herbart.* Bloomington, IL: Public School.

Pound, Linda. 2011. *Influencing Early Childhood Education.* Glasgow: Bell & Bain.

Ravitch, Diane. 2011. *The Death and Life of the Great American School System: How Testing and Choice Are Undermining Education.* New York: Basic Books.

1

A Prehistory of
Early Childhood Education

The teaching of young children is embedded in the history of education as a whole. A brief summary of that history will help provide the context for fully appreciating the uniqueness of the kind of schooling needed for children during their first five or six years of life.

At any time and place in history, educational theory and practice necessarily reflect the prevailing worldviews of the society and the culture in which they take place. Although we will only be concerned with the post-Renaissance phase of this history, a brief review of the pre-Renaissance stage will help put the present work in context. For Western Europe and the United States, three pre-Renaissance phases of education are usually distinguished. These phases were the *classical* phase of the early Greeks and Romans, the *scholastic and dialectic* teaching of the medieval Christian period, and the *humanism* of the early Renaissance.

An Uneven Historical Progression

I have to emphasize, however, that as far as education goes, the above time line is primarily a historical progression rather than a true developmental one. While there has been regular forward movement for some facets of educational history, it is far from being true for all. To illustrate, there has been a steady growth in the availability of education to all members of a society. During the Greek and Roman, medieval, and early Renaissance periods, education was primarily for the sons of the wealthy. Over the next few centuries, thanks to a combination of technological, economic, and social changes, education became more widely available, though still primarily for boys, of the lower-economic classes.

On the other hand, comparable advances in educational theory and practice did not parallel this progress. The third phase in this historical sequence, the

Renaissance *humanistic* phase, was a revolt against the Christian educational system that dominated the medieval period. Humanism was built on the resurrection and, one might argue, the deification of Greek and Roman literature, philosophy, and science. Yet the early humanists, in their zeal to teach students Latin and Greek, used harsh methods that would never have been used by teachers like Plato and Aristotle from the classical period.

The history of education is, therefore, not a regular progression of improvement and effectiveness. In some respects, it even appears to be more cyclical than evolutionary. This seems particularly true of the last few centuries, when the same educational ideas have seemed to go in and out of favor depending on the social, political, and economic climate. Consider the movement from *progressive education* to *curriculum reform* to *open education* to *back to basics* to *No Child Left Behind* that characterized education in the United States during the twentieth century. Indeed, there often seems to be no clear connection between explicit educational aims and theories and their translations into educational practice. For example, most effective teachers employ comparable methods of discovery learning, open discussion, and intellectual challenge, even though educators profess quite different educational philosophies.

What is perhaps most striking in reviewing these phases of educational evolution is how educators have advocated across the centuries the abiding educational insights applicable to children at all age levels. These insights include placement of the child before the curriculum, adaptation of the curriculum to the child, the primacy of observation and experience, the necessity of making learning interesting and enjoyable, and the priority of acquiring mental process over content. Yet these abiding bedrock principles of educational practice have never been universally put into practice in any one of these historical periods. It is a sad fact that what we do in education at any point in history often seems to have little or nothing to do with what we know to be good pedagogy for children.

In this book, I am primarily concerned with the three most recent phases of educational evolution—the *experiential*, the *universalism*, and the *scientism*—because it was only during these last phases that the teaching of young children came to be recognized as a legitimate pedagogical enterprise. Nonetheless, I do believe a brief summary of the educational practices of the first three pre-Renaissance periods of educational history is important to fully appreciate what came after them.

The Classical Period of Education, 600 BCE–476 CE

The Grecian Period, 600 BCE–146 BCE

The ancient Greeks did not believe that education was to be derived only from books. Blessed with a warm climate, many Greeks spent much of their time outdoors, often in open discussion in the marketplace. "Above all they knew, as not other peoples of their time, the value of moderation. The virtues of self restraint, self-knowledge, self-reverence expressed their motives" (Lawrence 1970, 26). In addition, the Greek gods were human in their emotions, thoughts, and deeds. Thus, for the early Greeks, religion was not a mystery that had to be conveyed by clergy; it was a set of stories or myths that could be understood by everyone and that had relevance to their daily lives.

Education varied among the different Greek city-states. Spartan education, for example, was much more militaristic than an education in Athens. With the exception of education in Sparta, most Greek education was private, for the wealthy families, and limited to boys. Formal education began at age seven, and classes were generally held in the teacher's home. A family slave, called a pedagogue, accompanied the boy to school and monitored his progress. The boys were taught reading, writing, mathematics, singing, and playing the flute and lyre. For boys twelve years and older, the curriculum was expanded to include sports suited for the adolescent body. These included wrestling, running, and throwing the discus and javelin (Marrou 1956). Most Athenian youths were expected to perform some form of military service, which was regarded as a form of education. They also had additional training in the fine arts, culture, science, and music. Education, including military service, ended for most of these students when they reached the age of twenty.

The richest and ablest students, however, continued their education with famous teachers. These extensions were, in effect, a type of graduate school. These advanced studies were led by the foremost philosophers of their time and gave rise to two alternative courses of study. The first, begun by Socrates and later continued by his student Plato at the Academy, was for those who wished to pursue learning for its own sake. Socrates regarded his school as a way to produce cultured gentlemen rather than to train students in a vocation. Although he taught oratory and rhetoric, Socrates focused on the Socratic method: asking the students questions that elicited preexisting, innate knowledge. The second style, introduced by Aristotle at the Lyceum school, was for those youths who saw education as a way of preparing themselves for careers in public life (by serving in the senate). The curriculum focused on oratory and rhetoric. Inasmuch as these students were preparing to become senators, they required the persuasive skills necessary to get their fellow administrators to act (Freeman [1907] 1969).

Ancient Greek civilization is credited with providing the foundations for Western civilization as we know it. Not only did Greek society provide an example of democratic society and education, but it also modeled an appreciation of music, poetry, literature, and science. This civilization lasted for more than five centuries and ended only when the Romans defeated the Greeks at the Battle of Corinth in 146 BCE, ultimately leading to the Roman authority over Greece (Roberts 2007).

The Roman Period, 750 BCE–476 CE

During the first five centuries following the founding of the Roman Republic, there was little evidence of any formal system of education. The Roman principle of *patria potestas* acknowledged the father (the paterfamilias) as head of the household and granted him ownership of his children. Education took place within the home. Parents taught their children the domestic, agricultural, and military skills required of any citizen of the republic. Perhaps most important was the inculcation of Roman values, morals, and social responsibilities. All of these were considered essential to the cohesion and civil functioning of the society.

The Roman educational program expanded, beginning to reflect the Greek influence around 200 BCE, with the first dedicated *ludi* (play) schools, which were primarily aimed at socialization and instruction in the basic skills of reading and writing. This influence became more pronounced after the Roman conquest of many of the Greek eastern provinces around 250 BCE. At the lowest level, the Roman schools resembled those of the Greeks and were often taught by Greek slaves. School was open to boys as well as girls, and students paid for their education. A teacher often conducted classes in different places and taught for either boys or girls (Roberts 2007).

As Rome grew in size and power after the Punic wars, the family lost much of its importance as the cornerstone of the society. The family education common under paterfamilias was gradually replaced by an educational system that borrowed from, but did not replicate, that of the Greeks. Children, after the age of six or seven, went to school outside the home and were taught reading, writing, and counting. After the age of twelve, boys from upper class families went to a grammar school where they learned Latin, Greek, grammar, and literature. As in Greece, at age sixteen some boys went on to learn public speaking and rhetoric to prepare them for lives as orators.

But there were two major differences between the Greek and Roman educational orientations. To the Greeks, the arts were central to their educational philosophy and incorporated many of the subjects covered by our contemporary liberal arts curricula. The Romans considered the arts unimportant and thought of them in a more limited way than we do today. They did, however, incorporate one facet of the Greek arts: Greek literature. The other difference was athletics. For the Greeks, athletics reflected their belief that a healthy mind could exist only in a healthy body. It also reflected their belief in the importance of perfection and beauty. For the Romans, athletics was only the means to keep their soldiers in good physical condition.

As it evolved, the late Roman system of education became a tier system much like our own today. Students progressed through tiers, and their progress was determined more by their ability than by their age. Although there are some parallels to our educational system, there are important differences. In our educational system, those who attend higher education do so to attain advanced professional and occupational skills. But in Roman society, vocational skills, such as those needed to be a tradesman or farmer, were learned on the job. Those students who went on to higher education prepared themselves for public service as statesmen or orators.

The Medieval Period of Education, 500–1400 CE

The historian Gibbon ([1782] 2008) dated the fall of the Western Roman Empire to November 476 CE, when a German chieftain, Odoacer, deposed Romulus Augustus, the last emperor of the Western Roman Empire. But obviously the empire had been in decline for some centuries. In addition, the Eastern Roman Empire did not fall until the Turks captured Constantinople on May 29, 1453. Historians have continued to reassess this period that was once called the Dark Ages. The term *medieval* is now used to reflect the fact that the period was much more differentiated than the term *Dark Ages* would suggest.

In Europe during the early Middle Ages, most of the people were uneducated, and this was reflected in a lack of central authority and continued conflict. The nobility had castles to protect and knights who fought their battles. Keeping the peasants uneducated tended to keep them subservient so there was no incentive for higher social classes to support general education.

Knights were the exception to the period's disregard of education. The boys who were to become knights were taught reading, writing, and a number of practical skills. Usually an established knight taught the apprentice knights. Their education included the famous code of chivalry. Educating the knights was a way in which the nobility could look out for their own welfare. An educated army is more effective than an uneducated one.

Aside from the knight training, most of the education during the Middle Ages was through the monasteries and monastic orders. It was essential for the church to establish schools to train future priests. There were several variations. Bishops set up schools to train priests who administered to the bishops' dioceses. Some religious orders set up schools for both vocational and religious training. In other places, parish priests also taught a small number of peasant boys in the town to be literate. The curriculum was generally limited to learning medieval Latin, a kind of dialect of classical Latin, some arithmetic, and a few practical skills such as writing.

Around 1100 CE, education became more widespread. More Latin schools opened, and towns in both Italy and England supported them. In contrast to the church-oriented schools, these provided education both for those preparing for the ministry and those who were not. The curriculum was still quite limited and included reading texts of pious sentiments, grammar manuals, and a little bit of poetry, particularly that of Virgil. At the next level, students were taught *ars dictaminis*, the theory and practice of writing prose letters by following principles found in medieval manuals. The manuals offered rules for prose composition derived from Cicero's *De Inventione* and the pseudo-Ciceronian *Rhetorica ad Herennium*—two books written in the first century CE. Upper-level students, especially those beginning university study, might also study introductory logic or dialectic—a key part of the scholastic method (Ferzoco and Muessig 2000).

According to Kreeft (1990), a scholar of the medieval era, the aim of medieval education was to guide individuals toward leading a moral and God-fearing life. The clerics who dominated medieval education believed that knowledge was acquired from books and from debate, not from reality. The monastic teaching method was dialectic: "To the medieval mind, debate was a fine art, a serious science, and a fascinating entertainment, much more than it is to the modern mind, because the medieval people believed, like Socrates, that dialectic could uncover truth. Thus a 'scholastic disputation' was not a personal contest in cleverness, nor was it 'sharing opinions'; it was a shared journey of discovery" (Kreeft 1990, 14–15).

The late Middle Ages, coincident with countries becoming stabler and less combative, was important for introduction of the printing press and the use of movable type. The availability of inexpensive books changed the nature of medieval society. "Rather than being focused upon courts or churches, a literary culture began to emerge around the semi-autonomous printing press. Its agenda was set by demand and profit rather than religious orthodoxy or political ideology. Printing presses turned intellectual and cultural creativity into a collaborative venture, as printers, merchants, teachers, scribes, translators, artists, and writers all pooled their skills and resources in creating the finished product" (Brotton 2006, 49–50). Although the humanistic leaders of society tried to use the printing press to their own advantage, it could not put back into the bottle the cultural genie the printing press had released.

The Renaissance Period of Education, 1400–1700 CE

Modern education is a product of the Renaissance. The Renaissance was a perfect storm of scientific experimentation, cultural rediscovery, technical innovation, courageous exploration, and revolutionary ideas about authority and government. But these movements did not happen all at the same time or all in the same place. Western Europe, for example, entered into the modern era earlier than Eastern Europe or the Middle East. Moreover, historians are constantly revising their interpretations of the events of modern history.

What cannot be denied is that the changes starting in the sixteenth century were as momentous as they were varied. Among the most significant of these changes were the voyages of discovery to the "new" continents and the Pacific Ocean. The Europeans' findings on these voyages not only changed the conception of the world but also contributed to enormous alterations in the structure of society and its economic and political systems. Perhaps the economic consequences were the most significant. The importation of spices, precious metals, and new plants and animals contributed to the emergence of a merchant class of entrepreneurs who took over the purchases and sales of these goods. This helped some societies move from a system of *orders based on birth*—royalty, nobility, clergy, and commoners—to one of *social class based on wealth* (Cameron 2006).

The Reformation

The rise of the social class system further increased the unhappiness of most of the common people with the practices of the Roman Catholic Church. There was unhappiness with the pope, who seemed too interested in affairs of state and too little interested in the spiritual well-being of his followers. Likewise, people were also angered at the lower church officials who sold indulgences (excusing one's sins) to the wealthy, and who, along with other excesses, lived lavishly and kept mistresses. In keeping with the revolutionary orientation of the Renaissance, the authority of the Roman Catholic Church began to be openly and boldly attacked.

Although there were many who overtly challenged the church, it was the German monk Martin Luther, the most outspoken of the challengers, who brought this issue to a head. The selling of indulgences, which, by implication, meant that people could buy their way into heaven, particularly incensed him. Luther expressed his unhappiness with church corruption by penning his 95 Theses in 1517. They called for a full reform of the Roman Catholic Church. In his theses, Luther made three major points, which became the grounds of the Reformation, the bases for all modern Protestant denominations:

1. People could earn salvation only in God's forgiveness. In contrast, Catholicism taught that faith and good works were needed for salvation.
2. The pope is a limited authority. The Bible is the one true authority.
3. All people with faith in Christ are equal. People do not need priests and bishops to interpret the Bible for them. They can read it themselves and make up their own minds.

On October 31, 1517, Luther posted his 95 Theses on the church door in Wittenberg, Saxony, Germany. Thanks to the printing press, invented several decades earlier, Luther's theses were printed and distributed throughout Germany and eventually the rest of Europe. Luther captured the rebellious spirit of the times, and people throughout Europe began following his dictates. As a consequence, many different Protestant sects emerged and were often in conflict with one another as well as with the Roman Catholic Church.

The rejection of the Roman Catholic Church led countries like Germany, Switzerland, and England to declare a national religion. Wars and edicts against certain religions were unintended consequences of this religious diversity. This tumult set the stage for the turbulent seventeenth and eighteenth centuries.

The invention of the printing press had other consequences, particularly for education. Books could be mass-produced at low cost, which encouraged the spread of literacy and of broad public education. It thus gave a boost to the rise of the humanist philosophy that dominated the sixteenth century. Humanism was founded on the belief that a better world would be created from an education based on the rediscovered, reinterpreted literary works of Greek and Roman antiquity. It is concerned with human needs and goodness rather than the divine or supernatural. Humanism is generally regarded as the transition between the ancient, prescientific world and the modern world.

Humanism had two major contentions, which are still argued by some contemporary humanists (Bloom 1987). The first proposition was that mastery of the rediscovered classics of the Greco-Roman period would make the student a better, more refined, more rational individual. This training would also prepare the student for reflecting on and coping with the moral and ethical problems of the rapidly changing social world. Second, a humanistic education would provide the student with the prerequisite skills to serve as an ambassador, lawyer, priest, or secretary. Training in translation, public speaking, and letter writing were also highly marketable skills in the mercantile economy. Thus humanism had the goals of making students both better people and more employable ones.

While the goals of humanism were laudable, the methods used to achieve them were not. The humanists' rejection of medieval scholastics and dependence on dialectics led to a reorganization of the schools and universities in much of Western Europe. The new education was based on the idea that classical culture provided the best preparation for both intellectual and practical vocations. Will S. Monroe describes well the character of this curriculum:

> To accomplish this purpose [of achieving a classical education] as soon as the child was considered sufficiently matured for linguistic discipline, and this varied from the sixth to the ninth years, he was initiated into the mysteries of Latin eloquence. His preliminary training consisted in a verbal study of the Latin grammar for purposes of precision in speech and successful imitation; but, as the grammar was printed in Latin, with hundreds of incomprehensible rules and exceptions, all which had to be "learned by heart," the way of the young learner was, indeed, a thorny one. True, the classical authors were later read, but chiefly for the purpose of gleaning from them choice phrases to be used in the construction of Latin sentences or for purposes of disputations in

dialectics. Logic and history were given most subordinate places in the course of study, the former merely that it might give greater precision in writing and speaking, and the latter that it might furnish illustrations in rhetorical exercises. (1900, 2–3)

The humanistic educators placed great emphasis on students in primary schools, secondary schools, and universities speaking Latin. Knowing Horace and Virgil by heart was the primary goal of every student. Aside from memorization, the focus of education was on grammatical structure, with understanding the content and intent of the author only a matter of secondary concern. Instructors were admonished to set an example by speaking only in Latin. Indeed, students were forbidden to speak their native language and were punished if they did so. Not surprisingly, a system of spying arose whereby some students would report on others who spoke the "vulgar" native language. Nonetheless, as might be expected, young people still spoke their native language when they were alone (Monroe 1900).

This type, but not all types, of humanistic education was offered only to men. Humanists held that there was a different training for women. This different preparation derived from the fact that men owned the households and women ran them. Renaissance society offered few nonhousehold roles for women, but it did not deny them the opportunity to obtain an education. Yet this education was valued only insofar as it contributed to the women's attractiveness as potential wives and homemakers—not as a means of having an occupation outside the home.

Humanist Leon Battisa Alberti describes what he regarded as a humanist role for women: "The smaller household affairs, I leave to my wife's care. . . . It would hardly win us respect if our wife busied herself among the men in the marketplace, out in the public eye. It also seems somewhat demeaning to me to remain shut up in the house among women when I have manly things to do among men, fellow citizens, and worthy and distinguished foreigners" (Brotton 2006, 46).

The First Educational Reformers

While the humanists did a great service in bringing back the literature and culture of the ancient world, they did a disservice in their blind devotion to the past and their use of rote methods of instruction. It was this devotion to learning from books rather than from nature that nurtured the first educational rebels, among them Francis Bacon and John Milton.

Francis Bacon, 1561–1626

The Renaissance also gave rise to modern science. Although Aristotle and Plato remained the major sources for scientific observation and thinking during the early phases of this period, their authority was increasingly challenged. The discovery of the Americas by the Europeans made it clear that the earth was round and not flat as was often assumed by many in the ancient world. And Galileo (1564–1642) rejected Aristotle's theories of motion, acceleration, and the nature of the universe. His refined telescope allowed him to confirm the claim of Copernicus (1473–1543) that the earth was not at the center of the universe but was one of the infinity of heavenly bodies. Galileo, like Copernicus, was an advocate of observation and experiment over philosophical speculation.

Francis Bacon, however, took these scientific developments even further and articulated the foundations of modern science. Bacon challenged the argument that knowledge was best gained by logical deduction as epitomized in the syllogism

> All men are mortal,
> Plato is a man.
> Therefore Plato is mortal.

From the Aristotelian perspective, logic and rhetoric are truer and more reliable than is observation. Bacon argued, however, that the premises of the syllogism had to be demonstrated and could not be taken on faith, particularly when the primary premise could never be proven. To prove that all men are mortal, one would have to wait for all men to die. In contrast to deductive reasoning, Bacon argued for the use of inductive reasoning, arriving at general conclusions only after amassing a multitude of facts. For Bacon, science had to be based on observation, experiment, and induction, not on reasoning from unproven premises.

John Milton, 1608–1674

The poet John Milton was greatly troubled and angered by humanistic education. In his *Tractate of Education* (Ainsworth 1928), he used harsh language to attack the teaching methods of the humanists. He complained of the many mistakes of the Latin schools and was critical of the unrealistic demands these schools made on students and the fact that they made learning unpleasant and ineffective. He also argued that the Latin-school approach was overly linguistic, abstract, and divorced from the real world. But the teaching of Latin was what most incensed Milton. He argued that instruction in Latin was mechanical and that far too much time was spent on the subject.

Milton, like Bacon, not only criticized but also offered his own suggestions regarding what effective schooling should entail. He advocated children beginning with the simplest subjects—"those most obvious to the sense" (Ainsworth 1928, 54). Following Bacon, he also admonished teachers to employ the inductive method starting with the study of sensible things. The more abstract subjects are to be taught only after the mastery of the sensible. He had an encyclopedic view of education that would cover everything from geometry and arithmetic to grammar, poetry, and logic. In contrast to humanistic education, which was largely speculative and contemplative, Milton proposed a curriculum that would prepare the student for living both a practical and a religious, moral life.

Summary

All of the demographical, political, technological, intellectual, and philosophical changes of the sixteenth, seventeenth, and eighteenth centuries are what gave rise to the modern world and to modern education. At the heart of modernity was the primacy of the individual over the state and the church, and of observation and experimentation over deductive logic and rhetoric. The primacy of the individual is the basis of democratic and parliamentary governments. And as Thomas Jefferson appreciated, an effective democracy rests on an educated constituency. But modern education has not found it easy to shake off some of the humanistic curricula and teaching practices or the ongoing conflict over whether education is to serve the individual, society, or both.

The earliest Giants included in this book were arguing directly against humanistic educational practices. But it is a testament to the hardiness of humanism that many of the later Giants were still fighting, if indirectly, against the negative educational practices associated with that orientation. This is not meant, however, to gainsay the lasting positive benefits of the humanistic revival of the ancient Greek and Roman literature and cultures to modern society and education.

References

Ainsworth, Oliver Morley, ed. 1928. *Milton on Education: The Tractate of Education with Supplementary Extracts from Other Writings of Milton*. New Haven, CT: Yale University Press.

Bloom, Allan. 1987. *The Closing of the American Mind*. New York: Simon & Schuster.

Brotton, Jerry. 2006. *The Renaissance: A Very Short Introduction*. New York: Oxford University Press.

Cameron, Euan, ed. 2006. *The Sixteenth Century*. New York: Oxford University Press.

Ferzoco, George, and Carolyn Muessig. 2000. *Medieval Monastic Education*. New York: Leicester University Press.

Freeman, Kenneth John. (1907) 1969. *Schools of Hellas: An Essay on the Practice and Theory of Ancient Greek Education from 600 to 300 B.C.* New York: Teachers College.

Gibbon, Edward. (1782) 2008. *The History of the Decline and Fall of the Roman Empire*, Vol. 1. New York: Quill Pen Classics.

Kreeft, Peter. 1990. *A Summa of the Summa*. San Francisco: Ignatius.

Lawrence, Elizabeth. 1970. *The Origins and Growth of Modern Education*. New York: Penguin.

Marrou, H. I. 1956. *A History of Education in Antiquity*. Translated by George Lamb. Madison: University of Wisconsin Press.

Monroe, Will S. 1900. *Comenius: The Beginnings of Educational Reform*. New York: Scribner.

Roberts, John. 2007. *Oxford Dictionary of the Classical World*. New York: Oxford University Press.

2

John Amos Comenius

1592–1670

History is not always kind to innovators, and it has been particularly unkind to John Amos Comenius. Given little mention in contemporary histories of education, Comenius nonetheless made major and lasting contributions that have shaped many facets and levels of contemporary education. The breadth and depth of his contribution is truly extraordinary. As Maurice Walter Keatinge writes, Comenius was the man

> whose theories have been put into practice in every school that is conducted on rational principles, who embodies the materialistic tendencies of our "modern side" instructors, while avoiding the narrowness of their reforming zeal, who lays stress on the spiritual aspect of true education while he realises the necessity of equipping his pupils for the rude struggle with nature and with fellow-men . . . [yet] produced practically no effect upon the school organization and educational development of the following century. (1910, 98)

The failure to fully appreciate Comenius's contribution lies in circumstances unrelated to his educational achievements. Rather, it had to do with Comenius's unfortunate boyhood acquaintance Drabik, with whom Comenius remained in contact throughout his life. As a young man, Drabik re-created himself as a seer and a prophet. Comenius was taken in by Drabik's self-serving descriptions of forthcoming events. Naively, Comenius wrote articles in support of Drabik's predictions, which turned out to be false. When the truth came out, the public rejected not only Comenius's writings supporting these prophecies but the whole of his huge educational opus. His books and essays were only rediscovered and reprinted in the nineteenth century. Likewise, Comenius's barely marked grave was also found at that time, and his remains reinterred with a proper tombstone. In the last century, there has been a growing interest in the man and his work (for example, Bergson 1911, Anastasas 1973, Gardner 1993). This interest will no doubt continue to enhance his reputation and acknowledge the lasting importance of his work.

The Man

The Early Years, 1592–1611

John Amos Comenius was born in 1592 in Moravia, a province in what is now the Czech Republic. His father was a prosperous miller who belonged to the Moravian Brotherhood, a Protestant sect characterized by its extreme simplicity. Its members dedicated themselves to living as pure a life as possible in accord with the demands of a literal interpretation of scripture. Throughout his life, Comenius maintained a strong relationship with the brotherhood and, at various times, served as a teacher, a minister, and a church leader for the group.

Because of the religious conflicts and prejudices of the times, the brotherhood was forced to leave Moravia and other provinces as well. As a result, Comenius led a nomadic life and, once he reached adulthood, was never able to return to his homeland. His nomadic existence was also assured by the death of both parents while he was still a child. Relatives looked after his rearing and schooling but without great warmth or affection. He entered the Latin school in his teens, at a later age than most of his peers. As an adult, his memories of the thousands of rules he had to learn, the deadly study of grammar, and the drudgery of translating Latin authors without a good working dictionary contributed to his deep and abiding sympathy for the struggles of the elementary school student. The hate he felt for his educational experience may well have contributed to his later decision to become an educator.

The University Years, 1611–1628

In 1611 Comenius went on to Herborn University, where he intended to study for the ministry. It was at Herborn where he became acquainted with the work of the educational philosopher Ratke. This thinker's radical ideas for educational change helped nourish Comenius's still-emerging sense of self as an enlightened educator. Although Comenius did not pursue them immediately, Ratke's ideas became embedded in his psyche. Ratke argued that there is a natural sequence in the development of the human mind and in the acquisition of knowledge. He contended that this sequence should be followed in designing a course of instruction. Among other innovations, Ratke also insisted that children first be taught in their native tongue. These ideas, among others Ratke advocated, eventually became part of Comenius's own educational philosophy.

Yet at that point in his life, Comenius still thought of himself as having a life in the ministry and went on to the University of Heidelberg, where he matriculated in philosophy and theology. However, he had to drop out after a few months due to lack of funds. Comenius traveled to Prague on foot. Because he was still too young to enter the ministry, he took a job as a teacher in a brotherhood-run elementary school in Prerau, a town in the Olomouc region of what is now the Czech Republic. In that role, he was able to introduce some of the educational ideas he had acquired at Herborn. He was most concerned with the way Latin was taught and wanted to create a text that would make it much easier for children to learn that language.

In 1616 Comenius was ordained and became the minister of a church in Fulneck, a town in the Silesian region of what is now the Czech Republic. Comenius continued his elementary school teaching while still performing his ministerial duties. In fact, he was so admired for his teaching that he was chosen as the superintendent of education in the town.

Even after assuming his new role as superintendent, he did not give up his ministry and continued to meet both the spiritual and educational needs of the community. The three years he spent in Fulneck were perhaps the happiest and most conflict-free years of his life. During this period, he married and had two children. But these tranquil years were ended with the outbreak of the religiously inspired Thirty Years' War (1618–1648). To the Catholic Spaniards, the Moravian Brotherhood was an apostate group. In 1620 the Spaniards invaded Fulneck, pillaging and burning the town. Comenius's home, his library, and his unpublished educational manuscripts on which he had labored for years were lost.

Fleeing Fulneck, Comenius was given refuge by Count Karl von Zerotin on his Bohemian estate. The trials of being an exile were compounded by the deaths of his wife and children due to disease. But the persecution of the Moravian Brotherhood continued, and an edict in 1627 ended the protection of the brotherhood by the

Bohemian nobles. Comenius and other members of the brotherhood set out for Poland. Crossing the mountains, Comenius was able to look back for the last time at his beloved Bohemia and Moravia. He later wrote, "My whole life was merely the visit of a guest; I had no fatherland" (Monroe 1900).

The Years in Poland, 1628–1641

In the Polish city of Lissa, Comenius and several hundred other members of the brotherhood were welcomed to the estate of Count Raphael, who was also a member of the Moravian sect. During his thirteen years in Lissa, Comenius was able to pursue an idea that had gradually taken hold of his imagination. This idea was a pansophic (encyclopedic) educational system that would cover all extant knowledge and that was organized into an age-graded curriculum, which extended from infancy through the university. This was *The Great Didactic*, which he completed in outline form during his stay in Lissa.

Comenius approached his grand design on two fronts: one philosophical and the other practical. These remained the two central themes of his educational discourse for the rest of his life. While in Lissa, Comenius wrote some of his other most important educational works: *Janua Linguarum Reserata* (a revolutionary introduction to Latin), *Orbis Pictus* (The World in Pictures), and *School of Infancy* (a primer for parents). In Lissa, Comenius also taught elementary school and introduced a grading of the schools and a detailed description of a course of study for each grade.

The publication of *Janua* and *Orbis Pictus* were well received, and Comenius's educational work began to be recognized at home and abroad. It was not long before his educational ideas and methods began to be implemented in schools all over the world. He lectured in many countries on the European continent and in 1641 was invited to Britain. But despite the writings of Bacon decrying the state of education in England, British Parliament was too involved with the uprising in Ireland and then the civil war against King Charles I to be concerned with educational reform. Comenius had hoped for financial support from the English to fill out his grand design of conducting universal research on curriculum and the founding of pansophic colleges, which would be comprehensive schools that taught the whole of human knowledge. Comenius regarded the pansophic colleges as the capstone of his educational system and whose graduates would exemplify the social, practical, and spiritual rewards of a universal education. This idea of a universal college that would serve all the people of the world was Comenius's fervent dream to which he devoted all of his energies.

Devastated by the failure of the English to provide financial support for his grand educational project, Comenius left London for Sweden, where he brokenheartedly resigned himself to giving up his grand educational scheme. From Sweden he went back to Lissa. In that city, however, his teaching and writing brought little income, and his poverty made it necessary for him to seek a patron to support his work.

The Years at Elbing, East Prussia, 1642–1648

Comenius found such a patron in Louis De Geer, a rich Dutch merchant who was then living in Sweden. But De Geer had little interest in such grand designs as *The Great Didactic*. He offered to support Comenius if he would undertake writing more effective schoolbooks, provide more rational methods of teaching for the instructors, and introduce a more intelligent grading of the schools. Comenius accepted the offer and moved to the town of Elbing on the Baltic Sea in East Prussia, where he and his second family settled in 1642.

In order to provide for his family and others of the brotherhood (for whom, as a leader and pastor, he continued to feel responsible), Comenius had to abandon his dream of creating a universal educational system. Perhaps because he did not find writing textbooks particularly challenging, Comenius allowed himself to be diverted by accepting a teaching position in Elbing and by frequent trips to Poland to attend ecclesial conventions and to minister to the needs of the brotherhood. However, De Geer became impatient with him and appointed a commission to review his work.

In 1646 Comenius went to Stockholm to report on his educational efforts. The commission reviewed his progress and gave a very favorable report. By that time, Comenius had completed a number of projects: a book on language teaching, which dealt with the nature, function, and laws to be observed in language instruction; a lexicon based on these laws; and a series of graded reading books. De Geer urged him to prepare these materials for publication.

The Return to Lissa, 1648–1650

Another detour in Comenius's career came in 1648 with the death of Justinus, the senior bishop of the Moravian Brotherhood. Comenius was chosen as his successor.

This appointment meant that Comenius had to move back to Lissa and give up his arrangement with De Geer. Comenius's strong sense of responsibility was shown by the fact that once in Lissa he sent the finished books to De Geer as rapidly as he could. Comenius was actually happy to leave the town of Elbing, where he felt isolated and, in some ways, betrayed. He had assumed his connection with Sweden, where De Geer lived and wielded considerable influence, would end a ban that had exiled the brotherhood from Bohemia and Moravia. However, the Peace of Westphalia, which ended the Thirty Years' War, did not withdraw the ban, and the brotherhood remained excluded from their homeland.

In his role as bishop, Comenius devoted his full time to the needs of the brotherhood from 1648 to 1650. Still, the church had little money, and Comenius began to consider lucrative offers from other regions to revise their educational systems. One such offer came from Transylvania in Hungary. The offer was appealing. In addition to a liberal salary, he would be provided with the complete backing to set up a school system according to his philosophy. He was also offered a printing facility for the printing of his books. Recognizing that this arrangement would benefit the brotherhood as well as his own work, Comenius petitioned the brotherhood to be relieved of his position as bishop for a few years.

Last Years in Hungary and Holland, 1650–1670

The brotherhood granted the petition, and Comenius and his family once again moved to a new community, this time in the city of Saros-Patak, a cultural center in northern Hungary. He immediately drew up a plan for a seven-year school. Comenius stayed in Saros-Patak for four years, during which the first three years of the seven-year plan were completed. The innovations that Comenius introduced were an immediate success. In part at least, the positive outcome of the program was attributable to the fact that the teachers were those Comenius himself had trained in Lissa.

Comenius returned to Lissa in 1654 to reassume the role of bishop. But his stay there was brief for the Swedes attacked Lissa; Comenius escaped, as he put it, almost "in a state of nudity" (1858, 101). As he had in Fulneck, Comenius once again lost both his library and his many unpublished manuscripts. He wrote of the loss of these manuscripts, on which he had labored for years: "The loss of this work I shall cease to lament only when I cease to breathe" (Monroe 1900, 70).

Comenius escaped to Silesia and shortly afterward to Frankfurt in Germany. Still not feeling safe, he journeyed on to Hamburg, Germany. In Hamburg, he suffered a severe illness that incapacitated him for two months. When he learned of Comenius's illness, Lawrence De Geer, the son of Comenius's deceased former patron, wrote to him and told him to come directly to Amsterdam in Holland. During Comenius's time with his father, the young De Geer had formed a deep and abiding affection for Comenius and a profound respect for his educational ideas. He wanted to ensure that Comenius had a safe and secure place to reside. In 1656 Comenius made his final move to Amsterdam.

This was a happy move for Comenius. The Dutch Republic was the most liberal region in Europe, open to a wide variety of religious beliefs and opinions. Although in his sixties—old for the time period—he continued to be productive and published a one-thousand-page edition of his collected educational writings. He also continued serving as minister to his disheartened brotherhood who had also escaped to Holland. In addition, thanks to the efforts of the young De Geer, he was sought out to teach the children of the wealthy merchant class in Amsterdam. He was comfortable both financially and intellectually in this new setting.

Comenius could well be regarded as a genius, and one who could rightly be named the father of modern education. In person he was a humble, gracious, and generous man. As Palacky writes, all those who knew him attested to his goodness, kindness, and faithfulness:

> In his intercourse with others, Comenius was in an extraordinary degree friendly, conciliatory, and humble; always ready to serve his neighbor and sacrifice himself. His writings, as well as his walk and his conversation, show the depth of his feeling, his goodness, his uprightness, and his fear of God. He never cast back upon his opponents what they meted out to him. He never condemned, no matter how great the injustice that he was made to suffer. At all times, with fullest resignation, whether joy or sorrow was his portion, he honored and praised the Lord. (Monroe 1900, 81–82)

The Work

Comenius was a reformer—but an evolutionary reformer rather than a revolutionary one. For example, he was opposed to the way in which Latin was taught, but he was not opposed to the teaching of Latin. I have included Comenius among the philosophers because of the sweeping scope of his conception of pedagogy and his contributions to the institution of education as a whole. But he might equally have held his own place among the second group of practitioners in this book. His focus on methodology and his many innovations with respect to both teaching methods and curriculum rival those of Pestalozzi, Froebel, Montessori, and Steiner.

Philosophical Work

Comenius's most overarching work was *The Great Didactic*. Will S. Monroe describes the encyclopedic scope and aims of the work:

> Not only should education be common to all classes of society, but the subjects of instruction should be common to the whole range of knowledge. Comenius holds that it is the business of educators to take strong and vigorous measures that no man in his journey through life may encounter anything so unknown to him that he will be unable to pass sound judgment upon it and turn it to its proper use without serious error. . . . But even Comenius recognized the futility of thoroughness in a wide range of instruction, and he expresses willingness to be satisfied if men know the principles, the causes, and the uses of all things in existence. It is a general culture—something about a great many things—that he demands. (1900, 88–89)

Indeed, Comenius agreed with Plato that "if properly educated, man is the gentlest and most divine of created beings; but if left uneducated or subjected to a false training, he is the most intractable thing in the world" (Monroe 1900, 86).

Considering the exponential growth of knowledge and technology over the past four centuries, Comenius's vision of pansophic education—that individuals could be taught all that there is to know—seems impossible today. Indeed, today it is rare for an individual to know all there is to know within his or her own discipline or profession. But it was not this way at the time of Comenius's writing. The inductive, experimental sciences introduced by Bacon were in only their infancy, the New World was only in the process of being discovered, and the modest range of arts and mechanical skills could all be covered. Comenius looked to nature as a guide for both his teaching methods and for the organization of the curriculum.

He believed that his educational precepts were grounded in the way nature operates and that education would be easy and enjoyable:

1. if it is begun before the mind is corrupted.
2. if the mind is prepared to receive it.
3. if we proceed from the general to the particular, from what is easy to what is more complex.
4. if the pupils are not overburdened with too many different studies.
5. if the instruction is graded to the stages of the mental development of the learners.
6. if the interests of the children are consulted and their intellects are not forced along lines for which they have no natural bent.
7. if everything is taught through the medium of the senses.
8. if the utility of instruction is emphasized.
9. if everything is taught by one and the same method. (Monroe 1900, 91)

Comenius was as attentive to method as he was to the child being taught. In *The Great Didactic*, he laid out in detail methods for how to teach the sciences, the arts, language, morals, and religion. For each discipline he outlined specific steps that had to be taken to master the subject matter. With respect to language, for example, he argued that language instruction should be first tied up with the study of objects, and it should reflect the interests and comprehension of the children. He writes, "They waste their time who place before children Cicero and the other great writers; for, if students do not understand the subject-matter, how can they master the various devices for expressing it forcibly?" (Monroe 1900, 100).

In reading *The Great Didactic*, one cannot help but be impressed, indeed overwhelmed, by Comenius's foresight. Although he lived at the very beginning of the Renaissance, Enlightenment, and Age of Reason, many of his ideas are remarkably contemporary. As illustrated above, he paid equal attention to the developing child, the method of instruction, and the nature of subject matter being taught. The later Giants further elaborated and articulated these ideas that are today conceptualized as DAP. Even today we see these three essential components only in quality early childhood education programs and in some private schools for older children and youth. We can turn now to some of the more practical contributions of Comenius's work.

Contributions to Practice

The School of Infancy

In his advice to parents, Comenius was quite contemporary. He urged mothers to breast-feed their children and complained about those mothers of wealth who made use of wet nurses. As children moved beyond breast-feeding, their food should be soft, sweet, and easily digestible. He strongly advised mothers not to give their children highly seasoned foods and, above all, not to give them medicines. Apparently in Comenius's time, as is true today, there were hucksters hawking panaceas that often did more harm than good. Comenius believed that infants reared on such medicines would grow up to be "feeble, sickly, infirm, pale-faced, imbecile, [and] cancerous" (Monroe 1900, 114). He cautioned parents to ensure that their infants and young children had abundant fresh air, sleep, and exercise.

Comenius also emphasized the importance of math and language development. With respect to math, he contended that very young children should be able to count to ten and be able to distinguish different quantities. But he also recognized that going beyond those attainments was too difficult for children in the first years of life. He did argue that very young children could learn some beginning geometry by distinguishing among geometric shapes and between larger and smaller shapes. But he recognized that such children could not really understand true measurement until they reached the age of reason at six or seven.

Comenius also had much to say about language development in young children. He was adamant that children should learn to identify things like shapes, plants, and animals either before or at the time that they are given words for these objects. He emphasized that it is important that children speak correctly. He also believed that children should first learn to speak and comprehend their own mother tongue before learning another language. And he challenged his contemporaries by insisting that Latin not be taught until at least age twelve. During the early childhood years, children could profit from listening to poetry as well as jingles and nursery rhymes. They might not always understand the words, but they would enjoy the rhythm and rhymes of the language. In many ways, Comenius anticipated what is now considered the best preparation for reading—namely, language enrichment.

Comenius believed that children should be introduced gradually into language learning, going from the simple to the complex step by step. He wrote four Latin instruction books. In order of difficulty but not of publication, they are *Orbis Pictus,* the *Vestibulum,* the *Janua Linguarum Reserata,* and the *Atrium.*

Orbis Pictus

Orbis Pictus translates to "The World in Pictures." This book is generally regarded as the first illustrated book for children. While the idea of an illustrated textbook was not original to Comenius, he was one of the first to use it in elementary language instruction. Comenius, in keeping with his pansophic outlook, included a wide variety of subject matter in *Orbis Pictus.* A sense of the subjects covered is given by some of the chapter titles: "God," "The World," "The Heavens," "Fire," "The Air," "The Water," "The Clouds," "The Earth," "The Fruits of the Earth," "The Metals," "Tame Fowls," "Singing Birds," "Birds That Haunt the Fields and Woods," and "Ravenous Birds." Under the pictures in each chapter are two columns, one describing the picture in the vernacular and the other describing it in Latin.

With *Orbis Pictus,* Comenius hoped to achieve several different goals. One of these was to entice children to learn by using pictures, which are attractive and interesting to them. Another was to turn the child's attention to words and things. Finally, Comenius believed that interest and attention are the prerequisites for readiness to learn. Pictures thus facilitate the learning process and the child's willingness to follow a teacher's instructions. *Orbis Pictus* gained enormous popularity and was translated into many languages and continued in print well into the seventeenth and eighteenth centuries.

Janua Linguarum Reserata

Comenius wrote *Janua Linguarum Reserata* (The Door of Languages Unlocked) during his stay in Lissa. Comenius fashioned his book after a *Janua* published several decades earlier by a Jesuit priest. But Comenius geared his *Janua* to the elementary and secondary student. Again, its aim was encyclopedic, and in one hundred chapters, Comenius covered everything from the origin of the world to the mind and its faculties. As in the *Orbis Pictus,* the text was presented in adjoining columns, one with the subject in German and the corresponding column in Latin.

Comenius had a definite method in mind for the use of this text. Each chapter was to be read ten times. At each reading the student had to engage in an ever more complex rendering of the material. The method took the student from a literal translation of Latin into the vernacular, to a later logical analysis of reading, to a final reading in which students challenge one another to quote certain passages of Cicero or Virgil. This followed Comenius's belief that mastery of a language can only be demonstrated in its effective use. The *Janua*, which appeared before the *Orbis Pictus*, earned Comenius worldwide fame that was reinforced with the later appearance of the *Orbis Pictus*.

Atrium

Atrium (The Central Court) was meant as a more advanced text for those students who had completed the *Janua*. In Comenius's scheme, the *Janua* provides the materials for the building, while the *Atrium* provides the decorations. It essentially deals with each of the parts of speech, including nouns, pronouns, and adjectives. In the book, Comenius introduces the parts of speech from the simplest to the most complex. Each part of speech is explained along with examples. Comenius really intended the *Janua* to be a simplified Latin grammar book, which reflected his belief that grammar should be taught late, not early, in language instruction.

Vestibulum

In practice, *Janua* proved more difficult than Comenius had anticipated. *Vestibulum*, Latin for the corridor from the outside of the Roman house to the atrium, was written while Comenius was at Saros-Patek. It was meant as a primer to *Janua*. As such, the sentences are shorter and deal with simpler subjects than *Janua*. The chapters deal with topics such as, in Comenius's terms, the accidents and qualities of things, the actions and passions of things, things at home and at school, and the virtues. Comenius expressed regrets that he could not illustrate this book. He believed the parallelism between words and things was the essence of his method, and illustrations would help cement the relationship. Like his other books, *Vestibulum* was widely published and translated.

It is to be hoped that Comenius will eventually gain the recognition his enormous contribution deserves. We can now look at Comenius's positions on the questions posed to all the Giants.

Common Themes

The Nature of the Child

For Comenius, the child has the predispositions for learning, but how those dispositions are realized is dependent on education.

> The seeds of knowledge, of virtue, and of piety are, as we have seen, naturally implanted in us; but the actual knowledge, virtue, and piety are not so given. These must be acquired by prayer, by education, and by action. He gave no bad definition who said that man was a "teachable animal." And indeed it is only by a proper education that he can become a man. (Comenius in Keatinge 1910, 204)

The Aims of Education

> That the education given shall be not false but real, not superficial but thorough; That is to say, that the rational animal, man, shall be guided not by the intellects of other men, but by his own; shall not merely read the opinions of others and grasp their meaning or commit them to memory and repeat them, but shall himself penetrate to the root of things and acquire the habit of genuinely understanding and making use of what he learns. (Comenius in Keatinge 1910, 234)

The Role of Play

Comenius viewed play as a means of learning.

> In such social plays with their companions there is neither the assumption of authority nor the dread of fear, but the free intercourse which calls forth all their powers of invention, sharpens their wits, and cultivates their manners and habits. (Monroe 1900, 117)

Conformance with DAP Principles

Comenius anticipated many of the principles set forth by NAEYC as fundamental to developmentally appropriate practices, including these two examples:

> **NAEYC**
> Development and learning proceed at varying rates from child to child, as well as at uneven rates across different areas of a child's individual functioning.

COMENIUS

We must wait for opportunities to train our youth in all things and not anticipate them. We must begin in good time but not before it, as that would be no help to nature but would corrupt it. (Comenius 1986, 92)

NAEYC

Many aspects of children's learning and development follow well-documented sequences, with later abilities, skills, and knowledge building on those already acquired.

COMENIUS

Education will be easy if the pupil is not overburdened by too many subjects . . . [and] if the intellect be forced to nothing to which its natural bent does not incline it, in accordance with its age and the right method. (Keatinge 1910, 127)

Commentary

John Amos Comenius was truly a genius. He not only understood child development as well as all the sciences, languages, and arts of his times, but also devised methods of teaching these subjects at all age levels. His *The Great Didactic* also set the four levels of schooling that are the standard in most developed countries. It is truly astounding to read his exposition of the principles of DAP written more than four centuries ago. While to my knowledge Piaget never read nor referred to Comenius, I was fascinated to read that they both shared the same vision of education: to teach individuals to think for themselves and not to accept the first ideas that come to them. I hope that Comenius will eventually receive the recognition he so clearly deserves.

References

Anastasas, Florence H. 1973. *And They Called Him Amos: The Story of John Amos Comenius: A Woodcut in Words*. Jericho, NY: Expostion Press of Florida.

Bergson, Henri. 1911. *Creative Evolution*. Translated by Arthur Mitchell. New York: Macmillan.

Comenius, Johann Amos. 1858. *The School of Infancy. An Essay on the Education of Youth, During Their First Six Years*. London: W. Mallalieu.

———. 1986. *Pampaedia, or, Universal Education*. Translated by A. M. O. Dobbie. Dover, UK: Buckland.

Gardner, Howard. 1993. *Multiple Intelligences: The Theory in Practice*. New York: Basic Books.

Keatinge, Maurice Walter. 1910. *The Great Didactic of John Amos Comenius*. London: Adam and Charles Black.

Monroe, Will S. 1900. *Comenius: The Beginnings of Educational Reform*. New York: Scribner.

3

John Locke

1632–1704

Impressions of bygone famous authors are often gleaned from their portraits and writings, but these may be quite misleading. This is certainly the case with John Locke. The portraits we have of him, together with his writings, give one the sense of a harsh, strict, and forbidding personality. However, Locke was a witty storyteller and conversationalist, and a sought-after guest by many of the most prominent English families of his time. In the same vein, Locke is often presented as an unrelenting empiricist who rejected innate, and any other, ideas that were not traceable to sense experiences. Yet he also recognized and valued the importance of inborn differences in ability and talent. Likewise, in contrast to the impression that he was all work and no play, he believed that serious endeavors were most effective when they were balanced with time for recreation and leisure (Woolhouse 2007).

The Sociopolitical Scene in Seventeenth-Century England

Locke grew up during one of the most tumultuous periods in English history. The ongoing challenges to the legitimacy of the church and the monarchy were certainly influential in shaping Locke's ideas about the importance of individual authority and of personal experience in human development. He was ten years old when the civil war between Charles I and Parliament began in 1642. The causal issues were both authority and religion. Charles wanted to usurp the powers of Parliament to help Catholicism be an accepted church within the nation. The royalist forces were winning until Oliver Cromwell took over the Parliamentary army. Cromwell not only defeated the royalists but took over Ireland and Scotland as well. Charles I was caught and beheaded in 1649.

Cromwell installed himself as lord protector, effectively serving as king. He abolished the House of Lords, the monarchy, and the Anglican Church. Charles II gained the throne in 1660 after Cromwell's death and a brief period of rule under Cromwell's son. Charles II's Restoration reestablished the House of Lords, the monarchy, and the Anglican Church. Charles II wanted his brother James II to take over the throne. But James II was a Catholic and was opposed by many in Parliament, which tried to pass a succession law that would give the throne to Charles II's illegitimate son Monmouth. However, Monmouth was beheaded for treason.

Charles II died in 1685, and his brother James II took the throne. But James II was very unpopular and alienated even his strongest supporters. In 1688 William of Orange was invited by Parliament to bring a Dutch army to England. James II, recognizing that he did not have the military support to mount a defense, found refuge in France. The ascendance of William to the throne was termed "the Glorious Revolution." It marked the transfer of power in the English government from the monarch to the Parliament.

During this turbulent period, Locke was a close associate of Anthony Ashley Cooper, the Earl of Shaftesbury, one of the richest and most powerful men in England. As a result of this association, Locke's fortunes rose and fell with those of his patron. Even so, Locke attended to the earl's affairs, tutored the earl's children and those of the earl's friends, and still managed to pursue his own political writing and scientific interests. Because of these distractions, however, Locke's major works were not published until after he was fifty. His essays made him famous, and he is now regarded as among the most influential political philosophers of the seventeenth century.

The Man

The Early Years, 1632–1646

John Locke was born in Bristol, England, on August 29, 1632. He came from a family of merchants—but not just any merchants. His great-grandfather, Sir William Locke, was said to have been the "greatest English merchant under Henry the Eighth" (Woolhouse 2007, 5). While some of William's sons and grandsons continued in the merchant business, others did not. William's grandson John, Locke's father, became a lawyer and later served as a manager, among other offices, of the extended family's properties and affairs.

Locke's mother, Agnes Keene, came from a landed family. She was said to have been "a most beautiful woman" (Woolhouse 2007, 5). Throughout their married lives, Locke's parents resided in Belluton, a house given to Agnes by her grandfather and that was located in Wrington, Somerset. John and Agnes had two other children: a second son, Peter, who died in infancy, and a third son, Thomas, who was born in August 1637.

Not much is known about Locke's mother other than his description of her as a "very pious woman and affectionate mother" (Woolhouse 2007, 6). His father had a more lasting influence and was the source for some of Locke's advice to parents in his book *Some Thoughts Concerning Education*. A contemporary of Locke described Locke's relationship with his father:

> Mr. Locke never mentioned him but with great respect and affection. . . .
> His father used a conduct towards him when young, that he often spoke of
> with great approbation. It was this being severe to him by keeping him in
> much awe, and at a distance when he was a boy; but relaxing still by degrees
> that severity as he grew up to be a man, till (he being capable of it) he lived
> perfectly with him as a friend. . . . He has told me that his father, after he was
> a man, solemnly asked his pardon for having struck him once in passion
> as a boy; his fault not being equal to that correction. (Woolhouse 2007, 6)

Locke's family was Puritan. It is unclear how religious an upbringing Locke had, but it is probable that religion was a major concern during his childhood. It could hardly be otherwise with the fierce battles being fought over whether the country should be Catholic or Protestant. That his father volunteered to serve in the Parliamentary (Protestant) army is another indication of the importance of national religion to Locke's family and in the country at that time.

Early Schooling at Westminster, 1646–1652

During the Parliamentary war against Charles I, Locke's father served under John Popham. After the war, Popham, a member of Parliament, nominated Locke to attend the prestigious public school Westminster, one of the best schools in the country. It was a boarding school, so Locke left home to attend it in 1646 at age fourteen. His father arranged for him to receive regular amounts of money to cover his expenses. Locke kept a very careful accounting of his expenditures and continued to do so throughout his life.

The curriculum at Westminster was still very much in the humanist tradition, and major emphasis was placed on learning Latin, Greek, Hebrew, and Arabic. Geometry, geography, and arithmetic were given only secondary importance. Classes started at five in the morning, and the school day was crammed full. Even during lunch and supper the students practiced reading Latin manuscripts. Instruction continued after supper as well.

The weekday schedule softened a bit on Saturday when the students only practiced Greek and Latin declamations. Sundays were a different story. After attending church services, the students memorized the catechism in Greek and practiced interpreting the Greek gospel. In the afternoon they wrote about the morning sermon and attended readings of the classical authors.

Locke was very critical of both the content and practice of this schooling, but he succeeded nonetheless. His academic achievements led to his election as a minor kings scholar. This allowed him to compete for a scholarship to one of the major universities with which Westminster was attached—namely, Christ Church Oxford and Trinity Church in Cambridge. Locke won a scholarship, and at age nineteen, he became a candidate for these universities. Candidates were allowed to choose which university they would prefer; Locke chose Oxford and moved there soon after his twentieth birthday in 1652.

The Oxford Years, 1652–1666

In many ways, the curriculum at Oxford was a replay of what Locke experienced at Westminster. He had to attend lectures on Aristotle, Cicero, and Quintilian as well as discourses on moral philosophy and logic. A variation from Westminster was that each student was required to have a tutor, a graduate of the college, and the student, not the college, paid the tutor. Locke's tutor's job was to oversee Locke's life and activities, to advise him on his course of study, and to recommend readings. This allowed much more flexibility than did the formal curriculum. Although Locke went along with the prescribed course of study, he was not very happy about it, as a friend recalled:

I have often heard him say that he had so small satisfaction there from his studies as finding very little light brought thereby to his understanding, that he became discontented with his manner of life, and wished his father had rather designed him for anything else than what he was destined to: apprehending that his no greater progress in knowledge proceeded from his not being fitted, or capacitated to be a scholar. (Woolhouse 2007, 18)

Locke's years as an undergraduate changed him in many ways. He now valued the friendship of his new college friends whom he regarded as witty, knowledgeable, and curious about the world. In his letters to his friends, he was dismissive of the provincialism of his small-town upbringing. He now regarded his visits to his parents' home in Somerset as boring, and he was always eager to return to Oxford.

Locke received his baccalaureate degree in 1656. His mother had died the previous autumn, and after graduation he returned to Somerset to spend time with his father. Despite his misgivings about university education, Locke returned to Oxford to pursue a three-year master of arts degree. He earned this degree in 1658 and was elected a senior student of Christ Church College. In December 1660 Locke was elected as lecturer in Greek at Christ Church and was chosen as lecturer in rhetoric in 1663. Neither lectureship was a permanent appointment.

Thanks to his scholarship, Locke was able to continue his studies and decided to pursue graduate work in physics and medicine. He was now twenty-seven, and his father urged him to consider marriage. His father even suggested that a widow of the father's acquaintance would make a suitable match. But Locke did not follow up on his father's suggestion.

The reason behind Locke's decision was that he had already met Elinor Perry, who was several years his junior, in Oxford. They attended parties and even exchanged valentines. Locke was truly smitten with Elinor, and when he was away from Oxford, he wrote letters saying how "melancholy" and sad it was to be away from her. Elinor was more restrained but often seemed to be leading him on. In response to her seeming words of encouragement, his letters became more impassioned. Her reply to these letters, according to Roger Woolhouse (2007, 27) was an admonition to "curb his pen."

Several years later, however, when Elinor moved to Ireland, she wrote Locke suggesting he join her and that she was now ready for a more serious relationship. By this time, Locke's ardor had cooled, and he wrote back that his duties and responsibilities required that he remain in England. Elinor married another man soon after Locke's response. Although Locke had many female friends, he never again had a serious romantic involvement with a woman.

At this stage in his career, Locke had to make a decision as to the future course of his life. According to the bylaws of Christ Church, fifty-five of the senior studentships were reserved for men in the clergy, or reading for the clergy, and only five could be held by others, two of which were in medicine and three in law and moral philosophy. Locke chose to be a doctor. He pursued his medical studies and received a license to practice medicine but never attained the degree of doctor of medicine.

One reason for Locke's choice of medicine was the fact that Robert Boyle (of Boyle's Law fame) took over as leader of the Oxford scientific group and became Locke's mentor. The empiricism of Boyle, and of his medical mentor, Sydenham, was very influential in Locke's own thinking. Under Boyle's direction, Locke undertook many physical experiments. Sydenham encouraged Locke to experiment with different pharmaceutical combinations aimed at finding better medicines. Sydenham rejected abstract theories of the causes of illness, which were prevalent at the time, and emphasized the importance of observation. This only reinforced Locke's own empiricist leanings.

In 1666 Locke left Oxford but continued his relationship with the university, renting lodging and returning periodically. Oxford was very traditional, and as some of Locke's views on religion, toleration, and authority became known to the dons (the university's academic leaders), he lost favor. It was the vindictive order of Charles II in 1684, however, that canceled Locke's studentship and ended his relationship with Oxford. This order met with the approval of the dons. Locke had already moved his belongings from Oxford in anticipation of this action by the dons. Locke later learned of a book burning on the Oxford campus of condemned authors, many of whom he had read and admired. It was the last such burning on the Oxford campus. Locke never returned to Oxford.

Locke and Lord Shaftesbury, 1666–1688

In 1666 Lord Shaftesbury traveled to Oxford to drink the mineral waters to help with his liver ailment. He asked Dr. Thomas, his physician at Oxford, to deliver twelve bottles of the water to him. Thomas was out of town and asked Locke, who had been working with him, to take Lord Shaftesbury the water in his stead. When they met and conversed, the two liked one another immediately. Soon after, Lord Shaftesbury asked Locke to be his personal physician and invited him to London to stay at Lord Shaftesbury's Exeter House, where Locke would have his own apartment. Locke agreed.

After moving to London, Locke advised and supervised an operation on Lord Shaftesbury to remove an abscess on his liver and to install a small silver tube to drain away future contaminants. The innovative operation was a success and further strengthened the bond between the two men. Locke soon took on more than physician responsibilities for Lord Shaftesbury. He also served as secretary, researcher, political operative, and friend. As a result, Locke was in the thick of English politics during the 1670s and 1680s.

Lord Shaftesbury also involved Locke in many of his financial dealings. Believing that England would profit from trade with the British colonies, Lord Shaftesbury urged Charles II to set up a board of trade to oversee commerce with the colonists. Locke was appointed secretary of the new board of trade. Lord Shaftesbury's interest in trade was not altruistic; he wanted to found profitable ventures in the American Carolinas. Locke was involved in writing the constitution for these new colonies. Lord Shaftesbury also asked for Locke's advice on the English monetary crises over the value of money, coinage, and interest rates. Locke wrote papers on these economic matters as well.

While living at Exeter House, Locke maintained his interests in philosophical matters that had been ignited at Oxford. He participated in regular meetings with a group of scholars interested in the same issues. It was during these meetings that Locke came to the conclusion that before deciding on philosophical issues, the first thing was to "examine our own abilities, and see what objects our understandings were, or were not fitted to deal with" (Woolhouse 2007, 98). It was this insight that led Locke to begin writing *An Essay Concerning Human Understanding*.

At this time in London, the air was saturated with the smoke of coal fires used to heat homes. Locke was asthmatic, and the smoke aggravated Locke's condition, so he often left London for periods to escape the pollution. In 1674 Locke traveled to France, ostensibly to be the tutor and guide of the son of one of Lord Shaftesbury's friends. But it was also to escape the London air. While in France he met with many scientists and continued his scientific experiments.

During Locke's stay in France, Lord Shaftesbury was accused of treason and was imprisoned for a year (1678) in the Tower of London. Lord Shaftesbury was released after a rumor spread that there was a Catholic conspiracy to assassinate Charles II and put his Catholic brother James II on the throne. Over the next several years, Lord Shaftesbury took advantage of the rumor to get Parliament to pass an exclusion bill that would bypass James II and put his Protestant half brother Monmouth on the throne. The bill never passed, and Lord Shaftesbury became a fugitive and fled to Holland in 1682. He died there a year later.

In 1678 Locke returned to London and continued work on *Essay* and other writings. But in June 1683, another plot to assassinate the king and his brother was revealed. Though Locke had nothing to do with it, because of his relationship to Lord Shaftesbury, he was branded as a traitor. In September 1683 he went into exile in Holland. It was during his exile in Holland that Locke finished *An Essay Concerning Human Understanding*. During this period he also published an epistle (a literary letter for the public) on toleration in Latin.

In 1688 King James II continued efforts to support the Roman Catholic Church, which led Parliament to invite William of Orange to bring an army to England and him (William) to assume the throne. King James II fled, and William became king and his wife, Mary, queen. With King James II gone, Locke was free to return to England. Locke was asked by Lord Charles Mordaunt to accompany his wife and the new queen on their voyage to England. Locke accepted and accompanied the new queen on the royal yacht so she could rejoin her husband (Woolhouse 2007).

The Last Years, 1688–1704

When he returned from Holland, Locke was invited to live with Sir Francis Masham and Lady Masham in their home, Oates, in Essex. While living at Oates, Locke published drafts of *An Essay Concerning Human Understanding* and *Two Treatises of Government* in 1690. And in 1693 he published *Some Thoughts Concerning Education*, which is discussed in the next section. For some reason, Locke did not want his authorship of *Two Treatises* to be known and went to considerable trouble, including using a pen name, to conceal the fact that it was his work. In addition, he was very unhappy with the printed edition of *Two Treatises* and revised it several times, but he remained unhappy with the result.

In 1696 the board of trade was revived, in part through Locke's intervention. The board dealt with many different issues, including the governance of the colonies, the Irish wool trade, and the suppression of piracy. Locke served as a member of the board until 1700. But he was only in London for the summer months because of his asthma. Locke remained at Oates for the rest of his life and died on Saturday, October 26, 1704.

Locke left behind a distinguished body of work. In addition to those previously mentioned, he wrote *A Letter Concerning Toleration, Two Treatises on Government, Second Treatise on Government, The Reasonableness of Christianity as Described in Scriptures, On Politics and Education*, and *Of the Conduct of the Understanding*. His complete works have been released in nine- and ten-volume collections, a testament to the voluminous and enduring quality of his writings.

The Work

Although our main concern is with Locke's work on education, it is nonetheless useful to present at least the basic propositions of *Essay Concerning Human Understanding* because in many ways it provides the rationale and justification for a number of the child-rearing practices he advocates. His ideas about learning, for example, derive directly from his belief that the mind at birth is a blank page. Likewise, his thoughts on discipline reflect his ideas of justice in *Two Treatises on Government*.

An Essay Concerning Human Understanding

An Essay on Human Understanding is in the direct lineage of the Enlightenment rejection of royal and papal authority. *Essay* is divided into four books. Book I gives a detailed rebuttal of the notion of innate ideas. In Book II, Locke presents his theory of ideas, which is in effect a cognitive psychology of thinking. Book III is devoted to language, and Book IV is given to the discussion of abstract knowledge, including intuition, mathematics, science, faith, and opinion. For our purposes, we need only summarize the major theses of the first two books.

Book I

Locke's main proposition in the first book is to make the case that the mind at birth is a blank page (the term *tabula rasa* is often attributed to Locke but does not appear in the essays) and that we are not born with any innate ideas. He writes that the supposed universality of such ideas is false because there are no universally accepted truths. He pointed out that the supposed universal principle of identity (the Aristotelian syllogism: If a=b and b=c then a=c) is not understood by children and those of limited mental ability. As discussed in the upcoming chapter on Piaget, children do attain the identity principle but only after the age of six or seven.

Book II

In contrast to Book I, Book II deals with what humans can and cannot know, due to the limits of our understanding. Locke argues that we can only know what comes to us through our senses or through reflection, which is our perception of the operations of our own minds. Locke thus identified primary qualities that are intrinsically part of the object; a sugar cube, for example, continues to be sweet no matter how many times you divide it. Such qualities are passive in contrast with those that are actively constructed by the mind, such as numbers, causes, and effects.

In this book, Locke lays down the premises of learning, which became in the first half of the twentieth century the psychology of behaviorism—the dominant psychology of its time. But his empiricism has other implications as well. If humans are not born with innate ideas, and if all our ideas come by way of our senses, then we are all born equal, for we are all born with the same senses and with the same blank page. This is a concept that Thomas Jefferson, a student of Locke, wrote into the Declaration of Independence. Locke also argued that our reason leads us to the knowledge "of this certain and evident truth, that there is an eternal, most powerful and most knowing being which whether anyone will please to call God, it matters not" (Locke [1690] 1975). By presenting the God concept in this way, Locke divorced it from its Western Judeo-Christian identity and reasoned that God, by any other name, would have the same attributes. Here Locke influenced the writers of the US Constitution. His view allowed them to profess a belief in God without tying it to Christian theology. It was thus a factor in the constitutional separation of church and state.

Some Thoughts Concerning Education

Locke wrote *Some Thoughts Concerning Education* in response to a request from a friend asking for advice about raising his son. In answer to this request, Locke wrote a series of letters, which he later brought together as a book. Locke actually had a chance to test his ideas in the training of the grandson of his hosts at Oates. In the introduction of the book, Locke emphasizes the importance of the early years of life for the formation of character:

I myself have been consulted of late by so many, who profess themselves at a loss how to breed their children, and the early corruption of youth is now become so general a complaint, that he cannot be thought wholly impertinent, who brings the consideration of this matter on the stage, and offers something, if it be but to excite others, or afford matter of correction: for errors of education should be less indulged than any. These, like faults in the first concoction, that are never mended in the second or third, carry their afterwards incorrigible taint with them thro' all the parts and stations in life. (Locke [1690] 1975, xii)

Although Locke's views on government are quite liberal and democratic—he believes all men are created equal—he nonetheless appears still tied to the English class system and says nothing about the education of women:

I would have everyone lay it seriously to heart and, after having well examined and distinguished what fancy, custom, or reason advises in the case, set his helping hand to promote everywhere that way of training up youth with regard to their several conditions [social classes], which is the easiest, shortest, and likeliest to produce virtuous, useful and able men in their distinct callings: though that most to be taken care of is the gentlemen's calling. For if those of that rank are by their education once set right, they will quickly bring all the rest into order. (Locke [1693] 2007, 10)

Here Locke is suggesting that if upper classes are correctly educated, they will have no trouble keeping the lower classes content with their lot.

The original book was divided into twenty-two ten-page sections dealing with a range of issues from child rearing to education. For the purposes of this book, only the recommendations that pertain to young children are summarized. Locke begins with a discussion of health and hygiene and echoes the ancient Greek adage of a "sound mind in a sound body." Locke was very opposed to meeting the infant's wish and desire for unhealthy foods and contended that from an early age children must discover the "power of denying ourselves the satisfaction of our own desires, where reason does not authorize them" and that even infants should be "us'd to submit their desires, and go without their longings" (Locke [1693] 2007, 32).

With respect to discipline, Locke advocates the practice his father employed, mainly start strict and allow more freedoms as the child grows older: "I imagine every one will judge it reasonable, that their children, when little, should look upon their parents as their lords, their absolute governors, and as such stand in awe of them; and that, when they come to riper years, they should look on them as their best, as their only sure friends, and as such love and reverence them" ([1693] 2007, 35). Locke also recognizes that one can go overboard in this direction: "On the other side, if the mind be curbed, and humbled too much in children; if their spirits be abas'd and broken much by too strict an hand over them, they lose all their vigour and industry, and are in a worse state than the former" ([1693] 2007, 36). And he opposes physical punishment: "Beating them, and all other sorts of slavish and corporal punishments, are not the discipline fit to be used in the education of those we would have wise, good, and ingenuous men; and therefore very rarely to be applied, and that only in great occasions, and cases of extremity" ([1693] 2007, 39).

In regard to learning, Locke writes, "Though it be past doubt, that the fittest time for children, to learn any thing, is when their minds are in tune, and well disposed to it; when neither flagging of spirit, nor intentness of thought upon something else, makes them awkward and averse" ([1693] 2007, 57). With respect to beginning reading, and I would guess he would say the same for arithmetic, he strikes a very contemporary note:

> Thus much for learning to read, which let him never be driven to, nor chid for; cheat him into it if you can, but make it not a business for him. 'Tis better it be a year later before he can read, than that he should this way get an aversion to learning. If you have any contests with him, let it be in matters of moment, of truth, and good nature, but lay no task upon him about ABC. (Locke [1693] 2007, 124)

Locke is clearly aware of age changes in mental ability:

> But when I talk of reasoning, I do not intend any other, but such as is suited to the child's capacity and apprehension. No body can think a boy of three or seven years old should be argued with as a grown man. Long discourses, and philosophical reasonings, at best, amaze, and confound, but do not instruct children. When I say, therefore, that they must be treated as rational creatures, I mean that you should make them sensible, by the mildness of your carriage, and the composure even in your correction of them, that what you do is reasonable in you, and useful and necessary for them, and that it is not out of *Caprichio* [from *capriccio*, meaning "whim" in Italian], passion or fancy, that you command or forbid them any thing. (Locke [1693] 2007, 63)

Locke also suggests that it is important to excite children's curiosity but not to offer them simplistic answers to difficult questions: "Perhaps it may not sometimes be amiss to excite their curiosity, by bringing strange and new things in their way, on purpose to engage their enquiry, and give them occasion to inform themselves about them: and if by chance their curiosity leads them to ask, what they should not know; it is a great deal better to tell them plainly, that it is a thing that belongs not to them to know, than to pop them off with a falsehood or a frivolous answer" ([1693] 2007, 101). Locke's book on education affords his answers to the themes addressed in this book.

Common Themes

The Nature of the Child

Locke emphasized the malleability of the child, both of mind and body.

> I imagine the minds of children as easily turned this way or that, as water itself: And though this be the principle part, and our main care should be about the inside, yet the clay-cottage is not to be neglected. (Locke [1693] 2007, 2)

The Aims of Education

For Locke, early education is essential in the formation of the child's character and the prevention of corruptions in later life.

> These, like faults in the first concoction, that are never mended in the second or third, carry their afterwards incorrigible taint with them through all the parts and stations of life. (Locke [1693] 2007, ii)

So for Locke, in keeping with his social conservatism and in sharp contrast to his political liberalism, education served mainly as a means of maintaining the status quo.

The Role of Play

Locke gave many examples of the benefits of toy and game play, but he also believed that playtime was better spent if it was put to more useful purposes.

I have seen little girls exercise whole hours together and take abundance of pains to be expert at dibstone, as they call it. Whilst I have been looking on, I have thought it wanted only some good contrivance to make them employ all that industry about something that might be more useful to them; and methinks, 'tis only the fault and negligence of elder people that it is not so. (Locke [1693] 2007, 224)

Conformance with DAP Principles

NAEYC

Development and learning proceed at varying rates from child to child, as well as at uneven rates across different areas of a child's individual functioning.

LOCKE

There are a thousand other things, that may need consideration; especially if one should take in the various tempers, different inclinations, and particular defaults, that are to be found in children, and prescribe proper remedies. The variety is so great that it would require a volume; nor would that reach it. . . . There are possibly scarce two children who can be conducted by exactly the same method. (Locke [1693] 2007, 318)

NAEYC

Early experiences have profound effects, both cumulative and delayed, on a child's development and learning; and optimal periods exist for certain types of development and learning to occur.

LOCKE

'Tis that which make the great difference in mankind. The little or almost insensible impressions on our tender infancies have very important and lasting consequences: and there 'tis, as in the fountains of some rivers, where a gentle application of the hand turns the flexible waters in channels, that make them take quite contrary courses and by this direction given them at first in the source, they receive different tendencies and arrive at last at very remote and distant places. (Locke [1693] 2007, 11)

Commentary

As Locke makes clear, individual differences are a necessary consideration at any level of education. But they are of particular significance when undertaking the instruction of young children. Young children are growing more rapidly than at any other time in the human life cycle. Because of this rapid rate of growth, individual differences are magnified, and a group of three-year-olds, for example, will be more variable in their physical, social, emotional, and intellectual development than would a comparable group of eight-year-olds. Smaller class size is the best way to address individual differences at all grade levels, but it is crucial in the instruction of young children. Locke also anticipates the tremendous importance of the infancy years for later personal and social development. Locke's view of development has become the accepted wisdom of contemporary psychology and psychiatry. So Locke, in his own way, made very important contributions to DAP.

References

Locke, John. (1690) 1975. *An Essay Concerning Human Understanding*. New York: Oxford University Press.

———. (1693) 2007. *Some Thoughts Concerning Education*. Sioux Falls, SD: NuVision.

Woolhouse, Roger. 2007. *Locke: A Biography*. New York: Cambridge University Press.

4

Jean-Jacques Rousseau

1712–1778

The lives of Comenius and Locke are interesting, but the life of Jean-Jacques Rousseau is fascinating. The fascination comes, in part at least, from the fact that Rousseau, in his book *The Confessions* (Rousseau [1781] 1953), revealed himself in a way that had never been done before. In this book, Rousseau wrote about his passions, his hopes and fears, and his sexual exploits. He also confessed his most repugnant as well as his most admirable deeds. Rousseau's *The Confessions* is regarded as one of the first autobiographies. Yet it is also a work of bibliotherapy, in which he eases his guilts and anxieties by putting them into written form.

The fascination has other ingredients. Rousseau, alone among the Giants, had no formal schooling and was entirely self-taught not only in literature, politics, and history but in music and drama as well. Of all the Giants, he is one of the most gifted and the most versatile. He wrote a successful opera, a best-selling novel, extremely influential political tracts, and a book on education, in which he introduces the child as a constructor of his or her own reality. This concept is the foundation for the contemporary constructionist approach to psychology. His psychological and sociological insights resonate in contemporary psychoanalytic and sociological thinking.

Rousseau must also be given credit for contributing to the romantic movement in literature and the arts. In his *Confessions and Reveries of the Solitary Walker* (Rousseau 2004), Rousseau gave evocative, idyllic descriptions of sunsets and pastoral settings. Both his opera and novel celebrate the morals and values of life in small, rural societies. Romantic writers like Johann Wolfgang von Goethe, William Wordsworth, and Friedrich Schiller were inspired by Rousseau's celebration of the individual and by his reverence for beauties of nature.

Rousseau was also the most complex, contradictory, and unstable of all the Giants. From an early age, he gave evidence of what today we would call masochistic tendencies. These were coupled with a sense of inferiority stemming from his low social status, his bashfulness, and his small stature. Together, these traits, in my opinion, led to use of the ego defense that Anna Freud (1946) terms *reaction formation*, or turning feelings and thoughts into their opposites. This defense served to alienate him from his friends and contributed to his later paranoia. It was also the basis of his innovative philosophy. What others regarded as positive progress in government, science, and the arts, he regarded as negative—as corrupting man's natural goodness and freedom. That was the underlying message in all his work.

By suggesting a possible psychological component to Rousseau's achievements, I in no way want to reduce or to minimize the enormity of his contribution. Indeed, what he accomplished is made even more remarkable by the fact that he was working under such formidable psychological, and later in life, physical handicaps.

The Man

The Early Years, 1712–1718

In *The Confessions*, Jean-Jacques Rousseau offers the following description of his birth and family: "I was born in Geneva in 1712, the second son of Isaac Rousseau . . . and Suzanne Bernard" (Damrosch 2005, 7). Suzanne died nine days after giving birth to Jean-Jacques. For the rest of his life, he suffered guilt (and self-punishing tendencies) over being the cause of his mother's death. This guilt was made even more onerous by the fact that his father "seemed to see her again in me, but could never forget that I had robbed him of her" (Rousseau [1781] 1953, 19).

One of Suzanne's legacies was a large number of romantic French novels (Cranston 1982; Damrosch 2005). Rousseau's father had wide-ranging intellectual interests and made it a practice soon after Rousseau was born to read to his son every day. Thanks to Isaac's diligence in this regard, Rousseau taught himself to read. As he grew older, Rousseau read books to his father while Isaac was at his watchmaker's bench.

In 1725 Rousseau, at age thirteen, was apprenticed to a young engraver, Ducommun, who turned out to be a cruel and miserly mentor. They did not get along, and Rousseau showed little aptitude for engraving. The situation grew increasingly intolerable. In 1728, when he was sixteen, Rousseau took a holiday with friends outside the city. Geneva was a gated canton. At the end of the day, the boys reached the gates after they had been closed and locked. This had happened before, and Rousseau had been severely punished for it. On this occasion, he decided not to go back into the city and to seek his fortune elsewhere.

Rousseau knew the countryside and some of the farmers in the area, so he was able to find food and lodging. After several days, he met a Catholic priest who was charged with getting Protestants to return to the faith. Geneva was harshly Calvinistic, and Rousseau had been raised on tales of mean, cruel priests. But the priest, Pontverre, was pleasant and shared his food and wine with Rousseau. He encouraged Rousseau to seek a haven with a Catholic lady living in nearby Annecy. The lady in question was Madame de Warens. Rousseau's relationship with Warens changed his life.

Youth, 1718–1742

Psychoanalyst and psychohistorian Erik Erikson describes adolescence as an age when the young person seeks to establish a sense of personal identity, a unified sense of self that consolidates the past and gives guidance to the future (1950). Failure to arrive at an identity can lead to a young person experiencing what Erikson describes as *role diffusion*, which is the inability to bring together the various facets of self and social roles, resulting in a sense of insecurity and dependency. This period in Rousseau's life is a good example of role diffusion.

Rousseau walked to Annecy (he loved to walk and did so even when he was offered rides) to do as the priest suggested. When he met with Warens, whom he expected to be a matronly type, he found, to his surprise, a young, attractive, and charming woman only twelve years his senior. He was immediately enthralled with her and was eager to take her advice. Warens encouraged him to go to Turin, Italy, and convert to Catholicism, because that would increase his chances of finding a livelihood in Catholic France. At the Turin monastery where he underwent the conversion, he was alongside some unsavory professional converters who used conversion to gain food and shelter.

After taking his vows as a Catholic, Rousseau returned to Annecy and moved in with Warens. While living with her, he continued his reading, developed a passion for music, and learned to copy and write musical scores. Warens, concerned that he was not making progress in finding a profession and independence, encouraged him to leave and to try to find an occupation. In 1730 Rousseau spent time in Neuchâtel and Lausanne, attempting to earn a living as a music teacher but without much success. Rousseau also served as a footman, in livery for a woman who was dying of cancer.

After these aborted efforts to become independent, he made a brief trip to Paris but found the city dirty, smelly, dark, and dank. In 1732 Rousseau joined Warens in Chambery, where she had moved. Soon after, she found him a job as clerk in a land office. But he found copying documents dull and boring and his coworkers the same, so he stayed at the job for only eight months.

During this period, Rousseau was discovering facets of his own nature. He knew that he did not like to work for anyone else, particularly as a servant, and needed to be his own master. At the same time, he recognized what he considered an innate and human tendency toward idleness that he had to overcome with energetic self-will. His visit to Paris also reinforced his belief in the degeneracy of city life and the purity and simplicity of living off the land.

In 1732 Rousseau left and then returned to Warens, staying with her until 1738. During this period of his life, he was not working and could read and engage in musical productions, and meet and discourse with interesting people. In 1738 another young man, Jean-Samuel-Rodolphe Wintzenreid, took over the managerial responsibilities of Warens's affairs and replaced Rousseau in Warens's affections. Rousseau moved to her country house in Les Charmettes where he spent his time reading and walking. In 1740 Warens arranged for him to tutor the sons of Gabriel Bonnot de Mably, who lived in Lyon. It was here that Rousseau discovered that he was not cut out for teaching; Mably was forgiving but agreed that the arrangement was not working. Rousseau moved back to Paris in 1742 hoping to earn a living as a musician. He created what he believed was a simplified form of musical notation, which he submitted to the prestigious Académie des Sciences. It was actually well received, but the reviewers, many distinguished writers and musicians, pointed out the system worked well for melody but not for harmony. Nonetheless, the positive recognition helped to confirm Rousseau's growing sense of identity of himself as a thinker and a writer.

The Productive Years, 1742–1762

When Rousseau moved back to Paris in 1742, he became close friends with Denis Diderot, one year Rousseau's junior. In many ways they were opposites. Rousseau was small, slight in build, socially bashful, insecure, and inept at social banter, as he writes, "Wit comes to me half an hour after other people" (Damrosch 2005, 157). Diderot was tall, robust, and a brilliant conversationalist. Perhaps because opposites attract, they became close friends, and Diderot encouraged Rousseau in his musical and political writing.

In 1745 Rousseau met Therese Lavasseur, an illiterate scullery maid at Rousseau's rooming house in Paris (Cranston 1982). She was teased and ridiculed by the other lodgers, but Rousseau was impressed by her "sweet gaze" and "modest demeanor" and defended her (Damrosch 2005, 187). She and Rousseau became lovers, and they stayed together for the rest of his life. A year after the couple met Lavasseur gave birth to the first of their five children. The first, like the four that followed, was given to a foundling home soon after birth. Years later, after Rousseau had become famous, this abandonment of his children was made public and became a social scandal. Rousseau defended himself by saying that he was too poor to raise his children properly.

He was indeed poor and in debt. In 1746 the Dupins, a wealthy bourgeois family knowing of his exceptional literacy skills, took him on as a kind of research assistant for their book projects, one on chemistry, another on government, and a third on the equality of women. His five years of researching these projects gave Rousseau a further opportunity to deepen his education. While working with the Dupins, he also continued his relation with Diderot and other Enlightenment thinkers who were challenging traditional authority and values. While Rousseau did not agree with their rejection of religious authority, he was sympathetic with many of their other ideas.

In 1749 Diderot was asked, on the basis of his having successfully translated a dictionary, to write a more general dictionary called a cyclopedia. This project became the *Encyclopedic Dictionary of the Arts and Sciences*, in short, the *Encyclopedia*. The first volume appeared in 1751 and quickly became the bible of the Enlightenment movement. Diderot asked Rousseau to write chapters on music, which he agreed to do.

During this same period, Diderot was publishing writings on radical materialistic ideas that extrapolated Locke's ideas that there were no innate ideas to conclude that the divine origin of religion was fiction. Since all knowledge came through the senses, a blind person might never arrive at the conception of God. This was too much for the authorities, and Diderot was imprisoned. He was released after four months with the provision that he was never again to publish anything at variance with existing morals and values.

Rousseau frequently visited Diderot while he was imprisoned at Vincennes. On one of his early visits, he shared with Diderot news of an essay contest being conducted by the journal *Mercure de France* on "whether the restoration of the sciences and of the arts has contributed to purify morals" (Damrosch 2005, 212). On a later visit to Diderot, Rousseau had a revelation so powerful that he had to sit down to still his heart and thoughts. His revolutionary insight was that science and the arts were not progressive, as the writers of the Enlightenment contended, but rather regressive and destructive of individual freedom and authenticity. When Rousseau shared his thoughts with Diderot, his friend did not agree but encouraged Rousseau to enter the contest.

Rousseau worked hard on the brief essay *Discourse on the Sciences and Arts* and submitted it. In 1750, six months after sending in the essay, Rousseau learned that he had won the prize. He was, in this essay, finally able to bring together the disparate thoughts regarding the human condition that had come together on his way to Vincennes. His essay marshaled powerful arguments to support his contention that the sciences and the arts actually undermined individual freedom rather than liberated it. With this publication, Rousseau was able to find his identity both as a writer and an original social and political thinker.

The essay made Rousseau famous and changed his life. His success gave him the confidence to devote his full time to other writing projects. Once he found his identity, he worked furiously. The first product of this industry was the one-act opera *Le devin du village* (The Village Soothsayer), which was first produced in 1752 and was an immediate success. It was performed at Versailles, and Louis XIV was greatly impressed by it, as was his mistress, Madame Pompadour. But Rousseau did not accept an invitation to Versailles and the pension that Louis XIV would have given him. He also began to dress in shabby clothes and gave up his wig, sword, and watch. He hoped in this way to demonstrate that he was not corrupted by the society that he was criticizing.

In 1756 Rousseau and Lavasseur moved to l'Hermitage in Montmorency outside of Paris at the invitation of admirer Madame d'Epinay. While there Rousseau began work on his novel *Julie, or The New Heloise*. Two years later he rented Petit Montlouis, a nearby small house. While living there Rousseau worked in a small, attached pavilion, where he completed *Julie* as well as *The Social Contract* and *Émile*. Although Rousseau enjoyed the country and his solitude, he nonetheless had to put up with the endless visitors to the now famous author.

The novel *Julie, or The New Heloise* was published in 1761 and became a huge best seller. But the acclaim that came with the success of *Julie* was short lived. The French government, on the grounds of political and religious heresy, condemned *The Social Contract* and *Émile*, which were published the following year. The Parliament of Paris issued a warrant for his arrest. Rousseau was forewarned and fled to Geneva.

The Last Years, 1765–1778

In 1765 Rousseau was ordered to leave Switzerland by the Genevan ministers because of the criticism of religious education in *Émile*. The philosopher David Hume had invited Rousseau to England, and he and Lavasseur went there to escape arrest. But Rousseau came to believe that Hume was plotting against him—one symptom of growing paranoia. While in England, however, Rousseau began work on *Confessions*. Four months after going to England, Rousseau returned to France under an assumed name because the warrant for his arrest was still in force, but his feeling of persecution was increasing. He did not feel safe in one place and fled to several cities, ending in Bourgeon in eastern France.

Rousseau's difficulties were made even more onerous by a medical problem requiring frequent urination, which went undiagnosed. One of the reasons he did not go to Versailles to meet with Louis XIV was his fear that he might have to leave the meeting due to his condition. Years later the problem was recognized as an enlarged prostate, and Rousseau received a large number of catheters to aid him in urinating. This problem, together with his bashfulness and lack of skill in social niceties, led him to ignore the many invitations to the salons of wealthy Parisians.

During this time (1766–1769), Rousseau continued working on the manuscript of *The Confessions*. In 1770 he returned to France under his own name. He expected to be challenged by his enemies, but they never materialized. In a poor section of Paris, Rousseau and Lavasseur rented a tiny apartment on the sixth floor, which could only be reached by a dark and treacherous stairway. To support himself and Lavasseur, Rousseau took in music copy work for which he charged a minimal fee. When customers tried to pay him more than the fixed amount, he declined to take it. By refusing to take more than he had earned, or felt he deserved, Rousseau believed he was being true to the values he had proclaimed in his written work.

Isolated and embittered, believing in conspiracies against him, Rousseau tried to regain his reputation by giving readings of sections from *The Confessions*. As in so many other spheres of his life, Rousseau tried to turn the negative revelations about his misdeeds into something positive—that he was at least being honest about himself. The Paris police, however, put a stop to these readings. While continuing his copying work, Rousseau began another work of self-justification: *Dialogues: Rousseau, Judge of Jean Jacques*, which was never published.

In 1776 Rousseau began writing the *Reveries of the Solitary Walker*, which he never completed. In *Reveries* he describes an incident that happened on the streets of Paris in 1776. He was walking along when a coach came thundering by accompanied by a huge Great Dane running alongside it. Rousseau was unable to avoid the animal and was bowled over by it. He was left unconscious and probably suffered a concussion. Although Rousseau's health had improved, it began to deteriorate after the accident. In his weakened condition, living in the walk-up apartment was no longer possible.

The Marquis René-Louis de Giradin knew Rousseau from the music copy work Rousseau had done for him. He invited Rousseau to stay at Ermenonville, his chateau, outside of Paris. He and Lavasseur moved into a charming guest cottage on the estate in 1778. Rousseau enjoyed the gardens very much and took pleasure in walks about the estate. In late June 1778, Rousseau took his usual early morning walk and stopped at a café to have a coffee. While at the café he complained of tingling and later of a violent headache. At the cottage, the headaches continued. Several days later he fell to the floor; Lavasseur could do nothing for him, and he died. The date was July 2, 1778. It was just a year before the French Revolution, which took as its rallying cry the values of his ideal community condensed into the motto *Liberté, Égalité, Fraternité*. De Giradin arranged to have Rousseau buried on the Isle of Poplars, a small, ornamental island on the lake of the estate.

In 1794, after the French Revolution, Rousseau's remains were moved to the newly constructed Panthéon in Paris. In the Panthéon, a monument to Rousseau stands opposite the one to Diderot. And Rousseau's coffin directly faces that of Voltaire, who always regarded Rousseau's work as of little or no value.

The Work

All of Rousseau's works—the novel, the ballet, the opera, and the texts *Émile* and *The Social Contract*—carry the same underlying message: the form of government under which individuals live determines every facet of human life, and most forms of government rob people of their freedom. Even *The Confessions* reveal how the different societies in which he lived help shape his ideas. According to Rousseau, the Baconian idea of social progress through reason and empirical research, the center of Enlightenment thought, was basically wrong. This point was most strongly made in *The Social Contract*. Although *The Social Contract* has enormous social consequences, for our purposes we need to focus only on *Émile*. In many ways this book anticipated the major themes of modern developmental psychology.

Like all Rousseau's works, *Émile* was not only an educational critique but a social one as well. It recounts the childhood and youth of a boy named Émile. He opens the book with this statement: "Everything is good as it comes from the hands of the Maker of the world, but degenerates once it gets into the hands of man" (Rousseau 1956, 11). Rousseau continues by arguing that there are three kinds of education: education that comes from the development of our faculties, education that comes from our experience with things, and education that comes from man—that is, society. He thought that the education from things gives rise to individuality and authenticity, while the education of society leads to immorality and lack of true selfhood.

In *Émile*, Rousseau confronts the fundamental paradox of education for individuality and freedom as opposed to education for becoming a conforming member of society. Freire (2000) puts this contrast most tellingly by calling the conflict one of education for *liberation* as opposed to education for domestication. Rousseau saw most education as being *domestication* and, in the process, suppressing individual freedom and authenticity. *Émile* is a thought experiment. It is meant to illustrate what a man might become if raised only by his experience with things before being exposed to the domesticating influence of society. Rousseau recognizes that such rearing is impossible in fact, but he uses Émile's innocence to show what society does to young people.

The book recounts the life of Émile in five books, one for each stage of development: infancy, boyhood, the approach of adolescence, adolescence, and marriage. For our purposes, we need only to summarize the first two books.

Infancy

The period of infancy, defined by Rousseau as the first two years, is largely given over to the mother and nursing. As do Comenius and Locke, Rousseau criticizes the practice of wet-nursing. He says that half the children in the France in his day die before age eight. Rousseau also echoes Locke in saying that children should not get used to eating at specific times. To ensure children's freedom to grow and explore, clothing should not be too tight and infants should by allowed to crawl about in well-padded rooms. He argues against trying to teach children to walk or talk, because they can learn these very well on their own.

Boyhood

For Rousseau, the boyhood period extends from infancy up to early adolescence, around age twelve. Surprisingly, Rousseau argues that it is not until adolescence that children attain the ability to reason. It is surprising inasmuch as the ancients (particularly the Greek and Roman societies mentioned in chapter 1) described age six or seven as the age of reason and used it as the criterion to begin formal education. And it was Locke's awareness of this new ability to reason that led him to argue that after age six or seven children could understand the idea of rules and of breaking them. Rousseau rejects Locke on this issue and suggests that it is foolish to reason with a child until adolescence.

On other points, Rousseau agrees with Locke on the importance of habit and the need for parents to avoid both overindulgence and undue harshness. And as Locke does, Rousseau argues that parents must distinguish between their children's needs and wants and satisfy only the former. Children should act, he says, not out of obedience but rather out of necessity. But Rousseau again appears to disagree with Locke with respect to authority. Locke contends that authority is a powerful tool of discipline and that approval and disapproval are superior to physical punishment. Rousseau, in contrast, argues that adults should not claim any authority over the child but only ensure that the child knows that "he is weak and you are strong and therefore that he is at your mercy" (Rousseau 1956, 39). Rousseau says that if there is something the child should not do, he should be prevented from doing it without forbidding, explanation, or reason. This amounts to a kind of learning from the law of necessity. Nonetheless, this method still sounds quite authoritarian.

Rousseau also argues that the first impulses of nature are always right, and if children engage in wrong action, it is not out of ill intention and should not be punished or chastised; rather, the behavior should be ignored. He writes that if parents leave things about that a child breaks or harms, it is the adult's fault, not the child's. On such occasions, adults should not even give any evidence that they are annoyed or upset. Adults teach the wrong lesson when they blame the child for the adults' carelessness. In this regard, Rousseau writes a passage that has become the rallying cry for child-development advocates.

> Nature wants children to be children before they are men. If we deliberately depart from this order we shall get premature fruits which are neither ripe nor well flavoured and which soon decay. We shall have youthful sages and grown up children. Childhood has ways of seeing, thinking and feeling peculiar to itself: nothing can be more foolish than to seek to substitute our ways for them. I should as soon expect a child of ten to be five feet in height as to be possessed of judgment. (Rousseau 1956, 38–39)

For the first stages of children's lives, Rousseau puts down what he regards as the most important and most useful rule in education, "It is not to save time but to waste it" (Rousseau 1956, 41). He explains that the first twelve years of life are when acquired vices and bad habits are established and that these are difficult to eradicate once they are in place. Wasting time means not teaching the child anything that could be misunderstood or misinterpreted. In effect, the child should learn only what is necessary for survival. "If . . . your pupil came to the age of twelve strong and healthy but unable to distinguish his right hand from his left, the eyes of his understanding would be open to reason from your very first lessons" (Rousseau 1956, 41).

Given this position, Rousseau argues against the typical elementary school curriculum of his day. He contends that the study of languages is "one of the futilities of education" (Rousseau 1956, 48). As for geography, it is taught with verbal and graphic symbols that the child cannot understand. It is even more "ridiculous" to set children to study history that is far beyond their comprehension (Rousseau 1956, 48). He says that children can have no real understanding of events without knowing their causes and their effects.

His recommendations with respect to reading are equally radical. Not many parents or educators today would agree that "reading is the greatest plague of childhood" (Rousseau 1956, 51). For Rousseau, children should begin to read only when there is some need for them to do so. Children can learn most of what they need to learn from verbal conversation and through experience with things. He contends that reading is a "torment" to children because they are compelled to learn it and to use it for purposes that are not their own (Rousseau 1956, 51).

Rousseau argues that teachers begin teaching geography by walking and showing children "the real thing"—that is, the countryside, directions, and topography (Rousseau 1956, 53). In whatever study he undertakes, Émile (as a model for all children's education) is encouraged to make his own equipment of the most elementary sort. A balance can be made of a stick resting on stone with objects at either end. Rousseau suggests that the laws of statics and hydrostatics can be learned in the bathtub by inverting a glass into the water. The failure of the inverted glass to fill with water indicates that air has weight (Rousseau 1956, 78).

Rousseau claims that he hates books. But the one he recommends to the character Émile is *Robinson Crusoe*. Rousseau would like Émile to see Crusoe as a model of making do without the ready-made tools of society. He would have Émile imagine himself as Crusoe and re-create some of the things Crusoe has created. In this way, Rousseau believes that Émile would learn to be self-sufficient, even without society. But more important, it would give Émile a sense of security and self-confidence once he does enter society.

Like Comenius and Locke, Rousseau argues that education should begin with the young child. The three also agree that children's mental abilities develop over time and that education should be adapted to the level of the child's intellectual development. All three argue vigorously against physical punishment as a discipline technique. Where they differ is on the specifics of education.

Common Themes

The Nature of the Child

Rousseau, like Locke, believed that character was learned, but unlike Locke, he believed it was sophisticated society that corrupted character.

> Everything is good as it comes from the hands of the Maker of the world, but degenerates once it gets into the hands of man. (Rousseau 1956, 11)

The Aims of Education

For Rousseau, the aims of education were first and foremost for the individual rather than for society.

> Plants are fashioned by cultivation, men by education. We are born feeble and need strength; possessing nothing we need assistance; beginning without intelligence, we need judgment. All that we lack at birth and need when grown up are given us by education. (Rousseau 1956, 11)

The Role of Play

> Work and play are all the same to him. His games are his occupations: he is not aware of any difference. He goes into everything he does with a pleasing interest and freedom. It is indeed a charming spectacle to see a nice boy of this age, with open smiling countenance, doing the most serious things in his play or profoundly occupied with the most frivolous amusements. (Rousseau 1956, 67)

Conformance with DAP Principles

NAEYC

Development and learning occur in and are influenced by multiple social and cultural contexts.

ROUSSEAU

And is it [Rousseau's educational system] practicable? That depends upon the conditions under which it is tried. These conditions may vary indefinitely. The kind of education good for France will not suit Switzerland; that suitable for the middle classes will not suit the nobility. The greater or less ease of execution depends on a thousand circumstances which it is impossible to define. (Rousseau 1956, 7)

NAEYC

Many aspects of children's learning and development follow well-documented sequences, with later abilities, skills, and knowledge building on those already acquired.

ROUSSEAU

Though memory and reasoning are essentially different faculties they depend on each other in their development. Before the age of reason the child receives images but not ideas. The difference between them is that images are simply the exact pictures of sense-given objects, whereas ideas are notions of objects determined by their relations. (Rousseau 1956, 46)

Commentary

Early in the twentieth century, cultural anthropologists like Margaret Mead and William Sapir were arguing the important role that culture played in child rearing and development. But it was not until the 1960s and the increase in cross-disciplinary research—such as the psychosocial stages introduced by Erik Erikson, John Bowlby's biopsychology concept of attachment, and the rediscovery of Lev Vygotsky's social cultural determinism—that psychologists came to fully appreciate the importance of the sociocultural determinants of society and culture on child development and human behavior. It is a testament to Rousseau's foresight that he already appreciated the central role of culture and society on child development. But unlike some of the current advocates of the sociocultural approach (Woods 2013), he did not downplay the all-important role of biological development. Rousseau's insistence on children learning from their own experiences with the natural world before learning about the social world anticipated contemporary concerns such as Richard Louv's finding of nature deficit disorder in today's children (2005).

References

Bowlby, John. 1969. *Attachment: Attachment and Loss, Volume One*. New York: Basic Books.

Cranston, Maurice. 1982. *Jean-Jacques: The Early Years and Work of Jean-Jacques Rousseau*. New York: Norton.

Damrosch, Leo. 2005. *Jean-Jacques Rousseau: Restless Genius*. New York: Houghton Mifflin.

Erikson, Erik. 1950. *Childhood and Society*. New York: Norton.

Freire, Paulo. 2000. *Pedagogy of the Oppressed*. Translated by Myra Bergman Ramos. New York: Continuum.

Freud, Anna. 1946. *The Ego and the Mechanisms of Defense*. Translated by Cecil Baines. New York: International Universities Press.

Louv, Richard. 2005. *Last Child in the Woods: Saving Our Children from Nature Deficit Disorder*. Chapel Hill, NC: Algonquin Books.

Rousseau, Jean-Jacques. (1781) 1953. *The Confessions of Jean-Jacques Rousseau.* New York: Penguin.

———. 1956. *The Emile of Jean-Jacques Rousseau; Selections.* New York: Teacher's College Columbia University Press.

———. 2004. *Reveries of the Solitary Walker.* Translated by Peter France. New York: Penguin.

Woods, Ruth. 2013. *Children's Moral Lives: An Ethnographic and Psychological Approach.* West Sussex, UK: Wiley-Blackwell.

5

Johann Heinrich Pestalozzi

1746–1827

If history has been unkind to Comenius, it has been particularly cruel to Johann Heinrich Pestalozzi. Of all the Giants, Pestalozzi has had the most widespread, profound, and lasting effect on elementary education in the modern Western world. His was a life of dedication and selfless denial in the service of a single humanitarian goal: education of the disadvantaged.

Although well known and celebrated in his lifetime, he is much less well recognized and valued today than many of the Giants who followed him. One likely reason for this lack of recognition is that he left no organized or named system of education, such as those left by his followers Froebel, Montessori, and Steiner. Another reason is that his theoretical writings were tangential and obscure while his fictional descriptions of rural life were well received. Pestalozzi's true educational creations were not the words he wrote but rather the teaching practices he introduced, the children he taught, and the assistants he trained. For this reason, although his educational legacy lives on, its originator is all but forgotten.

Yet Pestalozzi's success came only after numerous professional and financial failures. After each failure, however, his unwavering belief in his educational ideas gave him the burning energy to pursue those ideas until the very last day of his life. One of his first failed efforts was very personal. Inspired by Rousseau's *Émile*, he sought to rear his own son, Jean-Jacques, in the manner prescribed in that book. The disastrous results of this educational experiment on his own child—and of his more ambitious next one—led him to progressively create an elementary curriculum that did succeed.

But it was far from a straightforward progression, in part at least due to his overly ambitious agendas. This trait, together with his poor management and leadership skills, contributed to the closing or moving of some of the educational communities he created. Toward the end of his life, these character traits also contributed to a bitter conflict between his two most devoted followers and to the disrepute and closing of his most long-lasting and successful school.

In fairness to Pestalozzi, it has to be said that some of his educational communities were forced to close or to move because of the geopolitical upheavals taking place during his lifetime. Among these were the French Revolution; the extended series of conflicts that included the seven coalition wars against Napoléon I, the Napoleonic Wars, and the Battle of Jena in 1806; and the war-ending Congress of Vienna in 1814–1815. The rise of urban industrialization and the rural cottage industry also began during this same time period.

Paradoxically, though some of Pestalozzi's schools were closed or moved because of sociopolitical changes, these same changes were instrumental in making his work known around the world. After Napoleon was defeated by Germany in the Battle of Jena, Prussia decided to create a new society and to revise its educational system. Wilhelm von Humboldt, a renowned philosopher and statesman, was put in charge of the task. Following the advice of the German philosopher Johann Gottlieb Fichte, he looked to Pestalozzi's educational system as the most advanced and most effective system available.

In 1806 Humboldt sent many aspiring teachers to Pestalozzi's last and most successful school at Yverdon. After being trained by Pestalozzi and his assistants, these young men (teachers were all male at this time) returned to Prussia to revise the Volksschule curriculum and to set up teacher training seminaries. Over the years, the Prussian schools built on Pestalozzi's methods came to be viewed as the most modern and progressive in the world. They attracted many visitors from all over Europe and abroad, including the United States. In the 1880s the Oswego movement in New York, and Superintendent Francis Parker's schools in Quincy, Massachusetts, were but two examples of how Pestalozzi's educational practices were taken up in the United States.

It is perhaps because so much of Pestalozzi's educational theory and practice have become accepted educational wisdom that Pestalozzi's influence on contemporary educational theory and method is not fully appreciated. Equally important, perhaps, was his inability to put into words what he was so able to put into practice.

The Man

With the Giants of philosophy, it was easy to separate the life story and the work. Not so with Pestalozzi, whose life story was his work. Although he wrote a good deal, much of it was rambling, tangential, and incoherent. What he accomplished with children far surpassed what he achieved with words. Therefore, I devote more time to his life and proportionately less, in relation to the other Giants, to his words.

The Early Years, 1746–1761

Johann Heinrich Pestalozzi was born in Zurich, Switzerland on January 12, 1746. His father, John Baptiste, was a surgeon who specialized in visual disorders. His mother, Susanna Hotz, also came from an upper class family—her father was a doctor and her uncle a general. Misfortune hit the family early in Pestalozzi's life. John died when Pestalozzi was five, leaving the family almost penniless. His mother was left with three children: Johann Heinrich, his older brother, and a younger sister.

Before his death, John Baptiste pleaded with the trusted family servant Barbara Schmid Babeli to stay with the family after his death. She promised she would do so and did indeed remain with the family until Susanna died some forty years later. Babeli never married and turned down more lucrative positions to stay with the struggling Pestalozzi family. It was Babeli who took care of the family's finances and stretched them to the limit. She would wait till the end of the day when the farmers were eager to get rid of the fruits and vegetables to bargain for a lower price. Pestalozzi's mother and a charitable woman named Elizabeth became the models for Gertrude, the heroine of Pestalozzi's educational novels (Guimps 1890).

At school Pestalozzi was not academically adept. Although he understood what was being taught, he was often inattentive. His spelling was atrocious, and his teacher thought him slow. While his fellow students liked him for his kind disposition, they also took advantage of his good nature. Pestalozzi tells of the day in Zurich when there was an earthquake. The teachers and children all rushed downstairs, but Pestalozzi was told to go back up to the classroom to fetch caps and books. Because of his social awkwardness and learning problems, his fellow students called him Harry Oddity of Fool Borough.

From the time he was nine, Pestalozzi spent a few weeks each summer with his grandfather Andrew Pestalozzi, who was a pastor in the lovely town of Höngg on the banks of the Limmat River. These were the happiest times of Pestalozzi's childhood. Andrew often took Pestalozzi along when he visited schools, the sick, and the poor in his parish. It was on these visits that Pestalozzi first became aware of impoverished conditions under which the peasants lived. He was deeply moved by their plight and decided to become a pastor like his grandfather, who was such a good servant to his flock.

Rebirth at the University, 1761–1771

In mid-eighteenth-century Zurich, the schooling sequence was elementary school, grammar school, and then college. After completing grammar school at age fifteen, Pestalozzi attended the Collegium Humanitatis. In this environment, Pestalozzi flourished. He became deeply involved in his studies and felt confident to challenge his most-learned professors. But even more important to Pestalozzi were the friends he made and his involvement in political affairs. A group of young students who called themselves "the patriots" formed the Helvetic Society with the help of a professor. The prime goal of this society was to raise the country's moral standards. Like many idealist young people, they saw the injustices of society and naively believed that bringing these injustices to light through written pamphlets would bring about change.

Pestalozzi's closest friend during his university years was Johann Jacob Bluntschli, whom his friends called Menalk, a fellow student and a very principled young man who wished to help others reach moral perfection. He hoped to go into government service to further this ambition. Sadly, Menalk contracted a fatal illness and died in 1867. He knew Pestalozzi as an impractical dreamer and, as a last request, urged him not to undertake any far-reaching enterprise without the support of a friend "with a shrewder knowledge of men and affairs" (Silber 1960, 9). It was sound advice that Pestalozzi never heeded.

Menalk's death had one positive consequence. Menalk and Pestalozzi had also befriended Anna "Nanette" Schulthess, a young woman who belonged to one of the most respected Zurich families. She was attractive, bright, and well educated. Schulthess and Pestalozzi were drawn together by the death of their friend, and Pestalozzi fell madly in love with her. Actually, he had met her as a boy when, on one of those rare occasions when he had a few pfennig coins, he had gone to a confectionary store to buy sweets. The girl who waited on him told him not to spend his money so frivolously. It was Schulthess who gave him that advice.

Schulthess was eight years older than Pestalozzi and had not married because she had been very particular about choosing a mate. Their relationship grew, and the couple decided to marry. Schulthess's parents were not happy about this potential union and wanted Pestalozzi to prove that he could earn a living before they would give their consent. Pestalozzi had given up the idea of becoming a pastor because he could not accept the rigidity of the church; in fact, he broke into a giggle while delivering his first sermon. He also considered, but quickly rejected, the idea of becoming a lawyer. At the suggestion of friends, he decided to go into agriculture. Pestalozzi liked the idea, as it could be a way to help the struggling peasant farmers, so he went to learn modern farming methods at Rudolf Techffeli's experimental farm in Bern.

After serving his apprenticeship, Pestalozzi decided to buy land outside of Zurich to raise clover and madder (a plant that was used to create the red dyes being used in the growing cloth manufacturing industry). With some local bank support, he was able to purchase Neuhof, an estate with scattered parcels of some sixty acres of land, on which he proposed to create a model farm. With these acquisitions in hand, Schulthess's parents permitted the couple to marry, and they did so in September 1769.

Neuhof: The Agricultural and School Experiment, 1771–1779

Schulthess recognized Pestalozzi's genius and was able to overlook his untidiness and lack of concern about personal appearance as well as his tendency to take on much more than he could handle. She remained devoted and dedicated to him through all his later travails.

Their first years together were taken up with setting up the farm and remodeling the house at Neuhof. The couple moved into their new home in 1771. Pestalozzi worked hard at planting and caring for his crops. But the agricultural experiment did not go well. To begin with, Pestalozzi was taken in by an unscrupulous butcher who talked Pestalozzi into exchanging most of his fertile land for the butcher's much less suitable acreage. The butcher became the model for the cruel and avaricious Bailiff in Pestalozzi's most famous book, *Leonard and Gertrude* (Silber 1960). Pestalozzi also found it difficult to attend to the farm's details, such as bookkeeping and managing his accounts. The early years of the 1770s were also bad for farming, with too little rain and too much heat.

After three unsuccessful years of farming, Pestalozzi thought he might fare better if he added a spinning mill to the farm and if he opened a school for peasant children that would combine work and education. The school opened in 1774. He recruited some fifty boys ages six to eighteen to participate in the program. His plan was to create a homelike environment where love and companionship would be coupled with work and learning. Pestalozzi always saw himself more as father than as headmaster. He brought in master weavers and spinners to teach his students occupational skills. He also fed them and clothed them.

But the school was a financial failure. He was increasingly losing money. Many parents, after Pestalozzi had fed, clothed, and given their sons marketable vocational skills, withdrew them and put them to work elsewhere. This was just at the time when the students were skilled enough to have earned some money for the school. In 1779, after five years, the school had to close; Pestalozzi had exhausted his finances and his wife's inheritance. He blamed himself for the failure, recognizing his financial ineptitude. But he was now committed to his identity as an educator, and the experience helped him refine both his theory and practice.

Neuhof: The Literary Years, 1779–1798

With the closing of the school, Pestalozzi lost most of the land associated with Neuhof, but he still owned the house. Pestalozzi's friends encouraged him to write as a way to provide for his family. Even during the farm and school years, Pestalozzi kept a diary on the education of his three-year-old son. Some parts of this diary were later published in Johannes Niederer's *Notes on Pestalozzi* (Guimps 1890). He also published a collection of essays, *Education of the Children of the Poor*, that had first appeared in a journal published by a friend. Neither of these attracted much attention. But those who knew him recognized his literary talent.

With the school and farm closed, Pestalozzi spent his full time writing. In 1781 he published the first part of his novel, *Leonard and Gertrude*, which was a great success and earned Pestalozzi a gold medal and fifty florins from the Economic Society of Berne. By 1787 Pestalozzi wrote three more parts to form the complete work. In this novel, Pestalozzi's aim is to show, as Rousseau had done with *Émile*, how a natural education—in this case a primarily vocational one—could lead to intellectual and moral regeneration. But the novel was read as a romantic story and its teachings were largely ignored.

In a number of more didactic books spinning off of *Leonard and Gertrude*, Pestalozzi tried to make the messages more explicit. *Fables* was a book of 279 short fables that expounded his philosophy of life. With the exception of *Fables*, these works were pretty dull and did not receive much attention. Again at the urging of friends, Pestalozzi tried to put his educational theory into words. The result, *Researches into the Course of Nature in the Development of the Human Race*, was plodding and discursive and made it clear, to the author as well as to everyone else, that theoretical writing was not his forte. Nonetheless, his theme that knowledge of human development is essential to establish a solid basis for education was important. He was arguing for a developmental psychology of education.

The School at Stans, 1798–1799

In 1798 the French armies helped overthrow all but one of the independent Swiss states and encourage a more democratic republic. The residents of Unterwalden, the remaining Catholic canton after Napoleon's armies had devastated the others, were encouraged by the priests to resist joining the new central government. The French ruthlessly put down this rebellion, killing hundreds of peasants and burning and pillaging the villages. A great many children lost their parents and homes.

The new unified government of Switzerland, or the Helvetian government, included many of Pestalozzi's old classmates and friends who had belonged to the patriots at Collegium Humanitatis. They were very open to supporting a school run according to his educational and moral principles. After the tragedy at Unterwalden, the government tried to repair some of the damage that had been done supposedly under their auspices. The government had previously approved Pestalozzi's application to open a school and now decided to open it in Stans, the capital of Nidwalden (one of the forested cantons near Lake Lucerne), to serve the children who had been orphaned by war.

The school was to be housed in the Capuchin convent, which had been badly damaged during the war. The reconstruction of the buildings was not finished when the school opened in 1799. Pestalozzi and his program, arriving from a Protestant canton, were not well received by the Catholic population. But this new school was well financed by the generous government. The school opened with about fifty children, both boys and girls, in attendance and eventually grew to eighty.

Pestalozzi had his work cut out for him, and he undertook it alone, not for lack of resources, but by design. He believed that the atmosphere of the home was also the best atmosphere for a school. Every teacher, like every parent, must love every child in his care. Pestalozzi was reluctant to share this responsibility, so he took on the teaching himself. His wife and a devoted servant did the cooking and other chores.

Pestalozzi lived with the children day and night, ate with them, and prayed with them. Their education came from the children's own activities, including daily routines and outdoor excursions. Like Rousseau, he believed children learned best from the necessity imposed by circumstances rather than from verbal instruction. Over time, he was able to create the atmosphere that he had hoped for, and a spirit of love permeated the school.

But the international animosities continued and the wars were reignited. The second coalition army against Napoleon placed Unterwalden between the Austrian and French forces. There was little understanding on the part of the Helvetian government of what Pestalozzi had accomplished at his school, and it gave in to a request that the buildings at Stans be turned into an army hospital. The school closed after only five months, and the children with parents were sent back to them while the orphans remained with the Capuchin nuns, who returned to their convent when it was abandoned by the military.

The School at Burgdorf, 1799–1803

Pestalozzi's work at Stans did not go unrecognized, and his patriot friends quickly recruited him to move to Burgdorf, a small town with an ancient castle built on its commanding hill and located in the valley of the Emme River. After several brief teaching assignments, he was appointed to run a boys school housed in the castle. The Helvetian government gave him the castle rent free along with wood for fires and land for a garden. They also paid him a salary and provided funds for hiring assistants and domestic help. With a school of his own and government support, Pestalozzi was once again committed to perfecting his approach to elementary education.

For the first year, Pestalozzi did everything by himself. During the day, he taught an ever-growing student body with whom he tested out his educational ideas. At night he wrote elementary textbooks and books expounding his educational method. After a year, he was exhilarated but exhausted and was willing to accept help for the first time. By now he was sufficiently convinced of the soundness of his methods and was willing to train assistants. He recruited four relatively uneducated young men to work with him. In the fall of 1800, the castle was formally opened as an educational institute. It was to serve only those children whose parents could afford a small fee. Pestalozzi, however, did enroll a number of scholarship students.

The pupils, boys from five to ten years, were mainly day students, but a few students did board at the school. Pestalozzi also hired help to take care of the cleaning and cooking. The schedule was rigorous. The children were awakened at five thirty in the morning and did not go to bed until nine o'clock at night. "The day began with prayers, separate for the two denominations [Protestant and Catholic] and included more than eight hours of instruction in four periods, interrupted only by a short break before meals and a half hour's play time after them" (Silber 1960). Pestalozzi believed that if he kept students active learning good habits, they would have no time to learn bad ones.

Despite the long hours, the children seemed to thrive. This was clearly the result of the way they were taught. For Pestalozzi, the aim of education was not to impart facts but rather to facilitate the growth of the child's own mental powers. Accordingly, for Pestalozzi, the main thing was not what children learned but rather the process of learning itself. His methods were designed to further the child's progress by enabling the child to learn through his own activity, not through verbal instruction.

To this end, Pestalozzi devised a number of teaching tools. He believed, as did Comenius and Locke, that children had to start with the simplest materials and ideas and only gradually move to the more complex. To teach reading and spelling, for example, he introduced movable letters that could be rearranged into many different configurations. To teach math, he had children use concrete materials such as beans and pebbles so that when doing figures in their heads, they would have the concrete images to assist them. Likewise, he used apples and cakes that could be cut into slices to demonstrate the idea of fractions.

Out of necessity, Pestalozzi introduced several instructional methods that have become commonplace today. He used what today we call *ability grouping*, grouping children according to their level of mental development rather than their age. Because he had to deal with large groups of children at a time, Pestalozzi also practiced *collective instruction*, having children respond in unison as opposed to individual recitation, which was then the common practice.

After nineteen months of the school's operation, Pestalozzi invited government officials from Bern to come and evaluate the work of the school. The result was a very positive report that had far-reaching effects. For one thing, the government pledged continued financial support. Even more important, Pestalozzi's methods were made the unofficial teaching model for all the cantons. Each canton was invited to send teachers to be students at the castle. These teachers were to learn the methods and to implement them in their home schools. In addition, many of the children who were taught at the school later became teachers in their own towns and villages. Pestalozzi's methods were thus spread throughout Switzerland. Another effect of the report was that it gave a clear description of Pestalozzi's methods, which made Pestalozzi and his work known all over Europe.

Once Pestalozzi's work became well recognized, it was not without its critics. Perhaps the severest criticism came from conservative religionists who believed that because he did not employ the rote learning of the catechism and other traditional religious education methods, he had abandoned the tenets of Christianity. While Pestalozzi's ideas were unorthodox, he did believe (as did Comenius) that there was a divine spark of God in man, and that Christ was the example of how this spark could be brought to flame in all men with proper education. He simply believed that the traditional religious education was as faulty as the traditional secular one. For Pestalozzi, the love and care he and his coworkers gave the children was the best and surest way to instill a belief in divine goodness.

In 1803 sociopolitical forces interrupted Pestalozzi's work at Burgdorf just as they had at Stans. That year, as a result of Napoleon's Act of Mediation, the Helvetic Republic fell and federalism was restored in Switzerland. Asserting its regained rights, the canton of Bern repossessed the Burgdorf castle and Pestalozzi's institute was forced to move. Pestalozzi received many invitations to take his institute to other cantons and other countries.

One of the invitations came from the newly created French canton of Vaud. Advantages of that offer were that many of the supportive Helvetic ministers and many Burgdorf students lived there. A disadvantage was that Vaud was in French-speaking Switzerland, and neither Pestalozzi nor his assistants were very fluent in French. But it was still in Switzerland, so Pestalozzi moved the school to Yverdon in Vaud.

The School at Yverdon, 1803–1825

The town of Yverdon is located in a valley of the Jura Mountains on the banks of Lake Neuchâtel. Pestalozzi was given an ancient castle to house his institute. It was a very spacious building with many large halls for classrooms and dormitories. The castle had been remodeled and simply but adequately furnished. Because there was room, Pestalozzi was able to move his wife, daughter-in-law, and grandson to the castle. There was a large courtyard and a nearby meadow, and the lake was within short walking distance. The town of Yverdon gave the castle to Pestalozzi rent free for as long as he lived.

Within a year or two, the population at the institute in Yverdon had grown to more than 250 and included teachers, students, servants, and Pestalozzi's family. The student body came from many different European countries. In addition to those from Germany, France, and Switzerland, students from Russia, Italy, Spain, and the United States attended the school. Day students from Yverdon added to the mix. The attendees were boys of all ages from mainly middle-class families who could afford the small fee. A number of nonpaying poor pupils were also accepted. Pestalozzi's idea was that all students, regardless of family circumstance, should be treated equally. During his stay at Yverdon, Pestalozzi also started a school for girls, an expression of his belief that all children, including girls, should be given the same educational opportunities.

As at Burgdorf, the schedule was intense. "They had ten lessons daily, the first starting at six o'clock in the morning before they had washed or tidied their hair. But the lessons were a pleasure to them, including as they did nature observation, woodwork, gymnastics, and various games. Wednesday and Sunday afternoons were given over to long walks. In summer the boys went bathing, in winter skating and tobogganing; and often the young Sons of Switzerland could be seen marching, fencing, and shooting in a nearby meadow" (Silber 1960, 207).

Because many of the children were older than those who had attended the school at Burgdorf, the curriculum was expanded to include geography, history, the natural sciences, mathematics, music, handiwork, and religious education. All of these subjects were taught following the principles of starting from the simple to the complex and from the near to the far. The method followed Pestalozzi's basic principle of *Anschauung*, which translates as "observation" but for Pestalozzi was the whole operation of intelligence, always starting from immediate sense impressions and progressing to more general conceptions.

In the school, all the subjects were taught according to the *Anschauung* method. "They were taught to use their own eyes and hands and minds. Exercises in language and arithmetic were in the first instance, related to objects and circumstances in their environment before being applied to literature and pure mathematics, and geographical understanding was first aroused on walks and by making models before maps were used. Because of the considerable number of French speaking children, all lessons were given in both language" (Silber 1960, 207).

Writing was taught side by side with reading but only after children had mastered motor control. Children used movable letters, a Pestalozzi innovation, to aid them in learning to write. Additionally, "the different grades of each subject were taught at the same time of the day so that the children could pass from one stage to another according to their abilities and progress" (Silber 1960, 207).

Pestalozzi brought in specialists in fields such as geography, science, and math. These men then devised materials that encouraged *Anschauung*, wrote textbooks describing their work, and trained others in their method. In this way, Pestalozzi's principles of education were rapidly spread throughout Europe. In the United States, Pestalozzi's methods were introduced in schools in New Harmony, Indiana, and in Oswego, New York. Because parents had to pay a fee for their child's attendance, the institute in Yverdon attained a national and international reputation as a school for children of middle-class families. This was contrary to Pestalozzi's most fervent desire to create a school for poor children.

The first five years at Yverdon were extraordinarily successful not only in the primary mission of educating children but also in the secondary mission of establishing Pestalozzi-based schools in other European countries and abroad. But the idyllic days were not to last. Pestalozzi's two most valuable assistants, Johannes Niederer and Joseph Schmid, became increasingly antagonistic to one another.

Other factors entered in as well. The endless stream of visitors and temporary assistants, including Friedrich Froebel, were a disruptive factor. The language was also a barrier, particularly after large numbers of French students arrived who made fun of the bad French of the Swiss Germans. And because Pestalozzi took on many more nonpaying children than the fees could cover, the school came into more and more financial difficulties. The most serious event leading to the demise of the institute was the death of Pestalozzi's wife in 1815. She had been the mother figure of the institute, and her warmth and caring had helped keep the antagonisms from overflowing.

Pestalozzi based his method on the feeling of security provided by a loving community. The conflict between Niederer and Schmid led to the assistants taking sides and destroyed any hope of a loving relationship between the two competing groups and within the school as a whole. In desperation, Pestalozzi turned to Schmid to get things under control. Schmid introduced drastic financial cuts of staff and materials, which led to many faculty and students leaving the school. An effort to raise money by publishing Pestalozzi's complete works did not really solve the problem. Legal disputes between Niederer and Schmid made the situation even more difficult. But Pestalozzi continued to side with Schmid, even though many of his oldest and most trusted students, who resented Schmid's severe methods, refused to correspond with him as long as his loyalties remained with Schmid. The school at Yverdon finally closed in 1825, and Pestalozzi, his daughter-in-law, and his grandson moved back to the Neuhof house that Pestalozzi still owned.

The Last Years, 1825–1827

At Neuhof, Pestalozzi continued writing and hoped to open a school for poor children. He published a third version of *Leonard and Gertrude* and an unfinished *Swansong*, which was both an autobiography and an attempt to integrate his various curriculum innovations within a more comprehensive and unitary framework. But the ill will of his former assistants followed him, and a scandalous book about Pestalozzi by a colleague of Niederer put him into a serious state of agitated depression. His doctor sent him to Brugg, a spa city located at the confluence of three rivers. It was there that Pestalozzi died on February 17, 1827. He wished to be buried beside the school at Neuhof, and it was as he had wished.

The Work

Pestalozzi wrote on so many subjects—society, economics, culture, and religion, as well as education—that summarizing them here is truly impossible. In his book *Pestalozzi and Education*, Gerald Gutek (1968) has done an excellent job of putting together all facets of Pestalozzi's work. Here I will only try to summarize the two books that were most successful and that also expounded his educational theories.

Leonard and Gertrude

In this book, Pestalozzi tells the story of the pastoral village of Bonnal and its inhabitants, chief among them Gertrude; her easygoing drinking and gambling husband, Leonard; and their seven children. Pestalozzi intended in this book not only to give a vivid picture of typical rural life but also to demonstrate how a good person like Gertrude can bring about change and enlist the assistance of a benevolent Lord in doing so. The story is packed with stereotypical characters, including "the hypocrite, the fool, the gossip, the miser, the sot, the sycophant, the schemer, the just judge, the good parson, the intriguing woman from the court, the old schoolmaster enraged at a new departure in education, the quack doctor sentenced to dig the graves of those he killed" (Pestalozzi 1977, vii). The story is packed with action and powerful dialogue.

How Gertrude Teaches Her Children

Because *Leonard and Gertrude* failed to have its desired effect in making readers aware of the need for educational reform, Pestalozzi wrote a sequel, a book of letters, that set out the specifics of his educational method. Because it was discursive and tangential, *How Gertrude Teaches Her Children* never received the widespread acceptance of its predecessor. In *How Gertrude Teaches Her Children*, Pestalozzi details his premise that the basic elements of any subject matter are sequential quantity, form, and language. That is, the learner grasps first the quantity of things, then their shape and form, and finally their name or designation.

Common Themes

The Nature of the Child

Pestalozzi, like Rousseau, emphasized that character—good or bad—was the result of education. One of his many fables makes this point.

> Two colts, as like as two eggs, fell into different hands. One was bought by a peasant, whose only thought was to harness it to a plough as soon as possible; this one turned out a bad horse. The other fell to the lot of a man who, by looking it after well, and training it carefully, made a noble steed of it, strong and mettlesome. (Guimps 1890, 106)

The Aims of Education

For Pestalozzi, developing thinking skills was more important than acquiring knowledge and skills.

> The chief aim of elementary instruction is not to furnish the child with knowledge and talents, but to develop and increase the powers of his mind. (Guimps 1890, 241)

The Role of Play

Pestalozzi regarded play as a kind of action pleasure, deriving from the exercise of new mental attainments. He thus anticipated Freud's and Piaget's arguments that mental activity is pleasurable.

> When a child's sense impressions have resulted in clear and settled ideas, and when he can express these ideas in speech, he feels the need of examining, separating and comparing them; this is a pleasure in which life itself invites him, and in which he finds the surest aid for his judgment and power of thinking. (Guimps 1890, 379)

Conformance with DAP Principles

NAEYC

Many aspects of children's learning and development follow well-documented sequences, with later abilities, skills, and knowledge building on those already acquired.

PESTALOZZI

In each branch, instruction must begin with the simplest elements, and proceed gradually by following the child's development; that is, by a series of steps which are psychologically connected. (Guimps 1890, 241)

NAEYC

Children develop best when they have secure, consistent relationships with responsive adults and opportunities for positive relationships with peers.

PESTALOZZI

Since I had no fellow helpers I put a capable child between two less capable ones, he embraced them with both arms, he told them what he knew and they learned to repeat after him what they knew not. (Pestalozzi [1894] 1915, 44–45)

Commentary

Pestalozzi was the first to clearly articulate the principle that curriculum had to be adapted to the psychology of the child. Inasmuch as there was not the science of child psychology at that time, he, like Comenius, used analogies with nature to emphasize that children, no less than plants, require different types of environmental input at different stages of growth for full and healthy development.

In the second quotation, Pestalozzi clearly anticipates the current recognition of values and importance of peer tutoring and, implicitly, of multiage grouping. Perhaps Pestalozzi's greatest and most lasting contribution was his insistence that children first learn from their own actions with things in order to meaningfully conceptualize and name them.

References

Guimps, Roger de. 1890. Pestalozzi, *His Life and Work*. New York: Appleton.

Gutek, Gerald. 1968. *Pestalozzi and Education*. Prospect Heights, IL: Waveland.

Pestalozzi, Johann Heinrich. (1894) 1915. *How Gertrude Teaches Her Children*. Translated by Lucy E. Holland and Frances C. Turner. London: Allen & Unwin.

———. 1977. *Leonard and Gertrude*. Translated by Eva Channing. New York: Gordon.

Silber, Kate. 1960. *Pestalozzi: The Man and His Work*. New York: Schocken.

6

Friedrich Froebel

1782–1852

If history has been miserly in giving recognition to the contributions of Comenius and Pestalozzi, it has been generous in the acclaim it has given Friedrich Froebel. He is rightfully renowned as the inventor of the kindergarten, the champion of learning through play, and the first to engage women as the teachers of young children. At the same time, his educational theory—that human development is comparable to the development of crystals—and his educational materials and methods have not been widely adopted. His instructional aids—such as a ball, cylinder, and cube—that he called *gifts* were meant to teach children both simple and abstract concepts. The ball, for example, was first presented as a geometrical shape and later as the shape of the earth. Likewise, he called educational tasks, such as interweaving colored strips of paper, *occupations*, which were designed to encourage children's creative abilities. Despite the initial enthusiastic reception of Froebel's approach, with a few isolated exceptions, early childhood programs today bear little or no resemblance to the kindergarten envisaged by its inventor. Yet, Froebel remains the father of the kindergarten because he gave it the name.

The reasons for this short life span of the truly Froebelian kindergarten are many. The most important, perhaps, was that Froebel regarded the kindergarten as an educational program every bit as important, if not more so, than what was taught at the elementary and secondary levels. He thus demanded a great deal from the teachers who worked for him. They had to understand child development as well as how to use Froebel's gifts and occupations. They had to learn how the same gift could be used again and again at different ages to teach ever more abstract concepts. Froebel believed that with the correct use of his gifts and occupations, children could learn the underlying unity of self with mankind, nature, the universe, and spirit.

This complicated goal for children was difficult for teachers to understand and was made even more incomprehensible thanks to Froebel's abstract, tangential, and repetitious writing style. In addition, because the sequence of gifts and occupations was modeled after the growth of crystals rather than after the growth of children, the gifts and occupations often failed to engage children's interest. Hence the gifts and occupations were increasingly misused or simply given up. Nonetheless, some, including the occupation of paper folding, are still employed in some early childhood programs.

In Froebel's defense, it must be said that the early kindergartens, taught by those trained by Froebel or his disciples, did have a lasting and powerful, if unintended, consequence. Brosterman (1997) made this argument, contending that attendance at the true Froebelian kindergartens influenced many of the pre–World War I generation of Western architects and artists.

For example, Frank Lloyd Wright's mother bought him a set of the Froebelian gifts. Paul Klee, Piet Mondrian, Le Corbusier, Georges Braque, and other innovators attended Froebelian kindergartens. The colors, forms, and linearity of their work directly parallels the creations of children engaged with the gifts and occupations. Certainly correlation is not causation, but the coincidence of their work as children and as adults is surely not entirely coincidental. It is a powerful testament to the importance of early childhood education, Froebelian or otherwise.

Like Pestalozzi, Froebel was a poor manager and leader. But whereas Pestalozzi blamed himself for his failures, Froebel blamed others. And if Pestalozzi was too permissive as a leader, Froebel was too autocratic. With children, however, Froebel was quite another person. He enjoyed romping and playing with children in the forest and hills more than he did teaching them in the classroom.

The Man

The Early Years, 1782–1799

The German state of Thuringia is essentially a forest that runs northwest to southeast and sits on a continuous stretch of ancient rounded mountains. It was in the village of Oberweissbach within this state that Friedrich Froebel was born on April

21, 1782. His father was a pastor who ministered to six villages with a total population of approximately five thousand. Like Rousseau, Froebel lost his mother early, when he was only nine months old. The family servants and his older brothers took over Froebel's rearing in the absence of his father, who was busy caring for his flock. Froebel was especially close to his brother Christoph, who, of all the brothers, spent the most time caring for and protecting him.

At age four, Froebel's lack of parental care became active rejection when his father remarried. While initially the stepmother was kind to him, this ended abruptly after she became pregnant. Once she had a child of her own, she encouraged Froebel's father to turn against him. Froebel's father used the little time he did spend with his son in trying to teach the boy to read. Either because the father was a poor teacher or because Froebel was a poor student, or some combination of the two, Froebel had trouble learning to read. This problem was symptomatic of his later inability to express himself clearly in both speaking and writing.

The situation at home became increasingly intolerable as Froebel rejected any form of discipline his parents tried to impose. Relief came when a clergyman uncle on Froebel's mother's side visited the family. The uncle quickly took in the severity of the situation and invited Froebel to come and live with him for an indefinite stay. At age ten, Froebel went to live with his uncle in Stadt Ilm, located on the Ilm River in Thuringia (Snider [1900] 2004).

At his uncle's house, Froebel was treated with both kindness and trust. Kept largely at home by his parents, Froebel was now free to roam the beautiful surrounding countryside. He also attended school but found that he was at a disadvantage with the other children, who had many of the social and motor skills that Froebel lacked. But living with his uncle gave him a new sense of self-confidence, and he tried his best to adapt socially and to develop the strength and agility that was never required of him before.

Under the benevolence of his uncle, Froebel was able to finish school and to receive religious confirmation at age fifteen. Confirmation was the rite of passage to manhood and a time for deciding what to do with his life. Since his parents were obligated to help him find a vocation, he returned to live with them. Froebel hoped to go to the University of Jena, where his brothers had attended. But his parents were opposed, thinking him too stupid to be worth the cost. Rather, they decided that he would have to learn a trade. Accordingly, at age fifteen and a half, they apprenticed young Froebel to a forester with whom he lived for two years. At the end of this period, the forester asked Froebel to stay with him, but Froebel refused and returned to his parents' home.

The Search for Identity: Jena, 1799–1805

Froebel still hoped to go to the university but lacked the means. In 1799, however, he came into a small inheritance from his deceased mother. He convinced his father, with the help of his brother Christoph, to permit him to use the money to go to the university. The University of Jena is located in central Germany on the Saale River. Jena embodied the rich artistic and intellectual atmosphere of German art and science of that time. While at Jena (1799–1801), Froebel took courses in physics, architecture, and surveying, and he showed a special talent for mathematics and geometry.

Due to lack of funds, Froebel had to leave Jena before completing a course of study. Nonetheless, during his two-year stay, Froebel imbibed the spirit of the times not only in his courses but also in frequent informal meetings with other students. His one complaint about his university experience was that it lacked unity and coherence, a lack that he later tried to correct in creating his own pedagogy.

Froebel left Jena at age nineteen, still uncertain as to which vocational path he was to follow. Lacking other means of support, he returned to his parents' home for guidance. This time they sent him to live with some relatives who owned a farm in Hildburghausen, a town on the Saar River in central Germany. On the farm he was to learn agriculture. Shortly after he arrived at Hildburghausen, however, Froebel was called home because his father was very ill and had asked for him to return. The two reconciled with one another before his father died in 1802. With the death of his father, Froebel was now forced to find an occupation on his own. It was the start of a period of role experimentation in a path toward identity, similar to that experienced by Locke, Rousseau, and Pestalozzi.

Unsure of just what he wanted to become, Froebel first took up clerkship in Bamburg, a city in Bavaria. After a year of "scribbling," he decided the job was not for him. In 1803 he thought he might find his calling in land surveying. He had no training, but he had taken some courses on the subject at Jena. He did get some temporary work of this kind in and around Bamburg. Not happy with this endeavor either, Froebel tried working as a private secretary, a bookkeeper, and an accountant. Although some of these activities did satisfy his mathematical talents, the contents of the work were uninteresting. A friend urged him to become an architect. Froebel took this advice and, thanks again to a second fortuitous inheritance, moved to Frankfurt in 1805 determined to become an architect.

Identity Achieved: Frankfurt, Vyerdon, and Berlin, 1805–1816

Early in his stay at Frankfurt, Froebel met Dr. Anton Gruner, the head of a model school. Gruner was a student of Pestalozzi, whose methods he employed in his own school. Froebel visited the school and shared with the teachers some vague ideas of his own about education. Gruner overheard Froebel expound his pedagogical views and told Froebel, "Give up architecture; it is not your vocation at all. Become a teacher" (Froebel, 1889, 51). Froebel had his doubts. Gruner, however, convinced of Froebel's potential, offered him a teaching position at the school. After some hesitation, Froebel accepted the invitation and gave up the idea of becoming an architect.

When he began teaching, Froebel found that it satisfied both his philosophical and practical inclinations. Just as important, it reconciled the rebellious with the social side of his personality. He could protest against the outmoded educational practices of the time yet be caring and affectionate to the children in his charge. After two days of actually teaching, however, he realized how little he knew of classroom practice. He expressed his concerns to Gruner, who suggested that he go to study with Pestalozzi for a few weeks and arranged for Froebel to do so.

After his brief stay with Pestalozzi, Froebel returned to Frankfurt and taught at Gruner's school for two years. In 1808, in order to explore his own ideas about education, Froebel accepted the position of tutor to three sons of a landed couple. They provided Froebel and the boys a large meadow for them to use as a garden and play area. As a tutor, Froebel was free to innovate and introduce his own teaching methods. He devised a number of educational games for the boys to play, and this gave him the confidence that he could create his own curriculum materials. Nonetheless, he felt he still needed to learn more, so he took his three charges back to Yverdon in 1808 to learn Pestalozzi's methods firsthand and in depth.

Froebel and the three boys stayed at Yverdon for almost two years. Froebel was both pupil and teacher during this time. Although he was much impressed with the emphasis Pestalozzi put on children's learning from their own activities rather than from books, he was critical of other aspects of the program. It seemed to him that there was little integration among the subjects taught, and that Pestalozzi's own lack of knowledge of subject matter gave him little control over his teachers. The experience at Yverdon convinced Froebel that he needed to go back to university to learn more before he could start his own school. He returned to Frankfurt with the three boys and stayed with the family for another year.

In 1811 Froebel decided to go to the University of Göttingen, one of the most progressive schools of the time. One reason for his return was his difficulty with languages, particularly with grammar, which he hoped to remedy at Göttingen. But he soon gave up his hope of mastering languages and turned to the natural sciences, which revived his affinity for nature that he had first experienced in the forests of Thuringia. Crystallography particularly excited him, perhaps because it challenged his talent for geometry. At that time, Christian Weiss, a professor and renowned crystallographer, was teaching at the University of Berlin. Froebel decided to move to Berlin to study with him.

Froebel reached Berlin in 1812 and began attending Professor Weiss's lectures. Weiss taught that every crystal was formed from a liquid or gas, and as the crystal grew, it retained its unique, intricate, three-dimensional pattern of surfaces and angles. (Today we might say that each type of crystal has its own DNA.) In the laws of crystal formation, Froebel believed he had found the laws of growth that could be applied to all of nature—both animate and inanimate. These laws became the basis for his pedagogy.

The Prussian uprising against Napoleon in 1812–1813 again interrupted Froebel's studies. Though not born in Prussia, Froebel had a strong sense of being German (in the same sense that many nationalities in the United States identify with being American), and this entailed an obligation. Froebel enlisted in the army at age thirty-one. Among his comrades were two younger men, Heinrich Langethal and Wilhelm Middendorf, with whom he discussed his educational ideas and who were later to join and teach with him. Middendorf was to be become a lifelong and completely devoted friend, supporter, and defender.

The war ended with Napoleon's defeat and his exile to Elba. As a reward for his military service, Froebel was given a position in the mineralogical museum under Professor Weiss. Froebel's job was to categorize minerals according to a formula originated by Weiss. Froebel spent almost two years behind locked doors in a totally quiet room. Through intricate geometrical measurements, Froebel was able to identify and classify a variety of crystals into six major groups. He later said of this experience, "In the little crystal, I saw the hand of Providence for the development of the human race" (Snider [1900] 2004, 134).

Keilhau, 1816–1833

After almost two years of studying crystals, Froebel decided that he was ready to start his own school. He returned to his native Thuringia and opened an institute in the small village of Griesheim. This was the village in which the widow of his brother Christoph lived and where she was raising her daughter and three sons. Christoph's three sons and two other nephews of Froebel made up the student body of the new institute. Shortly thereafter Froebel moved the institute to more spacious quarters in nearby Keilhau, located in a picturesque valley in the southeast of Germany. The money to purchase the buildings and land at Keilhau came from the forced sale of a piece of property owned by Madame Christoph. After the sale, she, her sons, and Froebel moved to the new location.

Shortly after opening the institute in 1916, Froebel invited Langethal and Middendorf to come work with him. Middendorf arrived immediately and Langethal a year later. Barop, a relative of Middendorf, eventually joined them in 1823 but did not stay long. At the institute, the boys were allowed to roam the fields and forests, wear their hair long, and engage in mock fights and battles. They were also instructed in arithmetic and geometry as well as correct writing and speaking. In addition the boys were taught paper folding and modeling, forerunners of Froebel's later gifts and occupations.

Although the students were reveling in their freedom and actively engaged in their more academic work, there was little money for food or clothing. Madame Christoph came to the rescue again and sold her silver and other housewares to keep the school going. At the same time, Middendorf and, particularly, Langethal were urging Froebel to marry Henrietta Wilhelm Hoffmeister, whom Froebel had met in Berlin. She came from a good home and was well educated and refined. Froebel proposed in a letter and was accepted, but not without hesitation on the part of Henrietta's parents. Henrietta had a grown adopted daughter, Ernestine, whom she brought with her to Keilhau. The reason Langethal wanted Froebel to marry Henrietta appears to be because he was in love with, and intended to marry, Ernestine.

Froebel's marriage plans created what would be a lifelong vendetta against him. Several years earlier, when Froebel's beloved brother Christoph died, Froebel wrote a letter to Madame Christoph in which he wrote that he would be like a father to her sons. The widow misunderstood this as a promise of future marriage and was therefore willing to make financial sacrifices on his behalf. When Madame Christoph learned of the marriage plans, she demanded that Froebel give her back the money she had given him for the school. Because Froebel had no money, she accepted his written promise to pay her back at some future time. He never did repay the loan. Madame Christoph then left Keilhau but did not take her sons with her.

Finances continued to be a problem until Froebel's brother Christian decided to quit his successful business, give the proceeds to Froebel, and move his family to Keilhau. Christian brought with him his three daughters, two of whom would later marry Middendorf and Barop. So the institute eventually became a very close-knit family community.

As the institute gained in reputation, it attracted more students and became more financially viable, or at least passably so for the next six years (1820–1826). But neither Froebel nor his wife were good managers, and Froebel would not allow his financially experienced brother to take over the accounts. Even with the increased number of students, the school was still having trouble making ends meet. The rebellious side of Froebel's nature aggravated the situation. He developed a sense of his own infallibility and would accept no changes to what he thought was good management or sound pedagogy.

Froebel's' financial mismanagement and dictatorial manner created resentment among his teachers. Two of Froebel's best teachers Schoenbein, the discoverer of ozone, and Michelis, a distinguished scientist, left the school because they could not bear Froebel's interference with the teaching of subjects he knew nothing about. More serious a threat was another teacher, Herzog, who took up Madame Christoph's cause, turned her sons against their uncle, and encouraged them to leave the school, as he himself did.

After he left the school, Herzog publicized the story of Froebel's broken promise to marry his brother's widow and to repay the money she had loaned him. This publicity, together with his bad management and dictatorial manner, made Froebel's stay at Keilhau as headmaster untenable. By 1832, Barop, a better manager and teacher, took over the school, although Froebel remained the titular headmaster.

Froebel decided he had to found another school and returned to Frankfurt where he was reunited with Frau von Holzhause, whose three sons he had tutored years before. She introduced him to composer Franz Xaver Schnyder von Wartensee, with whom he shared his educational ideas. Schnyder von Wartensee was captivated by Froebel's desire to complete the reforms Pestalozzi had begun. Learning that Froebel was looking for a place to start a new school, Schnyder von Wartensee offered Froebel his castle in Wartensee on the shores of Lake Sampach in Switzerland. Froebel accepted the invitation and moved to Switzerland with his wife.

The Swiss Sojourn: Wartensee, Willisau, Burgdorf, 1833–1836

Froebel modeled the new institute at Wartensee after the one at Keilhau. But problems quickly arose. Herzog followed Froebel to Switzerland and again wrote articles defaming Froebel's character. Because of this, and other reasons, Froebel and Schnyder von Wartensee had a falling out, and after a year the school had to be given up. Some merchants in the nearby village of Willisau, however, invited Froebel to set up a school for their children. The people and the municipality supported the school, and more than forty students were immediately enrolled. In May 1833 the school at Willisau was formally opened.

Soon after the school opened, Middendorf left his wife and children to join Froebel and to help run the school. Two years later, Froebel was invited to run a training class for teachers in Burgdorf, located in the canton of Berne and in a tiny valley surrounded by the mountains of the Swiss Alps. Froebel moved to Burgdorf in 1835. Burgdorf had special meaning for Froebel because it was the place where Pestalozzi began his reform of elementary education.

At Burgdorf Froebel was appointed director of an orphanage of young children from four to six years of age. Froebel found that he was in his element with the young children. While he had enjoyed playing with the older children, teaching them never excited him. But with the young children, he was inspired to create songs, games, and exercises, and to read them stories and fables. Yet he still felt the lack of an overriding concept that would integrate all these activities within a broader conceptual whole.

One day while walking in the fields, he came upon some children playing ball in the meadow. He suddenly had the revelation that the ball represented not only roundness but also the earth and, indeed, the universe. This revelation gave him the idea that he could create materials that, with their use, the child could progressively acquire a coherent sense of self as an individual but also as one with humankind, nature, and the universe. These were the educational tools that he had vainly sought in other educational programs. According to Denton Jacquez Snider, Frobel said, "I shall now employ ball and cube as educative playthings for the little child, for my orphans. I shall put them together as one process or one play-gift; out of this I see developing a whole series of forms, through which the child playing, will enter the creative workshop of nature herself, and thus unfold into his spiritual inheritance" ([1900] 2004, 282). It is this kind of unity that Froebel wished to convey with his clarion call, "Come Let Us Live with Our Children" (Froebel 1904, 3).

Like Pestalozzi, however, Froebel also recognized that the mother was the first teacher and that if young children were to profit from his gifts, they had to start their education in infancy. Accordingly, he and his wife set about writing the book *Mother Play and Nursery Songs*, which would nourish the infant's language, intellect, and spirit (the book includes well-known songs, such as "Itsy Bitsy Spider"). During 1835 and 1836, Froebel thus began to create his kindergarten gifts and occupations and a play-song curriculum for mothers.

In 1836 Froebel returned to Berlin to settle the estate of his wife's mother. While there he visited the day nurseries for children whose mothers had to work. Because of industrialization the day nursery idea was already widespread. In Scotland James Buchanan created infant schools for the children of his weavers. This idea spread quickly and was the motivation for Robert Owen to open his own infant school in New Lanark, England, in 1816. So the idea of schools for young children was very much in the air when Froebel came to see its importance. But Froebel regarded these infant schools primarily as child care facilities for the working poor. In contrast, he saw early childhood as an educational level in its own right, and one that should be available to all children.

Blankenburg, 1836–1844

Froebel went back to Keilhau in 1836 hoping to start a school for young children on the premises of his old institute. But the acting head, Barop, rejected his unreasonable financial demands. Nonetheless, in 1837 Barop did give Froebel the funds to set up his school in an old powder mill in Blankenburg, a spa village in Thuringia. Middendorf came to work with him, again leaving his wife and children to do so. The students were young children from the town whose parents felt some trepidation about the school. In addition to teaching, Froebel began publishing the *Sunday Journal*, which explained the purposes and methods of the new institute. In the articles, most of which he wrote himself, he described the play gifts and how they were to be employed.

Froebel now regarded his early childhood pedagogy as having worldwide significance and began lecturing about it in many parts of Germany. But he still had not arrived at a name for the program. One day, while walking with Middendorf and

Barop over the Steiger Mountain to Blankenburg, he suddenly stopped and looked as if he were transfixed. Then he shouted to the mountains, "Eureka! I have it! *Kindergarten* shall be the name of the new Institution" (Froebel 1889, 137). This term expressed both the idea of a place for children and the idea of child growth and development. Froebel now had a name for his program and spent more and more of his time giving workshops and lectures about it.

Froebel set up his own printing press to publish his *Sunday Journal* and the *Mother Play and Nursery Songs*. His wife, who wrote most of the music and helped with the lyrics, died in 1839. Froebel was deeply grieved by this loss but continued his lectures, training, and teaching. He also completed the twenty gifts and occupations that made up the core of his program. A small workshop was also set up to manufacture his materials.

The Last Years: Hamburg, 1844–1852

In 1844 Froebel left Blankenburg to travel all over Germany for the next few years to lecture and give workshops on kindergarten education. In 1849 Froebel decided to marry his former student Louise Levin, who was many years his junior. Although he had wanted to return to Keilhau with her, the wives of Middendorf and Barop and other women would not have it, feeling scandalized by the idea of such a marriage. So in 1849 Froebel and his future bride set up a training school for kindergarten teachers at Bad Leibenstein, a renowned resort town in southern Thuringia.

In 1851, in Bad Leibenstein, the couple finally wed among many happy festivities and celebrations. But the happiness was not to last. Froebel's nephew, Karl Froebel, was a socialist and published the pamphlet *High Schools for Young Ladies and Kindergartens*. The pamphlet described not only an ambitious scheme for the education of women but also socialistic ideas that would do away with the present government. In that same year, the Prussian minister of education von Raumer, assuming that Friedrich Froebel had written the revolutionary pamphlet, closed all kindergartens in Prussia. His rationale was that kindergartens were subverting the government by teaching socialism. All attempts to clarify the differences between the uncle and nephew were ignored.

Froebel, whose orientation was religious rather than political, was devastated at this development and the failure of all attempts at reprieve. The closing of the kindergartens made it seem to him that all his labors were for nothing. But there were some supportive developments, including a teachers' conference in 1851 that highly acclaimed his work. Nonetheless, the closing of the kindergartens took its toll, and Froebel began to fade physically. As the end of his life approached, he resigned himself to not seeing the kindergarten flourish in his lifetime. He writes in his autobiography, "Now I know it will be centuries before my view of the human being as child, and the education corresponding to it can be accepted. But that troubles me no more" (Snider [1900] 2004, 441–42).

Froebel died on June 21, 1852. Middendorf designed the monument on Froebel's grave, showing a montage of Froebel's first gifts to children: the sphere, the cylinder, and the cube. The inscription echoes Froebel's famous call creating kindergartens: "Come Let Us Live with Our Children" (Froebel 1904, 3).

The Work

Froebel's three major works are *The Education of Man*, written in 1826; the *Pedagogics of the Kindergarten*, published in 1861 after his death; and his *Mother's Play and Nursery Songs*.

The Education of Man

In this book, Froebel gives his philosophy of education prior to inventing the kindergarten. At the heart of Froebel's position is his belief that we all have two selves: an inner self and an outer self. The inner self is spiritual—our good self; the outer is environmentally malleable—our bad self. As children play with the gifts and occupations, they discover the powers and limits of their actions and thoughts. They are thus able to realize their good, inner selves. It was something Froebel argued that children could not do with tasks set for them by others.

Froebel also recognized that play could be used by the outer self to give vent to selfish, egocentric, and hostile actions. Such actions were the result of being exposed to misguided parents and teachers. Froebel was convinced that children could gain control over the negative side of themselves only through play freed from external constraint. He argued that children need to stay in touch with their inner selves through self-initiated play at all levels of education and development.

Pedagogics of the Kindergarten

In this book, Froebel describes his gifts and occupations, their rationalization, and guidance for their use. The first gift given to the infant is the ball. Froebel argues that the ball is attractive to children of all ages and to adults as well (and is indeed so, judging by contemporary sports). He also argues that the ball—the sphere—is the basic form and that it represents a unity both at the concrete and abstract levels. Through interaction with the ball and the ministrations of the mother, the infant learns about his or her inner spiritual and outer sympathetic selves. Eventually, at later ages, the ball becomes the symbol not only of the earth and the universe but also of an inner unity with the spirit. A complete description of the gifts is provided by Kate Douglas Wiggin and Nora Archibald Smith in their book *Froebel's Gifts* (1895), and a thorough discussion of his occupations is found in their book *Froebel's Occupations* (1896).

Mother's Play and Nursery Songs

In his travels, Froebel listened to mothers singing and playing with their children. This was the basis for many of the songs and games that make up the book *Mother's Play and Nursery Songs*. "This book is a collection of fifty-five songs. Seven introductory songs express the feelings of a mother toward her infant child, and show how through playful incitement she seeks to develop its activity; forty-nine entries are little games which she may play with him, and the concluding song outlines the results presumably attained" (Blow 1894, 149–50). A thoughtful presentation of Froebel's *Mother's Play and Nursery Songs* is given by Susan Blow (1894).

Common Themes

The Nature of the Child

Froebel looked on the child as part of humanity, which is in turn part of nature and the universe as a whole. The child is at once a whole being but at the same time part of a series of much larger wholes.

> This original and fundamental nature of man, as being life in itself and therefore again giving life, makes itself know in man's impulse to creative formation. This fundamental nature makes itself known even in the child by the instinct for observing, analyzing, and again uniting—that is, by the instinct for formative and creative activity. Indeed, the fostering of this instinct in the child makes manifest the life of man, at the same time wholly satisfying the demands of that life. (Froebel 1904, 8)

The Aims of Education

Froebel regarded the aim of life as the need to attain a unity of self, society, nature, universe, and spirit. Education should enable the individual to achieve this aim.

> It is the aim of our endeavor to make it possible for man freely and spontaneously to develop, to educate himself from his first advent on earth, as a whole human being, as a whole himself, and in harmony and union with the life-whole—to make it for him to inform and instruct himself, to, recognize himself thus as a definite member of the all-life, and as such, freely and spontaneously to make himself known—freely and spontaneously to live. (Froebel 1904, 9)

The Role of Play

For Froebel, his playful gifts and occupations provide a means of progressive differentiation and higher-order integration.

> They [the gifts and occupations] proceed from unity, and develop in all manifoldness from unity in accordance with the laws of life. They begin with the simplest, and, at each particular stage, again begin with that which is relatively the simplest; but afterward advance in reciprocally beneficial relation to one another, and according to the necessary laws contained in the nature of the things themselves . . . in general with the development of life. (Froebel 1904, 18)

Conformance with DAP Principles

NAEYC
Play is an important vehicle for developing self-regulation as well as for promoting language, cognition, and social competence.

FROEBEL
A child who plays capably, spontaneously, quietly, enduringly, even to the point of bodily fatigue, becomes certainly also a capable, quiet, enduring man, self-sacrificingly promoting his own and others' welfare. (Froebel 1885, 30–31)

NAEYC
All the domains of development and learning—physical, social and emotional, and cognitive—are important, and they are closely interrelated.

Children's development and learning in one domain influence and are influenced by what takes place in other domains.

FROEBEL

Thus the work with colors does not in any way mean to develop a future painter, neither is the work in singing intended to train a future musician. The occupations simply have the purpose to secure in the young human being all-sided development and unfolding of his nature; they furnish in a general way the food for mental growth. (Froebel [1826] 2005, 327)

Commentary

What is perhaps most impressive of all Froebel's principles and his work in general, is Froebel's view of early childhood education as extraordinarily complex and intricate. Early childhood education, as he saw it, had to be rich and challenging and done in depth. Without overestimating the young child's abilities, he nonetheless saw the young child as capable of learning much more than what is usually thought possible. This may be the reason that some of those children who did experience kindergarten as Froebel designed it went on to artistic and architectural greatness. It still must be said that Froebel's greatest legacy to early childhood education and to DAP was his conception of the kindergarten and his insistence that play is an essential learning activity not only for children but also for individuals at all age levels.

References

Blow, Susan E. 1894. *Symbolic Education: A Commentary on Froebel's Mother Play*. New York: Appleton.

Brosterman, Norman. 1997. *Inventing Kindergarten*. New York: Abrams.

Froebel, Friedrich. (1826) 2005. *The Education of Man*. Translated by W. N. Hailmann. New York: Dover.

———. 1885. *The Education of Man*. Translated by Josephine Jarvis. New York: Lovell. (For access and information, see https://archive.org/details/educationofman00froe.)

———. 1889. *The Autobiography of Friedrich Froebel*. Syracuse, NY: C.W. Bardeen.

———. 1904. *Pedagogics of the Kindergarten*. Translated by Josephine Jarvis. St. Louis: Woodward and Tiernan.

Smith, Nora Archibald, and Kate Douglas Wiggin. 1895. *Froebel's Gifts*. Cambridge, MA: Riverside.

Snider, Denton Jacquez. (1900) 2004. *The Life of Friedrich Froebel: Founder of the Kindergarten*. Honolulu: University Press of the Pacific.

Wiggin, Kate Douglas, and Nora Archibald Smith. 1896. *Froebel's Occupations*. New York: Houghton Mifflin.

7

Rudolf Steiner

1861–1925

If the life of Rousseau is fascinating, the life of Rudolf Steiner is daunting. Like his idol Johann Wolfgang von Goethe, Steiner was a multifaceted genius. Stewart C. Easton, one of his biographers, writes:

> If Steiner had been nothing but a philosopher, or theologian, or educator, or authority on Goethe, or agricultural expert, or architect, or knowledgeable in medicinal plants, or dramatist, or gifted artistic innovator, inventor of eurythmy [speech as visible movement], an age that respects specialization would have reserved a respected niche for him. But Steiner was *all* these things at the same time. (1989, 9)

To be sure, Easton was a devotee of Steiner and may have overvalued some of his achievements. That said, it is also true that many of Steiner's ideas, such as the importance of organic gardening, anthroposophic (similar to homeopathic) medicine, and the use of stories and biographies as instructional tools, were far ahead of his time.

Despite his many contributions, Steiner is still largely unknown outside his relatively small circle of followers. Perhaps the major reason for this is anthroposophy, the esoteric philosophy Steiner created and to which he attributed all of his practical innovations. He saw anthroposophy as providing a spiritual rather than a materialistic way of understanding the world. In many respects, however, this spiritual view borders on the occult. Steiner advocated some startling propositions, such as reincarnation and communicating with the dead. His advocacy of these unorthodox ideas so sullied his reputation that his valuable ideas were dismissed along with the questionable ones.

I believe that Steiner's philosophy is best regarded as his way of understanding the extraordinary gifts he was given. As a child, he was able to see and to hear what his peers and the adults in his life failed to experience. His intellectual brilliance drove him to try to make sense of his seemingly clairvoyant talents. Many gifted children, like Wolfgang Mozart, have easily recognizable and socially valued gifts. In Steiner's case, it was only after he reached intellectual maturity that he was able to translate his gifts into practical achievements.

It was perhaps unfortunate that Steiner grew up during the last half of the nineteenth century when Spiritualism was very much in vogue. The popularity of Spiritualism emerged in response to the growing preeminence of the natural and social sciences in general and to the theory of evolution in particular. The evolutionary challenge to the biblical account of creation aided and abetted the materialistic view of man and nature that began to dominate European thinking during this time period.

According to materialism, the human mind was nothing but the firing of neurons in the brain. Soul and spirit had no place in this narrative. Materialism gave rise to an opposing narrative: the mental sciences movement. People in the mental sciences movement had a belief in the nonmaterialistic nature of mind and spirit. They viewed the mind and spirit as parallel to, but neither identical with nor reducible to, brain function. Steiner's anthroposophy is best understood in the esoteric atmosphere of these new mental sciences, which included Henri Bergson's *élan vital* (his idea of a dynamic force that drove the evolution of life but was not a bodily substance), Christian Science, transcendentalism, and Theosophy. In Spiritualism, Steiner found an explanation of, and a reason for, his talents.

Steiner suggests in his autobiography (and his biographers support) the idea that from an early age he lived in a spirit world that was as real to him as the physical one. Neither Steiner nor any of his followers succeed, from my reading at least, in defining or describing this spirit world. I believe it was Steiner's intuitive grasp of what others missed or ignored that, in retrospect as an adult, he described as the spirit world. As a child and through his young adulthood, he only appreciated that he had to keep these intuitions to himself.

In support of this interpretation of his intellectual abilities and the suppression of his intuitive gifts is the fact that Steiner pursued an academic career and earned his doctorate in 1891. I believe that it was only later when he was introduced to the spirit world of Theosophy that he found at least a partial explanation for his gifts.

It was his hope that by creating a spiritual science he could counteract some of the negative forces he saw deriving from an exclusively materialistic science.

And his efforts in this regard border on the unbelievable. Over 350 of Steiner's books and hundreds of his reviews and articles were published. Most of his books were stenographic transcriptions of his voluminous public lectures, and many appeared after his death. Once he created anthroposophy, he promoted his ideas with extraordinary energy and persistence. Indeed, Steiner's lecture and seminar schedule is one that verges on the humanly impossible. In addition, the sheer diversity of the topics he covered is truly staggering.

However, Steiner was not a charlatan. He had no patience for the hocus-pocus of séances, tarot cards, and the like, which sought to give material evidence of the spirit world. The very idea that some believed spirit had to take a physical form (for example, in table tapping) made him ill. And, unlike the Spiritualists, Steiner never sought to profit from his special gifts. He sincerely believed in the ideas he proposed, and he even devised mind-training techniques in hopes of helping others see the world as he did (Steiner 1995).

As a man, Steiner was small in stature and undistinguished in appearance but possessed a most-charming smile. He had a warm personality, what the Austrians describe as *gemütlichkeit*, roughly translated as "heartfelt graciousness." After Steiner became known as a spiritual leader, he was sought for advice and council by an unending, and exhausting, stream of admirers. His biographers give many examples of his attentive kindness and compassion even at times of extreme personal physical and mental depletion.

Given the volume of Steiner's opus, it is therefore really impossible in a brief sketch to do justice to his achievements. I will only go into detail in regard to his contributions to education. Certainly, while there is much that is hard to accept in Steiner's anthroposophy, there is also a great deal to admire and appreciate in his practical contributions.

The Man

The Early Years, 1861–1879

In the last half of the nineteenth century, the map of Europe was still very much a work in progress. The village of Kraljevec was on the border of Hungary and

Croatia and was part of the Austro-Hungarian Empire, which was created to stave off Prussian domination. The village is now part of the modern country of Croatia. It was in this village that Rudolf Steiner was born in 1861.

His father, Johann, had been a gamekeeper, descended from a long line of gamekeepers, for the Hoyos family. When Johann fell in love with one of the housemaids, Franziska, the then-reigning Count Hoyos, under whom Johann served, refused to let the two get married. The couple left the count's service, and Johann went on to learn to be a telegraph operator. With his new skills, Johann succeeded in obtaining a position as stationmaster in Kraljevec, located on the Adriatic Sea along the Southern Austrian Railroad between Vienna and Trieste.

When Steiner was about two years old, the family moved to Pottschach, a state in lower Austria, and they remained there until he was almost eight. The environment in which young Steiner grew up may well have contributed to his later reservations about science and industrialization. The setting of the village was magnificent, surrounded by mountains, including the Schneeberg (snow mountain) that dominated the area. It was an environment of great natural beauty. Moreover, most of the buildings, farming implements, and agricultural methods he observed were little changed from those used in the Middle Ages.

Young Steiner was thus surrounded by the rural world of the past at the same time he encountered the artifacts of modernity: the railroad, the telegraph, and the machinery of a nearby cotton mill—all of which intruded into the otherwise rustic scene. The tension between the natural world and that of machines was one Steiner felt throughout his life. It paralleled the tension he felt between the real world and what he later came to regard as the spiritual one.

In his biography of Steiner, Easton tells of an incident that Steiner recalled in a lecture he gave in Berlin. The incident occurred while Steiner was still living in Pottschach. He was sitting in the waiting room of the railroad station when a woman appeared to him who resembled someone in his family. He saw her open the door and approach him, and then she asked him, according to Easton, "to do everything he could for her now and later" (1980, 17). He was very much aware that the woman was not there in reality, but he was not frightened. Nor was he surprised to learn, a few days later, that a near relative had committed suicide on the day the woman had appeared to him. From an early age, Steiner learned not to share such experiences to avoid rejection and ridicule.

The family next moved to Neudörfl, a small Hungarian village close to the border with lower Austria. While the family still lived in Pottschach, Johann, after an argument with the schoolmaster, took his son out of the school and taught him at home. When the family moved to Neudörfl, however, he decided to send his son to the local school. Although Steiner found school boring, as most gifted children do, an admired teacher gave him a book on geometry. Steiner later wrote that through geometry he "first experienced happiness" and that working out the theorems gave him a feeling of "deep contentment" (Lachman 2007, 10).

When Steiner was eleven, his father had to choose between sending him to the gymnasium, where the focus was academic, or to the Realschule, which was in effect a trade school. His father thought that if he went to the Realschule he could learn to be an engineer for the railroad and thus have a secure future. So, from age eleven to age eighteen, Steiner attended the Realschule in the neighboring town of Wiener-Neustadt.

While attending the Realschule, Steiner earned some money by tutoring. It was during these years that Steiner's intellectual genius became apparent. Despite his heavy academic workload and the hour-long walk to and from the Realschule, he taught himself Greek and Latin so he could tutor children attending the gymnasium and the Realschule. He also found time to window-shop in the bookstores. In the window of a bookstore, he saw a copy of *The Critique of Pure Reason* by Emmanuel Kant. (Although epoch making, this book is notoriously difficult to read, even for philosophers.) Steiner spent his savings on the book, and at age fifteen he separated it into sections, which he read during his history class because the professor did nothing but read the history text to the students.

Steiner could not agree with Kant that there were limits to reason and that we could never know "*das Ding on Selbst*" (the thing-in-itself), the reality beyond the limits set by our senses. Steiner believed that the human mind could grasp reality directly and immediately and without the mediation of the senses. This is the way he interpreted his own seemingly extrasensory perceptions. The idea that there are limits to what we can know—Locke's basic thesis on which Kant elaborated—was a doctrine Steiner later attempted to counter with his own anthroposophy.

In 1879 Steiner graduated from the Realschule and was accepted at the Institute of Technology (a little like MIT) in Vienna. His father accepted a post in the village of Inzersdorf outside of Vienna so that Steiner could live at home and save the cost of lodging.

Vienna, 1879–1890

The years Steiner spent in Vienna were intellectually and culturally rich and stimulating. In addition to his courses at the institute, he also attended lectures at the University of Vienna. Outside his classes, Steiner spent much of his time at the Café Griensteidl, which, because of the many notoriously egocentric artists, writers, poets, and musicians who frequented it, was also known as the Megalomania Café. At the café, Steiner met and befriended many of the notable figures of his day. In addition, for the price of a cup of coffee, he also had a place to engage in long periods of reading and writing.

It was during the Vienna years that Steiner fell in love for the first and only time. The young woman in question was the daughter of a teacher whose son Steiner had befriended. He met her on a visit to their home. Later Steiner wrote that though they were both in love they were also both too shy to express their feelings. After Steiner left Vienna, the two corresponded for several years, but that exchange eventually ended.

Steiner had many close friends in Vienna but seemed particularly attracted to strong older women. And the attraction was mutual. For example, Rosa Mayreder, a well-known poet, painter, and writer, greatly valued his friendship, guidance, and council. When he left Vienna for Weimar, she wrote him, "Every day, indeed every hour, I become aware of the emptiness that our separation has left in my life" (Easton 1980, 33).

During Steiner's university years, Karl Julius Schröer, one of his professors, introduced him to the works of Goethe. Reading the works of the renowned writer, Steiner felt an immediate empathy and oneness with him. Goethe rejected the extremes to which the materialism of Isaac Newton was sometimes taken and argued that materialism falsified the world that he saw as a "living garment" (Lachman 2007, 13) that was constantly evolving and undergoing metamorphosis. These ideas were so in keeping with Steiner's own worldview that he felt he had finally found the mentor he had been looking for.

Professor Schröer appreciated Steiner's affinity for Goethe and suggested to Joseph Kürschner, who was editing a complete edition of Goethe's work, that Steiner be invited to edit Goethe's writings on natural science with an introduction and explanatory notes. This project not only provided Steiner with a modest income but also required a great deal of additional reading and writing in natural science, which helped hone his skills as a critic and author.

Because he did not always stay with his parents, Steiner often took a room at a cheap boardinghouse, which he found very uncomfortable. Professor Schröer introduced him to the wealthy Specht family, who was looking for a tutor for the sons. They hired Steiner, who moved in with them and lived with the family for the next five years (1884–1889). Although Steiner was by now a skilled tutor, Otto, one of the Specht boys, was a special challenge. He was born with hydrocephalus (water on the brain, leading to an enlarged head) and was thought to have an intellectual disability. Steiner intuited that the boy was, in fact, very intelligent but had a short attention span. To teach him, Steiner spent hours preparing materials that could be taught in short intervals.

The boy made steady progress, and after two years, Steiner insisted he go to school to learn the social skills that could only be learned by interaction with his peers. Otto progressed physically as well, and his hydrocephalus decreased to the point of being barely noticeable. Otto eventually went on to medical school, became a doctor, and then died while serving at the front in World War I.

After leaving the institute, Steiner became actively involved in the intellectual world of Vienna. In 1888 he became editor of the *German News Weekly* and began giving lectures on Goethe. Steiner also continued his academic work and submitted his doctoral dissertation in 1890. During this time, Steiner met, among many other leading intellectuals, Friedrich Eckstein, who was a philosopher of symbolism, an alchemist, and a musician. It was Eckstein who made Steiner aware of the many mental science movements of the time, including Theosophy.

Weimar, 1890–1897

In 1890 Steiner moved to Weimar where he joined a team of scholars working on a definitive edition of Goethe's works. Steiner was chosen as the best person to edit Goethe's scientific writings, based on the work he had done for the Kürschner edition. Once settled in Weimar, Steiner found many of his coworkers too academic, more interested in analyzing and dissecting Goethe's works than in understanding the true spirit of the master. In addition to his work on Goethe, Steiner also edited, wrote introductions to, and translated a number of books, including one on the philosopher Schopenhauer.

In the fall of 1891, Steiner took the oral exam for a doctorate in philosophy, mathematics, and mechanics at Rostock University. He received his doctorate in November and gave his first doctoral lecture in Vienna on Goethe's fairy tale *The*

Green Snake and the Beautiful Lily. In 1892 Steiner took lodging with Anna Eunike, a widow with four daughters and a son. With a secure home, he began his practice—maintained until his death—of giving lectures on a wide variety of subjects and of writing an astonishing number of books, articles, and reviews.

Berlin: The Theosophy Connection, 1897–1914

Steiner moved to Berlin in 1897 (and maintained a residence there until 1923), and there became actively involved in the intellectual, artistic, and literary life of the city. He continued actively writing and lecturing on Goethe as well as other topics. In 1899 Eunike, who had also moved to Berlin, invited Steiner once again to move in with her. Steiner was more than happy to do so inasmuch as he hated living in an apartment. He married Eunike that same year. Although it was clearly a marriage of convenience, Steiner refused to discuss it, saying, "Private relations are not something to be publicized. They do not concern the public" (Easton 1980, 91).

While occultism has been present throughout history, it gained momentum in the mid-nineteenth century. A leading figure in this invigorated spiritual movement was Helena Petrovna Blavatsky, a half-German, half-Russian woman with extraordinary psychic powers (what today we might call extrasensory perception, or ESP). Blavatsky published several books, including *Isis Unveiled* and the posthumous *The Secret Doctrine*. In these books, she told of what she had learned of the spirit world during her trances. In 1875 she, together with Henry Steel Olcott and William Quan Judge, founded the Theosophical Society in New York. Although Theosophy itself dates back to antiquity, the aim of their conception of Theosophy was to understand the nature or divinity of humanity and the world through mystical means. Blavatsky and Olcott admired the Asian approach to the spirit world and moved the headquarters of Theosophy to India.

In 1899 Steiner published the article "Goethe's Secret Revelation," in which he interpreted Goethe's fairy tale as an affirmation of the poet's familiarity with the spirit world. The Berlin chapter of the Theosophical Society asked him to give some lectures to the members. These were well received, and he continued to give lectures on spiritual subjects for the next few years. In 1902 he was asked to head the newly formed chapter of German Theosophy.

Through his lectures, Steiner met Marie von Sivers, who owned the Theosophical Society headquarters in Berlin. She eventually became his spiritual partner in the sense of accepting and furthering his Theosophical beliefs (Steiner 2006). After

Anna's death, she also became his second wife. Steiner was now lecturing and writing exclusively on spiritual matters. In 1904 Annie Besant, who had taken over the leadership of the Theosophical Society after the death of Blavatsky and Olcott, asked Steiner to take over the Theosophical-based Esoteric School for Germany and Austria. But Steiner insisted that he would take a Western spiritual path, rather than an Eastern one, because he wanted to relate his theories to Christianity.

The tensions between traditional Theosophists and Steiner and his followers continued to grow because many of Theosophy's tenets (such as Blavatsky's claim that certain races such as the Aryan were superior to others) were antithetical to Steiner's beliefs. The tensions were further exacerbated by Sivers's emphasis on the importance of the arts in spiritual life and by Steiner's increasing positive researches into Christianity and its relation to the esoteric world. The final break came in 1909 when Besant and C. W. Leadbeater, who replaced Olcott after his death, attributed messianic status to a beautiful, young Indian boy, Jiddu Krishnamurti, and proclaimed him to be the new world teacher.

Steiner was disgusted by the whole affair, and in 1912 the German Theosophy group split apart, with the majority joining Steiner's new Anthroposophy Society. Although Steiner acknowledged that the basic tenet of his approach, that the human being is both physical and spiritual, was borrowed from Blavatsky, his cosmology differed in important respects. Steiner defined anthroposophy as "a path of knowledge to guide the spiritual in the human being to the spiritual in the universe" (Steiner 1973, 13). He regarded anthroposophy as a true science and thought that through means of dedicated mental effort it could be researched and objectified like the data of any other science. Anthroposophy opposed the Theosophy of Blavatsky and others because Steiner believed the spirit world could be observed directly through training in observation and meditation. In contrast, Theosophy believed the spirit world could only be contacted through trances and spiritual mediators.

During this period, Steiner experienced several personal losses. His father died in 1910, and his wife Anna died the following year. Lending credence to the adage that all bad things come in threes, his coworker Sivers became ill in 1911 as well. While these events slowed Steiner down, they did not end his frenetic pace of travel, writing, and lecturing. This same year, he wrote his second mystery drama and formed the first building committee for the Goetheanum (a building Steiner designed to honor Goethe and to become the headquarters of the new Anthroposophy Society).

The Anthroposophy Society, 1914–1923

In 1914 a general assembly of the Anthroposophy Society took place in Dornach, Switzerland (near Basel), where the Goetheanum was to be built. A Swiss Theosophist, Emil Grossheintz, donated the land. This same year, Archduke Franz Ferdinand was assassinated in Sarajevo on June 18, and on August 1, World War I began. During the war, Steiner continued to travel between Germany and Dornach. On December 24, Steiner married his longtime coworker Sivers. This was done, in part at least, to prevent her from being deported as a Russian citizen.

During the war years, Steiner's lecturing was curtailed, but he introduced a new theme in talks and writing: the threefold nature—thinking, feeling, and willing—of the human being and of society. This threefold nature explains that in human beings thinking is related to the head and nervous system; feeling is attributed to the rhythmic system, including breathing, circulation, and heartbeat; and willing is powered by the metabolic system. Steiner regarded thinking as conscious, feeling as semiconscious, and willing as unconscious. Only when all three are in harmony can the individual realize his or her full human and spiritual potential.

Applying the threefold nature to the larger world, Steiner regarded society and culture as the thinking component, government as the feeling component (ensuring the rights of all individuals), and willing as the economic component (ensuring a reasonable distribution of wealth). Only if these three were brought into harmony would the society succeed and peace ensue. These thoughts were outlined in his book *Towards Social Renewal*, which is said to be one of the best-selling books published immediately after the war.

With the end of the war in 1918, Steiner renewed his frenetic pace of lecturing, writing, and counseling. He also devoted himself to practical projects, because it appears he now appreciated that these might well be the most lasting parts of his legacy. For example, Steiner created the first Waldorf school at the request of Emil Molt, owner of the Waldorf-Astoria Cigarette Factory. The school opened in 1919 in Stuttgart (more on this further in the chapter). In 1920, after working with two physicians, Steiner gave a lecture titled "Anthroposophical Medicine," suggesting that anthroposophical medicine is a supplement to traditional medicine (in some respects similar to homeopathic medicine).

Dornbach, 1923–1925

In 1923, in reaction to Adolf Hitler's denunciation of Steiner's work and claims that he was a Jew, Steiner gave up his residence in Berlin and moved to Dornbach, Switzerland, taking with him the Philosophical-Anthroposophical Press. The following year, continuing his efforts to apply anthroposophical insights, he introduced *biodynamic agriculture* and *curative education*. At the same time, friends recognized that he was beginning to tire, as for the first time Steiner canceled a lecture.

In 1925 he gave up lecturing and spent most of his time in the carpentry shop adjacent to the Goetheanum. He continued writing weekly installments of his autobiography until he died on March 30, 1925.

The Work

Although our major concern is with Steiner's educational innovations, it is necessary to briefly enumerate some of his other contributions:

- The Goetheanum burned down in 1923, and Steiner redesigned it to be made of reinforced concrete. Today it continues to serve as the headquarters and meeting place for the Anthroposophy Society.
- In collaboration with his wife Sivers, Steiner created the new art form *living speech*, in which "the participants develop physical movements and gestures which themselves communicate in a kind of moving language" (Lachman 2007, 129). This living speech is known as eurythmy, which is now practiced outside of Waldorf schools both as a dance form and as a therapy method.
- Steiner also contributed the concept of biodynamic agriculture, which we now call organic gardening.
- As a dramatist, Steiner wrote four mystery plays that continue to be performed in Steiner venues.
- In 1924 Steiner introduced the idea of curative education by building on his experience with Otto Specht. Curative education emphasizes individualized instruction geared toward an in-depth understanding of the child's problem. It is now practiced in the Camphill schools and communities. These are usually associated with Waldorf schools.

The Waldorf Schools

Emil Molt was a paternalistic employer at the Waldorf-Astoria Cigarette Factory in Stuttgart, Germany, who tried providing parenting lectures for his workers, but they were not well attended. The workers were excited, though, about having a private school for their children. Molt asked Steiner to open a school along anthroposophical principles, and Steiner agreed, and what we now know as a Waldorf school was created. Molt bought a former restaurant and had it remodeled into a school at his own expense. The school was proposed to Steiner in the spring of 1919 and was ready to open in September of the same year.

Steiner had set some preconditions. The school was to be run by the teachers and free from any constraints by the Stuttgart government for three years. In addition, the school was to cover the entire twelve grades. He also insisted that the school should be open to all children, regardless of class, race, or sex. It was one of the first schools to include both boys and girls in the same classroom. Twelve teachers were chosen. All were interviewed and personally selected by Steiner, but only a few were professional teachers. Steiner assigned himself the role of guide and spiritual adviser.

During the summer, Steiner gave a series of lectures and training sessions for the teachers on the spiritual bases of education. The school opened with 253 students made up both of the children of the workers and those of local anthroposophists. The school was so successful that by the end of the three-year trial period it had an enrollment of 1,100 and a long waiting list of aspiring students.

Steiner's spiritual perspective made his educational system unique. One of the things Steiner demanded of his teachers was that they understand in depth the development of the children in their charge. To encourage such understanding, he insisted that the children stay with the same teacher over a number of years. (This practice has now been adopted nationally in some countries, such as Denmark.) Also, following Goethe, Steiner believed in the power of color and introduced the idea that different colors facilitated learning at different age levels. Accordingly, classrooms in Waldorf schools are painted different colors depending on the age of the children.

Steiner's ideas about spiritual development dictated his educational philosophy. He believed that during the first seven years of life, children were ruled by their will and learned best by imitation—how adults act is more important than what they say. Steiner rejected the Enlightenment prejudice against rote learning and argued that it was helpful for children to learn, for example, the multiplication tables by heart before they had a full understanding of mathematics. Steiner also argued that children should not be taught to read before they lost their baby teeth at about age seven, because this is when they attain new mental abilities (Steiner 1996). In school-age children, Steiner believed, feeling took precedence over will-ing and thinking. Steiner writes, "The world of *feeling* is developed in the proper way through parables and pictures . . . especially through the pictures of great men and women, taken from history and other sources" (Steiner 1996, 34). He also writes that during this period it is "primarily a question of authority, (acquiring) confidence, trust and reverence" (Steiner 1996, 58). He also writes, "Children who are denied the blessing of having their musical sense cultivated during these years will be the poorer because of it for the rest of their lives" (Steiner 1996, 34).

Children gain the ability to think in abstractions during puberty. As Steiner writes, "With puberty, the time has arrived when human beings are ripe for the formation of their own judgments about what they have already learned. Noth-ing is more harmful to children than to awaken independent judgment too early. Human beings are not in a position to judge until they have collected the material for judgment. Every judgment that is not built on a sufficient foundation of gath-ered knowledge and experience of soul throws a stumbling block in the way of those who form it" (Steiner 1996, 37–38).

The threefold nature of willing, feeling, and thinking make up the basis for Wal-dorf education. All three are present at each developmental stage, but one usually takes precedence over the others. Steiner felt strongly that Western societies were too concerned with thinking and intellectualization and not concerned enough with feeling and willing. That is why he placed such emphasis on a rounded education—one that includes music, art, and dance. He believed that this integration could best be realized by having children write and illustrate their own textbooks and by teach-ing a progressively more difficult set of handicrafts like the progression from knit-ting to sewing and finally to weaving (Harwood 1958).

Common Themes

The Nature of the Child

Like Rousseau, Steiner appreciates that the child is not a smaller adult but instead has his or her own ways of thinking and knowing. Easton writes of Steiner's anthroposophical thinking:

> At the center of all anthroposophical thinking in the realm of education is the recognition that a child is not simply a small man or woman, and he should not be treated as such, reasoned with, preached to, filled with intellectual knowledge by adults, and expected to grow up in the image of his parents or teachers. A child is a potentially but not actually mature human being who will develop through the years of childhood at a pace that is virtually the same for all children, since the pace is governed not only by biological laws but by the laws of the soul and spirit. (1980, 259–60)

The Aims of Education

> The fact that we have both boys and girls at the Waldorf School seems to serve two purposes. One is to shape the teaching according to the needs of the whole human being, since with either boys or girls alone, education always tends to become one-sided. The other is to work toward the kind of human interrelationship required especially by today's society, in which women have either gained their place in society or are trying to obtain it. (Steiner [1923] 2004, 185)

The Role of Play

From his perspective, Steiner believed that play was necessary for the child to realize his or her talents and build a strong sense of self. He writes:

> It is best for the child if we allow play to be individually oriented since that creates inner strength. We must give special attention to what the talents and interests of each child are, for otherwise we would sin. (Steiner 1996, 87)

Conformance with DAP Principles

NAEYC

All the domains of development and learning—physical, social and emotional, and cognitive—are important, and they are closely interrelated. Children's development and learning in one domain influence and are influenced by what takes place in other domains.

STEINER

I have already said, that if nature is to harmonize with the natural development of the human organism, the child must be taught to write before he learns to read. The reason for this is that in writing the whole being is more active than is the case in reading. Writing entails the movement of only one particular member, but fundamentally speaking, the forces of the whole human being must lend themselves to this movement. In reading, only the head and the intellect are engaged, and in a truly organic system of education we must develop everything out of the qualities and forces of the child's whole nature. (Steiner [1928] 1972, 135)

NAEYC

Children's experiences shape their motivation and approaches to learning, such as persistence, initiative, and flexibility; in turn, these dispositions and behaviors affect their learning and development.

STEINER

"Physical environment" must, however, be taken in the widest imaginable sense. It includes not only what goes on around the child in the material sense, but everything that takes place in the child's environment—everything that can be perceived by his senses, that can work from the surrounding physical space upon the inner powers of the child. This includes all the moral or immoral actions, all the wise or foolish actions that the child sees. (Steiner 1965, 26)

Commentary

As the above quotations indicate, Steiner was one of the first to emphasize a holistic approach to the child, an approach that was first anticipated by Comenius. He also was the first to relate biological data, the development of adult teeth and puberty, to stages of mental and social development.

In my opinion, one of Steiner's greatest contributions was his inclusion of the arts, music, dance, and craft skills as essential to the curriculum at all age levels. Equally important was his innovative practice of having children research, write, and illustrate their own textbooks—effectively integrating the individualization and socialization aims of education. In creating their own texts, students are both nourishing individual mental abilities and learning about science, history, and culture. In many ways, Steiner's educational approach comes the closest to fully incorporating DAP.

References

Easton, Stewart C. 1980. *Rudolf Steiner: Herald of a New Epoch*. Hudson, NY: Anthroposophic.

———. 1989. *Man and World in the Light of Anthroposophy*. Great Barrington, MA: Anthroposophic.

Harwood, A. C. 1958. *The Recovery of Man in Childhood*. Great Barrington, MA: Myrin Institute.

Lachman, Gary. 2007. *Rudolf Steiner: An Introduction to His Life and Work*. New York: Penguin.

Steiner, Rudolf. (1923) 2004. *A Modern Art of Education*. Translated by Jesse Darrell, Robert Lathe, Nancy Whittaker, and George Adams. Hudson, NY: Anthroposophic.

———. (1928) 1972. *A Modern Art of Education*. Letchworth, UK: Garden City.

———. 1965. *The Education of the Child in the Light of Anthroposophy*. Translated by George Adams and Mary Adams. London: Rudolf Steiner.

———. 1973. *Anthroposophical Leading Thoughts*. Translated by George Adams and Mary Adams. London: Rudolf Steiner.

———. 1995. *Anthroposophy in Everyday Life*. Translated by Michael Lipson, Dietrich V. Asten, and Brian Kelly. Hudson, NY: Anthroposophic.

———. 1996. *The Education of the Child and Early Lectures on Education*. Translated by George Adams, Mary Adams, Robert Lathe, Nancy Whittaker, and Rita Stebbing. Hudson, NY: Anthroposophic.

———. 2006. *Autobiography: Chapters in the Course of My Life*. Translated by Rita Stebbing. Hudson, NY: Anthroposophic.

8

Maria Montessori

1870–1952

The history of scientific early childhood education begins with the work of Maria Montessori. Each of the earlier Giants argued that instructional practice should be attuned to the growing needs and abilities of children. It was left to Montessori, however, to take a scientific approach to meeting this challenge. She was a trained physical anthropologist as well as a doctor of medicine. When she turned her interests to education, she emphasized the importance of observation and experimentation, and she continually tested and refined both her methods and her materials of instruction.

Especially for her time, Montessori was an extraordinary woman. She overcame what seems to be insurmountable obstacles to become the first female physician in Italy. After receiving her medical degree, she held numerous prestigious academic posts, engaged in scientific research and publishing, and had a small private practice. In addition, her gift for public speaking made her a powerful spokesperson for women's rights and for the humane treatment of special needs and emotionally troubled children.

All those accomplishments are impressive, but Montessori became famous for the school for young children she created and for the teaching materials and teacher training methods she introduced. She recognized that children could do more for themselves if their environment was scaled to their size and strength. For example, it was Montessori who furnished the early childhood classroom with child-sized chairs, tables, and cutlery—these are now the norm in early childhood programs.

The Woman

The Early Years, 1870–1886

Italy in the mid-nineteenth century was one of the most backward of the modern Western European nations. Most of its people lived in small principalities, duchies, and kingdoms on the peninsula and were miserably poor and uneducated. In part, the backwardness of the country was due to control by other countries: first by France and then by Austria in 1848. There were few, if any, civil liberties, no free press, and an antiquated school system. It was only in the 1860s that King Victor Emmanuel of Sardinia drove out the Austrians. By 1870 he had united the country.

The leaders of the now-united Italy were eager for reform, and it was this eagerness for social and political change that Maria Montessori absorbed as she grew up. Montessori was born on August 31, 1870, in Chiaravalle, an Adriatic seaport village in the province of Ancona, Italy. Her father, Alessandro, came from a well-to-do Bologna family. For an Italian man of that time, he was well educated, with training in accounting. In 1865 his family moved to Chiaravalle, where Alessandro took a position with a tea and tobacco firm (Shephard 1996).

Montessori's mother, Renilde, also came from an upper-class family. She, too, was more highly educated than most Italian women of the time. Renilde loved books and had liberal ideas about the role of women in society. From an early age, Montessori's strong and independent spirit was encouraged and supported by Renilde. At the same time, Renilde was not a doting parent. When Montessori complained that she wanted something to eat while her mother was busy unpacking from a trip, Renilde gave her a moldy crust of bread and said, "If you can't wait, take this" (Kramer 1976).

When Montessori was five, Alessandro was promoted to a higher position in the company, and the family moved to Rome. The schools in Rome, however, were not much better than those in Chiaravalle. Perhaps because the teaching was so deadly—mainly memorization—Montessori did not stand out as a student. But she stood out in other ways. She was an exceptional child, and a number of telling anecdotes from her early years, repeated by each of her biographers (Standing 1957; Kramer 1976; Shephard 1996) that have become part of Montessori lore.

In one story, Montessori is said to have told a fellow pupil, of whom she disapproved, "You! You aren't even *born* yet" (Kramer 1976, 28). Another incident occurred when Montessori overheard a teacher speak negatively of the critical expression in Montessori's eyes. Montessori never raised those eyes in the presence of that teacher again. A more telling anecdote has it that, at age ten, Montessori suffered a serious illness that caused her mother to fear for her life. Montessori is said to have assured her mother by saying, "Do not worry Mother, I cannot die; I have too much to do" (Kramer 1976, 28).

When Montessori was twelve, the family had to decide whether to send her to a technical or classical school. In Italy girls were expected to attend the classical school, whereas boys had the choice. Montessori, however, had discovered that she had both a love and a talent for math. She therefore decided she wanted to become an engineer and insisted that she go to the technical school. Her mother supported her in this choice, and the two strong women were too much for Alessandro, who gave in.

At age thirteen, Montessori became a student at the local technical school. Only two girls were admitted to the school, and they were forbidden to speak with the boys. At recess the girls were kept in a guarded room. At that time, students focused primarily on recitation and memorization, with little focus on practical application. For example, they studied pictures of leaves in a book without going outside to collect and examine real ones. When reflecting on her own school experience, Montessori describes the children in the classroom as "butterflies mounted on pins" (Shephard 1996, 17).

Rome, 1886–1892

Montessori graduated with high marks in 1886 and then went on to the Technical Institute of Rome, where she hoped to pursue her desire to become an engineer. But, like many college students, she changed her mind when exposed to a broader range of subjects. She was particularly taken by her courses in biology and physiology. Her fascination with these subjects led her to consider the possibility of studying medicine.

When she told her parents of her desire to become a physician, her father—who could hardly accept her as an engineer—was violently opposed and refused to speak to her. Alessandro was joined in his opposition to Montessori's decision by most of her relatives. Renilde, however, again supported her daughter in this new career choice. With the encouragement of her mother, Montessori made an appointment to meet with Guido Baccelli, professor and head of the medical faculty at the

University of Rome. Although he gave her a polite hearing, he also made it clear that a woman would never be admitted to medical school. Montessori told him, "I know I shall become a doctor of medicine" (Kramer 1976, 34). She then proceeded to enroll in the premed program at the university and take courses in math, biology, physics, chemistry, and zoology. The demands of these courses gave her no time for the usual extracurricular pastimes of students. In 1892 she graduated with high grades and received the University of Rome's *diploma di licenza*.

Getting into medical school was another matter. Somehow—no one knows exactly how—Montessori did manage to get accepted. It has been suggested that Pope Leo XIII made it possible (Kramer 1976). He had said publicly that he believed medicine was a suitable profession for women.

Medical School and Academic Career, 1892–1900

However it was arranged, in 1892 Montessori was the first woman in Italy to be admitted to medical school. The University of Rome, however, was part of the Italian bureaucracy. Going to university was more of a matter of social class than of vocational preparation. Even among the students attending medical school, few expected to ever practice medicine. A university degree was more a symbol of social status than it was one of advanced education.

Being a woman at the university presented a number of special problems for Montessori. She was constantly being teased and taunted. During one lecture, a student behind her kept kicking the back of her seat. Montessori turned around and glared at him. The student later recalled that, after the look she gave him, he thought, "I must be immortal or a look like that would have killed me" (Kramer 1976, 46). In an attempt to avoid such treatment, her father escorted her to and from the university, and she made it a point to enter her classrooms last. But this meant that the male students often left her no place to sit.

In addition to the slights of her fellow students, Montessori also had to deal with her own reactions to the anatomy class and to dissections. In one class, she had a terrible reaction when the students were shown and had to examine fresh human body parts. Montessori went home, threw up, and decided to give up medicine. But she soon thought better of it and continued going to classes.

Dissection posed another problem because women were not allowed in the same room as men with a dead body. She had to do her dissection alone at night. She hired a man to smoke in the room to help her deal with the smell. Despite her problems with fellow students and her difficulties in dealing with dead body parts and cadavers, she persisted and eventually won the grudging support of her fellow students. She also won awards and coveted assignments at the university hospital.

Prior to graduation, each medical student had to give a public lecture. When a friend suggested to Alessandro that he attend his daughter's lecture, Alessandro was embarrassed because he had not known about it. He decided to attend. In her lecture, Montessori told with touches of humor how much her medical education meant to her. Instead of the derision she expected from her fellow students, she was given an ovation. After listening to his daughter and to the reception she received, Alessandro forever afterward referred to her proudly as "my daughter, the doctor" (Shephard 1996).

After graduation Montessori engaged in a number of activities that completely filled her days. In addition to a small pediatric practice, she also conducted research and consulted at an asylum for what today we call children with special needs. The inhumane ways in which these children were cared for led her to search for alternatives. She found these in the work of Jean Marc Itard and Edward Séguin (Itard 1801; Seguin [1866] 1971). Itard's accounts of his unsuccessful efforts to rehabilitate the Wild Boy of Aveyron were nonetheless replete with the methods he used to teach the boy language, manners, and personal hygiene. Montessori learned from these, but she took most of her guidance from Séguin, who had devised educational materials and methods, which he then used successfully with developmentally delayed and otherwise limited children.

The work of Séguin convinced Montessori of the value of special schools for these children, such as those already available in other European countries. She became more and more involved in working with this population. As a result, she was invited to speak about her work at major international conferences. Montessori soon became identified as a champion of the need for the sensory education of children with special needs.

Largely because of her advocacy, in 1900 an institute for children with all forms of limitations was established in Rome. It was called the Orthophrenic School. (*Orthophrenic* was the term used to cover all levels of intellectual disability as well as all other problems that prevented children from performing at normal levels.) Montessori was a natural choice to be appointed codirector of the institute. Giuseppe Montesano, a physician with whom she had worked at the children's asylum, was appointed the second codirector.

The institute was set up on the model of a teaching hospital in which the care of young patients also provided for the training of teachers in methods and techniques for educating orthophrenic children. At the end of the first term, a group of city officials visited the school and were amazed at the progress the children had made. Montessori spent the next two years of her life at the institute, training teachers in the special methods of observing and teaching children who had been previously institutionalized and forgotten.

Becoming a Teacher, 1900–1910

In 1900 Montessori abruptly gave up her position as codirector of the institute and went back to the University of Rome to take courses in education and physical anthropology, to visit schools, and to train teachers. She also continued studying the writings of Séguin and translating his books into Italian. She worked with his materials, continually refining them and adapting them for different types of children with limited abilities.

Ostensibly Montessori's reason for this change of direction was to test her idea that the methods used with orthophrenic children would benefit children of normal ability who had been environmentally deprived. The real reason, at least in part, was that she and Montesano had fallen in love and that she had become pregnant by him. Apparently both families were opposed to a marriage, and abortion in a Catholic country was not even considered. Yet an out-of-wedlock child would have destroyed Montessori's career, and at the urging of her family, in 1898 Montessori sent her child, whom she named Mario, to be reared by a farm family outside Rome.

When the couple decided not to marry, they also agreed that neither would marry anyone else. They continued to work together at the institute until 1900. In that year, Montesano broke their agreement and married another woman. That turn of events made it impossible for Montessori to continue working at the institute, yet over the next few years, she still continued to study and refine teaching materials and techniques for working with orthophrenic children.

During the same time period, a group of reform-minded developers decided to build low-income housing in the run-down San Lorenzo section of Rome. Such housing was needed to accommodate the flood of villagers from the country who came to Rome to work in the factories. Because both the mothers and fathers worked, their preschool-aged children were left free to roam the common areas of the buildings and to deface and soil them in the process.

The developers decided to open a preschool that would keep the children occupied and the buildings intact. Knowing her reputation, the builders asked Montessori to set up and run the school. To the amazement of her friends and colleagues, she accepted the offer. For her it was a gift that gave her the opportunity to try out her educational ideas. The school opened in January 1907 with fifty two- to six-year-old children and with an untrained teacher, Candida Nuccitelli. Nuccitelli lived in one of the buildings and knew many of the children. Someone suggested the name *Casa dei Bambini* (Children's House) for the project, and Montessori liked it and made it the official name of the school.

Montessori spent the next two years training Nuccitelli and other teachers, testing and modifying her materials, and introducing new ones. She had tables, chairs, dishware, and cutlery made for child-sized hands and fingers. Doorknobs were lowered, and stools were available for children to stand on to reach the washbasin. Her aim was to create an environment that enabled the children to do easily for themselves what before others had to do for them. This environment encouraged both freedom and spontaneity, the key words of her educational program.

In setting up the environment to the size and abilities of children, Montessori was following Séguin. He contended that orthophrenic children had to master the basic sensory and motor abilities that were prerequisites to more advanced skills. Séguin, for example, taught his students to hold a piece of chalk before showing them how to draw lines and letters. He also devised a wide variety of other exercises for the full development of all the senses. He believed such training was necessary before these children could be taught academic tools and skills.

Montessori followed the same paradigm with children who did not have mental or physical limitations. Her pupils acquired a variety of basic sensory and motor discriminations in preparation for learning academic skills. Students were taught to discriminate among colors, shapes, textures, and sounds, and to practice small and large motor coordination. Again she followed Séguin by having children learn to write before they were introduced to reading and by having them work with collections of objects before introducing them to printed numerals.

In addition, many of the materials were self-didactic and allowed children to solve problems by trial and error. With form boards, for example, a child had to place a geometric wooden form into its corresponding cutout in the board. Likewise, Montessori provided a set of different-sized metal cylinders that had to be inserted into corresponding-sized holes in a board. By means of repeated self-correction, the child could successfully complete these tasks.

Montessori also placed a great deal of emphasis on order. She believed that children thrived in an uncluttered environment. At her school, each child worked alone or with a few others on a small piece of carpet. When they were finished, they placed the material back in its place and went on to something else. Because the materials were adapted to the children's level of ability and interest, no external motivation was required, and the classroom was a quiet hum of happy, involved activity.

The experiment was a great success and the Casa dei Bambini became a magnet for visitors from all over the world. Montessori had become an international superstar. However, because the housing developers believed Montessori was exploiting the original intention for the school, she was permanently locked out of her school in 1909. But that did not stop her from continuing to train students, opening additional schools in Rome, and publishing the results of the work and her educational philosophy in her book *The Montessori Method*, which was published in 1909. By 1912 her book had already been translated into English as well as many other languages, and she became world famous.

Becoming Montessori, 1910–1952

Montessori's phenomenally rapid rise to fame was the result of a perfect storm of conditions. In the early years of the twentieth century, there was widespread unhappiness with the schools of the times and a new appreciation of education's all-important role in preparing children to live in newly industrialized societies. Many of the new industrial occupations, such as typist and typesetter, demanded literacy and numerical skills. The Montessori method promised to teach children these skills at an early age.

Additionally, the success of Montessori's school was also great copy for the explosion of print media both in Italy and abroad (Kramer 1976). Newspapers and magazines all over the world took up the story. The appeal of the Montessori program was that it taught young children the basic academic skills of reading and writing. But it also turned unruly brats into well-behaved children. Both of these achievements were attractive to political leaders, who could use the introduction of Montessori schools as evidence of their commitment to education and to controlling delinquency.

Starting in 1910, Montessori was in demand all over the world to give lectures and to train teachers. She decided then to give up most of her academic and medical appointments and to devote her full time to the promotion of her methods and materials. In so doing, she also gave up all of her steady sources of income and had to support herself and her family (her father was now retired) on the income from writing, lecturing, teacher training, and selling her classroom materials. In effect, her method had now become a business and was her sole source of income.

Having always lived a protected life and worked only for a regular salary, Montessori was not really prepared to be a businesswoman. Given the worldwide recognition and acclaim she was receiving, it is understandable that Montessori easily overestimated the income she would receive from her work. She also greatly underestimated the complexity and frustration of contractual agreements, billing, and collecting. Even more significant, by demanding that only materials and methods approved by her could bear her name, she set limits on the use and, therefore, the testing and verification of the effectiveness of her ideas and practices. As a result, she could no longer claim her program was based on open-ended science.

Over the next forty years, Montessori led a nomadic existence, traveling all over the world. As a result of two articles in *McClure's Magazine* in 1911 and 1913, she became well known in the United States, and Sam McClure, the magazine's publisher, invited her to the United States to give a series of lectures, including one at Carnegie Hall. Her first tour of the United States was highly successful, and she was given universal acclaim in the press and by the leading figures of the day.

She returned to the United States in 1915 to present a model school at the Panama-Pacific International Exhibition in San Francisco. Although the model school itself was a success, other avenues for furthering her work in the country were closed. Sam McClure had promised to build Montessori an institute in the United States, but the institute never materialized. And she had disputes with him about his payment of her expenses and fees. Montessori's success in the United States was not to last.

In addition to the conflict with McClure, other considerations led to her short-lived fame in the United States. She put off many of her former advocates by insisting that only teachers trained by her could open Montessori schools. Froebelian kindergarten teachers were angered by her refusal to allow them to include some of her materials in their programs. This foreshadowed similar schisms that would later occur between the purists and those who would adapt Montessori's approach into cultural variations of the method.

Although Montessori's work continued to be well regarded elsewhere in the world, it did not reappear as an important educational program in the United States until it was rediscovered in the 1960s. Its rediscovery, however, was quite ironic. It was not adopted as a model for the Head Start program for children of low-income families for whom it was ideally suited. Rather, it was embraced by well-off parents who also wanted to give their children a head start. Then and now, many Montessori schools in the United States remain private and expensive.

In 1912 Montessori's mother, who was the most opposed to any public recognition of Montessori's son Mario, died. When Montessori visited the adolescent Mario after his grandmother's death, he told her that he knew she was his mother and that he wanted to live with her. She welcomed the opportunity to have him in her home. But she maintained the fiction that he was her nephew. He traveled with her and became a coworker, a teacher trainer, and the manager of her financial affairs. He also served as her protector. Together they founded the Association Montessori International (AMI) in 1929. Mario served as president of the association, which was (and is) essentially an accreditation agency for Montessori teachers and schools.

Montessori continued to be popular in Europe. In 1915 the educational authorities in Spain invited her to set up a Montessori school and training institute in Barcelona. The government provided a beautiful old building with gardens, fountains, and plenty of room for outdoor play. She gave her first formal training courses there. In 1917 Montessori made her last visit to the United States to attend the wedding of Mario and Helen Christie, an American he had met when he traveled with his mother to San Francisco and stayed on to train teachers.

After World War I, Mario and Helen and their four children moved to Barcelona to be with Montessori. In Spain, Montessori experienced with her grandchildren the maternal pleasures she had been denied with her own child. Barcelona became the base from which she traveled to give her lectures and training courses. She now included methods and materials for older children, ages six to eleven, although she had never worked directly with this age group.

Between the two world wars, Montessori continued to give teacher training and lectures in Europe and South America. Closer to her home, a small group of young women opened a Montessori school for poor children in Vienna. Anna Freud, who was applying a psychoanalytic approach to education, was very interested in Montessori's work, and they met several times. Montessori, however, resisted introducing any therapeutic methods into her program, and she and Freud parted ways. Still, Freud did write an appreciative foreword to Rita Kramer's biography of Montessori (1988).

Montessori returned to Italy many times, and when Mussolini came to power, she met with him in 1921. He became an advocate and gave financial support for the opening of a Montessori school in Milan. In 1930 he held a celebration to honor her work, but it was really for his own propaganda purposes. Later, when Montessori saw the children in her schools wearing fascist uniforms and playing with guns, she broke with him and did not return to Italy until after World War II.

When the Spanish Civil War broke out in 1936, friends feared for the safety of the Montessori family and arranged for them to leave Spain on an English battleship, but without any of their belongings. One of Montessori's students, Ada Pierson, invited her, Mario, and the four children (Mario was now separated from Helen) to come to Amsterdam, where Montessori had been well received. They accepted the offer, and Holland became their new home.

When World War II began in 1939, Montessori was forced to flee again. Hitler believed her views were in conflict with Fascism and had her books burned, and a German mob burned her in effigy. Providentially, at this time Montessori was able to reestablish her relationship with Theosophy. In 1907 she had gone to hear a lecture by Annie Besant, who was then president of the society. Besant had glowing words to say about the Casa dei Bambini. Montessori, who was not yet famous in 1907, was awed that such a renowned person would speak well of her work. They became friends, and before World War I, Besant visited Montessori whenever she came to Rome. Their friendship waned, however, after Besant moved to India and became a champion of liberation and humanitarian causes.

When Besant died in 1933, George Sydney Arundale became the new president of the Theosophical Society. Arundale was also familiar with Montessori, and he and his wife visited Montessori in Amsterdam in 1937 and invited her to come to India. The Theosophists found Montessori's ideas congenial with their own, and many chapters of the Theosophical Society had Montessori Departments, which ran schools along Montessori lines. The Arundales wanted Montessori to take charge of the Montessori Department of the Theosophical Society of Allahabad—the Indian city to which Besant had moved later in life.

In October 1939 Montessori was forced to flee Holland. She accepted the Arundales' invitation, and she and Mario flew to India on a small plane. Mario left his children in the care of the Pierson family in Amsterdam, as they thought they would be gone just a few months. It turned out to be nearly seven years. Montessori received a warm welcome in India and even gave up her black clothes for white robes, which she believed were more in keeping with Indian culture. When England entered the war in 1939, Mario, who was an Italian national, was interned along with other nationals from Fascist countries. In 1940 the Indian government, as a seventieth birthday gift to Montessori, set Mario free. Montessori was very happy in India, and in contrast to her experience with leaders in Italy, Spain, and Germany, the Indian authorities lauded her.

After the war, Montessori and Mario flew back to Amsterdam in the summer of 1946 and were reunited with the children. Soon after, Mario married Ada Pierson. Though she was now in her eighth decade, Montessori continued traveling and giving lectures and training sessions. She lectured at international congresses in Italy, France, Austria, England, and Scotland. In 1950, her eightieth year, Montessori toured the Scandinavian countries before returning to Amsterdam.

When at home, and indeed wherever she was, she kept a demanding work schedule. She rose every morning at seven-thirty and, with only a short nap in the afternoon, worked until one o'clock of the next morning. She loved to eat, particularly pasta, and had grown quite stout but also increasingly frail. On May 6, 1952, she was seated in the house of friends in Noordwijk aan Zee, a little village on the coast of the North Sea. She had been thinking of taking a trip to Africa to give a lecture, but it was suggested that she was too weak to travel and that the lecture might have to be given by someone else. Mario was with her for the conversation, and she turned to him and said, "Am I no longer of any use then?" (Kramer 1976, 367). She died shortly afterward of a cerebral hemorrhage.

Montessori had always said she wished to be buried where she died. In accord with her wishes, she was interred in the courtyard of the Catholic church in Noordwijk. Her last wish reflected her belief that she was a citizen of the world and would be at peace anywhere in it.

The Work

Montessori published a large number of books. However, like Steiner, her students created many of them from her course presentations. She was truly remarkable as a lecturer and was said never to use notes and never to give the same speech twice. She was always introducing new ideas and perspectives. Increasingly in her later books, she became more religious and mystical, perhaps reflecting her Theosophical leanings. For our purposes, her most important book is *The Montessori Method*. Her other books are variations on the themes presented in that classic.

The Montessori Method

In this book, Montessori essentially recounts the history and pedagogical theory that she employed in setting up the Casa dei Bambini. She first goes into detail of how tasks should be given—by preparing the environment rather than by direct instruction. In this way, the child's self-discipline is a natural outcome. The rest of the book shows how much she owes to Séguin, whom she duly credits. Her extended discussion of muscular education and education of the senses is built directly on Séguin. The same is true for her chapters on exercises for the practical life and those on reading, writing, and mathematics.

It was Montessori's genius, however, to go beyond Séguin and expand and elaborate on the materials that he introduced and to articulate the pedagogical principles that generated them. Her general philosophy stresses the importance of the sensitive periods of development, repetition, and a prepared environment that encourages liberty, spontaneity, and the internalization of self-discipline. These principles retain their validity. Today the Montessori method remains a specific way of teaching with the particular materials she introduced. However, many of her innovations, such as child-sized chairs and tables, are used in virtually all early childhood education programs. Likewise, a number of the materials used in non-Montessori programs, such as form boards, are modeled after the Montessori materials.

Common Themes

The Nature of the Child

Montessori saw the child as born with potential for attaining many positive qualities that could only be fully realized with the proper education.

> The children in a Montessori class are given the freedom that is the liberty of the human being, and this freedom allows the children to grow in social grace, inner discipline, and joy. These are the birthright of the human being who has been allowed to develop essential human qualities. (Montessori 1966, xvii)

The Aims of Education

Montessori regarded scientifically informed education as a means of advancing and promoting the whole of civilized society.

> Today, however, those things which occupy us in the field of education are in the interests of humanity at large, and of civilization, and before such great forces we can recognize only one country—the entire world. (Montessori [1912] 1964, 5)

The Role of Play

While Montessori often implied that play was the child's work, she was not opposed to recreational play, imagination, and fantasy. But she thought they had no place in the classroom.

> Yet when all are agreed that the child loves to imagine, why do we give him only fairy tales and toys on which to practice this gift? If a child can imagine a fairy and fairyland, it will not be too difficult for him to imagine America. (Montessori 1967, 177)

Conformance with DAP Principles

NAEYC

Early experiences have profound effects, both cumulative and delayed, on a child's development and learning; and optimal periods exist for certain types of development and learning to occur.

MONTESSORI

The sensitive period refers to a special sensibility which a creature acquires in the infantile state, while it is still in a process of evolution. It is a transient disposition and limited to the acquisition of a particular trait. Once this trait, or characteristic, has been acquired, the special sensibility disappears. (Montessori 1966, 38)

NAEYC

Play is an important vehicle for developing self-regulation as well as for promoting language, cognition and social competence.

MONTESSORI

The children in our schools have proved to us that their real wish is to be always at work—a thing never before suspected, just as no one had ever before noticed the child's power of choosing his work spontaneously. Following an inner guide, the children busied themselves with something (different for each) which gave them serenity and joy. (Montessori 1967, 202)

Commentary

Like the other Giants, Montessori saw development as a product of both nature and nurture. Her description of sensitive periods reflects the importance she places on this interaction.

With regard to the second principle, that children take joy in work, it merely restates Montessori's dictum that: "Play is the child's work." In my opinion, Montessori did not really mean to say that work and play were the same thing. She appreciated that play can be painful and work can be joy. In fact, what separates the two is not joy or serenity, but rather their relation to reality. Play always involves a modification of reality in the service of the self. Work, in contrast, always involves a modification of the self in the service of reality.

Montessori's genius was in devising tasks that brought work and play together. For example, the form boards, which demand that the child find the right cylinder for the right hole, enrich the child's problem-solving abilities (modification of reality in service of the self) at the same time the child is learning size and weight discriminations (modification of the self in the service of reality). Like Locke, she believed that learning is most effective when it is combined with play. But that the two are not identical.

Montessori was an original. Like the contributions of many of the other Giants, hers have become so much a part of our conventional wisdom (child-sized chairs and tables are but one example) that we no longer even think of them in connection with Montessori. That, in many respects, is the true test of Gianthood in the context of DAP.

References

Itard, Jean Marc Gaspard. 1801. *De l'éducation d'un homme sauvage*. Paris: Chez Goujon fils.

Kramer, Rita. 1976. *Maria Montessori: A Biography*. Chicago: University of Chicago Press.

———. 1988. *Maria Montessori: A Biography*. New York: Perseus.

Montessori, Maria. (1912) 1964. *The Montessori Method*. Translated by Anne E. George. New York: Schocken. (See: http://books.google.com/books?id=vopsPFT9HCEC.)

———. 1966. *The Secret of Childhood*. Translated by M. Joseph Costelloe. Notre Dame, IN: Fides.

———. 1967. *The Absorbent Mind*. Translated by Claude A. Claremont. New York: Holt, Rinehart and Winston.

Seguin, Edward. (1866) 1971. *Idiocy and Its Treatment by the Physiological Method*. New York: A. M. Kelley.

Shephard, Marie Tennent. 1996. *Maria Montessori: Teacher of Teachers*. Minneapolis: Lerner.

Standing, E. M. 1957. *Maria Montessori: Her Life and Work*. Fresno, CA: Academy Literary Guild.

9

Sigmund Freud

1856–1939

Of all the Giants, Sigmund Freud is by far the most widely known, the most broadly influential, and the most stridently controversial. He also has had, by far, the most biographers. These include the classic three-volume work of Ernest Jones (1953) and the brilliant study by Peter Gay (1988) as well as the popular *Sigmund Freud* from Kathleen Krull (2006). Accordingly, in the brief sketch that follows, it is impossible to convey the richness of Freud's life and the extent of his written work. I only touch on what seems most relevant to conveying the man and his contribution to early childhood education.

Like Charles Darwin's theories, those of Freud brought about a paradigm shift (Kuhn 1996) in our accepted ways of thinking about our common humanity and our personal selves. Darwin deflated the biblical account of creation, while Freud punctured our belief that we are entirely rational beings. Significant portions of both theories are now widely accepted.

Darwin's theory, among other things, liberated the social sciences from philosophy. Once humankind was regarded as yet another animal species, it was opened to scientific exploration. Psychology, sociology, and anthropology became disciplines in their own right. And the new sciences of psychology and psychiatry were created to deal with the enlightened understanding that mental illness and intellectual disability have natural, not religious or demonic, causes.

These developments were a necessary prelude to the innovations Freud introduced. At the heart of his contributions was the insight that *unconscious psychological events could be the cause of both physical and mental illness.* Among many other consequences, this idea created the new field of psychosomatic medicine. Regarding

141

children, Freud argued that even young children were, in the broad sense, sexual beings. The concept of infantile sexuality added an entirely new dimension to the theory and practice of early childhood education.

Like Pestalozzi, Froebel, Montessori, and Vygotsky, Freud eventually acquired a close group of devoted, trusted disciples. Again, like these other Giants, when any of these followers defected, they were rejected from the Giant's magic circle. Like Montessori, Freud also resisted any changes or additions to the constructs he introduced. Unlike most of the Giants, however, who were nomadic, Freud stayed in Vienna for almost his entire life. For this reason, it is possible to describe the evolution of his ideas without situating them in the succession of cities and countries in which he worked.

The Man

The Early Years, 1856–1873

Amalia Freud was only twenty-one when she gave birth to Sigmund Schlomo Freud on May 6, 1856. She was the third wife of Jacob Freud, a wool merchant, who was twenty years her senior. At the time of Freud's birth, the family lived in the Moravian town of Freiburg (now Pribor), a small market town in the Czech Republic. Jacob was not a very successful salesman, and the family lived in a crowded, one-room apartment.

Eleven months after Freud's birth, Amalia had another son, Julius, who died from an infection before he was a year old. This added pressure to some already-troubling family dynamics that may well have contributed to some of Freud's later thinking. Jacob had two grown sons by an earlier marriage. One of Jacob's son's, Emanuel, was married and had children of his own. The other son, Phillip, was a bachelor of about the same age as Amalia. Both sons lived close to their father. As a child, Freud played with Emanuel's son, John, who was a year older than Freud.

When Freud was three, Jacob took the family to Vienna in hopes of having more financial success and also to escape the hostile anti-Semitism in Freiburg. Emperor Franz Joseph of Austria gave Jews some civil rights in 1849, and full citizenship was granted them in 1867. But Jacob's hopes of doing better in Vienna were not realized, and the Freuds lived in a tiny apartment in a crowded neighborhood that was home to most of the new Jewish émigrés.

Amalia went on to have six more children (five girls and one boy), all of whom survived. But she nonetheless doted on her firstborn—*mein goldener Zigi* (my golden Zigi), a nickname she affectionately used for Freud. He was a precocious child, and family life soon became centered on his intellectual activities. He ate his meals alone, and his sister had to give up piano lessons because the noise interfered with his studies. Freud was a hard worker. For six successive years, he was first in his class. In his early teens, Freud already had a working knowledge of Greek, Latin, German, and Hebrew. He also taught himself the basics of English and Italian. He began reading William Shakespeare at the age of eight, and the Bard and Goethe were his favorite authors (Storr 1989).

After graduating from the gymnasium at age seventeen, Freud was ready to enter the university. He intended to study law because it seemed the profession most suited to his desire to be of service to others. But Freud's plans changed after visiting the 1873 World Exhibition in Vienna. At the exhibition, Freud saw the latest creations of science and technology—steam engines and machines of mass production—and the latest in medical science. He also attended a lecture where he heard a scientist read Goethe's essay *On Nature*. As a result of these experiences, Freud wrote to a friend, "I have determined to become a natural scientist. . . . I will examine the millennia-old documents of nature" (Gay 1988, 24).

Medical Education and Training, 1873–1886

In 1873 Freud enrolled in the University of Vienna. His first interest was zoological research. To pursue this interest, he obtained a position as a research assistant in the laboratory of Ernest Brücke, a distinguished physiological authority. Freud admired Brücke, took him as a mentor, and accepted his scientific worldview. Brücke and his coworkers were determinists, who argued that all bodily processes had to be explained in physical and chemical terms. This view essentially denied any spiritual or occult interpretations of biological functioning. Freud later extended this deterministic view to psychological phenomena, which, he argued, were never a matter of chance. It became a basic tenet of all his theorizing.

Although Freud was happy working in Brücke's lab, he was, for financial reasons, still living at home. After eight years, which included a year of compulsory military service, Freud accepted that he could no longer afford to continue as a laboratory assistant. He took Brücke's advice, completed his medical training, and received his MD degree in 1881. For the next three years, he worked at the Vienna General

Hospital, where he intended to get the practical experience that would prepare him to open his own private practice.

In 1882 Freud met and fell in love with Martha Bernays, a friend of his sisters. Martha came from an orthodox family of intellectuals and was well educated for a woman at that time. Freud sent her letters and daily roses. Martha lived in northern Germany, so their engagement was a long-distance one. Freud had a very traditional conception of a woman's role, and Martha acceded to it, writing back to him, "I want to be whatever you want me to be" (Krull 2006, 42). It was a prolonged engagement because Freud did not want to marry until he opened his own presumably remunerative private practice.

Freud's three years of hospital experience taught him that he really could not stand the sight of blood and that he did not like to inflict pain. These dispositions ruled out surgery and other medical specialties as options. What did capture Freud's interest was the growing field of neurology, the study of the nervous system and the brain. Whereas the heart had long been regarded (even by Aristotle) as the seat of thought and feeling, neurology now located these processes in the cerebral cortex.

Accordingly, Freud chose to specialize in neurology and obtained a fellowship to study with celebrated Parisian neurologist Jean Martin Charcot during the 1885–1886 winter months. Freud was fascinated by Charcot's work on psychological disturbances with no known physical causes (the hysterias) and his use of hypnosis to cure them. Freud's decision to specialize in the treatment of the hysterias was a direct result of his sojourn in Paris with Charcot. He returned to Vienna in 1886, opened a private practice in April, and married Martha on September 13 of the same year.

Freud and Martha had six children, the last of whom was Anna, born in 1895. It was a very harmonious and loving marriage and family. Martha attended to the family and had little to do with Freud's practice and intellectual endeavors. He, in turn, was a devoted father who, despite his voluminous workload, always took time for his wife and children. He was very interested in their schoolwork and took time to read and play with them.

Becoming Freud, 1886–1902

When Freud opened his own practice, he posted an advertisement describing himself as a doctor of *nervous disorders*. He had few patients at first, but then he began to get referrals from other doctors who had cases they could not treat. In addition, Freud was getting referrals from Josef Breuer, a fellow physician and friend. (Breuer was also the family doctor to the Stott family, whose sons were tutored by Steiner.) Although Breuer was an inner ear specialist, he also treated his rich patients for many other ailments, including hysteria.

One of Breuer's patients was an extremely intelligent and gifted twenty-one-year-old woman, who was given the pseudonym of Anna O. Anna O. had a wide range of physical symptoms unrelated to any organic condition. Breuer first saw her in 1880 and continued to treat her for another year and a half. During their sessions, she herself noted that when she talked about the fantasies and experiences that disturbed her, she felt better. She called the process "chimney sweeping," and she also came up with the phrase "the talking cure." Years later, Breuer revealed that Anna O. had made sexual advances to him and that they repulsed him. He thus anticipated what Freud came to describe as transference, which could be used to therapeutic effect.

Breuer shared his "talking cure" of Anna O. with Freud. In his own practice, Freud had already rejected electric shock and hypnosis, believing them to have little therapeutic value. Like Breuer, he found that when his patients recalled past unpleasant events, this had a cathartic effect for them. Freud came to regard hysterical symptoms as expressions of unpleasant memories. These memories were hidden, or repressed, but if brought back to consciousness could relieve the symptoms. Freud and Breuer published their cases and a description of the talking cure in the book *Studies on Hysteria* (Breuer and Freud 2000).

Anna O. was not the only patient who contributed to Freud's psychoanalytic technique. When Freud was treating Baroness Fanny Moser, she asked him if he would please stop interrupting her and let her talk. When he did this, she was able to make connections between seemingly unrelated thoughts. Freud then incorporated *free association*—letting the patient say anything that came to mind without interruption—into this therapeutic practice, and it became a basic tenet of psychoanalytic treatment.

After the publication of *Studies on Hysteria*, Freud and Breuer became increasingly alienated. One of the reasons was Freud's belief that he had discovered the psychological cause of the hysterias: an early traumatic sexual experience. Breuer could not accept this sexual hypothesis and told Freud so. Breuer's rejection of his sexual theory so angered Freud that he no longer considered Breuer a friend. Despite the fact that Breuer had been both intellectually and financially support-ive of Freud for more than ten years, Freud's friend became an enemy never to be forgiven. (Many years later when both Freud and Breuer were old men, Breuer met Freud on the street and opened his arms to greet his old friend; Freud ignored him and walked on.) Freud knew and accepted this facet of his own personality. In *The Interpretation of Dreams*, Freud writes, "An intimate friend and a hated enemy have always been indispensable requirements for my emotional life" (1913, 385).

Freud soon found a new intimate friend in Rudolf Fleiss. Fleiss was a Berlin nose and throat specialist whom Freud befriended and with whom he engaged in a long-term correspondence. Fleiss's friendship supported Freud over the last decade of the nineteenth century, during Freud's most creative period. When they were first published, Freud's highly unorthodox ideas were widely rejected and ridiculed by most of the medical community, and Fleiss was a source of unfail-ing support and reassurance during this time. But years later, Fleiss, too, would become the enemy.

During this same period, Pierre Janet, a French psychiatrist, was using methods similar to those of Freud and called his treatment psychological analysis. Although Janet also employed the talking cure, he, like Charcot, still thought the hysterias were rooted in some unknown neurological disorder. But Freud's theories and treatment methods, which he began to call psychoanalysis by 1897, attempted to be more universal. To assure himself that his theories were common to everyone and not limited to his neurotic patients, Freud undertook a self-analysis. If he found in himself what he observed in his patients, then he would affirm that his theories about human dynamics were indeed common to all.

In the course of his self-analysis, Freud recalled that as a child he was attracted to his mother and resented his father. He related this to the Sophocles drama *Oedipus Rex* and called the phenomenon the Oedipus complex, which he said was a uni-versal phenomenon. This is but one example of Freud's tendency to overgeneralize. In this example, he ignored those family configurations, like that of single parents, where an Oedipus complex was unlikely.

Another discovery from his self-analysis was that dreams are an important ave-nue for uncovering unconscious motives. Freud had collected his own dreams since he was a child, but he now began collecting dreams from Martha, the children, and his patients. In 1900 he published *The Interpretation of Dreams*. Freud regarded this as his most important work and says of it in his preface to the third English edition, "Insight such as this falls to one's lot but once in a lifetime" (1913, xix).

For almost half a century, Freud did all his writing and saw all his patients in the same apartment above a butcher shop on Berggasse 19 in a middle-class section of Vienna. It seems appropriate therefore to give an account of his office, his famous couch, and his daily routine. Krull describes his office this way:

> Always the room would be hazy—he smoked as many as twenty cigars a day, claiming that they helped focus his mind. The floor was covered with plush Persian carpets, the walls lined with books and sculptures displayed in oak bookcases. Gas lamps gave a soft glow, while a small coal-burning stove provided warmth, as well as moist air from the glass tubes attached to it. No noises came from the street because the office was in the back of the building. (2006, 72)

The couch (now famous) was made of horsehair and covered with pillows and a Persian rug to use as a blanket, and on the wall above the couch was a painting of Oedipus and the Sphinx. Later, when he could afford it, Freud had the room soundproofed. Freud would sit behind the couch on a large, green leather armchair where he could not be seen by the patient. When he and the patient were comfortable, he would suggest, "Say whatever comes into your mind." Freud accepted whatever the patient said, did not tell the patient what to do or say, and did not make judgments. Eventually, after many sessions of listening, he would begin to give interpretations.

When it came to taking on patients, Freud was very discriminating. Applicants had to be intelligent, open to change, motivated, and less than fifty years old. Before accepting patients, Freud also insisted on a week trial period, after which he would accept or reject the individual as a patient, or an *analysand* (the term he preferred). Those he accepted had to agree to come for five to six hours a week for a period of months or even years. Because they had to pay for each session in advance, most of Freud's patients were wealthy people, although he did accept some interesting cases pro bono.

Freud followed a fixed daily routine. He saw patients between eight in the morning and noon, after which he wrote up his notes; he did not take them while listening to patients. The main meal of the day was lunch, served at precisely one o'clock, and Freud rarely spoke during this time. After lunch Freud took a walk along Ringstrasse, a tree-lined boulevard offering many shops and cafés. Each day he went to the barbershop to have his beard and moustache trimmed. On some days he would stop to buy cigars or frequent an antique shop to add to his collection of antiquities.

Freud resumed seeing patients from 3:00 to 9:00 p.m., after which he had supper. Sometimes after supper he would walk with Martha and the children to a café for ice cream and pastries. On returning home, Freud wrote until early in the morning. On Saturdays he gave lectures at the university and played cards with friends; on Sundays he had dinner with his mother and his five sisters. In the summers, Freud vacationed with the family in the Austrian Alps. Freud followed this daily and yearly routine for almost fifty years.

Fame and Notoriety, 1902–1923

In turn-of-the-century Europe, Freud was often dismissed as a "witch doctor" or "crank" coupled with anti-Semitic slurs. *The Interpretation of Dreams* initially sold only a few hundred copies. But there were some favorable reviews, including one by physician Wilhelm Stekel. At Stekel's suggestion, Freud formed a group to meet regularly to discuss psychoanalysis. In 1902 the Wednesday Psychological Society began its regular meetings. The members consisted of a mix of Freud's supporters, several Jewish doctors, some non-Jewish doctors, and a few men from other professions.

The group met regularly on Wednesday evenings from nine to twelve at Freud's apartment at Berggasse 19. The members included many who would eventually become famous in their own right—in addition to Stekel, early members included Max Kahane, Rudolf Reitler, and Alfred Adler. More members, including Sándor Ferenczi, Carl Jung, Otto Rank, Ernest Jones, and A. A. Brill, later joined these men. The meetings were devoted to discussing case histories, analyzing public and fictional figures, dissecting each other's dreams, and even revealing embarrassing or troubling personal feelings, thoughts, and actions. Freud, however, excused himself from indulging in these revelations inasmuch as he had already analyzed himself.

The dynamics of the group were complicated. On the one hand, one of the group members said, "We were like pioneers in a newly discovered land. . . . A spark seemed to jump from one mind to the other" (Krull 2006, 96). But on the other hand, it was Freud's group, and he was somewhat difficult to deal with. Although the members were eager for his approval, it was not always clear how best to get it. Freud was afraid that those who agreed with him might steal his ideas, but he resented those who disagreed with him. He eventually settled into the role of father figure and was addressed as professor.

Freud's new group of admirers now took the place of the Fleiss friendship, which ended in 1906 over a bitter dispute as to the originator of the concept of bisexuality. Now that Freud had fresh intimates, Fleiss became the enemy. Perhaps because of the support of the Wednesday Psychological Society, Freud felt secure enough to publish what he felt was his second most important, and most controversial, book, *Three Essays on the Theory of Sexuality*.

In a group of creative individuals, it was not surprising that the atmosphere became less than cordial over the next few years as members began to offer their own theories. Adler proposed that it was the drive to power, not sexuality, that was the basic human dynamic. Freud could not accept this heresy. Adler left the society and took nine members with him. After the break, Freud was opposed to any sharing of ideas between the two groups.

Despite the departure of the Adlerians, the Wednesday group continued to grow. In 1908 it became too large for Freud's home and was formalized as the Vienna Psychoanalytic Society. That same year, the first psychoanalytic conference was held in Salzburg, Austria, with Freud as the featured speaker. The conference was a success, and it gave birth to the *Jahrbuch für psychoanalytische und psychopathologische Forschungen* (*Journal of Psychoanalysis*) and to the formation of Wednesday Psychological Societies in cities from Budapest to New York. Psychoanalysis had become an accepted theory and treatment of emotional disorders in some circles. In other circles, the theory was still highly suspect; for example, in England in 1911, an entire audience of 250 physicians walked out of a conference rather than listen to a presentation of Freud's ideas.

Despite negative reactions, the psychoanalytic movement continued to grow. As it grew, Freud became concerned about the pervasive perception of psychoanalysis as an Austrian Jewish cult. He was also concerned about who would take over the leadership of the organization after he was gone. He hoped that the choice of a non-Jew to follow him might change that perception and began to look at his personal followers for a leader. While Jones was non-Jewish and an ardent supporter, he was not an innovator. Jung, on the other hand, was a brilliant Swiss physician twenty years Freud's junior, whom Freud met in 1907 and who quickly became Freud's disciple. Jung also became Freud's chosen heir. In 1909 Freud was invited to give lectures at

Clark University in Worcester, Massachusetts, and Freud asked Jung to accompany him. But the relationship was already beginning to fray. A day before setting sail, when Jung recounted a dream about mummies, Freud fainted. When he recovered, Freud interpreted Jung's dream as representing the younger man's wish for Freud's death. After that episode, Freud's relationship with Jung deteriorated as Jung deviated more and more from psychoanalytic theory. The relationship ended by 1913.

Despite Freud's disagreements with Jung and his general dislike of the United States (perhaps because it was too radical a change from strict routine at home), the trip was a success. Freud was greatly impressed by how freely and openly his ideas were discussed and often accepted in the United States. Interest in his work extended far beyond the medical field; the general public was equally intrigued by his fascinating case studies. Freud felt validated: "It was like the realization of an incredible daydream" (Krull 2006, 107). Freud's experience was the reverse of Montessori's. While she was first accepted in the United States and later rejected, Montessori continued to be well received in Europe. In contrast, Freud's popularity in the United States never waivered, but he has never been fully accepted in all parts of Europe.

But the spread of psychoanalysis was abruptly halted with the onset of World War I. In 1914 the assassination of an Austrian duke by a Serbian revolutionary led Austria-Hungary to declare war on Serbia. Russia sided with Serbs as did France and later England. Twenty-five countries, including the United States, were ultimately involved, and intellectual interchange and travel were virtually impossible during the war years.

Initially Freud took the side of his country and was proud, if distressed, when his three sons joined the army. But when he began to realize the destructive capabilities of modern warfare—airplane bombardment, submarine attacks on shipping, poison gas, and more—he took it as powerful evidence for his theory that we are guided more by our unconscious motives than we are by reason.

During the war, Freud continued seeing patients and continued writing and maintaining a voluminous correspondence. World War I helped support the case for psychoanalysis. Many soldiers returning from the war suffered nonphysical injuries, which were labeled shell shock. (Today post-traumatic stress disorder is the medical term for these war-induced symptoms.) These soldiers were helped by the talking cure, which loaned credibility to Freud's theories and gave legitimacy to the training of psychiatrists in psychoanalytic theory and techniques. During the war, Freud also undertook the analysis of his daughter Anna. She later became a notable figure in her own right and originated the field of child psychoanalysis; eventually she and lifelong friend Dorothy Burlingham, a Tiffany heiress who was also analyzed by Freud, opened a school for emotionally troubled children.

The end of the war brought about the breakup of the Austrian-Hungarian Empire. It was a great relief that all Freud's sons had escaped serious injury. But times were difficult. Inflation destroyed Freud's savings along with those of his countrymen. Food was scarce, and there was little coal to heat homes. The flu pandemic was raging through Europe, and Martha came down with pneumonia but survived. However, Freud's daughter Sophie succumbed to the flu in 1920.

Although things improved a bit in the early 1920s, the harsh reparation demands of the Allies on Austria and Germany devastated both countries and brought about high inflation, unemployment, and food shortages. These conditions encouraged radical movements and paved the way for National Socialism and the rise of Hitler.

Surviving and Dying with Courage and Dignity, 1923–1939

Although Freud was well aware of these political events, he was also dealing with another problem. Early in his career, Freud complained of physical problems first to Breuer and then to Fleiss. He suffered from migraine headaches, and according to Max Schur, his last physician, Freud had cardiac symptoms as well (Schur 1972).

On April 25, 1923, Freud wrote to Jones, his earlier disciple, that he had noticed a growth on his jaw and palate, which had been removed. It was, however, not done under the best conditions or by the best surgeon. Remedying the botched job required further surgery and the removal of some of his jawbone. In order to eat and talk, Freud had to be fitted with a prosthesis, which he called "the monster" (Krull 2006, 123). The device disfigured Freud's mouth and made it difficult for him to eat and speak. This was a mortifying experience for a man who had a melodious voice and a charming mode of speech and who was meticulous about his appearance.

The growths clearly had been the result of Freud's cigar addiction. He refused, however, to give up cigars and continued to have nonmalignant lesions, which required an additional thirty surgeries. Although he suffered constant, often-excruciating pain, he refused all drugs except aspirin and did not complain. He kept on with his daily routine and published important books, theoretical articles, and case histories, as well as pieces on psychoanalytic technique. He also continued with his voluminous correspondence, which at his death totaled more than twenty thousand letters.

During this period, political nationalism and extremist movements were gaining support. When Hitler became German chancellor in 1932, he closed all democratic institutions and began using anti-Semitism as an emotional rallying cry and as a scapegoat for all his nation's ills. Hitler's ruthlessness became more and more apparent. He removed the Austrian National Socialists who had supported him and had them shot. In Berlin, Freud's books, along with those of Einstein, were publicly burned. Even with these warning signs, Freud was reluctant to leave his accustomed routine. He welcomed new patients and was visited by both former patients and famous admirers. He resisted the invitations to move to England or the United States to escape Hitler's persecution. In 1938 the gestapo came to his home and took Anna to their headquarters. Anna was released after questioning, but this event forced Freud to change his mind and decide to move his family to England.

Leaving Austria was not easy, and though Freud was able to get exit visas for his immediate family, he could not get them for his sisters, who later died in the Holocaust. In England, Freud's friends set up an office that closely resembled the one he had at Berggasse 19. Freud continued to see patients and write, but those tasks ended when the lesions became cancerous and horrifyingly painful. When Freud engaged his last physician, Schur, he made a request, "Promise me one thing, that when the time comes you won't let me suffer unnecessarily" (Schur 1972, 408). Schur agreed.

In September the pain became unbearable, and Freud asked Schur for an overdose of morphine. Freud died on September 23, 1939. His ashes are kept in a Greek urn, one from his own collection, in the Freud Museum in London.

The Work

Freud was a prolific writer, and his letters, essays, articles, brief and long books have been published in many formats, perhaps the most inclusive being a twenty-four-volume collection. Accordingly there is no way to briefly summarize his work. From the point of view of early childhood education, however, a few of Freud's contributions have special significance.

The Concept of Infant Sexuality

Freud's concept of infant sexuality is often misunderstood because it is often taken in the adult sense of sexual attraction and intercourse. But Freud saw sexuality in broader terms. In the second essay of his book *Three Essays on the Theory of Sexuality* ([1962] 2000), Freud indicates that when he speaks of infantile sexuality, he is speaking of it in the larger sense of an appetitive drive. From this perspective, hunger and tension in the bowel and bladder zones are precursors to sexual arousal and follow a similar cycle. That is, in each case there is a gradual buildup of excitation followed by a sudden, pleasurable reduction of tension.

Freud did suggest, however, that the satisfaction obtained from the precursor sexual zones were more in the nature of forepleasure and not the same as the pleasure of orgasm. He also contended that if a child was overly deprived, or overly indulged, in oral or anal activities, he or she could become fixated on obtaining pleasure from those zones. This could lead to sexual perversions, such as sadism or masochism, or contribute to character structure: Oral characters, to illustrate, gain pleasure and reduce tension by eating, drinking, or smoking. Anal characters gain pleasure and reduce tension by excessive neatness and by orderliness, stinginess, and inflexibility.

Freud's Three Models of Personality

Over the course of his career, Freud elaborated on three psychological models that, taken together, give a comprehensive picture of the human personality.

The Dynamic Model

This was the first model Freud employed, and it is basically a hydraulic one. The sexual drive, in all its sequential manifestations, creates a pressure to be discharged but is kept from doing so through psychological repression. As a result, the built-up pressure finds release in physical symptoms that have no physical determinants. The symptoms displace or redirect the pressure from the sexual drive to the body's musculature, which can produce paralysis of an arm, a leg, or the vocal muscles.

The Developmental Model

In *Three Essays on the Theory of Sexuality*, Freud introduces a developmental model of the personality. He argues that the sexual drive, in the broad sense described above, moves from the oral to the anal to the genital zones during the first five years of life. From age six to age twelve, the sexual drive is in a period of dormancy. Freud termed this the *latency* period. In adolescence, the Oedipus complex is reawakened, but now the young person must find a nonparental figure as the object of his or her sexual desire. It is also a period when a person consolidates his or her personality or personal identity.

The Structural Model

In his book *The Ego and the Id* (1960), Freud introduces a threefold structure for the mind. The *id* represents the unconscious impulses and wishes of the individual, the "seething cauldron" of desire. The *ego* emerges from the failure of the id to realize its goal and develops to serve the adaptive function of mediating between the id and reality. For example, an infant cries when it is not fed, and the ego will enable the infant to delay gratification.

At about age four or five, the girl or boy identifies with the parent of the same sex in order to vicariously satisfy the Oedipus (Electra, in the case of the girl) complex. Through this identification, the child internalizes the moral precepts of the parent, which become the *superego*. The superego is the conscience, and the ego must now mediate between the demands of the id and the constraints of the superego.

These three models provide a whole new perspective for the understanding of young children and of providing for their education.

Common Themes

The Nature of the Child

Freud was the first to introduce the concept of infant sexuality.

> We do wrong to ignore the sexual life of children entirely: in my experience children are capable of every psychical sexual activity and many somatic ones as well. Just as the whole human sexual apparatus is not comprised in the external genitals and the two reproductive glands, so human sexual life does not appear only with puberty, as on a rough inspection it may appear to do. (Freud 1962, 280)

The Aims of Education

For Freud the aim of education, on the part of both parents and schools, is to assist the child in mastering his or her instincts and emotions in constructive, psychologically healthy ways.

Education can, without further hesitation be described as an incitement to the conquest of the pleasure principle, and to its replacement by the reality principle; it offers its aid, to the process of development which concerns the ego; to this end it makes use of rewards of love by those in charge. (Freud 1991, 6)

The Role of Play

According to Freud, play is not work but rather the use of imagination to go beyond reality.

The child's best loved and most absorbing occupation is play. . . . He rearranges the things of his world and orders it in a new way that pleases him better. It would be incorrect to think that he does not take this world seriously; on the contrary, he takes his play very seriously and expends a great deal of emotion on it. The opposite of play is not serious occupation but—reality. (Freud 1963, 35)

Freud also writes that while play is characteristic of children, it doesn't disappear in the adult but reemerges in the form of daydreaming and is the basis for artistic creativity.

Conformance with DAP Principles

NAEYC

Many aspects of children's learning and development follow well-documented sequences, with later abilities, skills, and knowledge building on those already acquired.

FREUD

Thus we can now define the forms taken by the sexual life of the child before the primacy of the genital zone is reached; this primacy is prepared for in the early infantile period before the latent period and is permanently organized from puberty onward. (Freud 1943, 287)

NAEYC

All the domains of development and learning—physical, social, and emotional and cognitive are important, and they are closely interrelated.

Children's development and learning in one domain influence and are influenced by what takes place in other domains.

FREUD

It may well be that nothing of considerable importance can occur in the organism without contributing some component to the excitation of the sexual instinct. (Freud 1973, 205)

Commentary

Freud is unique among the Giants of DAP in his insistence on the importance of the sexual life of the young child. His contribution adds a whole new level of understanding of young children's thoughts and actions. He also gave new meaning to the significance of the early years and a fresh understanding of parent-child relations and interactions. Likewise, his descriptions of the sexual stages of development have now become part of our everyday lexicon, as have his concepts of the id, ego, and superego.

For both Freud and Piaget, play is always a transformation or reconstruction of reality in the service of the self. And it was Freud's psychosexual theory that was the starting point for Erik Erikson's description of psychosocial development, although Erikson went beyond Freud to cover the whole of the human life cycle. Yet it is Freud's illumination of the importance of unconscious processes that has most enlightened our understanding of human psychology in general and the psychology of the young child in particular. We now appreciate that much of the young child's behavior can be understood as the product of unconscious fears, frustrations, and anxieties.

References

Breuer, Josef, and Sigmund Freud. 2000. *Studies on Hysteria*. Translated and edited by James Strachey. New York: Basic Books.

Freud, Sigmund. 1913. *The Interpretation of Dreams*. Translated by A. A. Brill. New York: Macmillan.

———. 1943. *A General Introduction to Psychoanalysis*. Garden City, NY: Garden City.

———. 1960. *The Ego and the Id*. Translated and edited by James Strachey. New York: Norton.

———. 1962. *The Standard Edition of the Complete Psychological Works of Sigmund Freud: Early Psycho-Analytic Publications, Volume III* (1893–1899). Translated and edited by J. Strachey. London: Hogarth.

———. (1962) 2000. *Three Essays on the Theory of Sexuality*. Translated by James Strachey. New York: Basic Books.

———. 1963. *Collected Papers*. Edited by Philip Rieff. New York: Collier.

———. 1973. *The Standard Edition of the Complete Psychological Works of Sigmund Freud*. Translated by James Strachey. London: Hogarth.

———. 1991. *General Psychological Theory: Papers on Metapsychology*. New York: Touchstone.

Gay, Peter. 1988. *Freud: A Life for Our Time*. New York: Norton.

Jones, Ernest. 1953. *The Life and Work of Sigmund Freud*. New York: Basic Books.

Krull, Kathleen. 2006. *Sigmund Freud*. New York: Viking.

Kuhn, Thomas S. 1996. *The Structure of Scientific Revolutions*, 3rd ed. Chicago: University of Chicago Press.

Schur, Max. 1972. *Freud: Living and Dying*. New York: International University Press.

Storr, Anthony. 1989. *A Very Short Introduction*. New York: Oxford University Press.

10

Jean Piaget

1896–1980

Second only to Freud, Jean Piaget is easily the next most well known and influential of the Giants. Like Freud, Piaget created a new discipline, genetic epistemology, which is, in effect, an experimental philosophy. Piaget put to test the basic question of epistemology: how do we come to know the external world? Exploring the development of intelligence, perception, memory, and imagery in children was a vast enterprise, and Piaget felt he had little time for anything else. Almost all his life was devoted to his work; even family, friends, and leisure were subordinated to his efforts. To illustrate, he saw only one film in his life and read Marcel Proust for recreation.

It was a huge sacrifice that paid major dividends for psychology and education. Thanks to his single-minded dedication, he published more than sixty books, a great many book chapters, monographs, and hundreds upon hundreds of articles. All of the earlier Giants had agreed that the most effective education starts from the psychology of the child. Yet it was not until the work of Piaget that we had a truly comprehensive, research-based picture of the development of children's thoughts and actions. Piaget's discoveries of children's unique worldviews and their progressive reconstruction of reality have transformed our ways of thinking about the psychology of human intelligence. They have also had a lasting impact on the training of teachers and the writing of science and math curricula.

Piaget's work was initially neglected, at least in the United States, because it was so much at variance with the then-dominant behaviorism of American psychology. It was only with the cognitive revolution of the 1960s (stimulated in part by Piaget's work) that Piaget's research and theories came to be more fully translated, and more fully appreciated, in the United States. Once recognized, his work stimulated a huge body of research in areas such as infancy, cognition, moral development, and many more.

Like Freud, whom he once met at a conference, and who, like himself, built his theory on Darwin's evolutionary ideas, Piaget spent most of his career in one city. Yet Piaget differed from Freud; with the exception of a few assistants, longtime devotees, and career-long colleague Bärbel Inhelder, Piaget did not surround himself with a dedicated group of followers. In 1955 he created the International Centre for Genetic Epistemology and invited scientists from many different fields to come for a year of research and study around a common topic. In 1964 I received a letter from Piaget inviting me to participate in the Centre during the 1964 and 1965 academic year. I accepted, and over the time I spent in Geneva, Piaget and I became friends. I was fortunate to be among those who could comfortably address him as *patron* (boss). He always welcomed fresh ideas and was never threatened by challenges to his own. Indeed, he once told me that "to the extent that there are Piagetians, I have failed." He continued to host the Centre until his death.

Given Piaget's single-minded dedication to his work, there are no full-scale biographies of Piaget's life, again in contrast to Freud, and just one detailed account of his early years—Fernando Vidal's *Piaget before Piaget*. He was not a letter writer (I have only two from him), and most of his friendships were, I believe, like ours—focused on the problems he was interested in studying. There is then, insofar as I can determine, little account of his personal life beyond his childhood and youth. So this chapter presents only a brief summary of his early life and his later academic achievements and appointments. The remainder of the chapter is an account of the evolution of his work. Indeed, he seemed to allow himself little time for anything else.

The Man

The Early Years, 1896–1918

Jean Piaget was born in Neuchâtel, Switzerland, on August 9, 1896. Piaget's parents were of middle-income background and lived at the foot of the mountains. Arthur Piaget, Piaget's father, was chair of the Department of Romance Languages and Literature at the University of Neuchâtel. He was a noted author and well-published scholar of Neuchâtel history. Piaget's father became famous for uncovering the fact that a revered document of Neuchâtel's history was actually forged and did not date back to medieval times (Vidal 1994).

Piaget's mother, Rebecca Piaget (née Jackson), was an intelligent, kind, and energetic person who was also emotionally troubled. Rebecca was quite religious and insisted that Piaget and his two younger sisters go to church. In his autobiography (Boring et al. 1952), Piaget wrote that the conflict between his father's scientific orientation and his mother's religious one was a constant source of tension in the family. At least some of Piaget's early scientific pursuits were motivated by a desire to escape an emotionally troubling home life.

Piaget's formal education was a traditional one for his time. He began Latin school at age ten and remained there for five years. Like Freud, Piaget was precocious. In 1907, when Piaget was ten years old, he asked Paul Godet, director of Neuchâtel's Natural History Museum, if he could work at the museum after it was closed. Godet agreed and became Piaget's mentor. Godet, an expert in mollusks, was a traditional biologist and taught Piaget how to observe, name, and classify mollusks. Piaget showed a talent for this work, and mentor and student published articles together. Godet died in 1911 (he left Piaget his mollusk collection), and Piaget paid tribute to him in the articles he then proceeded to publish on his own.

In 1912, at age sixteen, Piaget entered the literary (college preparatory) division of the gymnasium. He continued to do research and publish papers on mollusks. Based solely on his journal articles, he was offered a position at a natural history museum in Geneva, but he had to turn it down because he was still in school. The gymnasium was a three-year course of study, and when he graduated in 1915 Piaget went on to the University of Neuchâtel, where he was granted a *licence* (bachelor's degree) in natural science in 1918. In November of that year, he finished his doctoral thesis (on the mollusks of the Valais region) and was awarded his doctorate at age twenty-two.

All during his Latin school, gymnasium, and university studies, Piaget led a very active extracurricular intellectual life. In addition to his membership in the science-oriented Club of the Friends of Nature, he was also actively involved with many political and religious groups. Eventually, all this intellectual activity, combined with his personal rejections of the "demon of philosophy" and of his mother's religion, led to both ill health and emotional upheaval. Like many very bright and gifted adolescents, Piaget apparently suffered from being unable to find an identity among existing social roles and worldviews. After his graduation, he went to a mountain health resort in Leysin to give himself some distance from the pressures he felt at home.

While at Leysin, Piaget wrote and published a semiautobiographical novel, *Recherche*. Since Goethe's *The Sorrows of Young Werther*, the adolescent novel had become popular. In Goethe's novel, Werther's suicide over unrequited love prompted many copycat suicides among European youth. The novel became the model for the coming-of-age narratives of that period, which described adolescence as a period of *sturm und drang* (storm and stress).

In Piaget's novel, the hero Sebastien struggles with many of the same issues Piaget himself was coping with. In contrast to young Werther, Sebastien's sorrows were of an intellectual rather than emotional sort. *Recherche* is divided into three parts: The first deals with Sebastian's development, and the second with the crises that presumably brought Piaget to the mountain resort. The third is a theoretical essay in which Sebastien suggests the course and direction his life will take. In many ways, the three parts of the novel suggest the dialectic that characterized Piaget's later theories. Chapter 1 was the thesis (his religious upbringing and taste for philosophy), chapter 2 was the antithesis (the rejection of religion and philosophy), and the third was the synthesis (an integration of the underlying biological and psychological philosophies of his life). The novel's stages anticipated the progressive evolution and integration of Piaget's sociological, biological, and logical models of development.

Becoming Piaget, 1919–1980

Unlike the other Giants who went through long periods of role experimentation before finding an identity, Piaget found his early, within a few years after graduation. I describe the rest of his life as *becoming Piaget* because he was always opening new fields of research and continually changing and expanding his theories.

After receiving his doctorate, Piaget was still searching for a way to combine his biological, psychological, and philosophical interests. He spent 1919 at Bleuler's Psychiatric Hospital in Zurich, where Carl Jung had worked. There Piaget discovered that he was not really interested in personality and the affective life. From Zurich, Piaget went on to Paris, where he spent two years teaching psychology and philosophy at the Sorbonne. He also worked with Theodore Simon, who had collaborated with Alfred Binet in creating the Binet-Simon infant and child intelligence scale. After Cyril Burt, a British psychologist, translated the scale into English and added new items, Piaget was asked to translate these new English items into French and test them out.

In the process of examining children, Piaget found that he was much less interested in whether children got the answers right or wrong than he was in their spontaneous and often "wrong" answers. Like Freud, he began to pursue these "errors" as having meaning in their own right. Using the open-ended clinical interview techniques he had learned in Zurich, he had children elaborate on their original ideas. With this method of inquiry, Piaget found that children's spontaneous ideas were not truly "wrong" but simply represented a different, and age appropriate, way of thinking, even if considered wrong from an adult mental test perspective. In studying the development of children's thinking, Piaget finally found a way of combining his interests in philosophy, biology, and psychology. He published his first paper on intelligence in the French *Journal de Psychologie* in 1921.

That same year, Piaget accepted a position at the Jean-Jacques Rousseau Institute in Geneva working with the renowned child psychologist Edouard Claparede. With this Piaget's career was launched. In 1923 Piaget married one of his student assistants, Valentine Chartenay. In 1925 their first daughter, Jaqueline, was born; their second daughter, Lucienne, was born in 1927, and their son, Laurent, was born in 1931. Piaget continued his voluminous research and publications, and in 1929 the institute appointed him professor of the history of scientific thought. In 1940 he took over direction of the institute's psychology laboratory. During his career, he also taught at the Universities of Neuchâtel, Lausanne, and Paris. In addition to his teaching and research activities, he was also appointed to some prestigious international positions. He was chairman of the International Bureau of Education for more than twenty years and served as a Swiss delegate for the United Nations Educational, Scientific and Cultural Committee (UNESCO). Throughout his career, he also received numerous awards and over twenty honorary doctorates.

Once he was settled at the institute, Piaget set a pattern of work that he would follow for the rest of his life. At the beginning of each year, he and his teaching assistants would select a problem to study for the next two semesters. Together they devised an original set of tasks to explore the evolution of a particular concept. Under the supervision of his assistants, the institute students fanned out to the public schools of Geneva to collect their data. At the end of the year, the data was compiled, organized by age group, and presented to Piaget.

To appreciate what Piaget did with this material, it is necessary to describe his daily routine, which he followed to the best of his ability even when he was away from home. He got up every morning at four o'clock and wrote four or more publishable pages on square sheets of graph paper. These pages were then taken across the border into France to a printer, who typeset the handwritten text. After his writing stint, Piaget rode his bike to the institute, where he taught classes and attended meetings. I once attended one of his classes and was amazed to see him signing hundreds of blue books (to monitor attendance) while lecturing.

In the afternoons, Piaget took long walks in the nearby foothills of the French Alps. Once, on a visit, I walked with him across the border and was amused that the border guards knew him so well they never asked for identification. As we walked, I told Piaget a story that I thought would amuse him. One day I had to take my wife's station wagon to the store and took along my four-year-old son, Rick. Because he knew he was going to get a treat at the store, Rick said he was pleased that we were taking the station wagon. When I asked him why, he said, "Because we will get there faster." He confirmed one of Piaget's findings that young children identify speed with the length of the vehicle traveling. Piaget, however, responded in an unexpected way. "Oh, you Americans," he said, "you always have two cars!"

During these daily walks, Piaget pondered the issues he was working on at the moment. On another occasion, when we were both attending a conference in California, I met him on the beach near the conference—we both had played hooky. He explained, "*Je cherche une idée.*" ("I am on the track of an idea.") He read extensively at the end of each day before going to bed.

Each summer, as soon as classes were over, Piaget gathered up the research findings that were collected by his students during the year and left for the Alps, where he took up solitary residence in an abandoned farmhouse. The whereabouts of this retreat was as closely guarded as the names of depositors in numbered Swiss bank accounts; only Piaget's family, his longtime colleague Inhelder, and a trusted secretary knew where he was. During the summer, Piaget took walks, meditated, and wrote. Then, when the leaves began to turn, he descended from the mountains with the several books and articles he had written on his "vacation."

Over the years, Piaget and I continued to meet at conferences or when I visited with him on one of my trips to Europe. Once when I was in Israel, I called Piaget and told him I would like to stop by and see him on my way home. It was a bad connection, and I don't think he really knew who was calling him. He declined.

When I got home, I had my second letter from him—this one apologizing and saying that only after we had hung up did he realize who was calling. "Of course," he wrote, "you are always welcome." A few years later, driving home from my office at Tufts I heard on the radio of Piaget's death. As I drove on, I remembered his many kindnesses to me over the years and his wry sense of humor. It was September 17, 1980. Piaget was eighty-four years old and died of unknown causes in Geneva. His was interred at the Cimetière des Plainpalais in Geneva.

The Work

Piaget's work over his sixty years of research fell into three distinct periods based on the particular model he employed during each period. During the first period, he introduced a sociological model and explained development as moving from *egocentrism to sociocentrism*. For the second period, he added a biological model and added the terms *assimilation, accommodation,* and *equilibrium*. Starting in the early 1940s, Piaget added a logical model and employed the mathematical language of operations and groups. Not surprisingly, his books became increasingly more difficult to read as he sought to integrate each succeeding model into the earlier one.

The Sociological Model, 1921–1929

Piaget's discovery of children's spontaneous ideas about the world spurred a number of his studies about children's language and ideas about physical reality. Following the pattern of research design, data collection, and writing described above, Piaget published five books during this period. These are perhaps his most well-known books. In *The Language and Thought of the Child* ([1926] 1955), he found that young children were egocentric in the sense that they were unable to take another person's perspective when it was different from their own. This then became the model for explaining his findings in the other books of this period.

In his *The Child's Conception of the World* ([1929] 1951), Piaget reported that preschoolers believe that names are identical with the things they name—which is why they feel hurt by being called names. Young children also believe that dreams come to us from outside ourselves and remain outside. Similar findings were reported in the next book, *The Child's Conception of Physical Causality* ([1930] 1951). One example finding was that young children identify strength with movement—a stone is strong if it is rolling down a hill but weak if it is still. Likewise, in *Judgement and Reasoning in the Child* ([1928] 1951), Piaget found that a young child did not fully grasp relationships and did not understand, for example, that if the child had a brother or sister, the same was true for his or her sibling. In *The Moral Judgement of the Child* (Piaget 1948) Piaget reported, among other things, that young children judged culpability in terms of amount of damage done and only at a later age evaluated actions in terms of intentions.

Piaget attributed all his findings to the child's egocentrism, which created many forms of thought that resembled, but were not identical to, those of ancient philosophers. (Piaget thus disproved a popular theory at the time that suggested that the child recapitulates, or repeats, in his or her development the intellectual development of the human race.) Young children, for example, see names as identical to the objects named (nominal realism), attribute life to nonliving things (animism), and think that events that happen together cause one another (associative causality). But these ideas derive from the child's limited mental abilities and experience, not recapitulation. In his first five books, Piaget displayed his early research training in clear observation, classification, and naming. Such findings made him question the very origins of these spontaneous, unlearned modes of thinking and led to the adoption of his next, and quite different, model.

The Biological Model, 1929–1940

Although Piaget continued to do research on other issues, after the birth of his children, he began to keep careful records of his children's behavior and to engage in a number of innovative experiments with them. His aim in these investigations was to trace the origins of the ideas he had found in older children to their roots in infancy.

Piaget reported the results of his studies in three books, *The Origins of Intelligence in Children*; *Play, Dreams and Imitation in Children*; and *The Construction of Reality in the Child*. These three books are now generally regarded as classics in the field and have been one of the major forces behind the explosion of research in infant behavior in the United States and abroad. The publication of these books in the middle and late 1930s marked the end of the second phase of Piaget's work.

In these three books, Piaget introduced a biological model to explain his findings but included some of the earlier sociological ideas as well. Indeed, in *Origins*, Piaget dealt with the mental processes attributable to *nature*. In *Construction of Reality*, he dealt with the construction of concepts children acquired from experience and those that are attributable to *nurture*. In *Play, Dreams, and Imitation*, Piaget dealt with the development of the symbolism attributable to society. For Piaget, intellectual development was always a threefold product of nature, nurture, and society. What impressed Piaget about infant behavior was that it seemed to reflect a very elementary form of reasoning. This led him to adopt his last, most overarching model, the logical one.

The Logical Model, 1940–1980

The third and major phase of Piaget's endeavors began around 1940 and continued until his death. During this period, Piaget focused on how children and adolescents develop the mental abilities that gradually enable them to construct a worldview consistent with the reality experienced by adults. He was now concerned with how children progressively acquire the mental system that enables them to arrive at the adult, abstract versions of various concepts such as number (*The Child's Conception of Number*, 1952), time (*The Child's Conception of Time*, 1970), quantity, geometry, and speed (*The Child's Construction of Quantities: Conservation and Atomism*, 1941). Over the last forty years of his life, Piaget, along with his colleagues, amassed an astounding amount of information about the thinking of children and adolescents. This research is now central to the curricula of developmental psychology and education.

With his new operational model, Piaget was able to understand the development of intelligence as a process of maturing mental operations. This new model allowed him to arrive at a more comprehensive theory of intellectual development as described below. Although Piaget was criticized for his "quaint" methods, they continued to yield powerful and hitherto unknown facts about children's memory (*Memory and Intelligence*, 1973) and their use of imagery (*Mental Imagery and the Child*, 1971). Piaget remained very active until his death. In an age of computers, the Internet, and automation, the remarkable and unexpected discoveries of Piaget are evidence that in the realm of scientific achievement, technological sophistication is still no substitute for creative genius.

Piaget's Operational Theory of Intellectual Development

Piaget proposed that intelligence—adaptive thinking and action—develops in a sequence of stages that is related to age. For Piaget, intelligence was not a quantitative *individual* characteristic as measured by IQ but rather a qualitative species characteristic shared by all children. Each stage sees the elaboration of new mental abilities, which set the limits and determine what can be learned during that period. These stages are not preformed in the genome but are rather constructed during development; they are *epigenetic.*

Piaget argued that the order in which the stages appear holds true for all children. At the same time, he also argued that the ages at which the stages emerge would depend on the native endowment of the child and on the quality of the physical and social environment in which he or she is reared. In a very real sense, then, Piaget's theory is both a nature-nurture and sociocultural theory. It is also a dialectic theory—one that sees progress as a sequence of thesis, antithesis, and final synthesis of the two opposed positions. Using Piaget's terminology, Piaget saw development as a sequence of differentiation—of assimilation and accommodation eventually resulting in a higher level of synthesis or equilibration. It is also a neo-Kantian theory, because Piaget demonstrates that Kant's innate categories of knowing, space, time, number, and causality are not fixed but are developmental in nature.

The category of knowing determines how we perceive and understand reality. For example, our ideas of color are limited by the receptors in our eyes, but there may be colors that we cannot see. Likewise, all humans organize their basic experiences in terms of space and time because this is how our brains operate. It is because the complexity of categorical thinking changes with age that children's realities—as Piaget has demonstrated—differ from our own. Children, for example, generally cannot see reversible figures, such as the faces outlined by two sides of a vase, until after age six or seven. These earlier realities are not wrong, because they have to be understood as age-appropriate differences. Put somewhat differently, in the course of development, the child constructs and reconstructs reality in accord with his or her evolving categories of knowing. In this light, Piaget's way of looking at intellectual development has been called constructivism.

The Stage of Sensory Motor Coordinations (usually 0–2 years)

Piaget calls the first stage in the development of intelligence the *sensory-motor* period, and it is concerned with the evolution of those abilities necessary to mentally *construct* permanent objects. Although it seems to us that we know from birth that objects outside ourselves continue to exist when they are no longer present to our senses, this turns out not to be the case. For the infant, out of sight is literally out of mind. If an infant is playing with a rattle and it falls from the crib, she is not upset and finds some other way to amuse herself. After the first year, however, the infant has been able to construct a mental image of the object by coordinating all her sense experiences with it. By that point, if the same rattle disappears, she becomes upset and searches for it.

Object permanence is essential for all reasoning processes. It makes little sense to reason about things that have no permanence. The construction of permanent objects by the end of the first year helps to explain the separation anxiety that appears at the same time. It also helps to explain the terrible twos, because children want to grasp their individuality and assert their independence as permanent objects. In doing so, their negativism is an assertion of their separateness.

The Stage of Preoperations (usually 2–7 years)

This stage elaborates on the symbolic function—those abilities dealing with how we represent things. The presence of these new abilities is shown by the gradual acquisition of language, the first indications of dreams and night terrors, the advent of symbolic play (two sticks at right angles are an airplane), and the first attempts at drawing and graphic representation.

This stage is characterized by what Piaget called *transductive* thinking. In deductive or inductive thinking, one moves from class to individual or from individual to class (for example, All men are mortal; Socrates is a man; therefore Socrates is mortal). In *transductive* thinking, the relationships between things are at the same level. When asked to define words, for example, a preschooler will say, "a bike is to ride" or "an apple is to eat." For the preschooler, there are no larger categories in which to place objects—an object exists solely for the purpose it's used for. (In contrast, an older child would say that a bike is a "vehicle" or "means of transportation" and an apple is a "fruit," demonstrating a distinction between an individual object and the larger category the object belongs to.) Children at the preoperational stage reason from thing to action at the same level. It is because preschoolers think of everything existing at one level that they are not able to nest classes. A preschooler, for example, may know the number of boys and girls in his class but is baffled by the question, "Are there more boys or more children in the class?" The child at this stage is not yet able to understand that one can be both a boy and a child at the same time. It is only at the next stage that children are able to engage in truly deductive reasoning.

The Stage of Concrete Operations (usually 7–11 years)

When a child reaches school age, she acquires what Piaget calls *concrete operations*, internalized actions that permit the child to do in her head what before she would have had to accomplish through real actions. All Piaget's investigations, including his research on the concrete operations stage, focus on how the child copes with change and how she comes to distinguish between the permanent and the transient and between appearance and reality.

In his exploration of this stage, Piaget tested the child's abilities to discover that an object or quantity remains the same across a change in its appearance. In other words, that the object or quantity is *conserved*. The methods Piaget used to study how the child comes to deal with transformations are ingenuously simple and can be used by any interested parent or teacher. To give just one illustration from among hundreds, a child is shown two identical drinking glasses filled equally full with orangeade, and he is asked to say whether there is the same amount to drink in the two glasses. After the child confirms that this is the case, the orangeade from one glass is poured into a third glass that is taller and thinner, so that the orangeade now reaches a higher level. Then the child is asked to say whether there is the same amount to drink in the two differently shaped glasses. Before age six or seven, most children say that the tall, narrow glass has more orangeade. The young child cannot understand the transformation and bases his judgment on the static features of the orangeade, namely, the levels.

How does the older child arrive at the notion that the amounts of orangeade in the two differently shaped glasses are the same? The answer, according to Piaget, is that she discovers the equality with the aid of reason. If the child judges only on the basis of appearances, she cannot solve the problem. When she compares the two glasses with respect to width, she must conclude that the wide glass has more, while if she compares them with respect to the level of the orangeade, she must conclude that the tall glass has more. There is, therefore, no way, on the basis of perception, that she can solve the problem. If, on the other hand, the child reasons that what the tall glass of orangeade lost in width it gained in height, then the child would grasp that the amount remains the same.

On the basis of this and many similar findings, Piaget argues that much of our knowledge about reality comes to us not from without like the wail of a siren but rather from within by the force of our own logic. It is hard to overemphasize the importance of this fact because it is so often forgotten, particularly in education.

To those who are not philosophically inclined, it often appears that our knowledge of things comes directly from those things, as if our mind simply copied the forms, colors, and textures of objects. But as Piaget has made clear, the world we know is made up of mental constructions. There is a real world, but we can only know our reconstructions of it, not the thing-in-itself, as Kant put it. The importance of unconscious reasoning in the child's spontaneous construction of his or her world is thus one of the major discoveries of Piaget's third stage.

The Stage of Formal Operations (usually 12–15 years)

Long before there was anything like a discipline of child psychology, age six to seven was recognized as the age of reason. It was also assumed that once the child attained the age of reason there was no further growth in reasoning abilities. What Inhelder and Piaget (1958) found was that this was not the case. They discovered a second age of reason involving what they called *formal operations*, which do not appear until adolescence. This form of reasoning parallels the modern symbolic logic of George Boole (Boole 1854; Bell 1937). While the elementary school child is indeed able to reason, his or her reasoning ability is limited in a very important respect: it is limited to reasoning about things but not about verbal propositions.

The second age of reason corresponds to the ability to deal with second-order symbol systems. Algebra is a case in point. In written language, the letter *a* stands for a concrete sound, but in algebra, *a* stands for a variable number—it is a symbol for a symbol. The ability to understand historical time, celestial space, and nuclear physics all require formal operational thinking. Formal operations also permit adolescents to think about their thoughts, to construct ideals, and to reason realistically about the future.

No new mental systems emerge after the formal operations, which are the common coin of adult thought. After adolescence, mental growth takes the form—it is hoped—of a gradual increase in wisdom.

Common Themes

The Nature of the Child

For Piaget the child is constructing his intelligence—that is, his adaptive thinking and action—from the very beginning of life.

But if you study the *formation* of knowledge, which is my craft, you must constantly identify the intervening factors—those due to external experience, social life, or language and those due to the internal structure of the thinking of the subject which is constructed as it develops. (Piaget in Bringuier 1980, 18)

The Aims of Education

The principal goal of education is to create men who are capable of doing new things, not simply of repeating what other generations have done—men who are creative, inventive and discoverers. The second goal of education is to form minds, which can be critical, can verify, and not accept everything they are offered. The great danger today is of slogans, collective opinions, and ready-made trends of thought. We have to be able to resist individually, to criticize, to distinguish between what is proven and what is not. So we need pupils who are active, who learn early to find out by themselves, partly by their own spontaneous activity and partly through material we set up for them; who learn early to tell what is verifiable and what is simply the first idea to come to them. (Piaget in Ripple and Rockcastle 1964, 5)

The Role of Play

There are three main types of [play] structure which characterize children's games and determine their detailed classification. There are practice games, symbolic games, and games with rules [for example yoga, crosswords, and baseball, respectively], while constructional games constitute the transition from all three to adapted behaviors. (Piaget 1951, 110)

Conformance with DAP Principles

NAEYC
Development and learning result from a dynamic and continuous inter-action of biological maturation and experience.

PIAGET
Knowledge is neither a copy of the object nor taking consciousness of a priori forms predetermined in the subject; it's a perpetual construction

made by exchanges between the organism and the environment, from the biological point of view, and between thought and its object from the cognitive point of view. (Piaget in Bringuier 1980, 110)

NAEYC

All the domains of development and learning—physical, social and emotional, and cognitive—are important, and they are closely interrelated. Children's development and learning in one domain influence and are influenced by what takes place in other domains.

PIAGET

I think that, in addition to developmental factors—heredity or the maturation of the nervous system, external physical experience, the social milieu, language, and so forth—equilibration . . . plays a major role: the fact that the subject tries to give the maximum degree of coherence to his ideas and to resolve contradictions. (Piaget in Bringuier 1980, 62)

Commentary

I believe it is fair to say that Piaget was the first Giant to give DAP a solid experimental and theoretical foundation. He provided abundant evidence to support Rousseau's intuition that young children think differently than adults do. He thus made it clear that the education of the young child could not be simply a size-smaller first grade. He did this by showing the relation between the logical structure of the basic tool skills and the child's level of cognitive development. For example, the unit concept of number, the understanding that a number is both like and different from every other, requires the concrete operations that are not usually fully in place by age six or seven. Hence the folly of trying to teach young children arithmetic before this age. In the same way, the understanding of phonics (in English) also requires concrete operations inasmuch as the child must understand that one letter can be sounded in several ways and several letters can represent the same sound. To be sure, young children can learn numbers and letters, but this is far different from adding and subtracting or the verbal decoding required by reading.

Piaget's many other contributions with respect to the development of perceptions, memory, symbolism, and much more have still to be fully appreciated and incorporated into our educational system. But his work has built a solid experimental foundation of the fundamental tenet of DAP: that both child rearing and education have to start from an understanding of the child's level of intellectual development.

References

Bell, E. T. 1937. *Men of Mathematics*. New York: Touchstone.

Boole, George. 1854. *An Investigation of the Laws of Thought on Which Are Founded the Mathematical Theory of Logic and Probabilities*. Cambridge, UK: Walton and Maberly.

Boring, Edward Garrigues, Heinz Werner, Robert M. Yerkes, and Herbert S. Langfeld. 1952. *A History of Psychology in Autobiography*, Vol. 4. Worcester, MA: Clark University Press.

Bringuier, Jean-Claude. 1980. *Conversations with Jean Piaget*. Translated by Basia Miller Gulati. Chicago: University of Chicago Press.

Inhelder, Bärbel, and Jean Piaget 1958. *The Growth of Logical Thinking from Childhood to Adolescence*. Translated by Anne Parsons and Stanley Milgram. New York: Basic Books.

Piaget, Jean. (1926) 1955. *The Language and Thought of the Child*. New York: Meridian.

———. (1928) 1951. *Judgement and Reasoning in the Child*. Translated by Marjorie Gabain. New York: Harcourt, Brace.

———. (1929) 1951. *The Child's Conception of the World*. London: K. Paul, Trench, Trubner.

———. (1930) 1951. *The Child's Conception of Physical Causality*. London: K. Paul, Trench, Trubner.

———. 1948. *The Moral Judgement of the Child*. Glencoe, IL: Free Press.

———. 1951. *Play, Dreams and Imitation in Childhood*. Translated by C. Gattegno and F. M. Hodgson. London: Heinemann.

———. 1952. *The Child's Conception of Number*. Translated by C. Gattegno and F. M. Hodgson. London: Routledge and Kegan Paul.

———. 1971. *Mental Imagery and the Child*. Translated by P. A. Chilton. London: Routledge and Kegan Paul.

Piaget, Jean, and Bärbel Inhelder. (1941) 2000. *The Child's Contruction of Quantities*. Translated by Arnold J. Pomerans. New York: Routledge.

———. 1973. *Memory and Intelligence*. Translated by Arnold J. Pomerans. New York: Basic Books.

Ripple, Richard E., and Verne N. Rockcastle. 1964. *Piaget Rediscovered: Conference on Cognitive Studies and Curriculum Development*. Ithaca, NY: Cornell University Press.

Vidal, Fernando. 1994. *Piaget before Piaget*. Cambridge, MA: Harvard University Press.

11

Erik Erikson

1902–1994

In a variety of ways, the personal lives of the Giants contributed to their subsequent achievements. In the case of Erik Erikson, however, it was an abiding dynamic. The mystery of his birth was central to his formulation of *identity crises* as playing a critical role in human development. Erikson was different in other respects as well. He was the only Giant to do his major work in the United States rather than in Europe. Among the married Giants, he and Steiner were the only ones whose wives had their own careers and who collaborated with them in their work.

In one respect, however, Erikson was like most of the other Giants; he was nomadic. As a youth, he spent years traveling about Western Europe. During his career in the United States, he moved across the country several times but did not stay in one place more than ten years.

Of Danish decent, Erikson was born and grew up in Germany. Although he was a gifted artist, his lack of color sense, how to blend colors, limited his prospects in this domain. Thanks to a friend, he went to Vienna as a young man and became a member of the close-knit Freudian psychoanalytic community. His talents for working with young people were immediately apparent. This led to Anna Freud analyzing and training him and to him becoming one of the world's first male child analysts.

Although he published many articles, Erikson did not become nationally known until the publication of *Childhood and Society* in 1950. In that book, he went beyond Freud—as he had done in his clinical work—by emphasizing the daily, real-life events that contributed to psychological distress. The book also introduced his scheme for the eight psychosocial stages of human development. These stages are now widely taught in psychology, education, and sociology courses.

Of the stages that Erikson outlined, three of those stages take place in the first five or six years of life, which makes his work of particular relevance to early childhood education. Erikson's description of the psychosocial developmental of the preschool child is an essential complement to the emotional stages outlined by Freud and the intellectual stages introduced by Piaget. Together the three perspectives give us a panoramic description of the psychology of the young child.

The Man

In many ways, Erikson's achievements are linked to the places he lived and worked, and I use these as the chronological framework for his life.

The Early Years, 1902–1920

Karla Abrahamson came from a prominent Jewish family in Copenhagen. Her father, Joseph, was a successful dry goods merchant. Karla's mother, Henrietta Kalckar, died when Karla was fifteen. The family was active in the Jewish community and helped maintain a free soup kitchen for émigrés escaping the pogroms in Russia. When Joseph died in 1899, his oldest son, Axel, took over the business, and two of his younger sons became successful jewelers.

Karla, the only daughter, was regarded as the most beautiful of the Abrahamson women. She was brilliant and an intellectual who read and admired Søren Kierkegaard. Karla was also one of the few women of her generation to have attended the local gymnasium. In 1898 Karla, at age twenty-one, married Valdemar Isidor Salomonsen, a Jewish stockbroker. But the married couple did not spend more than a night together and the marriage was probably never consummated. It is said that Salomonsen confessed to Karla on their wedding night that he had engaged in fraud and other crimes and had to leave the country. He then disappeared.

Karla retained the Salomonsen surname for purposes of propriety. In 1902 Karla moved to Frankfurt, Germany, where she gave birth to Erik. There are many different versions of how she became pregnant (for example, with or without her knowledge) but it was clearly not by Salomonsen. If Karla knew who the father was, she refused to share this with her son, and finding out the identity of his unknown father became Eric's lifelong obsession.

After Erik's birth, Karla trained to become a nurse and moved to Karlsruhe, Germany. While in Karlsruhe, Karla learned that her husband, Salomonsen, had died shortly after Erik's birth. She was now free to marry again. Erik was a sickly child and was treated by pediatrician Theodor Homburger. Karla and Homburger fell in love and married when Erik was three. Erik accompanied them on their honeymoon. Karla later had two daughters, Ruth and Ellen, Erik's half sisters. Homburger adopted Erik, and he became Erik Homburger.

There was, however, a problem with this arrangement. Erik was blond, blue-eyed, and clearly Aryan in appearance. (He always believed his father came from the Danish nobility and had artistic talents.) It was soon obvious to Erik, as to everyone else, that he was not Homburger's child. This created issues because he was being reared as a Jew and was living in a Jewish community. At school, for example, the Jewish children called him goy while the Christian children called him Jew.

Erik attended the compulsory Vorschule (preparatory school) at age six and completed it at age nine. He then went to the Karlsruhe gymnasium on the academic track, which emphasized classical languages and literature, rather than the science and vocational tracks. Erik was an indifferent student who was frustrated that his gymnasium offered no outlets for his artistic gifts. He graduated at age eighteen and was awarded the Abitur, a certificate that was a necessary requirement for entering the university.

Wanderschaft, 1920–1927

After graduation Erik chose not to go to the university to study medicine as his stepfather wished. Rather, he began a nine-year *Wanderschaft* (a journey of self-discovery that Erik later called a moratorium, a time of trying out different identities) across Europe, taking art courses and earning a living by doing child portraits. He also secretly received money from his mother on return visits to Karlsruhe.

During his school years, Erik had only one close friend, Peter Blos. The two were drawn together not only because of common interests but also because Blos, as Erik assumed was true for himself, had a gentile father and a Jewish mother. Erik looked up to and admired Blos's father, who in some respects became a surrogate of Erik's unknown gentile parent.

Vienna, 1927–1933

In 1927 Erik received a letter from Blos, who had moved to Vienna. Peter was living with and tutoring the four children of Dorothy Burlingham, a Tiffany heiress whom Freud was analyzing. Burlingham was also close to Anna Freud, and the two were working together to create the new field of child psychoanalysis.

Together the women decided that they should open a school for children whose parents were being analyzed as well as for children who had emotional problems. They appointed Blos as headmaster of the new Hietzing school, and he recommended that Erik be hired as his assistant. Blos argued that although Erik had no teacher training, he was quite gifted. Erik moved to Vienna and began work at Blos's school. He also tutored Burlingham's children, who were very taken by him and his artwork.

Anna Freud learned of Erik's empathy with children and offered to analyze him for a low fee. It was a training analysis, not a therapeutic one, that was to prepare him to become a psychoanalyst. The analysis went on for three years. Because Erik had little formal training as a teacher, Anna Freud suggested that he get training in the Montessori method. Erik took the training and became a certified Montessori teacher. He felt that Montessori's approach was congenial with his own growing concern for stressing the social environment of child development.

During his years in Vienna, Erik came to know Sigmund Freud and even traveled with the Freud family on some of their vacations. It was a period during which Freud was beginning to deal with the adaptive, reality-testing processes of the ego and not just its mediating role between the id and superego. This orientation also appealed to Erik's concern with the adaptive self in human development. During this time, Erik was surrounded by many of the major figures in early psychoanalysis, such as Heinz Hartmann, August Aichhorn, Paul Federn, and Wilhelm Reich. Erik attended seminars, took classes at the university, and absorbed the intellectual ferment of that period. But he was also troubled by the unwillingness of the analysts to deal seriously with anything but the inner workings of the mind. In subtle ways, he suggested in his case presentations alternative interpretations to dreams and associations that tied them to immediate real-life events—to the outer life as well as the inner one.

In 1929 Erik met Joan Serson, a Canadian-born, American-trained student (at Barnard College), who came to Vienna while researching her doctoral dissertation on modern dance. She was a tall, attractive woman. Erik met her at a masked ball; the couple fell in love and began living together. In 1930 Joan became pregnant. They were married shortly after in three different ceremonies—Christian, Jewish, and civil. Joan was surprisingly well received by Erik's parents and stepsisters, perhaps because he was happy and now had a profession.

The marriage resulted in a tug of war for Erik's allegiance between two strong women. Joan was critical of the closed-mindedness of the Freudians and supported Erik's emphasis on life circumstance as the genesis of emotional problems. Anna Freud, on the other hand, made efforts to get Erik to focus on the inner life. After completing his analysis, Erik was accepted as a full member of the Vienna Psychoanalytic Society. This recognition gave him immediate entry in psychoanalytic societies anywhere in the world.

After his certification as a psychoanalyst, Erik and Joan moved to Denmark. In Denmark Erik hoped to set up a practice and to make contact with Karla's family and perhaps find out who his father really was. But the Danish authorities would not grant him citizenship. At the same time, Joan's mother was living in the United States and encouraged them to come to America. Hans Sachs, an analyst living in Boston, invited them to come to that city where, he promised, they would be well received and where Erik would be among the very few child analysts.

Boston and New Haven, 1933–1939

In 1933 Erik, Joan, and their two sons, Kai and Jon, moved to the United States. Erik spoke only a hundred or so words of English and had trepidations about his ability to make a living in this new country. Yet the Statue of Liberty and New York's skyscrapers impressed him, as did the warm welcome the immigration officers gave him.

The family moved to Boston, and Erik's therapeutic talents quickly gained him an excellent reputation. He was able to help patients who had made no improvement while being treated by better-trained and more-experienced analysts. Erik also helped the children of his colleagues and continued to do so throughout his career. He used very unorthodox methods. He made it a point, for example, to have dinner with the family of the child he was treating.

Equally unheard of was having adult patients join Erik and his family for a meal. In contrast to Freud, who did not like looking patients in the eyes, Erik felt he needed to have visual contact. It also turned out that learning English was not the problem Erik had feared. He learned the language quickly, partly from his patients but also with help from Joan. After a year, he was giving case presentations and lectures in English.

In addition to his private practice, Erik also consulted at the Judge Baker Children's Center and joined Henry Murray's Social Relations Group in the Psychology Department at Harvard, where he was given an assistantship. But Edward Boring, chairman of the psychology department, was bothered by Erik's lack of academic training and made it clear he had no future at Harvard.

Lawrence Frank, an executive of the Rockefeller Foundation that had supported Erik's assistantship at Harvard, was aware of Erik's problems with the school. He suggested that Erik move to New Haven, Connecticut, to join a presumably more hospitable group at the Institute of Human Relations at Yale. Frank negotiated a three-year grant to support Erik's work at the institute. So the family moved to New Haven in 1936.

Initially Erik was well received at the institute. But things did not work out as planned. He was excluded from Arnold Gesell's Clinic of Child Development, where he had hoped to do his research. In part, this exclusion was due to differences in scientific approach (Erik used qualitative methods and the clinic used quantitative ones). At Yale Erik once again came up against the experimental bias when Clark Hull, a leading behaviorist, undertook a program at the institute to unite behaviorism and psychoanalysis by using quantitative experiments. But Erik's exclusion, particularly on the part of the Gesell group, also had some anti-Semitic undercurrents, which raised conflicts in the academic community.

Nonetheless, Erik found more congenial colleagues elsewhere on the Yale campus, mainly in the Department of Anthropology. He felt much more at home with the anthropologists, who were, like himself, observers and classifiers rather than experimentalists. Erik was particularly impressed by social anthropologist Edward Sapir's attempt to integrate anthropological and psychoanalytic concepts.

Through Sapir, Erik met Margaret Mead. The two were mutually impressed with each other and became lifelong friends. The energetic Mead introduced him to the quieter and more retiring anthropologist Ruth Benedict, with whom he became friends as well. Erik's friendship with Mead gives additional credence to the fact that he felt comfortable in the company of strong women—not only Mead and Benedict but his wife and Anna Freud as well.

While at Harvard, Erik had met H. Scudder Mekeel, an anthropologist with some analytic training. In 1937 Erik accepted Mekeel's invitation to attend a summer institute at the Oglala Sioux reservation in Pine Ridge, South Dakota. Erik was impressed by the openness of Sioux child rearing and the mutuality of the community. But the Sioux were also the tribe that slew Custer and in turn were slaughtered in the Battle of Wounded Knee. Erik was well aware of this history, and it contributed to his understanding of how a proud people can be humiliated by a stronger power. This humiliation was aided and abetted by moving the tribe to a reservation. The visit to Pine Ridge added to Erik's conviction regarding the contribution of life circumstances to mental health. He wrote a paper on the Sioux, and it was later printed in his book *Childhood and Society*.

Berkeley, 1939–1950

The research and publication potential that Erik had hoped to realize at Yale never materialized. Marian Putnam, his research associate at Yale, had an alternative. Jean Walker MacFarlane, who was at the prestigious Institute of Child Welfare at the University of California, Berkeley, was beginning a longitudinal study of children. The Rockefeller Foundation supported it. Putnam recommended Erikson for a five-year grant to participate in the project. The arrangement gave him leeway to engage in other activities in addition to his work at the institute.

The family, now including daughter Sue, agreed to move to California. Before doing that, however, Erik applied for US citizenship and was granted it in 1939. In the process, he changed his name from Erik Homburger to Erik Homburger Erikson—later Erik H. Erikson and eventually Erik Erikson. His son Kai suggested the name change, which followed the Scandinavian tradition of naming the son after the father's given name—that is, Erikson, or "son of Erik." The change elated the two Homburger boys, who would no longer be called Hamburger by their peers.

By 1940 Erikson was spending most of his time seeing patients but took on other responsibilities as well. After the attack on Pearl Harbor in 1941, psychologists and psychiatrists were called on to help the war effort in various capacities. Psychologists ran the Office of Strategic Services (forerunner of the CIA) and were charged with evaluating new recruits. Hundreds of thousands of draftees were examined for any signs of mental illness that might preclude their ability to serve in the armed forces.

Erikson was called on to help understand the German psyche. He wrote a paper on Hitler's youth, which reflected how his personality and the time period interacted to make Nazism possible. His published paper on Hitler's adolescence was later included in *Childhood and Society*. Erikson also worked with returning veterans. He was impressed by the fact that men who were psychologically healthy when they went to war came back mentally and emotionally distressed.

In dealing with these men, Erikson rejected traditional psychiatric labels and instead began describing these men as suffering from *identity confusion*. They had been taken from their jobs, their homes, and their families and were required to bear arms and kill other men. He regarded this disruption of their sense of self and identity as the problem. Erikson advised therapists that they could best help the veterans and their families by encouraging them to resume normal activities as soon as possible.

This work further contributed to Erikson's belief in the importance of the social-environmental configuration on human development and on emotional well-being. Additional support came from his visits to the salmon-fishing Yurok American Indian tribe of Northern California. Although quite different than the Sioux, the Yurok, too, had a culture that was quite at variance with the surrounding American society. They, too, Erikson believed, suffered the identity-confusion consequences of being marginalized.

After the war, Erikson was fully engaged in his private practice, serving as a training analyst, and teaching occasionally at University of California, Berkeley. In 1949 Donald Mackinnon, a Berkeley psychology professor, set up the Institute of Personality Assessment and Research (IPAR), which became an affiliate of the Department of Psychology at UC Berkeley. IPAR was modeled after Murray's Department of Social Relations at Harvard. Mackinnon had worked with Erikson and wanted to appoint him a member of IPAR.

With strong support from the Rockefeller Foundation, Erikson was appointed full professor of psychology and a lecturer in psychiatry. But the personal gratification of that appointment was soon all but erased by the rise of McCarthyism, the nationwide search to identify, punish, and ostracize those found to have Communist leanings or associations. In 1950 a loyalty oath was made part of the annual contract each UC Berkeley faculty member had to sign to continue his or her employment. If a faculty member did not sign, he or she had to appear before a committee and explain the refusal. Erikson wrote a powerful letter explaining his position against the loyalty oath, refused to sign the oath, and resigned his professorship on June 30, 1950. One of his reasons was that it was too similar to what some of his extended family had experienced during the Nazi era in Europe.

This was also the year *Childhood and Society* was published. It was a two-part compilation. The first section included some of his clinical casework papers and his previously published studies of the Sioux and Yurok. In the second section, he republished his theoretical accounts of the lives of Hitler and Maxim Gorky (which he used to bolster his concepts of ego identity and identity crises). Most important, in this book he also introduced his model of the eight stages of human development. Although the book did not do well at first, it became a best seller on campuses once it came out in paperback.

Stockbridge, 1950–1960

In 1948 psychiatrist Robert White of the Menninger Foundation had accepted an offer to become head of the Austen Riggs Center in western Massachusetts. The Austen Riggs Center was a residential treatment facility for well-to-do patients. White took with him a group of psychologists and psychiatrists, among them Freudian scholar David Rapaport. White had long been impressed with Erikson and wanted to bring him to Riggs as well. To entice Erikson, he said the position would allow him to consult on a regular basis at Benjamin Spock's Arsenal Nursery School at the University of Pittsburgh. Spock and Erikson had worked together before and had become friends. White also arranged for Erikson to be appointed visiting professor at the University of Pittsburgh.

Erikson accepted the position and the family moved to Stockbridge, Massachusetts. At Riggs, Erikson saw patients, attended case conferences, and became close friends with Rapaport, who tried to build bridges between Erikson's sociohistorical emphasis and traditional psychoanalysis.

With Erikson's arrival, Riggs began to cater to adolescents and young adults rather than older patients. This gave Erikson an opportunity to work with young people suffering from identity issues. He was particularly interested in how identity issues affected major historical events, and he became focused on Martin Luther as a paradigm for the role identity crises in individual and social change. From 1956 to 1957, he took a sabbatical from Riggs to write *Young Man Luther*.

During Erikson's sabbatical, I had a postdoctoral fellowship from the National Institute of Health and became Rapaport's research assistant. Erikson was away writing *Young Man Luther*, but he did return on several occasions, and I had the opportunity to meet him and sit in on a few of his case conferences. At each conference, he listened carefully to the presentation and then gave very unexpected and insightful interpretations and helpful suggestions to the therapist.

In 1958 Erikson published *Young Man Luther*, in which he depicted Luther's rebellion against the Roman Catholic Church as his way of resolving his personal identity crisis. He also argued that Reformation was the seminal factor in Renaissance thinking. The book met with mixed reviews. Some religious leaders found it at variance with historical research on both Luther and the Renaissance. Erikson's friends suggested that the book had to be looked at as a challenge to traditional psychoanalytic thinking.

Erikson, however, did not see himself as neo-Freudian but rather as extending traditional psychoanalysis beyond the limits Freud had set—from the inner to the outer and from childhood to the whole life cycle. At Riggs, Erikson began to lose interest in clinical work and felt the need to teach, write, and be in the company of more scholars than were available at Riggs. So Erikson told his friends at Harvard that he would be open to a position there and encouraged them to do what they could in that regard.

Cambridge, 1960–1970

Erikson's friends at Harvard—including David Reisman, Talcott Parsons, and Henry Murray—came together and approached McGeorge Bundy, then dean of Harvard, to find an endowed professorship for Erikson. Endowed professorships were one way the administration could bypass often-biased university departments to hire people with cross-disciplinary interests. An endowed professorship for Erikson was set up with money from the Field Foundation and other donors. It was a very liberal arrangement. Erikson was to teach two courses: a large undergraduate course (Social Science 139) and a graduate seminar. He was allowed a sabbatical at the end of every second year, as opposed to the usual six for most faculty members. During his tenure at Harvard, he also gained grants to spend time in India when he began work on *Gandhi's Truth*.

During his early years at Harvard, Erikson became increasingly interested in the life of Gandhi. He was now personally moving beyond the identity crises of youth to the midlife crises of generativity (the stage at which individuals see themselves as having responsibility for the welfare of succeeding generations). He gained grants to spend time in India and began traveling to the country in 1962. Like Montessori, he fell in love with the people and the culture, if not with the food and the poverty. In his research on Gandhi, Erikson was troubled by the contradiction between Gandhi's personal cruelty and his public image of sympathy and caring. He resolved this issue by including in the book a personal letter to Gandhi addressing this discrepancy between public and private behavior.

Gandhi's Truth: On the Origins of Militant Nonviolence was published in 1969 and met with immediate critical success. It won the Pulitzer Prize for nonfiction and the National Book Award in philosophy and religion. The *New York Times Book Review* listed it among the twelve best books of 1969. Despite the accolades, the book did not do as well as the publisher and Erikson had hoped. Perhaps this was due, in part, to the fact that there was not a lot of US interest in India in general and Gandhi in particular.

During his years at Harvard, Erikson also published *Insight and Responsibility* (1964) and *Identity, Youth, and Crisis* (1968), each elaborating on his themes of the challenges posed to youth by social change and the need for generativity in midlife. In 1970 Erikson turned sixty-eight, the mandatory retirement age for Harvard professors. He was now free to spend his full time on consulting and writing.

California, 1970–1988

After Erik left Harvard in 1970, he and Joan decided to move back to California to escape the harsh New England winters. They purchased a home in Tiburon overlooking San Francisco Bay. But they often retuned to Cotuit for the summer and reunions with the family. After leaving Harvard, Erikson was given many honorary doctorates, including those from Harvard, Yale, and Berkeley. He also received a great many other prestigious nonacademic honors. And he still maintained a full schedule of writing, consulting, and meeting with scholars. But he and Joan also enjoyed swimming, dancing, and socializing with friends.

Erikson continued to give invited lectures, which appeared as books, including *Dimensions of a New Identity* (1974) and *Toys and Reasons* (1977). As he aged, Erikson became increasingly interested in his last stage of integrity versus despair, and he tried to articulate it as he experienced it. These considerations resulted in his last book, *The Life Cycle Completed* (1982).

Cambridge and Harwich, 1988–1994

In the late 1980s and early 1990s, Erikson had health problems and grew more infirm. Although weakened, he continued to meet with friends and help them with their writing. In the late 1980s, the Eriksons moved to Cambridge, where Joan had hoped to have more help in caring for him. It didn't work out as planned, and eventually Joan purchased a small house in Harwich, a charming village on Cape Cod, where she could care for him on her own. He died in Harwich on May 12, 1994. A ceremony in his honor was held in Harwich and attended by friends, colleagues, students, and former patients from all over the country.

Commemorative services were also held all over the United States and abroad. Erikson was buried in Harwich. Joan, who worked closely with Erik and who edited all of his books, continued working and writing and introduced her own conception of the last stage of life. Some falls and infections led to her decline. She died in 1997 and was buried next to her husband of sixty-two years.

The Work

For the purposes of this book, I will only summarize Erikson's first three stages of psychosocial development, which deal with the early childhood years.

Infancy: Trust vs. Mistrust

According to Erikson, the first dimension of social interaction emerges during infancy (the Freudian oral stage) and involves basic trust at the one extreme and mistrust at the other. The degree to which a child comes to trust the world, other people, and herself depends to a considerable extent on the quality of the care she receives. The infant whose needs are met when they arise, whose discomforts are quickly removed, and who is cuddled, fondled, played with, and talked to develops a sense of the world as a safe place and of people as helpful and dependable. When, however, the care is inconsistent, inadequate, and rejecting, it fosters a basic mistrust. Mistrusting experiences can support an attitude of fear and suspicion on the part of the infant toward the world in general and people in particular that will persist through later stages of development.

It should be said at this point that the basic problem of trust versus mistrust (and all the stages) is not resolved once and for all during the first year of life; it arises again at each successive stage of development. There is both hope and danger in this. The child who enters school with a sense of mistrust may come to trust a particular teacher who has taken the trouble to make himself trustworthy. With this second chance, the child can overcome the early mistrust. On the other hand, the child who comes through infancy with a vital sense of trust can still have his sense of mistrust activated at a later stage—if, say, his parents are divorced and separated under acrimonious circumstances.

Toddlerhood: Autonomy vs. Shame and Doubt

Stage two spans the second and third years of life (the anal stage in the Freudian scheme). Erikson describes the emergence of autonomy during this period. This autonomy dimension builds on the child's new motor and mental abilities. At this stage the child can walk and climb, open and close, push and pull, and hold and let go. The child takes pride in these new accomplishments and wants to do everything for herself. This includes pulling the wrapper off a piece of candy, selecting the vitamin out of the bottle, or flushing the toilet. If parents recognize the young child's need to do what she is capable of doing at her own pace and time, then the child develops a sense of being in control of muscles, impulses, self, and, not insignificantly, her environment. This self-mastery is what Erikson means by the sense of autonomy. This stage clearly reflects Erikson's Montessori training and his emphasis on spontaneity and freedom.

When, however, caretakers are impatient and do for the child what the child is capable of doing for himself, they reinforce a sense of shame and doubt. To be sure, every parent has rushed a child at times, and children are hardy enough to endure such lapses. It is only when caretaking is consistently overprotective and criticism is harsh and unthinking that the child develops an excessive sense of shame with respect to other people and an excessive sense of doubt about his own abilities to control himself and his world.

A child who moves through this stage with a sense of autonomy buoyantly outbalancing his feelings of shame and doubt is well prepared to be autonomous at later phases in the life cycle. In contrast, a child who leaves this stage with less autonomy than shame or doubt will be handicapped in her attempts to achieve autonomy in adolescence and adulthood. Again, however, the balance of autonomy to shame and doubt set up during this period can be changed in either positive or negative directions by later events.

Early Childhood: Initiative vs. Guilt

At this stage (the genital stage of classical psychoanalysis), the child, age three to five, is pretty much master of her body and can ride a tricycle, run, cut, and hit. The child can thus initiate motor activities of various sorts on her own and no longer merely respond to or imitate the actions of other children. The same holds true for the child's language and fantasy activities. Erikson argues that the social dimension that appears at this stage has initiative at one of its poles and guilt at the other.

Whether a child will leave this stage with his sense of initiative outbalancing his sense of guilt depends to a considerable extent on how parents respond to the child's self-initiated activities. A child who is given the freedom and opportunity to initiate motor play—such as running, bike riding, sliding, skating, tussling, and wrestling—has his sense of initiative reinforced. Initiative is also reinforced when parents answer the child's questions (intellectual initiative) and do not deride or inhibit fantasy or play activity.

On the other hand, if a child is made to feel that her motor activity is always noisy and disruptive, that posing questions is a nuisance, and that her play is silly and stupid, then she may develop a sense of guilt over self-initiated activities that will persist through later life stages.

All of these stages have relevance for early childhood teaching and curriculum. Equally important was Erikson's concern for sociocultural variations of parental behaviors such as manners and prejudices, and the unconscious attitudes these practices instill.

Common Themes

The Nature of the Child

The prolonged childhood is what Erikson regards as distinctive about children's nature.

> It is human to have a long childhood; it is civilized to have an ever longer childhood. Long childhood makes a technical and mental virtuoso out of man, but it also leaves a lifelong residue of emotional immaturity in him. (Erikson 1950, 17)

The Aims of Education

It is only a seeming paradox that newly born Man, who could, in principle and probably within some genetic limits, fit into any number of pseudo-species and their habitats, must for that very reason be coaxed and induced to become "speciated" during a prolonged childhood by some form of family: he must be familiarized by ritualization with a particular version of human existence. (Erikson 1977, 79)

The Role of Play

Like Freud, Erikson regards play as a creative activity that in adulthood gives rise to the arts.

Thus, wherever playfulness prevails, there is always a surprising element, surpassing mere repetition or habituation, and at its best suggesting some virgin chance conquered, some divine leeway shared. (Erikson 1977, 17)

Conformance with DAP Principles

NAEYC
Many aspects of children's development and learning follow well documented sequences, with later abilities, skills, and knowledge building on those already acquired.

ERIKSON
Each critical item of psychosocial strength [the eight stages of man] discussed here is systematically related to all others, and that they all depend on the proper development in the proper sequence of each item. (Erikson 1950, 271)

NAEYC
Development and learning proceed at varying rates from child to child, as well as at uneven rates across different areas of a child's individual functioning.

ERIKSON
Ben [Rogers, in *Tom Sawyer*] is a growing boy. To grow means to be divided into different parts which move at different rates. A growing boy has trouble in mastering his gangling body as well as his divided mind. (Erikson 1950, 211)

Commentary

Erikson is unique among the Giants in that he focused on development across the whole life cycle. His stages of psychosocial development complement the stages of both Freud and Piaget, and their three stages combined give a comprehensive picture of early childhood development. It was a positive picture inasmuch as he saw negative experiences at one stage capable of being remediated at a later one. But he recognized that the reverse was also true and that a good beginning could be undone by later experiences. Like Vygotsky, he emphasized the role of society, but in the realm of personality formation rather than in the domain of higher mental processes. What comes through Erikson's writing in general and his stages in particular is a positive, hopeful sense of the human condition while acknowledging the negative potential of humanness.

References

Coles, R. 1970. *Erik H. Erikson*. Boston: Little, Brown.

Erikson, Erik. 1950. *Childhood and Society*. New York: Norton.

———. 1958. *Young Man Luther*. New York: Norton.

———. 1964. *Insight and Responsiblity*. New York: Norton.

———. 1968. *Identity, Youth, and Crisis*. New York: Norton.

———. 1969. *Gandhi's Truth: On the Origins of Militant Nonviolence*. New York: Norton.

———. 1974. *Dimensions of a New Identity: Jefferson Lectures on Humanity*. New York: Norton.

———. 1977. *Toys and Reasons: Stages in the Ritualization of Experience*. New York: Norton.

———. 1982. *The Life Cycle Completed*. New York: Norton.

Friedman, Lawrence J. 1999. *Identity's Architect: A Biography of Erik H. Erikson*. New York: Scribner.

12

Lev Semenovich Vygotsky

1896–1934

Russian psychologist Lev Semenovich Vygotsky provides a fascinating counterpoint to the basic assumptions of the Giants. Broadly speaking, he was a potential, rather than a true, Giant of early childhood. Vygotsky did not live long enough to fully articulate his innovative theories and to support them with a substantial body of research. Nonetheless, Vygotsky's emphasis on the impact of culture and society on human development provides an important alternative to the nature-nurture emphasis of many of the Giants.

Vygotsky was a cultural psychologist committed to a "psychological theory in which the human being is the subject of cultural, rather than natural, processes" (Kozulin 1990, 1). With this commitment, Vygotsky built on the then-prevailing Western sociological and anthropological theories and also on the Marxist philosophy of sociocultural economic and historical determinism. From Vygotsky's sociocultural perspective, there is no significant human nature; rather, the individual is entirely shaped by the culture and society in which he is reared.

Most of the other Giants viewed the formation of mental abilities at all age levels as simply a part of the natural maturing process, regardless of social environment. Vygotsky's commitment to the sociocultural origins of the higher mental processes puts his views sharply at odds with many of the other Giants.

Vygotsky's Sociohistorical Context

Vygotsky believed that a thinker could be fully understood only in the context of the historical, cultural, and social context in which she lived and worked. And this

195

is certainly true of Vygotsky himself. Accordingly, a little background on the Russian society and culture in which Vygotsky matured will not explain his genius, but it will perhaps account for the particular direction it took and the ways in which it was realized.

Vygotsky was born in 1896, the same year as Piaget. The prerevolutionary environment of Russia was, however, a far different one from the Swiss sociocultural climate. Piaget grew up in Switzerland, which had been established as a democratic confederacy in some form since 1815 and was an accepted and prosperous country of armed neutrality in Western Europe. In contrast, Russia, at the time Vygotsky was reaching maturity, was still ruled by the Romanoff royal family and its cruel, authoritarian laws and prohibitions. Vygotsky grew up as a member of a despised Jewish minority, while Piaget was reared as a member of the elite social class. Not surprisingly, while Piaget regarded himself as an evolutionist, Vygotsky saw himself as a revolutionary.

Both men lived at a time when the social sciences finally broke from philosophy and strove to establish their disciplines as legitimate fields of study. The dominant ideology of the time was an environmental approach to psychology with the belief that, with the exception of a few basic instincts, all human behavior was learned. Psychologists such as Ivan Pavlov (1927) and John Watson (1930), anthropologists such as Franz Boas (1911), and sociologists such as Emile Durkheim (1982) and George Herbert Mead (1934) espoused this view. Environmentalism reinforced Vygotsky's sociocultural perspective, but it was a position that Piaget sought to disprove.

Vygotsky was influenced not only by the social science of his day but also by the arts and literature of his native country. Although Russia was far behind Western Europe with respect to democratization and industrialization, it was not intellectually or artistically isolated. Indeed, Russia experienced the same turn of the century intellectual and artistic ferment and experimentation that enriched the West. Among the contemporaries of Vygotsky were writers Maksim Gorky and Vladimir Nabokov; poet Boris Pasternak; composers Sergey Prokofiev, Igor Stravinsky, and Dmitry Shostakovich; painters Marc Chagall and Wassily Kandinsky; film innovator Sergey Eisenstein; and famed stage director Konstantin Stanislavsky. Vygotsky knew some of these individuals personally and absorbed much of their cultural creativity.

Prerevolution Russia was thus a contradictory society of ruthless cultural, religious, and racial prejudice on the one hand and of intellectual and artistic freedom on the other. This contradiction had its parallels in the psychologies of that time. The Freudian emphasis on biological drives was opposed by the environmental emphasis of the behaviorists like John Watson. A comparable discrepancy existed between reductionists like Wilhelm Wundt, who emphasized an individual's reaction times to sensory stimulation, and holistic Gestalt theorists like Wolfgang Köhler, who insisted that the whole of something is greater than the sum of its parts. These and similar "crises" in psychology were some of the forces that drove Vygotsky to formulate his own theory of human thought and action.

The Man

The Early Years, 1896–1913

Lev Semenovich Vygotsky was born in the town of Orsha located in southeastern Russian (now Belarus). He was the second of eight children of a middle-income Jewish family. Vygotsky's father held a number of managerial positions in insurance and other companies. His mother was recalled as a warm, intelligent woman with a love for literature, which she passed on to her son. The family was financially comfortable and contributed to the cultural life of the town. While Vygotsky was still a boy, the family moved to Gomel, the second-largest city in what is now Belarus.

When Vygotsky was eight years old, the Jewish sector of Gomel was the target of a pogrom. Men on horseback rode through the town pillaging, injuring, killing, and destroying. At that time, pogroms were an unrelieved threat to the Jewish settlements in the outback of the Russian Empire. Unlike the citizens of other communities, however, the Gomel townspeople fought back and repelled the onslaught. Later the citizens who had resisted the raid were put on trial for injuring some of the attackers, and Vygotsky's father courageously agreed to speak in defense of those individuals who had stood up for themselves.

For Vygotsky, it was his first direct experience of the anti-Semitism he would encounter later during his efforts to gain entrance into the university. But his father's valiant stance also provided him with a model of challenging established authority—whether it was political or scientific. Aside from this experience, Vygotsky's childhood was relatively uneventful. He was regarded as a precocious boy and was privately tutored. After his bar mitzvah in 1909, Vygotsky entered the Jewish gymnasium, or high school, in Gomel. While at the gymnasium, Vygotsky was primarily interested in the humanities and was particularly passionate about Russian poetry and prose. He especially admired the writings of Aleksandr Pushkin and Pasternak. Fyodor Dostoyevsky's novels and Russian translations of Shakespeare's plays also captivated him.

During the gymnasium years, Vygotsky also joined a discussion group that brought together Jewish students who were interested in Jewish history and culture. Before World War I, Zionism was a heated topic of discussion in many of the Jewish communities in the Russian rural areas. Its popularity reflected the longing to escape the dreaded pogroms and the anti-Semitic governmental restrictions. One of the reasons Vygotsky later found Marxism appealing was its promise to do away with sexual, racist, and religious discrimination.

Youth, 1913–1924

Vygotsky graduated from gymnasium in 1913, winning a gold medal for his scholarship. He had long harbored the hope of attending Moscow University. There was, however, a quota system that severely limited the number of Jewish students accepted each year; despite that, Vygotsky expected his high grades and strong recommendations would win him acceptance. This expectation was dashed when he learned that acceptance would not be decided on the basis of merit but by a lottery system. Fortunately, Vygotsky was one of the winners of the lottery and was accepted at the university.

But acceptance also presented its own problems. Vygotsky's interests were clearly in the humanities, so it would have made sense for him to work toward a liberal arts degree. But with such a degree, his only job opportunities as a Russian Jew were teaching at one of the few Jewish gymnasium schools. His other options were medicine and law. With a professional degree, he could practice outside the limits set for Jewish teachers. So Vygotsky, after some consideration of becoming a doctor, enrolled in law school.

At the same time, he also took courses at the Shanyavsky Public University, majoring in philosophy and history. Shanyavsky was relatively intellectually free in comparison with the heavily state-controlled Moscow University. At Shanyavsky, Vygotsky was surrounded by the controversy between the archaists, who were dedicated to the established canons in literature and the arts, and the innovators, who were dedicated to change and breaking the bonds of tradition. This dichotomy later figured in his own choice to approach psychology as an innovator rather than an archaist.

Vygotsky's interest in the humanities was apparent even as he was pursuing his law degree. While still a student, Vygotsky published book reviews and literary criticism. He wrote on Jewish questions, experimental literature, and new trends in the theater. These interests, however, had to be put in abeyance when he graduated in 1917. To earn a living, he returned to Gomel and took a teaching position in a non-Jewish gymnasium, a job made possible by the elimination of discriminatory laws after the 1917 revolution.

From 1917 to 1924, Vygotsky taught literature and psychology to gymnasium students in Gomel. He also directed the theater section of the adult education center and gave many lectures to the community on topics ranging from literature to science. Vygotsky also created the literary journal *Verask*, in which he published many of his own articles that would eventually come together as his PhD thesis and then his book *The Psychology of Art* (1971). He pursued his educational interests by opening a psychological laboratory in the Teacher Training Institute. At the institute, he taught a course in psychology, the lectures for which were the basis for his book *Pedagogical Psychology* (1926). While in Gomel, Vygotsky also met Rosa Smekhova and married her in 1924.

A Brief Professional Life: Moscow, 1924–1934

In 1924 Vygotsky and Rosa moved to Moscow, where he expanded his range of activities. Although never trained as a psychologist, Vygotsky took a position at the Institute of Psychology and then moved to the Institute of Defectology—an institute that he himself created. He also directed a department for the education of children who were physically defective and intellectually disabled. Charged with ameliorating these disabilities, Vygotsky helped devise new methods of assessment and remediation that would counter the societal conditions that, from a sociocultural perspective, gave rise to these disorders.

Vygotsky first came to widespread attention of the Russian psychological community when he gave an address at the second all-Russian Psycho-neurological Congress in Leningrad in 1924. His thesis in that lecture, and one that he would pursue throughout his career, was that human consciousness, particularly the higher levels of consciousness, could not be ignored as they were by the reductionist and holistic psychologies of his day. In arguing for the study of higher mental processes, Vygotsky—like his contemporary Piaget—was anticipating the cognitive revolution in psychology that came about in the 1960s.

With his presentation, Vygotsky put himself in direct opposition to both the reductionists, who were concerned with relegating thought and action to sensations and reflexes, and the holistic Gestalt psychologists, who were concerned mainly with perception and problem solving. Although Vygotsky did not win many adherents with his arguments, he did catch the attention of Alexander Luria, then secretary of the Moscow Institute of Psychology. Luria invited Vygotsky to join their research group. Once established at the institute, Vygotsky attracted a small group of devoted colleagues, including Luria, Aleksei Leontiev, and students who worked as a team with him on a number of different projects. These projects included studies of psychology, reflexology, and mental abnormality. Vygotsky's close collaboration with his students and coworkers sometimes makes it difficult to determine who did what. But it is generally accepted that Vygotsky was the group's conceptual and theoretical leader as well as its innovator and motivator.

Over the next ten years, Vygotsky maintained a fiercely demanding schedule of lecturing, teaching, experimenting, and writing. Much of his writing was done while living in a one-room apartment with his wife and two daughters. In addition to all his many professional responsibilities, he also took on heavy editorial work to support his family. It is truly miraculous that he could have written his six books and hundreds of articles under these conditions. His accomplishments appear even more miraculous considering that he suffered from tuberculosis for the last twelve years of his life and was in and out of the hospital or bedridden a great deal of the time. One can only admire and stand in awe of such effort and dedication.

Because it was recognized that Vygotsky might die at any time, he and his coworkers tried to lay the groundwork for the fields in which a sociocultural theory could be applied and expanded. The sense of urgency helps explain why Vygotsky's own writing was often hurried, obscure, and difficult to follow. It also helps account for the often schematic and anecdotal reporting of his and his coworkers' research studies.

During this period of frenetic activity (1924–1934), there was considerable intellectual freedom in Russia. Vygotsky and his group of coworkers notably had access to foreign literature, and they themselves were able to publish their work without censorship. Vygotsky's own theories changed and grew during this period, but the development of his thinking is difficult to document because the availability and publication of his work did not follow any apparent chronological order. Vygotsky had laid out a plan of lifelong research similar to that of Piaget. However, he was never able to complete it, as he died of tuberculosis on June 11, 1934, at age thirty-seven. His devoted and committed colleagues and students published much of his work after his death.

In the 1930s, Joseph Stalin sought to secure his power by ruthlessly eliminating his enemies. As part of this purge, he instituted strict political control over Russian science. Many scientists were not only discredited but also sent to Siberia or tried and executed. Vygotsky had been spared that fate, but after his death, his books and writings were banned from Russian libraries and his work put down as anticommunist. His contributions to education, and the understanding of intellectual disabilities and mental illness, and mental illness remediation, were discredited and no longer followed.

It was only after the death of Stalin in 1953 and the gradual establishment of a more liberal government that Vygotsky and his work became acceptable in Russia once again. Many of his articles and books were published or republished, and his theories came to influence not only Russian psychology but also Russian education and work with the intellectually disabled and mentally ill. The cognitive revolution in American psychology in the 1960s helped bring the work of both Vygotsky and Piaget into the mainstream of American psychological research and theory.

The Work

The extreme conditions under which Vygotsky lived and worked—living in cramped quarters, carrying a tremendous workload alongside family responsibilities, and knowing that he might die at any time—make it understandable that his written works pose a real challenge to his interpreters. Vera John-Steiner, Michael Cole, Ellen Souberman, and Sylvia Scribner, the editors and foremost promoters of his work in the United States, write in their preface to *Mind in Society: The Development of Higher Psychological Processes* (Vygotsky 1978):

> Vygotsky's style is extremely difficult. He wrote copiously and many of his manuscripts have never been properly edited. In addition, during frequent bouts of illness he would dictate his papers—a practice which resulted in repetitions and dense or elliptical prose. Gaps in the original manuscripts make them even less accessible now than they might have been at the time they were written.

In the United States, Vygotsky's work is perhaps best known through his books *Thought and Language* (1967) and *Mind in Society* (1978). These books present much of Vygotsky's sociocultural, historical theory as well as brief descriptions of some of the research studies he offers in support of his propositions. For the purposes of the present book, I briefly summarize some of the basic tenets of Vygotsky's theory and a few examples of the supporting research given in those two books.

Mental Tools

For Vygotsky, tools are the cultural instruments, such as memory aids, language, mathematics, and the example of other individuals, that eventually become the higher-level mental processes. These tools differ from one society to another and hence explain social and cultural differences.

Internalization

Vygotsky's central point, and the one that puts him apart from the other Giants, is his argument that the sociocultural tools, which were once external, become internalized mediators of the higher-order mental processes. For example, he contends that the language of young children becomes progressively internalized as mental thought processes—they no longer speak aloud as they accomplish a task, but they still have similar internal thoughts. Likewise, after a certain age, a child who once solved a finger maze manually can solve the problem mentally without actually touching the maze. In short, it is through language and other symbol systems like mathematics that society and culture give rise to higher-level thinking processes.

Mediation

Vygotsky's basic proposition is that the higher-order mental processes, such as reasoning, concept formation, attention, and memory, are derived from culture and society rather than from inborn biological processes. To explain this idea, Vygotsky used an example from Pavlov's conditioning experiments. *Mediation* is the difference between a simple stimulus response connection (stimulus→response) and one that includes an intermediary, in this case, the organism (stimulus→organism→response). Mediation covers all the processes that operate between the stimulus and the response. These processes are initially external, like language, but become internalized parts of the organism in the course of development. Put differently, as a result of the internalization of tools, the individual no longer acts directly on the environment. Rather, all her interactions are mediated by the mental tools taken from the culture and society.

Learning and Development

Vygotsky distinguishes between learning and development. He regards development as all the biologically linked spontaneous achievements of the child. Learning has to do with all the achievements due to culture and society.

To make this distinction concrete, he uses the example of the intelligence test, which he argues measures development. Two children may attain the same IQ but with adult assistance may raise their IQs considerably but to different extents.

The difference between what a child acquires on his own and what he achieves with the aid of social tools is the zone of proximal development (ZPD). From Vygotsky's perspective, a child cannot attain full adult mentality without the aid of sociocultural learning.

Unfortunately, Vygotsky did not live long enough to fully articulate and experimentally prove or modify his position. For example, in *Thought and Language* (1967), he takes issue with Piaget's first model of mental development that moves from egocentrism (failure to take the other person's point of view) to sociocentrism (the ability to see another's perspective). Vygotsky argues that just the reverse is true and that language develops from sociocentrism to egocentrism.

In Piaget's commentary (1962) on Vygotsky's book (which he had first read long after Vygotsky's death), Piaget says that while there are many points on which he agreed with Vygotsky, Vygotsky misunderstood egocentrism. Vygotsky took the word to mean self-centered thinking. Piaget pointed out that he only meant the child was unable to differentiate between his point of view and that of others—that is what accounted for the self-centeredness of the young child. It is not necessary to go into Piaget's response in detail. It suffices to state that Piaget deeply regretted not having met Vygotsky and having the opportunity to discuss the points of disagreement.

It really is unfortunate that Piaget and Vygotsky never met; in many ways the aims of Vygotsky's proposed research paralleled those of Piaget. Vygotsky was an open-minded scientist and his theories were complicated and deeply rooted in philosophy, history, and the social sciences. Had he lived and not been constrained by Stalin's brutal attack on what Stalin regarded as capitalistic science, Vygotsky might well have brought his theories into line with more contemporary research and theory.

Common Themes

The Nature of the Child

> The internalization of socially rooted and historically developed activities is the distinguishing feature of human psychology, the basis of the qualitative leap from animal to human psychology. (Vygotsky 1978, 57)

The Aims of Education

For Vygotsky, the aim of education is to take mental development beyond what would be realized by maturation alone.

> To implant [something] in the child . . . is impossible. . . . It is only possible to train him for some external activity like, for example, writing on a typewriter. To create the zone of proximal development, that is, to engender a series of processes of internal development we need the correctly constructed processes of school teaching. (van derVeer and Valsiner 1991, 331)

The Role of Play

Vygotsky said that there is " no such thing as play without rules" (Vygotsky 1978, 94). He regarded make-believe play as having three major components: creation of an imaginary situation, taking on and acting out rules, and following a specific set of rules determined by specific social roles (Vygotsky 1978).

> Thus, in establishing criteria for distinguishing a child's play from other forms of activity, we conclude that in play a child creates an imaginary situation. (Vygotsky 1978, 93)

Conformance with DAP Principles

NAEYC
Development and learning advance when children are challenged to achieve at a level just beyond their current mastery, and also when they have many opportunities to practice newly acquired skills.

VYGOTSKY

The zone of proximal development . . . is the distance between the actual developmental level as determined by independent problem solving and the level of potential development as determined through problem solving under adult guidance or in collaboration with more capable peers. (Vygotsky 1978, 86)

NAEYC

Play is an important vehicle for developing self regulation as well as for promoting language, cognition and social competence.

VYGOTSKY

In this way a child's greatest achievements are possible in play, achievements that tomorrow will become her basic level of real action and morality. (Vygotsky 1978, 100)

Commentary

Vygotsky is unique among the Giants for his insistence on the all-important role that culture and society play in the attainment of higher-level mental processes. He is therefore one of the major influences, together with Erikson, to have brought these variables to the forefront of contemporary psychological and educational theory and research. While the higher-level mental processes are not as free of biological constraints as Vygotsky argued (recent research shows that the prefrontal cortex develops in adolescence and can account for some typical adolescent behavior), he has helped to give sociocultural factors the important recognition they deserve.

References

Kozulin, Alex. 1990. *Vygotsky's Psychology: A Biography of Ideas*. Cambridge, MA: Harvard University Press.

Piaget, Jean. 1962. *Comment on Vygotsky's Critical Remarks Concerning the Language and Thought of the Child, and Judgment and Reasoning in the Child*. Cambridge, MA: Massachusetts Institute of Technology Press.

van der Veer, René, and Jaan Valsiner. 1991. *Understanding Vygotsky: A Quest for Synthesis*. Cambridge, MA: Blackwell.

Vygotsky, Lev. 1926. *Pedagogical Psychology*. Translated by Robert Silverman. Boca Raton, FL: St. Lucie.

————. 1967. *Thought and Language*. Cambridge, MA: Massachusetts Institute of Technology.

————. 1971. *The Psychology of Art*. Translated by Scripta Technica. Cambridge, MA: Massachusetts Institute of Technology Press.

————. 1978. *Mind in Society: The Development of Higher Psychological Processes*. Cambridge, MA: Harvard University Press.

13

The Evolution of Developmentally Appropriate Practice

The preceding chapters followed the evolution of DAP from its beginnings in philosophy to its implementation in practice and then to its grounding in scientific research and theory. This chapter compares and contrasts all the Giants from three perspectives. The first section describes the personality traits of the Giants that contributed to their extraordinary achievements. The next section briefly reviews the original ways of understanding experience and learning that each of the Giants contributed to early childhood educational practice. The concluding section presents each Giant's unique perspectives on the nature of the child, the aims of education and play. The diversity of their approaches and answers to these questions provides a rich and comprehensive picture of the growing child and of his learning potential.

Personalities of the Giants

The Giants were a product of eras and places where they lived as well as of their personal talents and histories. Yet each one was able, in one way or another, to rise above the prejudices and accepted wisdom of his or her times and contemporaries. In so doing, each was able to offer fresh insights into both the nature and the nurture of the young child.

Dedication to an Idea

One of the most striking traits common to these singular individuals was that each was devoted to an idea—to its promotion and implementation—that became an all-consuming driving force that continued unabated until his or her death:

- For Comenius the propelling idea was *a universal educational method and curriculum* extending from infancy to early adulthood, as he wrote about in *The Great Didactic*. The curriculum was intended for girls as well as for boys and for young people in all stations of life.

- Locke's compelling idea was more philosophical. He wanted to demonstrate the *limits of the human mind for understanding the world and the self*. He was particularly opposed to the concept of innate, unlearned ideas.

- What drove Rousseau was his iconoclastic belief that *sophisticated society was corrupting* and that one could find true freedom and authenticity only in small, rural communities.

- Pestalozzi dedicated his life to the idea of an *activity- and observation-based elementary education*, as opposed to the book-dominated humanistic one. He believed activity-based education would lift children out of poverty by giving them academic and mechanical skills needed to earn a living in an increasingly industrialized world.

- The *kindergarten* became Froebel's obsession. After he formulated the concept, Froebel funneled all his energies to the construction and use of his gifts and occupations for kindergarten children.

- Steiner conceptualized *anthroposophy*, and it became his mission to propagate the idea to which he attributed all his multifaceted contributions.

- Montessori devised the *Montessori method*, which she promoted as the most effective and beneficial way to educate young children.

- For Freud, *psychoanalysis* and its extension into a variety of human domains kept him working, despite intolerable pain, until his death.

- Piaget sacrificed much of ordinary life to pursue his *genetic epistemology* and to extending it to all facets of human thought and action.

- With regard to Erikson, the concepts of *identity* and *the human life cycle* were what drove all his thinking and writing.

- For Vygotsky, his belief in the *social-cultural-historical determination of human thought and action* was the dynamic behind the remarkable achievements of his regrettably short life.

Discipline, Hard Work, and Sacrifice

Additional outstanding traits of the Giants were their self-discipline, their capacity for hard work, and their willingness to sacrifice family and relationships in pursuit of their goals. I think it is fair to describe all the Giants as having, to some degree, obsessive-compulsive character traits. This compulsion to realize a vision took charge of their lives and made everything else subordinate to it. Piaget was the extreme, but Comenius, Locke, Steiner, Montessori, Freud, and Vygotsky nearly match his intensity. Compulsivity was but one of Rousseau's dominating traits. Pestalozzi, though unschooled, wrote a number of books and spent both days and nights at his schools. As he aged, Erikson became increasingly more compulsive about his writing. Froebel was perhaps the least disciplined in this regard, but even he spent several years in a closed room classifying crystals.

Late Bloomers

A third commonality, if not a trait, was the fact that all the Giants found their professional identities later in life. This is in contrast to, for example, the mathematical and physical sciences and the arts, where talent often appears early. To be sure, Montessori, Freud, Piaget, and Vygotsky all showed their genius early, but they did not really find their unique professional niche until well into their adulthood. Comenius was in his late thirties when he conceived of his ideas in *The Great Didactic*. Locke's *Essay Concerning Human Understanding* came out when he was in his late fifties. Rousseau published his *Social Contract* and *Émile* at age fifty. *The Interpretation of Dreams* went to press when Freud was in his mid-forties. Piaget published *The Language and Thought of the Child* in his late twenties, but the distillation of his major work in *Psychology of Intelligence* did not appear until he was in his early fifties. *Childhood and Society*, the book that made Erikson famous, came out when he was nearly fifty. The major works of Vygotsky were completed when he was in his thirties.

The explanation for the late blooming of social scientists seems fairly straightforward. It simply takes longer to become an innovator in the social sciences because these sciences are still, in some respects at least, relatively unexplored and underconceptualized. In this regard, it is interesting to point out that Freud, Piaget, Vygotsky, and Erikson were basically observers and classifiers rather than experimentalists in the strict sense. Indeed, much of their work would not be accepted for publication in any of today's psychological journals. Yet they are the most quoted in psychology textbooks and are the most well known outside their disciplines.

Contributions to Experiential Learning

Psychologists define learning as the modification of behavior as a result of experience. For the most part, however, psychologists have focused on the behavior being modified rather than the experience that modifies it. This is understandable, inasmuch as experience is necessarily subjective as well as objective and therefore is difficult to define. This is true to some extent even if the experimenter controls the subject's experience—for example, Pavlov and his famous studies. Burrhus Frederic Skinner emphasized this point when he introduced the concept of "operant conditioning" (1938), in which the unconditioned stimulus was unknown. In so doing, he acknowledged the difficulty of identifying and defining the learning experience in an objective way. Accordingly, psychologists have focused more on the behaviors being learned rather than on the experiences that give rise to them.

In contrast, the Giants of DAP were very much concerned with the nature of experience and its role in the learning process. Each Giant added a unique perspective to the experience and learning process. That is to say, these workers focused to a greater extent on the stimulus, the source of the experience, than on the response to it. In so doing, they added a great deal to our understanding of the role of experience in learning. Philosophers Comenius, Locke, and Rousseau each addressed the issue of the *kinds* of experience essential for education in general. Educational practitioners Pestalozzi, Froebel, Steiner, and Montessori each dealt with the issue of how these modes of experience are best combined into effective learning processes. Researchers and theorists Freud, Piaget, Erikson, and Vygotsky helped us understand *why* children's otherwise seemingly inexplicable behaviors could be attributed to unconscious experiences.

Taking their contributions together, the philosophical and practical Giants recognized three conscious sources of knowledge:

1. Experiences as a result of interacting with the natural world
2. Experiences derived from encounters with the social world
3. Experiences created by the individual's own activity

Freud, Piaget, and Erikson also introduced the idea of another type of learning experience:

4. Unconscious experience

In addition to these broad general categories, each of the Giants added his or her own subcategory of experience. With regard to what *kinds* of experiences students should have, Comenius made the point that experiences can vary from the simple to the complex and insisted that education should follow this sequence. Locke argued that there are conceptual as well as sensory experiences but that the conceptual experiences always derive from the sensorial. Rousseau added the difference between experiences of the natural versus the social world.

Comenius (along with Locke and Rousseau) also recognized that there were bad as well as good experiences, which education might not be able to correct. Locke was specifically concerned that the English children from upper-class families were acquiring bad linguistic habits from their servants. Rousseau turned Locke's critique on its head and argued that it was the snobbish behavioral examples set by the sophisticated upper classes who were corrupting the peasantry. All three philosophers help us appreciate that both "bad" and "good" social experiences can come from any social class and that those value judgments in themselves are relative.

The practitioners helped articulate *how* experiences could be translated into practical learning. It was Pestalozzi who understood that, in education at least, the social and natural experiences can and should complement one another. He insisted that children learn social skills and knowledge through the use of natural experiences, such as counting stones to learn numbers or walking through the town and country to learn geography. He thus emphasized manipulative and exploratory experiences. Froebel, in contrast, was most concerned with children becoming innovative through their self-initiated learning experiences. Froebel thus focused on self-created learning experiences. Combining the two approaches, Steiner insisted that children learn best through the holistic integration of natural, self-created, and social experiences; he demonstrated this by having older children research, write, and illustrate their own textbooks. Through this approach to schooling, Steiner introduced the concept of integrative experience. Montessori argued that there are sensitive periods during which the training of the senses is facilitative of all later learning.

It was Freud who revealed that unconscious emotional experiences could explain why children engaged in certain play behaviors (for example, children like playing peekaboo because it helps reduce their separation anxiety). Piaget documented that many of a child's cognitive achievements could be attributed to her unconscious intellectual functioning (for example, a child argues that the number of pennies grouped together are the same as the number spread out but is not aware of how he reached that conclusion). Erikson contended that many social misunderstandings arise from unconsciously acquired sociocultural habits (for example, a Vietnamese child at a non-Asian friend's house loudly burps after dinner believing, as he learned from his culture, that this is a compliment to the chef). Finally, for Vygotsky, the unconscious is the source of creativity in art and accounts for its uniqueness.

The Giants have broadened our conception of the range of experiences from which children can learn and profit. Each of their contributions and ideas gives early childhood educators understanding and tools to provide an educational program that addresses the whole child in all her individuality.

Common Themes

The Nature of the Child

Each Giant focused on a particular facet of the nature of children, reflecting his or her own background and personal predilections:

- Comenius viewed the child from what today we would call an *ecological perspective*. He believed the physical environment in which the child was educated was a very important contributor to the effectiveness of the education.
- Locke was most impressed by the child's *malleability*, the extent to which the child could be molded by the environment. He also recognized that each individual's experiences were unique and that the range of individual differences was infinite.
- Rousseau argued that the child was a *constructivist* who did not copy the world experienced through the senses but rather reconstructed it in keeping with her own modes of thought.
- Pestalozzi regarded the child as a *social emotional being* with a need for the family's emotional support and security, even in educational settings. And that is what he tried to provide in his father-figure and teacher roles.
- Froebel recognized the child as a *creative* individual who could best realize that creativity through play with the gifts and occupations Froebel provided.

- Steiner was concerned that the *holistic* nature of the child was being neglected and believed that education had to provide for the child's artistic, musical, and movement potential and not just for the intellectual potential.
- The secret of childhood in Montessori's view is that the child is *self-actualizing*, when he or she is given an appropriately prepared environment and adult guidance.
- Freud's contribution to our conception of the child was his demonstration that the child is a *sexual being* (in the broad sense, meaning appetitive needs that go through the cycle of rapid build up of tension with sudden release and accompanying pleasure) from the beginning of life.
- Piaget demonstrated that the child, at least as early as the end of the first year of life, is a *rational being*. This is in contrast to the ancients, who argued that the child did not reach the age of reason until six or seven years old.
- Erikson added his concept of the child as a *generational being* who was a bearer of the past as well as a harbinger of the future.
- Vygotsky saw the child as first and foremost a *user of cultural tools*, such as language.

These different depictions all carry a degree of truth and together give us a picture of the child's nature that is richer and more comprehensive than we could have gotten from any one Giant alone.

The Aims of Education and Play

In general, how each Giant viewed the aims of education, socialization, individualization, or some combination of the two strongly colored his or her understanding of the role of play in that education. For that reason, I will combine them in this discussion.

In this section, the Giants are grouped according to whether they regarded education and play as primarily socialization, primarily individualization, or some combination of the two. The Giants' approaches to education are also demonstrated through their political leanings within the sociohistorical situations of their times. It must be emphasized that all the Giants believed education necessarily involves socialization and individualization. Where they differed was with the level of importance they gave to these goals and with the means used to attain them.

Education and Play as Domestication

John Locke

Locke came from an upper-class English family and had liberal political ideas but was still a social conservative. He viewed education, particularly that of the boys from upper-class families for whom he wrote *Some Thoughts Concerning Education* (Locke [1693] 2007), as essentially necessary to preserve the status quo. For Locke, the aims of education were primarily social, although he did not want the individual's spirit to be crushed in the process. With respect to play, Locke contended that children learn best when learning is made a game. He regarded play either as a means to a social end or as a mere respite from work.

Johann Heinrich Pestalozzi

Pestalozzi viewed academic and technical education of the poor as the only way to ensure their rising out of poverty and avoiding potential criminality. Although he valued individuals, he saw education's goal as socializing all poor children toward economic independence. Pestalozzi's use of incredibly long hours of schooling makes it clear that he regarded socialization as the main aim of education. He regarded play, including festivals and pageantry, as a necessary reprieve from the task of learning.

Maria Montessori

Similar to Locke, Montessori came from an upper-class family, and like him, she was politically and socially liberal in some regards—believing in and fighting for women's rights—but conservative in others. Her method, devised for the education of low-income children, was initially focused on pre-academic skills. Although she emphasized freedom, it was always within social limits. I believe it is fair to say that she saw the aims of education primarily as socialization. Montessori regarded play as the child's work, by which she meant that the child's task is to learn about self and the world. Like Locke, Montessori thought play should be put to practical purposes and that pure play was primarily useful as a relief from work.

Lev Vygotsky

Vygotsky was also liberal on some issues and conservative on others. He was very much in favor of the Russian Revolution and was extremely critical of established psychology. With respect to education, however, he appears to be conservative. He contended that what one learned from teachers, society, and culture was more important than the contributions of individual development and self-initiated learning. For Vygotsky, play was primarily a mediator for the attainment of social rules. It seems fair to justify grouping him among those who view play as a means to end.

Education and Play as a Sequence of Individualization and Socialization

Jean-Jacques Rousseau

Rousseau, as a commoner living in prerevolutionary France, saw natural education, one acquired from interacting with the real world, as the only way to combat the corruption and abuse of the church and the nobility. Rousseau appreciated that socialization was necessary, but he believed an early natural education encouraging individualization was the best defense against the corrupting influences of sophisticated society. So he saw both individualization and socialization as necessary but sequential.

Rousseau thought of play as the disposition of childhood: "Love childhood. Look with friendly eyes on its games, its pleasures, its amiable dispositions" (Rousseau 1956, 33). Children learn the natural world through play. Adolescence is the time for formal, rule-based education. Play and formal education are sequential.

Erik Erikson

There is no doubt that Erikson was a liberal: he gave up a professorship at UC Berkeley rather than sign a loyalty oath. He also advocated for minorities, like the American Indians. With respect to the aims of education, he seems to echo Rousseau by suggesting that individualization and the sense of personal identity should precede socialization and the sense of generativity.

Erikson links play to the creation of both individual identity in adolescence and social generativity (creativity in the arts) in adulthood. Like Rousseau, he views play as contributing first to individualization and then to socialization.

Education and Play as Socialization and Individualization

John Amos Comenius

As a member of a liberal but religious minority sect, Comenius saw the aims of education as serving both the individual and society. Secular education of both men and women of all social stations of life would give each individual a chance for a happy, productive life. Spiritual education would ensure the moral underpinnings of the society. So Comenius, prescient in so many ways, saw education, from the outset, as having both individual and social aims.

Comenius thought that learning should be joyful (which can be regarded as playful) and also that the child should have a half hour of play for each hour of work. He thus saw play as having both educational and recreational roles at all levels of education.

Frederick Froebel

Froebel was a rebel as a child and youth and remained so when he became an educator. He believed that self-initiated play had to be present at all levels of development to ensure that the inner, creative self was not subordinated to the socialization imposed on the outer, social self. For him the aim of education was a simultaneous nourishment of both inner and outer selves with the goal of their eventual unity.

In Froebel's view, self-created play was the child's means of realizing both his inner spiritual self and his outer secular self at all stages of development. Only in this way could he achieve eventual unity between the two.

Rudolf Steiner

Steiner believed that the aims of education should speak to both the individual and the social facets of the personality. Such holistic education, in Steiner's view, prepares the young person to be individually free and socially responsible—both liberated and domesticated.

Steiner regarded the arts, music, dance, and athletics (which all can be regarded as individualizing) as an integral part of academic education at all age levels.

Sigmund Freud

Freud was a unique mixture of liberal and conservative. His theories were strikingly innovative, but his defense of them was conservative; he did not accept opposing views. Freud took similar positions to Comenius, Froebel, and Steiner with respect to the aims of education and play. He believed that education should ensure that "where id was, there ego shall be" (Sandler and Dreher 1996, 18), which indicates individualization. But he also recognized the necessary socializing force of the superego. I think it is fair to say that Freud saw the aims of education as supporting an ongoing battle between the needs of the individual (ego) and those of society (superego).

Freud regarded play as one way children adapt to social reality. In adulthood, play is the source of individual creativity. Freud thus saw play as socializing in childhood and individualizing in adulthood. In this regard, he took a position just the opposite of Rousseau and Erikson.

Jean Piaget

My impression is that Piaget was socially and scientifically liberal. If he was conservative, it was in his personal life with his regular habits of work and living. His two aims of education, described earlier, were for individual creativity and social responsibility. So Piaget, like Comenius and Freud, believed education had to combine individualization and domestication.

But, unlike Freud, Piaget held a similar view with respect to play. He said that there was "no assimilation without accommodation" (Piaget in Bringuier 1980, 42). That is, there is no adapting the world to the self (play or assimilation) without adapting the self to the world (work or accommodation). Put differently, no learning can take place without some contribution from both the individual and from experience. The inseparability of play and work holds true for all levels of development.

Conclusion

The Giants all agreed on the basic principles of DAP: Their differences with respect to the nature of the child and the aims of education and play are complementary rather than antagonistic. These differences also reflect the fact that whatever our training and background, how we view the world is, in part at least, colored by our personality predispositions.

Differing views of education will always be with us because they are, in part at least, reflective of abiding personality differences. Darwin, for example, noted the difference between lumpers—those who can't see the trees for the forest—and splitters—those who can't see the forest for the trees. Likewise, folktales distinguish between the fox, who sees the world from many different perspectives, and the hedgehog, who sees it from only one, and between the hare (in one interpretation), who is fast but overconfident, and the tortoise, who is slow and plodding but does not lose sight of the goal.

Yet the fact that there will always be conflicting views on the aims of education does not gainsay an underlying agreement about the principles of DAP. Whether we believe education should be primarily individualization, socialization, or some combination of the two, we still share a commitment to education. Our specific positions are based on opinions and values, not on facts. DAP is based on the *facts* of human development that have been amassed over more than one hundred years of research and over three centuries of practical classroom experience. That is to say, we can view education as a process of individualization, socialization, or some combination of the two and still employ age-appropriate materials and practices to attain these goals. Our educational opinions and values become a problem only when they blind us to what we know are in the best interests of children. The Giants never confused their personal opinions and values with sound pedagogical principles. We should all be inspired and challenged to follow their examples.

References

Bringuier, Jean-Claude. 1980. *Conversations with Jean Piaget*. Translated by Basia Miller Gulati. Chicago: University of Chicago Press.

Locke, John. (1693) 2007. *Some Thoughts Concerning Education*. Sioux Falls, SD: NuVision.

Rousseau, Jean-Jacques. 1956. *The Emile of Jean-Jacques Rousseau; Selections*. New York: Teacher's College Columbia University Press.

Sandler, Joseph, and Anna Ursula Dreher. 1996. *What Do Psychoanalysts Want? The Problem of Aims in Psychoanalytic Theory*. London: Routledge.

Skinner, Burrhus Frederic. 1938. *The Behavior of Organisms*. New York: Appleton-Century.

Index